PROFIT MARGINS

PROFIT MARGINS

THE AMERICAN SILENT CINEMA AND THE MARGINALIZATION OF ADVERTISING

JEREMY GROSKOPF

INDIANA UNIVERSITY PRESS

This book is a publication of

Indiana University Press
Office of Scholarly Publishing
Herman B Wells Library 350
1320 East 10th Street
Bloomington, Indiana 47405 USA

iupress.org

 The paper used in this publication meets the minimum requirements of the American National Standard for Information Sciences—Permanence of Paper for Printed Library Materials, ANSI Z39.48-1992.

Manufactured in the United States of America

First printing 2021

Cataloging information is available from the Library of Congress.

ISBN 978-0-253-05939-0 (hardcover)
ISBN 978-0-253-05938-3 (paperback)
ISBN 978-0-253-05937-6 (e-book)

CONTENTS

Acknowledgments *vii*
List of Abbreviations *ix*

Introduction: Advertising Looks at Cinema *1*
1. The Front Cover Medium: Lantern Slides, Temporality, and the Commercial Break *20*
2. Screen Sugar Pills: The Advertising Trailer and the Commercialized Intermission *105*
3. Watch This Space: Peripheral Advertising through Technologies *177*
4. The Cinema Wants to Be Free: Parks, Tickets, and Advertiser-Funded Cinema *236*

Conclusion: Intemperate Proclamations *288*

Selected Bibliography *303*
Index *321*

ACKNOWLEDGMENTS

THIS BOOK IS THE RESULT of more than a decade of research and writing, across multiple archives and universities. Invaluable contributions have come from Kathy Fuller-Seeley, Alisa Perren, Ted Friedman, and Cynthia Meyers, all of whom read and commented on multiple drafts of each chapter. Additionally, multiple anonymous reviewers for Indiana University Press provided essential feedback, as did several members of the Indiana University Press staff—most notably Allison Chaplin, Janice Frisch, Sophia Hebert, and Brian Carroll.

Numerous archivists across the United States were likewise vital to the project, many of whom I never met physically; I will leave them anonymous here on the grounds that I would omit more than I could possibly name in a sane amount of space. No less critical were the efforts of the Media History Digital Library, the Library of Congress, and Google, without whose optical character recognition (OCR) scanning and circulation of historical artifacts this project would not even have been possible. Additionally, any academic work is built on the shoulders of the community; some of the more prominent in this case include Matthew Bernstein, Malcolm Cook, Martin Johnson, Matthew Ogonoski, Patrick Vonderau, and Dana White, all of whom, whether they knew it or not, impacted the course of this book's development through conversation and assistance.

Countless others offered support and encouragement in various ways and at various times: my partner, parents, friends, and family; coworkers and grad school cohorts; advisors, teachers, and employers. There are too many to mention. A book is a communal work, and this book belongs to all of you as much as it belongs to me.

ABBREVIATIONS

ARCHIVAL COLLECTIONS

AIR—Alexander Industries Records, MSS 0056. Pikes Peak Library District, Special Collections in the 1905 Carnegie Library, Colorado Springs, Colorado.

CTP—Charles Trefts Papers, C3465. State Historical Society of Missouri Research Center, Columbia, Missouri.

JWT—J. Walter Thompson Company: Chicago Office Records, RL.00673; Information Center Records, RL.00713; and Staff Meeting Minutes, 1927–1938, RL.00749. Duke University, David M. Rubinstein Rare Book & Manuscript Library, Durham, North Carolina.

KCS—Kansas City Slide Manufacturing Company Records, K0637. State Historical Society of Missouri Research Center, Kansas City, Missouri.

PBC—Publicity Clock Company Advertising Cards and Brochures, RL.01057. Duke University, David M. Rubinstein Rare Book & Manuscript Library, Durham, North Carolina.

HISTORIC TRADE JOURNALS

Advertising & Selling (A&S)
Billboard
Camera Craft (CC)
Exhibitors' Herald (EH)
Exhibitors' Times (ET)
Motion Picture News (MPN)

Moving Picture Age (MPA)
Moving Picture News (MovPN)
Moving Picture World (MPW)
Nickelodeon/Motography
Printers' Ink (PI)
Printers' Ink Monthly (PIM)
Reel & Slide (R&S)
Variety

PROFIT MARGINS

INTRODUCTION
Advertising Looks at Cinema

> A moving-picture audience ought to be an inspiration to an advertising man. I have sat in a moving-picture theater full of kids and grown-ups and have thought, "If I only knew how to reach these people, I would know all about advertising."
>
> —Don Herold (September 1915)

IN THE AMERICA OF 1910, motion pictures and consumer-goods advertising were young industries that were still growing, changing, and defining themselves, and both craved respectability. The movies had become a regular part of daily life through the rise of nickelodeons in numerous cities, with a push for cultural respectability soon to come via the turn to feature films and palatial theaters at mid-decade. Advertising, already established as a recognizable component of modern life, was likewise attempting to improve its image, specifically via professionalization, reform (to finally rid itself of the stink of patent-medicine advertising), and public service (a favorite tactic of the billboard industry).[1] For both, reputation—being seen in the right places with the right people—was key.

It should come as no surprise that these two attractive young starlets had an on-again, off-again love affair. Indeed, the two had mingled openly from the earliest days; see, for example, the still-extant Edison film for Admiral Cigarettes from 1897, in which a showgirl in military dress emerges from an enormous package of Admiral Cigarettes and shares a smoke with iconic figures like Uncle Sam. From approximately 1908 to the early 1920s, that love affair entered full bloom as the two partners went through a protracted public dance, with advertisers attempting to integrate and regularize large-scale advertising in the cinematic space. It is that love affair—fumbling, hesitant, and often one-sided—that is the subject of this book.

In the pages that follow, I contend that in the America of the 1910s, advertising and the cinema were mutually defining institutions. For cinema—the younger and more desirable of the two—direct advertising was key to its developing self-confidence; advertising was the common rabble with which cinema was loath to associate for fear of being seen as a low-class medium. For advertising—the older and more philandering—the failure to successfully woo the film industry instilled a lack of confidence in moving media that would take years of amorous broadcasting experience to overcome.[2]

The relationship faltered over a foundational dialectic in early cinema: the fantasy of a passively captivated spectator versus the fear of a bored one. In other words, was a film viewer like a camera, uncritically recording whatever it witnessed? Or was a viewer like a photographer, choosing where to look and when to look away? Advertising, always seeking the most efficient means to a consumer's wallet, desperately hoped for cinema to be the former—a means of imprinting sales slogans directly on the brain. However, the film industry, stylish and eager to please, selected the latter definition both as a practical truth (if bad films did poorly, then the audience must not be passive) and as a component of a fashion-conscious branding strategy (good art aspires to good taste), thus crippling the fantasy that had drawn advertising in the first place.

However, the choice made by the bulk of the film industry to speak to its viewers as people who enjoy the finer things of life, rather than consumers of mass-manufactured goods, had a slow gestation, taking slightly longer than a decade to mature. During this period, in an effort to find a workable means to cohabitate with cinema, advertising proponents put pressure on multiple aspects of the industrial definition of the emerging medium. Film, at this point, was both national (at the level of studios and culture) and local (at the level of exhibition and experience); was a cutting-edge technology nonetheless surrounded by an entourage of much older forms (vaudeville, glass slides, stage performances); and was a key medium of modern communication, though paradoxically, it failed to earn the status of "speech" during the landmark Mutual Decision of 1915 (in which cinema was declared "a business pure and simple"—not part of the press—and thus not subject to First Amendment protections).

This period thus witnessed the rise of numerous novel advertising concepts, all geared toward exploiting different gaps in the motion-picture experience. These concepts—rapidly marginalized and/or abandoned by the evolving cinema—have been rediscovered and reborn for other moving media. The earliest variants of the broadcast spot, the corner "bug," and even the spatial thinking underpinning "squeezebacks" and online banners, to name just a few, emerged during the "long 1910s." In short, these are the years that witnessed the advent of modern moving-media advertising tactics and also their banishment from most picture theaters as a boorish intrusion on a refined lifestyle.

UPSTARTS AND CHARLATANS

Cinema advertising has always, of course, been a nebulous concept. Even twenty-first-century cinema advertising is a mishmash of different approaches, ranging from the pre-film advertising distributed by Screenvision and National CineMedia (NCM) to the placement of products onscreen and perhaps even within the narrative (such as the star turn of Reese's Pieces in *E.T.: The Extra Terrestrial* [1982]). Different approaches are often the purview of different companies, which negotiate with different elements of the film industry (producers or exhibitors) and have slightly different underlying philosophies. In short, any study of cinema advertising is in danger of becoming unwieldy with alarming speed. The actual subject of this book is thus productively delimited in four ways.

First, and most obviously, this is a synchronic and national study; this book analyzes only American cinema advertising during the "long 1910s" (roughly from the nickelodeon boom [1908] to the first experiments with sound-on-film systems [1923])—a slightly extended version of the period traditionally discussed by film scholars as the American "transitional era." As Richard Ohmann has said of mass magazines, the establishment of a media form is a matter of "process, not invention," and the "causes, effects, needs, and strategies" that make up a new form are most clearly visible during the early years of invention.[3] Thus, this book is focused on the years of invention, when the concept of cinema—particularly its relationship to consumption—was still developing. For this same reason, I have opted to delimit the study to the American context. Although cinema advertising was a global area of experimentation at this point, it is implausible to study silent-era cinema advertising as a global practice in these pages. Even if the materials for such a study were readily available in reliable translations, a global study would necessarily muddy the waters, as advertisers in each locale dealt with unique cultures, financial situations, and government regulations. American cinema in the long 1910s provides a sufficiently diverse array of local permutations and demands an isolated study of this length.[4]

Second, indirect advertising (covert name-dropping of a product without a sales pitch) has been omitted in favor of a focus exclusively on direct advertising (an overt sales pitch for a product). Although indirect advertising was a component of early silent film, with product placement, sponsorship, and the "educational" film all widely known, it came quickly under attack as doubly unethical—abusing the spectator by failing to announce its intentions and abusing the exhibitor by failing to pay for exposure (indirect advertisers typically paid film producers, not exhibitors).[5] The upstart field of direct advertising for the cinematic space largely arose as an alternative to the indirect advertising charlatans. During these early years, direct and indirect advertising were predominantly seen as distinct approaches with distinct concerns; although there are important moments of intersection, the isolation of direct advertising allows for both a more subtle and a more comprehensible study of its development.[6]

Third, and inverse to the previous, the definition of the cinema is more expansive here than in many related studies. Film histories have an understandable tendency to overemphasize the onscreen content. However, the cinema is made not only of light and shadow, but also of wood and brick; indeed, as mentioned above, the American silent cinema was a multimedia venue consisting of motion pictures, still photographs, and live music. A filmed and projected advertisement was but one of the methods of direct advertising within the cinema. Early cinema advertisers were aware that the movies were an environment as well as a technology and that the back of a seat had as much potential as the screen. As such, while screen content and aesthetic choices will receive due attention at various points, this is neither a study of screen images nor of the rhetorical structure of advertisements. It is a study of placement and the battle over territory. This book expands the definition of the cinema in order to approach direct advertising as an array of business decisions and theories, of which aesthetics are only a small part. It is, in fact, due to this concern for non–screen placement that I have opted to use the term *cinema advertising,* rather than the more commonly used term *screen advertising.*[7]

Fourth and finally, this book is a study of cinema-delivered consumer-goods advertising and how it impacted the cinema's branding strategy. Sales communication fragments into four different lines: advertising (both indirect and direct; the attempt to encourage purchasing), marketing (the development of sales strategies, including market research and pricing), branding (the intentional association of a product or company with a particular image or personality, such as the connotations of the Quaker in the trade character on a package of Quaker Oats), and public relations (maintenance of a public image through press releases, etc.). From the perspective of consumer goods, this is a study of advertising; from the perspective of cinema, this is a study of branding, marketing, and public relations. I believe this to be the most productive way to study 1910s cinema advertising in the United States for one key reason: a massive imbalance between the relative importance of the major players. Film frightened and/or confused mainstream advertising agencies, which were focused predominantly on entrenchment of print and billboard advertising. Most cinema advertising was, therefore, concocted by small companies from the margins of the advertising industry. These frequently fly-by-night cinema-advertising companies put pressure on the entirety of the film industry, up to and including the largest and most prominent theaters. The impact was thus predominantly on the film industry. Cinema advertising's impact on the mainstream advertising industry is a complicated and largely theoretical discussion—a conversation I have opted to hold until the conclusion of this book. This is, in short, solely a study of one industry attempting to purchase space within another and the impact of that effort on the latter industry's emerging self-definition.[8]

Refined and delimited, then, this is a study of the rise of cinema-oriented consumer-goods advertising using direct appeals and occurring within the United States. It is a study of the relentless advent of new cinema-advertising tactics and their equally rapid banishment into the margins by a rising, vertically integrating film industry. The focus in the following pages will always be on the debate—whether engaged in rhetorically (via the press) or practically (via experimentation and abandonment)—over the suitability of the cinema as an advertising venue. The goal is to understand the increasing disconnect between the desires of advertisers on the one hand and filmmakers, exhibitors, and audiences on the other.

REBRANDING THE SILENT CINEMA

In order to reframe our understanding of the American silent cinema as an advertising aware and influenced industry, this study predominantly draws on two recent paradigms in the study of media history: New Cinema History and media industries studies. New Cinema History, as framed by Richard Maltby and others, is a study not of the artistic qualities of films themselves, but of the cinema as a social experience; in other words, New Cinema History "rethink[s] the history of cinema as the history of the experience of cinema."[9] Our understanding of cinemagoing can be improved through a study of the ways in which the industrial decisions related to cinema advertising—including the development of standards of practice and the conflict between various power nodes of the industry (for example, production, exhibition, and regulation)—led to national, regional, and local variation in moviegoing experiences during the transitional era. A study of the interaction of these two growing industries—cinema and advertising (both riddled with internal conflicts and contradictions)—reveals the breadth of possible experiences of cinema, some of which became normative, while others remained outliers.

Consumer-goods advertisers called into question American cinema's relationship to its market by directly adapting the strategies of old media for use within the cinema space. Some approaches to cinema advertising treated film simply as a projected magazine, inserting advertising into the natural pauses (what would later be referred to, by broadcasters, as "interstitial pages of time").[10] Other methods treated film like theater, hanging advertising on the curtain during intermission. Still others defined the cinema as technological travel, splattering advertising on the walls like billboards along a highway. Although the cinema was readily understood as a cross between all three, advertising became a key point of contention in determining how similar cinema truly was to these other activities.

In short, we see the cinema in the process of defining itself via the actions, confrontations, and debates of its members with a potential partner industry. The film industry—as a part of the broadscale transitional-era rethink of standards of practice and market position that included the development of the palatial theater and the "prestige picture"—came to a greater understanding of the value of time, the behavior of audiences, and the psychological value of ticket costs (encountering and rejecting the concept of a dual market: the creation of one marketable object [film] for the express purpose of creating a second marketable object [the audience]).[11] The advertising industry, to their consternation, discovered that a temporal medium does not readily function like a physical medium, beginning the long and difficult journey to the mixed approach of the twenty-first-century moving-image model: spots, sponsorship, placement, and so on.

What follows, then, is a history of an under-studied shift during the transitional era of American cinema: the development of the cinema as a medium openly hostile to direct advertising. It is written with the interests of a historian of culture, technology, and industry and follows the shaky line of development of an idea as it threads slowly in and out of a particular cultural milieu.[12] Although I have my own opinions on the impact of advertising on culture and psychology, the approach here is intentionally politically agnostic, with the goal of letting the participants speak for themselves. It is my intention to analyze the actions and perspectives taken by the participants of the time and to elaborate on both articulated and unspoken theories and assumptions underlying these events and how those actions subtly shifted the experience of the cinema.

Although the book is, first and foremost, a socio-industrial study of a transition in the standards of practice of the cinema, what follows is also an important study for the history of advertising; it fills a notable gap in the literature between the print-centric advertising culture of the late nineteenth century and the rise of broadcasting in the early twentieth. Advertising history has long been dominated by studies of late nineteenth-century print culture and mid-twentieth-century broadcasting, with multiple book-length monographs focused on each of those two areas. In contrast, the (comparatively little) research into the 1910s has predominantly focused on the professionalization and entrenchment of print-centric ad agencies. The fringe experimentation with cinema during this period—preceding and prefiguring agency expansion and future tactics in moving media—is a forgotten phase of American advertising history situated importantly between print and broadcasting.[13]

Though early twentieth-century consumerism and regulation are very minor themes in comparison, what follows also provides evidence of the difficult territorial battles fought over the increasing integration of advertising into daily life. In fear of spectator hostility, as well as minor instances of state and local regulatory measures, the film industry engaged in a form of self-regulation: a very public push for an ad-free cinema.[14] Though I do not pursue the (often Marxist) questions of a political economist or a critic of the rise of consumption—aside from small references in chapter 4 to the commodification of the audience—scholars in these areas will find information within these pages directly relevant to their own research, as individual cultural actors on all sides of the debate engage with the rise of consumerism in ways both practical and idealistic.[15]

Finally, comprehension of each approach in this study requires an understanding of its essential formal properties, its antecedents, and what it influenced. New Cinema History isn't and needn't be hostile to an analysis of aesthetics; the experience impacts the design of texts as much as texts impact the structuring of experience. For example, the history of trailer advertising is inextricable from the history of animation—a scholarly blind spot currently being redressed by Malcolm Cook, among others.[16] The development of the film trailer—specifically its structural format of holding the title and release information to the final moments—must likewise be rethought in relation to earlier structural developments in consumer-goods trailers. The as-yet-unwritten history of film intertitles (particularly mid-1910s artistic backgrounds and/or animated letters), credits sequences, and company logos—all of which were frequently outsourced—will also have to reckon with the history of cinema advertising as a developmental phase. Scholars in all of these aesthetically oriented fields will find material of use in the pages that follow.

LOST AND FOUND

This book is the result of research that would have been impossible prior to the advent of document scanning, optical character recognition (OCR), and online repositories. A study of hundreds of minor companies throughout the United States, most of which have been defunct for a hundred years and many of which had an extremely brief life span, requires the accumulation of a massive number of small references. Simply tracking the published ads from a single company would have taken weeks of diligent effort in previous years. Something more complex—like a list of all mentions of the cinema, in both articles and ads, during the 1910s issues of *Printers' Ink,* a weekly trade journal for advertisers that published thousands of pages per year—would have been almost unthinkable, requiring a diligent reading of nearly every word of every issue.[17] A targeted research list can now be assembled in mere hours. The *Media History Digital Library* allows for the same type of rapid searching of numerous film periodicals. Although OCR can still miss important information even with careful manipulation of search terms, modern technology makes it much less cumbersome to seek out quick mentions of *trailer* and *slide* in small display ads and news blurbs.

The wealth of digitized trade materials—also including newspapers, census data, and various other small pieces of useful information—is unfortunately balanced by a corresponding absence: there are virtually no internal business documents from which to draw information. Aside from the Alexander Film Company material in Colorado Springs (which predominantly dates to the mid-1920s and later), nearly everything that has been archived for study was written for the purpose of sales. For example, we have numerous Kansas City Slide Company catalogs but very little internal correspondence or contract materials. Even basic behind-the-scenes data, such as an accurate list of incorporation and dissolution dates for the numerous businesses mentioned here, would take a Herculean effort to construct. More nuanced internal debates are predominantly lost to history.

As such, the focus of this study has been placed on the types of questions that can be answered by extant, obtainable information: the invention and spread of ideas and the geographical extent of their usage; standardization of forms; pricing and competition; the rise and fall in optimistic and hostile reporting; the professed and likely reasons for the success or failure of a business or an idea; and the underlying theories of audience attention and psychology driving the focus in each area. In other words, keyword searching has allowed for the clustering of ideas around definable technologies and concepts and has encouraged me to study the diverse array of activities and opinions that surround each term.

Methodologically, then, what follows is an attempt to explain the various perspectives waging war for the soul of the cinema in this moment and the reasons why particular individuals would promote particular approaches. The bulk of the interpretive work has been focused on rendering published statements useful by seeking contextual information on the backgrounds, beliefs, and biases of the author, the publisher, the region, and so on. To name just one important figure, F. H. Richardson, the projection expert for *Moving Picture World,* wrote numerous snide asides about advertising over the course of his career. However, the assumption that Richardson was idealistically opposed to cinema advertising would be incorrect. His opposition was purely technical and predominantly focused on lighting; if a theater's lighted advertising clock made it more difficult to concentrate on the film, the clock was "bad practice." In fact, Richardson was the owner of the Utility Transparency Company, which sold Make 'Em Yourself typewriter slides—a product used to make some of the cheapest-looking screen messages, including advertisements. Richardson's focus on the quality of projection did not imply a belief in the sanctity of the screen. His ill-humored but ultimately open-minded take on cinema advertising was likely influenced directly by his experiences in Chicago—one of the capital cities of American advertising in general and a hotbed of cinema advertising in particular.[18] *Moving Picture World,* Richardson's publisher, likely shared this perspective; the *World,* though clearly disinterested in reporting on developments in this field, often sold advertising space to cinema-advertising companies and was likely reticent to cut itself off from this revenue stream. Every effort has been made to fill in the gaps in the available research materials with this type of background knowledge, even where such knowledge is not overtly mentioned in the text. The men and women engaged in this field did so for specific personal reasons and had to engage, at times, with local tastes and regulations—complexities that leave traps for the unwary.

The study will proceed in four chapters and a conclusion. Each chapter tackles one particular approach—one keyword in early cinema advertising—and builds on the previous chapter, either chronologically (most of chap. 1 takes place before chap. 2) or by tactical progression (the tactics in chaps. 2, 3, and 4 were each envisioned as a type of corrective to a fault in chap. 1). Each of the four body chapters has been structured, like the book as a whole, to maximize clarity by isolating distinct but related topics. Each therefore opens with a short analysis of the standard aesthetic approach to the tactic, followed by a chronological history of its place in the market during the 1910s. Following the history are an analysis of the public rhetoric for and against the method and a case study designed to clarify a particularly thorny problem for purveyors of the preceding advertising tactic.

Chapter 1, "The Front Cover Medium," details the history of the magic-lantern advertising slide, which opened up a space for in-cinema advertising by staking claim to the gaps that necessarily existed between film reels prior to the advent of the multiple-projector model of exhibition and the seamless feature. In the early days of experimentation with cinema advertising, the screen was the first and most desired space, and the slide the cheapest option. Many nickelodeon theaters operated much like contemporary television stations, with regular advertising breaks at the end of each reel. As screening spaces improved with the addition of a second projector, an increase in the opulence of the space, and the elimination of other forms of entertainment in favor of film, slide advertising lost ground. However, slides set the standard; all other direct-advertising techniques concocted in the silent era would be attempts to correct the multiple failures of advertising slides.

Chapter 2, "Screen Sugar Pills," introduces the first and most obvious option in the efforts to fix slide advertising: a shift from still images to short film trailers. As an upgrade to the slide concept, trailer producers created roughly one-minute-long filmed advertisements. The brevity of these "minute movies" was inspired not only by the minimal content of slides, but also the need to make them easy to circulate; a trailer could be attached to the end of any reel of film that ran slightly short. Exhibitor reluctance to integrate such advertising throughout the program, however, combined with the trailer producers' need to regularize income resulted in the rise of cinema "space brokerage" and the advent of trailer reels: five to ten advertisements screened in succession in a bookend position of the program (indicating that the program had reached its end and was about to restart).[19] Over the course of this process, an early version of the commercial advertising spot was developed, though it almost immediately became isolated as a program chaser in a small subset of American film theaters.

Chapter 3, "Watch This Space," provides a discussion of a secondary plausible corrective to the faults of slide advertising: the abandonment of the screen in favor of alternative placement. Although they were only rarely integrated into cinema spaces—and remain little used in the contemporary resurgence of cinema advertising—lighted clocks, lighted signs, wall units, branded trash bins, and other elements of advertising at the periphery of the screen were created to stress the interactivity of the theatrical space. Designed as secondary sites of visual stimulation, offscreen advertisements were not only a conciliatory gesture in response to the audience's desire to not have advertising forced on them, but also a means to provide potential additional entertainment. Despite being almost immediately pushed out of active consideration—failing on the notion that offscreen materials were both tacky and caused significant light pollution in the predominantly darkened theater—these technologies provide a compelling case study of alternative definitions of spectatorship. For offscreen advertising, the cinema was a venue, not a screen, and could be reconceived with elements of spatial choice despite the obvious focus of attention.

Chapter 4, "The Cinema Wants to Be Free," presents the most ambitious attempt to correct the perceived problem of slide advertising's supposed incompatibility with ticket prices. For a small number of the cinema-advertising faithful, the answer to spectator irritation was, paradoxically, a vast increase in the quantity of advertising. Free cinema eliminated tickets altogether in favor of fully advertiser-funded cinema, ranging from simple coupon models to commercial breaks integrated with television-like regularity. With this chapter, the similarities between early cinema advertising and late twentieth-century television reach their clear apex, as free cinema is in many ways identical to later broadcast-advertising theories. Had any of these models become the common method of cinema spectatorship, film culture would have developed in a way more clearly in-line with other twentieth-century media, with free content underwritten by the frequent intrusion of direct-advertising messages.

The conclusion examines the advertising industry's continuing relationship with cinema and also inverts the focus by briefly studying the impact of cinema on the advertising industry and its pursuit of the starlets to come. Beginning with the key experiences and lessons revealed in the preceding chapters, the conclusion elaborates on the lasting influence of cinema advertising, both practical (through reinvention of old tactics) and theoretical (through persistent fears and common phrasing), on broadcasting and the web, as each form establishes the parameters of its own public romance. Meanwhile, the cinema—coy mistress that she has always been—carries on a back-alley dalliance for decades before finally allowing a little mainstream public affection. The twenty-first-century ubiquity of pre-film spots and product placement is a fittingly Victorian result of these early battles: a relationship accepted, admitted, and public, with a hint of lingering embarrassment.

NOTES

1. For professionalization, see Quentin J. Schultze, "'An Honorable Place': The Quest for Professional Advertising Education, 1900–1917," *Business History Review* 56, no. 1 (Spring 1982): 16–32; Peggy J. Kreshel, "John

B. Watson at J. Walter Thompson: The Legitimation of 'Science' in Advertising," *Journal of Advertising* 19, no. 2 (1990): 49–59; Kreshel, "Advertising Research in the Pre-Depression Years," *Journal of Current Issues and Research in Advertising* 15, no. 1 (Spring 1993): 59–75; and Roland Marchand, *Advertising the American Dream: Making Way for Modernity, 1920–1940* (Berkeley: University of California Press, 1985). For reform and public service, see Pamela Walker Laird, *Advertising Progress: American Business and the Rise of Consumer Marketing* (Baltimore, MD: Johns Hopkins University Press, 1998); Richard Ohmann, *Selling Culture: Magazines, Markets, and Class at the Turn of the Century* (London: Verso, 1996); Ellen Gruber Garvey, *The Adman in the Parlor: Magazines and the Gendering of Consumer Culture, 1880s to 1910s* (New York: Oxford University Press, 1996); Catherine Gudis, *Buyways: Billboards, Automobiles, and the American Landscape* (New York: Routledge, 2004); and Schultze, "Legislating Morality: The Progressive Response to American Outdoor Advertising, 1900–1917," *Journal of Popular Culture* 17, no. 4 (1984): 37–44.

2. If, as Charles F. McGovern has asserted, advertising "as the voice of capitalism . . . claimed the mandate to monopolize channels of common public discourse," this was the moment at which that claim was most seriously contested. McGovern, *Sold American: Consumption and Citizenship, 1890–1945* (Chapel Hill: University of North Carolina Press, 2006), 17.

3. Ohmann, *Selling Culture*, 13, 29.

4. There is a growing interest in global cinema advertising. See Michael Cowan's work on Weimar Germany, Malcolm Cook's research into British animation, and numerous studies in Bo Florin, Nico de Klerk, and Patrick Vonderau, eds., *Films That Sell Moving Pictures and Advertising* (London: British Film Institute, 2016).

5. See Gudis (*Buyways*, 4) for another example of an advertising medium—outdoor billboarding—in which the primary concern was developing an ethical approach to public display.

6. The early history of indirect advertising has been studied from various perspectives. See Kerry Segrave, *Product Placement in Hollywood Films: A History* (Jefferson, NC: McFarland, 2004); Jean-Marc Lehu, *Branded Entertainment: Product Placement and Brand Strategy in the Entertainment Business* (London: Kogan Page, 2007); Lee Grieveson, "The Work of Film in the Age of Fordist Mechanization," *Cinema Journal* 51, no. 3 (Spring 2012): 25–51; Stephen Bottomore, "Rediscovering Early Non-Fiction Film," *Film History* 13, no. 2 (2001): 160–173; Jay Newell, Charles T. Salmon, and Susan Chang, "The Hidden History of Product Placement," *Journal of*

Broadcasting and Electronic Media 50, no. 4 (December 2006): 575–594; and Vinzenz Hediger and Patrick Vonderau, eds., *Films that Work: Industrial Film and the Productivity of Media* (Amsterdam: Amsterdam University Press, 2009).

7. For studies focused on the form and rhetoric of screen advertising, see Florin et al., *Films That Sell,* and Michael Cowan's various studies of Weimar-era German advertising. Outside of the realm of consumer goods, see Lisa Kernan, *Coming Attractions: Reading American Movie Trailers* (Austin: University of Texas Press, 2004); Keith M. Johnston, *Coming Soon: Film Trailers and the Selling of Hollywood Technology* (Jefferson, NC: McFarland, 2009); and Ian Haydn Smith, *Selling the Movie: The Art of the Film Poster* (London: White Lion, 2018). A broader understanding of advertising content in this period can be found in Marchand, *Advertising the American Dream,* and Laird, *Advertising Progress,* among many others.

8. There are, of course, numerous other approaches one could take when examining the way advertising related to the cinema in this era, many of which will be mentioned briefly in the endnotes. For example, film industry self-advertising (in cinemas via trailers and handbills and out of cinemas via posters and tie-ups) grows and changes in response to the consumer-goods advertisements discussed in these pages. Likewise, the advertising industry's growing faith in picturization (which impacted advertising and branding via the rising importance of trade characters) was partially due to fear that increasing cinema spectatorship was proof that people did not really like to read.

9. Richard Maltby, Melvin Stokes, and Robert C. Allen, eds., *Going to the Movies: Hollywood and the Social Experience of the Cinema* (Exeter, UK: University of Exeter Press, 2008), 2. Daniel Biltereyst, Richard Maltby, and Philippe Meers, *Routledge Companion to New Cinema History* (New York: Routledge, 2019), 5.

10. Cynthia B. Meyers, *A Word from Our Sponsor: Admen, Advertising, and the Golden Age of Radio* (New York: Fordham University Press, 2014), 278.

11. For studies of dual-product market structures in other media, see Ohmann, *Selling Culture,* and David Croteua and William Hoynes, *The Business of Media: Corporate Media and the Public Interest,* 2nd ed. (Thousand Oaks, CA: Pine Forge, 2006), 28–29.

12. I have seen no evidence to suggest that advertisers abandoned the cinema because of difficulties in conceiving or creating persuasive advertisements to sell products in the cinematic space. Indeed, the opposite is

clearly true. There were numerous advertisements concocted for the cinema with an appeal and power that was surprising even to lifelong advertising men. It is for this reason that I keep the conversation, in this book, focused on industrial negotiations and eventual banishment. The use value of the space for advertising was almost never questioned at the level of content.

13. Key book-length studies of print culture, up to and including the early twentieth-century professionalization, include Jackson Lears, *Fables of Abundance: A Cultural History of Advertising in America* (New York: Vintage Books, 1993); Ohmann, *Selling Culture*; Garvey, *The Adman in the Parlor*; Laird, *Advertising Progress*; Gudis, *Buyways*; Marchand, *Advertising the American Dream*; and several articles by Quentin J. Schultze. Broadcast culture has been studied at length in Michele Hilmes, *Hollywood and Broadcasting: From Radio to Cable* (Urbana: University of Illinois Press, 1990); Hilmes, *Radio Voices: American Broadcasting, 1922–1952* (Minneapolis: University of Minnesota Press, 1997); Susan J. Douglas, *Inventing American Broadcasting, 1899–1922* (Baltimore, MD: Johns Hopkins University Press, 1987); Kathy M. Newman, *Radio Active: Advertising and Consumer Activism, 1935–1947* (Berkeley: University of California Press, 2004); Lawrence R. Samuel, *Brought to You By: Post-War Television Advertising and the American Dream* (Austin: University of Texas Press, 2001); Alexander Russo, *Points on the Dial: Golden Age Radio Beyond the Networks* (Durham, NC: Duke University Press, 2010); and Meyers, *A Word from Our Sponsor.*

14. Although a common refrain in studies of the rise of consumerism is that it led to fear of the "feminization" of culture—as advertising was often aimed at women—I have seen no evidence to suggest that the film industry's rejection of advertising was related to a gendered sense of its own audience. On feminization, see Newman, *Radio Active*, 8–10.

15. For critiques of the influence of consumerism and advertising, particularly with a media focus, see Dallas W. Smythe, "Communications: Blindspot of Western Marxism," *Canadian Journal of Political and Social Theory* 1, no. 3 (1977): 1–28; Newman, *Radio Active*; Thomas Streeter, *Selling the Air: A Critique of the Policy of Broadcasting in the United States* (Chicago: University of Chicago Press, 1996); and everything by Robert W. McChesney.

16. Malcolm Cook and Kirsten Moana Thompson, eds., *Animation and Advertising* (New York: Palgrave MacMillan, 2019). The minimal mention of cinema advertising in animation histories by Donald Crafton (*Before Mickey*) and Giannalberto Bendazzi (*Cartoons*) and histories of Walt

Disney by Timothy S. Susanin (*Walt Before Mickey*) and Brian Burnes, Robert W. Butler, and Dan Viets (*Walt Disney's Missouri*) all indicate that advertising has been unduly marginalized in the history of this particular field.

17. See, for example, the following, which mentions slides in passing only twice over the course of a very useful five-page article: O. B. Carson, "A Campaign That Gives 'Business Insurance' Against Irresponsible Competition," *Printers' Ink*, January 14, 1915, 31.

18. Numerous scholars have argued for the importance of interpreting the production perspectives of particular locales. See, for example, Michael Curtin, "Media Capitals: Cultural Geographies of Global TV," in *Television After TV: Essays on a Medium in Transition*, ed. Lynn Spigel and Jan Olssen (Durham, NC: Duke University Press, 2004), 270–302.

19. Effectively, film became a temporally bound, twentieth-century version of nineteenth-century magazine culture, where space-brokering contracts allowed agents (in this case the trailer producers themselves) to sell a certain amount of space, usually restricted to advertising sections bookending the content.

ONE

THE FRONT COVER MEDIUM

Lantern Slides, Temporality, and the Commercial Break

Films may come and films may go, but the advertising slide seemingly goes on forever.

—"Screenings," *North Tonawanda Evening News*, December 15, 1917

AT SOME POINT IN 2016, a major shift in the formal structure of the American cinematic experience went wholly unnoticed: Screenvision—which, alongside its competitor National Cine-Media, acts as space broker for the bulk of American theaters—removed digital slides from the list of advertising content it was willing to circulate.[1] This unceremonious end of the circulation of cinema slides on a major national scale effectively closed the book on a more-than one-hundred-year-old form.

Commercial magic-lantern advertising slides were a common and influential element of early cinema programs in America used to get the word out about such diverse matters as local piano-tuning services, a candidate's run for government office, and national brands' latest products. And, as the epigraph to this chapter humorously indicates, advertising slides could be interminable in numerous ways: the screening duration of a slide, the duration of a full slide-filled break in the program, and the repeated use of the same content (sometimes for months on end) all tend to exceed audience tolerance.[2] Even after its abandonment by the two big space brokers in twenty-first-century American cinema, the form itself likewise seems eternal. Still imagery that peddles merchants and services likely continues at the local level in theaters not affiliated with Screenvision or National CineMedia. A digital slideshow can be created with a laptop and screened in an independent local theater in minutes.

The history of the advertising slide is critical to the development of cinema advertising in the American context. In the early silent era, when the production and circulation of films were expensive endeavors, the cheapness of the glass slide allowed for adoption by advertisers of all sizes, creating a large early-adopter base.[3] This cost efficiency provided an easy point of entry for advertisers into a complicated new field, keeping development rapid and interest high despite persistent reluctance from exhibitors. More importantly, the unavoidable fact of reel-change pauses in early, single-projector theaters opened an obvious temporal gap in motion-picture display. Rather than simply attempting to fill this gap, early cinema advertisers endeavored to preserve and widen it. Although the drift of industrial sentiment was against them, this experimentation with an advertising caesura has become a defining feature of both broadcast and digital media. Participating sponsorship, the "spot" advertisement, and the concept of the commercial break are the historical shadow of the lantern slide.

The importance of the glass slide to the formal integration of advertising has an echo in advertising theory as well. Film was the first medium in which temporal, rather than spatial, sequencing was of prime importance. Prior to the advent of lantern slide advertising in motion-picture theaters, the driving theories of advertising placement stressed spatial nearness to a site of stimulation (interspersed with reading material or erected near a beautiful vista) or simple repetition of the message (papering every available surface with posters). Film—at least the celluloid

Figure 1.1. A stock slide from the Kansas City Slide Company, with professionally appended dealer information at the bottom. Note the alternation between white-figure layout and black-figure insets—the standard aesthetic approach at this company. The slide is also cracked, broken, and dirty, a purportedly common condition at the time. Author's personal collection.

portion of it—began the twentieth-century transition in media toward linear structuring and prompted considerable thought about the proper place of advertising under temporal restraint. Although we have since become accustomed to the description of an advertising spot as an "interstitial 'page' of time"—a magazine metaphor in which the experience of time is described in the terms of an experience of space—silent-era thinkers were more likely to refer to a screen advertisement as hijacking the front cover.[4] As the only temporal medium, every moment of screen time was an unavoidable focal point, lending screen advertising a sense of brashness and power exceeding what could be done in magazines. Indeed, the screen provoked a slippage between print and travel metaphors, as slides marked the first shift in placement ideology from the optional magazine and billboard ad to the mandatory stop sign. As such, the battle for advertising space in motion-picture theaters became a new front line in the longstanding battle over the rights of the audience.

The advent and marginalization of the slide are therefore crucial to the history of advertising not only in the cinema, but in all twentieth-century media. Though a seemingly outdated technology, even at its first appearance in cinema theaters, the form was very visible, was intermittently successful, and must be considered foundational for advertising development in twentieth-century electric media.[5] Twenty-first-century American advertising history makes little sense without a thorough understanding of the early history of the cinema slide.

DROP CURTAINS OF GLASS AND LIGHT

Lantern slides were generally still photographs printed onto a coated plate and displayed on a large screen. Projection could occur via either an attachment to the motion-picture projector or a specially designed projecting device (little more than a light source and a lens). A few manufacturers printed their slides on mica (which tended to fade but was light and hard to break, thus costing little to ship) or cut simple block letters into brass or other metals (which, though minimalist, were virtually impervious to heat and impact damage).[6] Glass plates, however, offering a suitable middle ground between premature fading and immortality, were the most popular and readily available material. Premade photographic glass plates could be ordered in bulk—twenty-four plates per box, fifty boxes per case—by those engaging in mass glass production.[7]

Amateur advertising slides could also be created via various home-production methods—including the use of scratch slides

(slides painted with an opaque coating on which messages are scratched), adhesive letters (affixed to plain glass), or even type or handwriting (sandwiched between two pieces of glass for screening).[8] The simplicity of these homemade options, however, rendered them decidedly less common for advertising use. Though advertisers appreciated cost efficiency, they rarely wanted their names associated with such aesthetically simplistic forms as homemade slides. Such slides were more commonly reserved for emergency communication between the theater and its patrons, such as calling a patron to the lobby.

Commercial mass reproduction of slides was a multistep process, the first of which was the making of a usable image. An artist would draw the advertisement at an overlarge size—up to sixteen square inches—and generally in black and white; photographs could also be used, but drawn images were cheaper to reproduce and thus far more common in early advertising slides.[9] The industry standard was to paint an image in white onto black paper, as a design "on a background of solid, impenetrable black" was considered more pleasing to the eye.[10] From a practical standpoint, this "white-figure" style would keep the focus on the copy (rendered as the brightest thing on the screen) and would simplify the process of hand coloring the slides (dye could be generally washed over particular areas, as the dark background concealed sloppy work).

Much like nineteenth-century advertising lithography, advertising-slide images were typically generic creations of the slide company's own copywriters, designed to advertise classes of (rather than specific) products—for example, the Kansas City Slide Company's "Don't Throw Away Your Old Suit" slide, designed to advertise cleaning services.[11] (See fig 1.1 on p. 22.) These stock slides were designed to be ordered from catalogs in order to turn a profit from repeated small sales (no more than a few copies at a time) to merchants across the country. The ultimate generic slides were billboard slides—abstract or scenic borders with a large, empty white space in the middle for custom copy. If stock slides failed to impress, artwork could be commissioned or reproduced from client copy for a "special" slide—mass-produced, in exactly the number desired by the advertiser, immediately after the drawing was approved.[12]

Regardless of whether the slide was stock, billboard, or special, written copy was always brief. In an echo of developing theories of billboard copy in the rapid-transit age—quick impact via imagery and ultra-brief copy—time constraints became the defining element of slide copy.[13] Although the viewers were not in motion themselves, one could never be sure how long a given projectionist would leave the slide on the screen, and film viewers were presumed to be "incredibly slow" readers under the best of circumstances.[14] Slide advocate Frank Farrington suggested no more than four words per line, while the Kansas City Slide Company advocated a ten-word maximum for finished slides.[15] Farrington also warned against all-capital lettering, as it slowed down comprehension.[16] A section of the image was always left blank in order to insert the name and address of the dealer who ordered the slide; although the positioning of this empty space could vary depending on the slide producer or the copy design, traditionally the dealer space was the bottom quarter. Handwriting of this dealer information, however, was typically considered an unnecessarily ugly practice.[17] The Kansas City Slide Company once described it as akin to "going to a ball in evening clothes and gym boots."[18] By 1913, multiple companies were offering to professionally append dealer information via a sticker or piece of celluloid before the slide went into the mail.[19]

Once the primary image was selected or created, it would be placed in front of a camera (all images were drawn at the same scale so that the camera wouldn't have to be refocused) to capture a negative. A pedal-operated printing box allowed a single operator to rapidly expose a large quantity of slides.[20] After bathing them in developing fluid and washing them, the technician would have a stack of black-and-white slides at a uniform (American) size of three and a quarter by four inches.[21] The printed glass slides would then be hand colored.[22] Finally, a mat (complete with the slide maker's name and address) and a second piece of glass were laid on top to protect the image coating, and the layers were bound together with paper tape.

Finished slides were available for purchase by any size business and even by proxy. National advertisers could make bulk orders to be sent to local dealers as "helps" (shorthand for a piece of advertising material sent out by the manufacturer to help the dealer move the goods). Unless the Kansas City Slide Company's 1913 catalog contained false information solely for "bandwagon advertising," major companies ordered such helps very frequently; Kansas City Slide claimed that national advertisers accounted for 75 percent of its business.[23] Local merchants could order one or a few slides solely for their own use. Exhibitors could even order multiple one-off slides on behalf of a few local advertisers as a way to both lower total shipping costs for merchants and engage in a bit of censorship over what would appear on their screen.

Once completed, a projected advertising slide, like a high-tech version of hanging a sign on a theater curtain (visible when the curtain was closed between each act), separated the pieces of the film program, acting as a buffer zone in the reel-change pauses between short films and between program repetitions as a whole. For films longer than one reel, slides would have acted as an intermission. As such, lantern advertising was delivered in the same space as the entertainment but in a form distinctly different from its "moving" nature (and possibly containing content disruptive to an ongoing multi-reel film narrative). Additionally, unlike the advertising curtain, where the quantity of advertisements had no necessary impact on duration, lantern slide advertising was "discrete" but problematically impermanent (or, as it would be termed in later critiques of radio, "fleeting"):

Figure 1.2. A custom slide from the Perfection Slide Company for Just Wright Shoes. The black-figure artwork would have resulted in significant white space and a very bright screen—an aesthetic most slide makers opted to avoid. Author's personal collection.

only one advertisement appeared at a time, giving it the best possible chance of being read, but an advertisement had to clear the screen (never to return during that program turn) before another could take its place.[24] As such, an onscreen disruption (or, if one chooses to discuss the slides individually, a collection of disruptions) would occur repeatedly, every fifteen minutes, as the theater changed reels, and the duration of the disruption would be measurable, roughly, by the number of slides shown. The advertising lantern slide was, therefore, the nearest sibling the silent-era cinema possessed to the contemporary television commercial spot; it was seen, at least in the early 1910s, as a caesura integrated into the film program at regular intervals and was as often as not regarded as an imposition to be avoided (perhaps with a trip to the restroom or a conversation with a friend).

THE NICKELODEON AND THE SLIDE BOOM

The lantern slide as a medium dates back to at least the seventeenth century, though nineteenth-century developments in lamp technology were responsible for its widespread use.[25] Despite their disparate dates of invention, early motion-picture exhibition tended to treat film and slides as fellow travelers, as early storefront theaters and itinerant exhibitors would integrate motion pictures and slides into a broad display of projected images. Indeed, well-known itinerant showman Lyman Howe toured with slides exclusively before transitioning to films at a later date.[26] In early nickelodeon screenings, with the demand for films exceeding the supply, many exhibitors turned to technologies like the stereoptigraph—a motion-picture projector with a lantern slide attachment—in order to easily integrate song and news slides into film shows. As such, the interaction of lantern slides with the early film industry is a concrete example of an old medium helping to delimit and define the horizon of expectations of a newer medium. Indeed, Charles Musser has argued that the experiential and communicative properties of motion pictures were largely worked out in direct comparison with stage performance (vaudeville) and the magic lantern.[27] As stable, film-oriented theaters emerged, the "combined show" was, for many, the pinnacle of nickelodeon exhibition.

However, these early pairings appear to have been largely entertainment oriented—the slides were generally song slides or news images.[28] Although there is evidence for the existence of direct advertising slides in the late 1800s—the advertising screenings of New York's Commercial Advertising Bureau, Fred A. Clark's ad-subsidized screenings in department stores, and an exhibitor who claims to have interspersed Civil War slides in the 1880s with advertising material—this use was presumably uncommon.[29] Indeed, all such screenings of advertising slides would likely have been experimental; every advertising slide would have been either a one-off or part of a very limited production run. The slide was, like the film, a medium predominantly of entertainment. Mass production of advertising slides in the United States coincides with the development of nickelodeon theaters in 1905.

By this time, the advertising slide had developed as an alternative to theater-curtain advertising—long a staple of stage-performance intermissions—but failed to be widely adopted. In New York City's Murray Hill Theatre, for example, a kinetoscope was used to screen advertisements on the curtain in late 1903 or early 1904.[30] By 1904, growth in the advertising-slide industry was significant enough that the Kleine Optical Company of Chicago began offering 250 different billboard slides on which to write advertising messages "with an ordinary fine pointed pen."[31] The Lee Lash Company—authors of the first monograph on theater-curtain advertising—subsisted on the fault line between the two forms, offering advice on curtains and slides simultaneously.[32]

The truly transitional moment was 1908, when the major film producers regularized output by shifting to studio-bound production of fiction films.[33] The massive upswing in available product, combined with the popularity of cheap amusements in the wake of the Panic of 1907, allowed for a boom in nickelodeon businesses and a corresponding boom in slide production.[34] The song slide was the pivotal transitional form—a proto-advertising slide that both stabilized the presence of slides in motion-picture theaters and provided a foot in the door for paid advertising within the cinema program.[35] Song-slide usage, already common in vaudeville, peaked around 1910, as sheet-music publishers used the sing-along slide performance in motion-picture theaters as a form of indirect advertising to increase the popularity and sales of their new songs. Slide historian John W. Ripley asserts that nearly every motion-picture theater regularly integrated song slides at this time in order to avoid the interminable "reel change" announcement slide.[36] In short, the song slide, a means to both fill program time and add a touch of class to early exhibition, was also a key point of entry for the commercialization of theatrical spaces.[37]

The increasing number of theaters likewise produced a greater need for announcement slides—such as "Ladies, Please Remove Your Hats"—and increased the circulation of news slides (a slide alternative to the irregularly circulated filmed news footage that existed prior to the 1911 advent of newsreels). The demand for such content boosted the flow of film exhibitor dollars into the slide industry. Nickelodeon exhibition, flooding the slide makers with cinema-related cash, triggered a dramatic increase in both the circulation and quality of slides. Slide makers attempted to outclass each other with their products and to shame exhibitors into purchasing the latest and best slides. For example, the Levi Company traded on recent improvements to slide quality as early as December of 1908, when it declared that only a "Bumble Puppy" would still be using announcement slides of the previous generation.[38] New companies, offering either more aesthetically pleasing, more humorous, or sometimes simply cheaper announcement slides, flooded the market to compete for these dollars.

It was this 1908 flourishing of the slide market that also gave rise to the nationally circulated, massively reproduced advertising slide. Frank B. Howe, a slide maker writing for *Camera Craft* magazine in 1917, asserted that "the development of present day slides," including the advertising variant, could be traced to 1909. As late as 1906, Howe asserted, "the only variety of slide in use was the . . . 'picture slide' . . . [used for] lectures, travelogues, and home entertainments."[39] Howe's history appears to be accurate. The earliest known examples of mass-produced advertising slides appear in 1908, and we can reasonably date the proliferation and standardization of the form to a point just prior to 1910.

There were two important logics underlying this transition. First, the era from 1910 to 1915 witnessed "rapid growth" in national consumer advertising.[40] With a rising interest in marketing to immigrants and the poor via mass repetition of imagery (technically advertising to the illiterate), the advertisers were also in the market for new, image-based ways to reach the masses.[41] Second, the burgeoning cinema-slide market boosted interest in cinema applications. The rapidly developing slide industry became a cut-throat business almost overnight, as every successful new concept was imitated by a multitude of competitors within months of its premiere. See, for example, the Brayton Manufacturing Company's "baby show" scheme—nothing more than pictures of cute babies—which was immediately cloned by multiple companies in the summer of 1909.[42] At times the industry would descend to literal photocopying; unscrupulous businesses would rent slide series from a competitor and rephotograph them, eventually renting out the duplicates as their own work.[43] As such, companies were seeking not only new product lines to sell, but also ways to reduce their price point so as to gain market share through lower prices. Advertising could serve both of these ends. Though the relationship that developed between advertisers and slide makers was not a unique one (many forms of cinematic advertising developed in quick succession), it is apparent why the two would have been drawn together at this juncture: advertisers were seeking an audience, and the rapidly proliferating slide businesses—in desperate need of regular income—were seeking other revenue streams.

Between 1908 and 1910, the trade press indicates a dramatic upswing in advertising-slide production. The first to offer advertising slides via an ad in *Moving Picture World* in April 1908 was Boston's Preston Lombard, who offered "Announcement, Advertising, [and] Special" slides.[44] The Young Advertising Service of Manning, South Carolina, was also engaging in ad-slide sales by July 25, 1908; *Moving Picture World* declared that the company had "originated a good advertising proposition" in which it had "arranged with several moving picture establishments for space upon the canvas between acts."[45] Within four months, on November 7, 1908, commercial lantern slides were common enough for *Moving Picture World* to caution against their proliferation: "Quite a business was done Election Night [November 3] in several dime theaters . . . with advertising slides. We venture to caution these places, however, that this advertising the grocery, shoe, drug, and other stores in their neighborhood will in time drive the people away from their shows. They come there and pay to see moving pictures and illustrated songs and not to get quotations on green apples from some local grocer."[46] During the latter half of 1908, then, the notion of the advertising slide arose—perhaps independently in multiple cities—as a viable product for use in nickelodeons. Importantly, the unproven assumption that advertising was incompatible with the cinema audience's desires was asserted almost immediately. Both the use of slides and the assumption that they were an inherent evil in the cinema would swell enormously over the course of the next five years.

Slide manufacturers, both established and newly formed, quickly jumped into the advertising-slide field; between April 1908 and the end of 1910, at least twenty-three slide makers offered advertising slides through display ads in the pages of *Moving Picture World*.[47] Most companies boosted their product by declaring that "advertising slides will pay your expenses," as the Brayton Manufacturing Company had done in a trade ad on May 15, 1909.[48] Growth was rapid and, in the early days, beneficial. By June 12, *Moving Picture World* argued that the boom in the field over the previous year had created "a pleasing change . . . in the quality and character of the . . . announcements and advertising slides shown in nickel theaters," crediting Brayton in particular with elevating the quality of the form.[49]

The established centers of entertainment slide production—New York, Chicago, and Philadelphia—were also the hub cities for the ad-slide trade.[50] Companies dotted the countryside, however, with an unexpectedly large number of advertising-slide manufacturers sprouting across the state of Missouri, for example, presumably to take advantage of a nationally central location.[51] As such, it is undeniable that the advertising slide went through a phase of rapid development between 1908 and 1910, attaining early widespread adoption by both slide manufacturers and film exhibitors.

Though it is clear that the nascent field was in full swing by the end of 1910, it is equally clear that small manufacturers and local merchants were the predominant clients in the early years. The unsettled and local nature of early slide business can be seen directly in Sandusky, Ohio, where a pair of sixteen-year-old boys began an advertising-slide company and, by late May of 1909, were "getting out, after school hours and on Saturdays, two-hundred advertising slides a week."[52] The fact that young boys in Sandusky had heard of the concept implies its commonality, while their audacity in starting up and (briefly) succeeding with a business of this type strongly implies that, to this point, local manufacture was still more common than postal order or dealer "helps." By early 1911, columnist Thomas Bedding, in an article in *Moving Picture World,* came near to directly stating that such conditions persisted. Bedding admitted surprise that the "soulless" advertising man, who would "advertise on a funeral hearse" if given the chance, had not adopted the motion-picture theater for advertising purposes. While his mocking tone was not exactly inviting to advertisers, it is clear from his article that "Mr. Postum, Mr. Moxie, [and] Mr. Munyon," among other major advertisers, were not at this point attempting national brand advertising through the medium of slides.[53] As such, the quantity of active advertising-slide producers in these first few years likely greatly exceeds the number advertising nationally in trade presses like *Moving Picture World,* as the bulk were producing local slides for local use.

There are several plausible reasons for the rapid proliferation of commercial slide companies at this time. Part of the proliferation might have been caused by successful companies giving birth to competitors—as the Neosho Slide Co. did when A. V. Cauger moved 150 miles north and formed the Kansas City Slide Co. around 1910.[54] The fledgling industry was also amenable to small start-ups. Though large companies existed (Kansas City Slide already had thirty-two employees in 1912, which ballooned to sixty-three by 1914), the North American Slide Company of Philadelphia was able to operate with only three employees from 1916 to 1919.[55] Two blocks up the street, the No-Destructo Slide Company employed only six Philadelphians in 1916.[56] The explosion of spending in an industry of mostly small businesses would also undoubtedly have drawn unethical prospectors in search of a quick buck. Such appears to be the reason for the existence of the Marshaw Slide Manufacturing Service, which so frequently cashed checks without filling orders that *Moving Picture World* published two articles provoked by the outpouring of complaints.[57]

Most important, however, was the established relationship between slides and motion pictures in nickelodeon exhibition practices. Dedicated film theaters delivered a series of short films—one reel (roughly fifteen minutes) in duration—from a single projector. Both song and announcement slides had developed as common means of filling the pause created during a reel change. This gap was a clear and established zone of indeterminate (but definitely nonfilmic) content, during which a seated audience patiently waited for the next film. With exhibitors already seeking ways to fill this technologically mandated pause and turning to slide manufacturers to do so—especially the promotionally inflected song slides—advertisers interested in reaching the large and growing customer base of the motion pictures had an obvious form on which to focus their attention. Offering to pay the cost of announcement slides in exchange for including advertising, or, better yet, offering to pay the exhibitor a small weekly fee for the space (helping them "pay the rent"), advertisers would not have found it difficult to stake claim to a part of the temporal flow that the film industry proper seemed incapable of or uninterested in filling. Though dated, lantern slide advertising emerged specifically as a way to capitalize on a large audience rendered idle by a reel change.

PRICE-CUTTERS, PREDATORS, AND PROFESSIONALS

Despite early improvement, the young commercial slide industry was rapidly flooded with small businesses "incompetent in the extreme" and was so devoid of standards of practice that it looked as though it would soon self-destruct.[58] The slide industry's most pronounced problem was price-cutting, resulting in largely unsatisfactory slides being made just as slides were becoming common in theaters. As photography journalist T. Stanley Curtis asserted, in late 1911, "a number of men who possessed more business acumen than photographic or artistic talent . . . have entered the field and flooded it with worse than mediocre work, cutting their prices to the detriment of the conscientious slide makers." Curtis also helpfully added that "it was at the time when the demand increased so suddenly that the 'shyster' slide-makers started their work," implying the importance of the nickelodeon boom to the rise of "shysters" without directly stating the fact.[59]

By early 1909, the Ohio Transparency Company was already using a price-cutting reference as its company slogan: "The Best not the Cheapest."[60] By the middle of 1911, the Niagara Slide Company humorously attempted the reverse tactic, taking out a display ad in which it claimed it had been "arrested . . . for selling slides too cheap."[61] Publicly declared prices—still common in slide company self-advertising during these early years—also show a clear downward trajectory. The Brayton Manufacturing Company was advertising hand-colored advertising slides from custom copy for fifty cents each in December 1908.[62] In March of 1909, the Levi Company dropped its price to thirty-five cents per slide, attributing the reduction to "increased facilities."[63] Later that same year, the Marshaw Slide Manufacturing Service matched that price.[64] In mid-1912, the Erker Bros. Optical Company of St. Louis used the thirty-five-cent price as a launch special for its new designs and even offered to cut further (four dollars per dozen, or thirty-three and one-third cents per slide) for larger orders.[65] That same year, George Birt of Indianapolis offered advertising slides for thirty cents each and had cut corners so badly that his slides were nothing but black letters on color-tinted glass.[66] By 1913, the Greater New York Slide Company had dropped its offer as low as eighteen cents per slide, if ordered in quantities of one hundred and (quite accurately) called it "an *extremely* low price for good advertising slides."[67] In the surviving data, the historical low point is found in a one-year contract, commencing in late 1914 and signed by the Advertising Slide Company of St. Louis, in which the company agreed to a price of sixteen cents per slide.[68] However, slide maker Frank B. Howe, in his 1917 historical overview of the market, even asserted that hand-colored custom-designed slides could be had for as little as ten cents during this period.[69] Under such conditions, it is unsurprising that companies could form and fold in less than a month—as Louisville's Advertising Specialty Company did in early 1912.[70]

Compounding the problem, popular images were rapidly and heavily pirated by unscrupulous opponents. Such companies would even publicly boast of their superior renditions of the work of others. A 1913 catalog from the Kansas City Slide Company, for example, included a page with eight slide images, four of which were the original designs of their competitors, while the other four were their own "superior" renditions.[71]

In this wildly competitive market, a subset of slide companies—the larger companies regularly advertising in the trade press—attempted to add elements to their business model to help carve out a stable and profitable niche. Most of these elements ran directly parallel to principles of the established, print-focused advertising agencies: cultivating a notion of professional expertise, space brokering, and offering services like distribution and screening assistance.[72] An oligarchy of high-end slide makers developed through these efforts to combat the price-cutting problem.

"Professional" rhetoric—assertions that one could be a slide advertising expert—ran rampant in these early years, as companies attempted to mimic the full-service notion of traditional agencies by marketing themselves as not only manufacturers of slides, but creators of both visual and written copy. The Brayton Manufacturing Company, in its first full-page display ad, used the word *Artists* five times (along with the words *Original* and *Alive*) as a buffer between the two columns.[73] The following month, Brayton asserted that profit was just a side effect of its public respect as "artists" and claimed that "money-making is not our business or pleasure."[74] As early as 1911, the Lee Lash Company asserted that the weight of experience—its long history of "censorship" of advertising curtains—had given the company keen insight into advertising copy.[75] By 1912, the Thornton Advertising Company encouraged advertisers to see its hiring of B. S. Presba—described as a man with years of experience in slide advertising—as "evidence that . . . [it had] standardized Theatre Slide Advertising, and brought it to such a state of efficiency that it demands careful attention."[76] In 1913, the North American Slide Company brought the term *expert* into the industry for the first time when it declared that its slides were "made by experts—the copy prepared and the drawings made by trained specialists," resulting in its slides having "character . . . snap and go."[77] Within a decade—by 1922—the Kansas City Slide Company declared in its monthly catalog update, "Slide News," that the price of slides was for the art rather than materials; as such, a decrease in the price of glass would not decrease the cost of slides because they were "drawn by high-salaried experts."[78]

This, however, was simply the explicit rhetoric. Many companies also tacitly declared expertise by publishing catalogs of stock slides—implying clearly that their creativity was what was for sale. Although A. V. Cauger of the Kansas City Slide Company claimed to have been "the first concern in the slide business to put out an illustrated list," the Levi Company catalog was already in its second edition as early as 1908—two years before the Kansas City Slide Company opened for business.[79] Within a few years, many of the more prominent slide producers—including Brayton, Scott and Van Altena, the Niagara Slide Company, the Erker Bros. Optical Company, and Burden and Salisbury—directly mentioned catalogs in their self-advertising, and many others were likely circulating catalogs without leaving a paper trail in the trade press.[80] By 1917, the practice was so common that photography expert Thomas P. Mason asserted that anyone thinking of starting a commercial slide company should, as their first act, "classify his possible customers according to their lines of business and then make up . . . some ready-to-serve designs" that could be made and sold immediately through a catalog list.[81] In the absence of (or possibly in addition to) a catalog, some companies would even send one slide free as an example of the high quality of their work. Both the Mica Non-Breakable Slide Company, in 1912, and the Columbia Slide Company, in 1915, even offered to make a free sample from the advertiser's copy.[82] Either through direct claims or the weight of catalogs, advertisers were encouraged to see slide copy as an expert service.

"Professionalization" was not just implied in copy-writing practices. In an attempt to indicate that slide advertising was a stable and accepted medium, slide producers either offered or explicitly guaranteed distribution in various ways. Space brokering—the very same concept the print-based agencies had used in the late 1800s to stabilize magazine and newspaper advertising—was the method of choice for the Motion Picture Advertising Company and Lee Lash Company, both of New York City, and the Auerbach Advertising Agency of Butte, Montana.[83] Space brokering in motion pictures consisted of the signing of exclusive contracts with a number of theaters and then reselling the contracted advertising space to clients as part of the cost of a slide purchase.[84] The Lee Lash Company had enough theaters under contract that a one-year advertising deal running until May 31, 1913, was valued at $87,946.[85]

In the absence of space brokering, two other forms of guarantee were attempted: offering a check-up service or offering to aid in contracting theaters. At least one, the Thornton Advertising Company, took the former course and attempted "to absolutely guarantee service" by using a system of "territorial managers" to personally double-check that slides were being screened as promised and in good condition.[86] Although Thornton is the only example I have uncovered, this method would have been relatively easy for small, locally focused slide producers to integrate. Multiple slide concerns—such as the Harold Ives Company and the Neosho Slide Company—went the latter route and offered to aid in contracting with theaters for screenings of finished slides.[87] These methods of guaranteeing circulation in the absence of space brokering contracts with theaters were attempts to prove that slide advertising was not a scattershot and unprofessional affair and that the professional slide maker had the experience and knowledge necessary to get advertising slides onto screens.

In short order, the larger slide producers began describing themselves as full-service agencies for motion-picture theater advertising. In 1912, the Neosho Slide Company declared that it made slides "complete from the design to the guaranteed delivery of the slides to your trade."[88] By 1914, the Kansas City Slide Company was offering contracts for service that included new slides weekly that were conceived, made, and mailed with no need for continual advising by the advertiser.[89] In 1921, the Standard

Slide Corporation's notion of a full-service slide-manufacturing company was clear from the following description: "We prepare the layout of the copy for the slide; explain how the slides can be used to the best advantage; secure the dealer's cooperation and take entire charge of the distribution of slides direct to dealers with return card check-up."[90] Integrating elements of all of the above—copy writing, consultation, and distribution assistance—the slide manufacturer as professional expert on slide advertising became common by the mid-1910s, as slide manufacturers effectively became cinema-based ad agencies in an American advertising culture where medium exclusivity was still a common way of differentiating advertising companies.

Much of the above professionalization, despite the slide industry's largely catalog-based (and therefore local-merchant-based) business, included one further rhetorical spin designed to imply strength and stability: the implication was always that slides were plausible for national campaigns. The attempt to draw national advertising contracts as a way to legitimize and stabilize both a company (through windfall profits) and the industry (by association with mainstream advertisers) was often rhetorically baldfaced. Overt name-dropping of national manufacturers who had once used a slide maker's service proliferated in self-advertising. Often such mentions included example images printed as part of the display ad. For example, well-known brands and manufacturers like Arrow Collars and the American Tobacco Company appeared in the self-advertising for the Greater New York Slide Company and Niagara Slide Company respectively.[91] The Advertising Slide Company of St. Louis even circulated a portfolio of previous work for national advertisers like Coca-Cola, Sunkist Oranges, and the Heinz ("57 Varieties") Corporation.[92] Other companies overwhelmed a lack of concrete detail with large numbers—like Neosho's 1912 declaration that "40 National Advertisers" were using its distribution service or the Novelty Slide Company's boast that "115 National Advertisers" had at one point signed a contract for its slides.[93] Perhaps the best evidence of the perceived importance of the blessing of national advertisers comes from the Thornton Advertising Company; in 1912, and apparently in the absence of any firsthand national campaigns, the company circulated an enormous list of the former clients of B. S. Presba, though these clients predated his association with Thornton itself.[94] The presumed endorsement of national advertisers, on top of full-service appeals, made top-flight ad-slide manufacturers look quite stable.[95]

LOST IN THE WOODS

Despite all these efforts, the advertising-slide business, in the short term, was a troubled realm. Price competition by small, often fly-by-night producers had placed individual company profit above market health and had devastated the public reputation of the form. Regardless of the attempts by the larger manufacturers to attain professional credibility, cut-rate slide producers and their many clients created an avalanche of shoddy product and poor display practices and a massive backlash against advertising slides.[96] To the vexation of the larger slide makers, in-cinema advertising became not only common, but so often incompetently produced that public complaints proliferated. A parade of exhibitor rejections and legal restrictions of slides appears in the historical record between 1912 and 1916.

As spectator complaint expanded, many exhibitors took it upon themselves to try to force advertising off of cinema screens. At least one prominent member of the film press—*Moving Picture World*'s own Epes Winthrop Sargent—playing on growing anti-advertising feelings, made claims to a supposedly higher moral standing that the "manager" had over the "billposter." Sargent asserted the need to "have respect for your business even if you have none for yourself." For Sargent, the exhibitor who would turn a screening of *Quo Vadis* into a "store show" by breaking it up with slides indicating "that the bull Ursus kills represents a well known brand of smoking tobacco" was the epitome of capital-influenced moral degradation.[97] Exhibitors themselves often simply refused to run ad slides, occasionally using such a decision as a reason for chest-thumping in the press. A few theaters in Louisville, Kentucky, for example, voluntarily abandoned slides altogether in 1912 on the grounds that "the public . . . [was] not meeting the show-slide with particular warmth, and that not enough business [could] be secured to make the shortening of the shows worth while."[98] The Dreamland Theater, of Augusta, Georgia, was more boisterous in its rejection, asserting not only that "no advertising slides go on our screen . . . at any price," but also that it would not even place advertising in its printed programs.[99] Multiple public refusals of this nature are recorded in the motion-picture trade press.

Two specific legal attacks on slide advertising have also come to light. In 1915, Bloomington, Illinois, added an extra twenty dollars per year to the licensing fee for theaters using "advertising slides or curtains."[100] Acting as both a deterrent (for theaters that did not want to pay an extra twenty dollars before inaugurating a possibly damaging advertising line) and a sign of acceptance (simply an added tax on increased profits), the Bloomington advertising fee indicates not only the commonality of debate of the topic, but also the public's difficulty in knowing quite how to respond to it. The double-edged law implies the existence of both quality professional slides and cheap profiteering. Legislators in Boston attempted to pass a bill in 1916 of much less ambiguity: the bill would have made it illegal to show any advertising onscreen in Boston—"with the exception of . . . religious or charitable institutions or events, or when it refers to his own theatrical affairs"—with a mandatory fine of fifty to two hundred dollars for violators and a license revocation for repeat offenders.[101] By the mid-1910s, then, public condemnation of slides had reached such a fever pitch that local government was stepping in.

In the absence of the defunct song slides and with the growing reluctance to use advertising slides to fill the gaps between reels, the advertising slide began slowly slipping out of typical theater programs. Many exhibitors turned increasingly to self-promotion to fill gaps. During the early 1910s, an increasing use of homemade slides to announce either the next film in the program or the program for the following day led to an eventual professionalization of the "coming-attraction" or "advance" slide. In 1911, F. H. Richardson, in early advertising for his typewriter slides, declared that "up-to-date theaters use them for announcing future programs"—a practice that surely dated back to old scratch and handwritten slides in the earliest film theaters.[102] Earlier that year, exhibitor Samuel Acri, in a letter to the editor of *Moving Picture World,* requested that the practice be professionalized. Acri asked studios to circulate advance slides with images and names of actors and actresses on the grounds that the drawing power of certain performers could improve box-office receipts if it was used to advertise.[103] Over the following years, the coming-attraction slide would be tested in a number of formats by independent studios in an effort to increase the competitive value of their films. In July of 1912, both the Crown Feature Film Company and Universal were offering "announcement" slides for their upcoming productions.[104] Reliance offered advance announcement slides—made by high-class slide producers Scott and Van Altena—by 1913.[105] Between 1912 and 1913, a number of general slide producers also began circulating coming-attraction slides (apparently without studio consent or funding), including the Novelty Slide Company and the Manhattan Slide Company.[106] By early 1913, however, the practice was still so haphazard that the Windsor Cut-Out Slide Company of Baltimore was offering, for seventy-five cents per week, rudimentary coming-attractions slides that featured nothing but a list of the next program's titles cut out of plain paper.[107] Discussion of the Windsor slides, in *Moving Picture World,* provides evidence for the growing use of the pause

Figure 1.3. An advance slide for the Dorothy Phillips feature *Once to Every Woman*. Though it features complicated border work and was circulated by a film studio, the aesthetic arrangement (figure upper left, description upper right, gap for local information at the bottom) follows the established standards of stock slides from consumer-goods advertising slide makers. Author's personal collection.

between reels to streamline audience pleasure. Rather than frittering away the pause on advertising or songs, only to have spectators get up to leave in the early moments of a film (after realizing that the program has started to repeat), Windsor advocated for the use of film-title slides not only to announce the next program, but even to announce the next picture in the current sequence. In this way, patrons would "have a chance to leave before the [actual film] is thrown on the screen."[108] The advance slide, then, became a standard form of exhibitor discourse with patrons in the early 1910s, both to keep the program running smoothly and to entice patrons to return for more.

Other forms of theater self-publicity joined the coming-attraction slide in the pauses in the program. One example was the Novelty Slide Company's advocacy of regular screenings of a slide indicating that the theater was "A Member of the Exhibitor's League of America." This information would supposedly indicate that one's program was consistently of the highest quality.[109] Such self-advertising tactics are indicative of a transition in exhibition philosophy before 1915, when exhibitors would attempt to either phase out the reel change pause (by installing a second projector and moving to a model with only one intentional intermission between turns of the program) or use the pauses for theater business.[110] This streamlining of the program sequence purportedly for the benefit of patrons, while not completely incompatible with continued advertising-slide use, reduced the amount of space available for their integration.

Quality cutting had clearly damaged both exhibitors' and advertisers' faith in the standard advertising slide. It therefore seems reasonable to assume that the commonly reported "hissing" at slides by angry spectators was not a natural response to an unwanted imposition into the film program, as silent-era critics would contend. Rather, slide hatred was the outgrowth of a particular historical moment in which the slides themselves were ugly and often screened for months on end, even when dirty and broken, and in which the quantity had escalated beyond the tolerance level.[111] Indeed, a 1921 article in *Moving Picture Age* declared that "almost any theater owner will agree that it is the poor slides that draw the kicks. For this reason the . . . theater manager . . . must insist on good slides."[112] Though a minority of voices likely continued to oppose advertising slides throughout the silent era—decrying them as a generic evil of the motion-picture theater—the origin of viewer and exhibitor displeasure was abusive early business practices that put slide-industry competition above spectator desires.[113]

Although the print-based ad agencies were, even then, waging a successful battle against public distrust, the lantern slide industry—less entrenched in the business model of exhibition than print ads were to magazines and newspapers—struggled to fight a battle against public distaste in the absence of clear financial underwriting of the exhibition field.[114] The evolving oligarchy of large manufacturers, while shifting their business model to full-service and their rhetoric to national advertiser appeals and professionalization, paralleled their self-elevation with critique of the problems in their industry. Decrying price-cutters as the bane of the slide field, this minority of major slide makers both admitted and condemned the state of their industry in an attempt to put themselves above the fray. In seeking to rationalize and solidify their industry and to shift the public perception of slides from parasite to legitimate cinema adjunct, major slide manufacturers did not simply offer better product, but argued explicitly that quality was the opposite of low cost. High price became almost synonymous with quality production.

Although T. Stanley Curtis asserted in late 1911 that the price-cutting situation was starting to improve, the movement for higher-quality slides would not become apparent in slide-maker self-advertising until 1912 and 1913.[115] As early as 1912, direct mention of prices in display advertising began to disappear. Many, including the Kansas City Slide Company, eventually began to hold the line on prices in order to keep quality up—their minimum price for stock advertising slides was fifty cents each in 1913.[116] Signs of the coming transition to pricier slides appear in the advertising from the Niagara Slide Company in 1913, which held to the then-common thirty-five-cent price tag only for duplicates; the first iteration of any ad slide would cost fifty to seventy-five cents.[117] The Neosho Slide Company was attempting a rhetorical flourish to justify higher prices as early as 1914, claiming "the best is always the cheapest" (a bit of linguistic double-talk that, though still capable of drawing business from someone scanning the page for the word *cheapest*, actually meant that the greater returns from a more expensive ad paradoxically made it a "cheaper" advertisement).[118] In its previously cited 1912–1913 contract, the Lee Lash Company legally claimed the value of its slides at one dollar each—a claim that was not contested.[119] In 1914, the Perfection Slide Company offered any two slides, out of a pictured eight, for $1.50.[120] By 1915, a letter to the editor of a journal for piano tuners indicated that Neosho's price for stock slides was also seventy-five cents at that point, and the Best Slide Company took to openly deriding price-cutting in its catalog, saying "the price cutter never commands respect."[121]

Though it is difficult to name a date for when, or even if, the major players in the industry entirely won the price-cutting conflict and rallied around a stable minimum of pricing, it is clear that the problem dragged on, in some regions, at least as late as 1917. *Camera Craft* magazine published two articles that year in which descriptions of price-cutting were worded to imply that it was a current problem. Frank B. Howe's previously cited article of February 1917 claimed that coming-attraction slides could still be had for nine cents and asserted that only two companies were then holding the line on prices.[122] Thomas P. Mason, though he was writing six months later and claimed that good slides were worth between $.75 and $1.50, still took the time to mention that one could not cut costs to twenty-five cents or less and maintain quality because "it costs an average of thirty cents each to make and market the slides."[123] As such, fading low-end manufacturers might have persisted in price-cutting up until the start of American involvement in World War I.

"UNITY OF ACTION SPELLS SCREEN SUCCESS"

By roughly mid-decade, the slide industry had taken on the appearance of a speculative bubble that had already burst. The boom around 1910 and the near bust by the early teens—due to price-cutting, the rise of two-projector theaters, and increasingly vocal opposition from some exhibitors and legislative bodies—appeared to outweigh the improvements in professionalization via full-service claims and improved production quality. Indeed, the increasing use of reel-change pauses and intermissions for theater self-advertising appeared to be the final straw for a medium that was a technological relic even at its advent. Despite this, a number of slide companies had developed enough market clout to persist in the uphill battle to stabilize, legitimize, and even expand the field.

The avenue to eventual stabilization, both regionally and nationally, came when attempts to control and eliminate price-cutting pushed the oligarchs to unite, simultaneously creating combines of even greater market power and expanding the national reach of a single advertising contract. Early rumblings occurred in the hub cities of Chicago and New York. In 1913, Chicago's International Slide Advertising Company attempted to engage all local exhibitors as stockholders. Using a dividend structure to encourage exhibitors to use the most expensive slides possible, International hoped to boost both the quality of slides and the income from them. The plan faltered quickly, likely because International had invited exhibitors to the meeting under false pretenses (having advertised it as a formative meeting for an Independent Exhibitors' League).[124] The following year in New York, where cut-rate producers were so common as to threaten the entire local industry, a small group of manufacturers decided that a slide monopoly would be more effective against price-cutting. Late in 1914, an undisclosed ringleader company (most likely Joseph F. Coufal's Novelty Slide Company) sent letters to all the prominent New York concerns suggesting a group meeting. This ringleader argued that a single large company could stamp out price-cutters more effectively while simultaneously offering more drawing power for national advertisers.[125]

Though nothing appears to have come of these initial efforts, two years later a New York association, rather than an amalgamation, of quality slide producers went into effect. Led by the Novelty Slide Company, seven powerful New York slide companies banded together in an official association. Envisioned as a slide-centered adjunct to the National Association of the Motion Picture Industry (NAMPI—an early film industry organization designed to "clean up" the movies), the group operated under the slogan "Unity of Action Spells Screen Success."[126] This association was designed "to promote the quality of the lantern slide, and to insure for exhibitors a standard of workmanship in slides"—in part by "standardization of prices with a fixed minimum," banning the "imitat[ion] of another's design," and by eliminating free samples, free design work, and other "illegitimate competitive methods."[127] The association thus directly attacked poor business practices in the field. Though no extant information on this organization stresses advertising as a fundamental issue, it is worth noting that of the seven charter members—Novelty Slide Company, Manhattan Slide and Film Company, Perfection Slide Company, Commercial Slide Company, Greater New York Slide Company, Excelsior Illustrating Company, and Long and Heller Inc.—all but the latter had been soliciting the business of national advertisers for years.[128] The additional fact that, by 1920, "the kind of slides in demand are used mostly for advertising purposes" effectively turns any action by slide companies into a decision regarding advertising dollars.[129]

The association of price with quality—so obvious in Coufal's slide-maker association—was paralleled by attempts to encourage both advertisers and exhibitors to engage in more responsible screening practices. For advertisers, this was accomplished through a transition to long-term service contracts that included mandatory slide changes on a regular basis. For exhibitors, this included exhortations to limit the quantity of slides integrated into the program.

Changing the slide weekly, or at worst biweekly, became something of a mantra for those interested in regularizing the form. G. R. Lowe of the Neosho Slide Company, "Old Man Best" of the Best Slide Company, and independent advisors Frank Farrington and Ernest A. Dench all encouraged the use of a new slide every week.[130] Most worded the advice pessimistically, citing advancing levels of irritation, though D. H. Harris optimistically declared that "change of copy . . . brought the largest response."[131] Keeping the patrons from seeing the same slide multiple times was deemed essential to evading spectator irritation.[132] For a cinema culture not yet used to reruns (a common experience for the television and home-video generations), repetition of slides was seen as an inherent fault.

In another surprising echo of the history of advertising lithography, proliferation also became a key issue for lantern slides.[133] It is not uncommon to run across, in the trade press of the early 1910s, hyperbolic condemnation of the quantity of advertising slides. To name just two examples, in 1911, Charles A. Young reported that Chicago's Elmo Theater was opening its program with "two dozen or so" ad slides, while in 1914, "a correspondent" in Guthrie, Oklahoma, noted "a twenty- or thirty-minute siege of advertising slides at moving picture houses."[134] Excessive slide usage was common enough that many slide proponents felt moved to suggest a specific numerical limit. In late 1911, *Motography*'s resident projection specialist, William T. Braun, proposed that "no more than two or three should be run at each show" and asserted that further congestion could be relieved by dispersing that limited number into multiple reel changes.[135] By 1913, John B. Rathbun—author of a guide to film production and exhibition—asserted that "three slides should be the limit in any case" and warned strongly against screening any outside of the intermission "after the theater is darkened for the show."[136] The most permissive (and most common) quantity that has turned up in my research was twelve per program. Ernest A. Dench asserted in 1916 that in a good theater, "the slides do not exceed one dozen."[137] Exhibitor S. L. "Roxy" Rothapfel proposed the same number that year as well.[138] The spectatorial experience was to be disturbed minimally and always with fresh, professional-looking advertising material. Although no published sales material from slide companies declares such to be the case, it is plausible that both space brokering and other forms of exhibition assistance were inaugurated specifically for this reason—as a way for slide producers to help limit the number of slides any given theater would screen.

Through these efforts by top-flight slide producers to legitimize and professionalize the field at the expense of any small slide producer attempting to compete on price alone, large national advertisers were becoming sold on the value of slide advertising. More and more consumer-goods manufacturers dabbled in the field, to varying degrees of success. The makers of Calumet Baking Powder found, in a survey of dealers in 1912 and 1913, that slide advertisements were dramatically increasing sales; in one extreme case, a dealer, after regular slide advertising for two months, saw a 50 percent increase in total sales.[139] The trade press for druggists had declared slides the best form of advertising for soda as early as 1914.[140] The "Question Box" section of the 1914 *Monthly Bulletin of the National Commercial Gas Association* was also enthused, as all but one dealer reported good results from slide advertising, provided regular changes were maintained and seasonal articles were stressed.[141] Goodyear was also sold on slide advertising by 1914, and its "Dealer Help Book" for that year asserted that the movie-theater patron "sees [advertising] at a time when his mind is not only most influenced by what you have to say, but when you are sure of his WHOLE attention."[142] Some combination of slide-producer professionalization, cinema psychology rhetoric, and measurable financial impact had developed a distinct appreciation of the short, direct advertising slides in cinema programs.

As the quality of slides improved, a few exhibition groups changed their tune. Two state exhibitor leagues—Ohio and Michigan—along with the exhibitors association of St. Louis (which consisted of fifty theaters) went so far as to allow theaters to pay their monthly dues to the association by running a slide for which the association, rather than the theater, was paid—effectively making the association itself a space broker. Although all three groups made allowances for exhibitor reluctance, allowing them to pay dues in cash if they desired, the fact that regional exhibition groups had accepted slides to such a degree indicates a generally dwindling exhibitor hesitancy.[143] Likewise, tirades about abusing cinema patrons all but disappeared from the trade press after 1916.[144] Every published mention of slide advertising from 1918 to the early 1920s was an unreserved recommendation. Surprisingly, then, the era of slide hate—so overblown in the historical memory of the form—was actually relatively brief and very early. It was largely a memory by the mid-teens. While it may be a stretch to assume that advertisers, exhibitors, and spectators had found mutually acceptable ground, at the very least, the public debate had burned itself out and moved on to other areas (like product placement, industrial films, and advertising trailers, all of which were much more common after World War I). The advertising-slide industry was, with the disappearance of large-scale public condemnation in print, left to persist or dissolve on a company-by-company and exhibitor-by-exhibitor basis.

POLITICS, PHILANTHROPY, AND PATRIOTIC PERSUASION

The fact that advertising slides persisted, even in the wake of the advent of advertising trailers (see chap. 2), indicates that the implied reduction of antipathy was, in practice, an actual one. This stabilization of the commercial advertising-slide industry was historically abrupt and must therefore have owed a debt to

Figure 1.4. A slide for the US Fuel Administration, produced by the Unique Slide Company; one of countless examples of patriotic or philanthropic advertising circulating during the war. Author's personal collection.

tangentially related experiences in exhibition at mid-century. It cannot be coincidence that the apparent stabilization of the form occurred, much like all early twentieth-century advertising, in the years immediately surrounding World War I, when an avalanche of patriotic advertising was created for the war and consumer-goods advertising increased in response to the excess profits tax.[145] Indeed, a cursory glance at the wartime issues of *Moving Picture World* easily gives the (inaccurate) impression that the advertising slide was dead and gone. The few wartime mentions of consumer-goods advertising slides in the journal were entirely self-congratulatory descriptions of their supposed disappearance under the weight of patriotic slide needs. An early editorial comment on patriotic slides attempted to differentiate them from commercial advertising, calling ad slides "business" and saying "no one 'talks business at a club,'" while political talk was inexplicably described as "wonderfully appropriate."[146] Thornton Fisher, in a delightfully snide tone, included a paragraph of "Reminiscences" in a 1918 column, remembering the "old" days: "When they used to throw slides on the screen between pictures. After having basked in the light of love's fond dream in one reel your vision would suddenly be startled by a slide announcing 'Henry Beermeister, Delicatessen, Liverwurst and Sausages,' or 'Visit Smith's Emporium. Clothes for all the family. Your father bought his pants from us. Why not you?'"[147] For Fisher, the content and directness of commercial messages were startling and baffling—different in both tone and topic from what had previously transpired on the screen. One is forced to wonder why a turn to politics would not have been considered equally abrupt.

Despite the obvious connection, the film industry was seemingly incapable of describing this outpouring of unpaid charity and propaganda slides during film screenings (including at least 100,000 Liberty Loan slides) as a furthering of cinema advertising.[148] This reluctance is doubly surprising with the knowledge that the same major slide manufacturers were central to both advertising and propaganda.[149] Rarely, in published material, was a political exhortation considered startling to an entertainment-seeking audience. This is likely due to the fact that charity and political advertising was tacitly or literally forced on exhibitors.[150] Two stories of exhibition groups grumbling about charity slides were recounted in the pages of *Moving Picture World* in 1915, when the exhibitors lamented the abuse of their generosity. Social welfare groups pressed so strongly for free assistance that refusal to help was tantamount to antisocial behavior.[151] Election slides were equally problematic. Jamestown, New York, exhibitor

M. L. Woods refused to run political slides in late 1916 in his two theaters on the grounds that they "stirred up strife and confusion, and attracted the attention of our regular patrons from the screen."[152] As such, political and charitable slides were opposed both for their refusal to pay and for their incompatibility with entertainment programs; both critiques echoed attacks on cinematic advertising.[153]

Once the Creel Committee began inundating exhibitors with demands for patriotic inclusions, the compulsion for assistance included a real threat of punishment. New Hampshire exhibitor Charles H. Bean made the threat nearly blatant in his letter, late in 1917, in which he encouraged cooperation with Creel Committee requests in the following terms: "In view of the fact that the United States Government has been lenient with motion picture exhibitors on the recent proposed tax of 10 per cent of gross receipts . . . every exhibitor . . . should show its appreciation and patriotism . . . by doing his bit in helping lend the fullest support of his screen to our government."[154]

In November of 1917, one exhibitor—J. H. Ruerup of Bozeman, Montana's Gem Theater—had his exhibition license revoked after purportedly declaring "to hell with the government" and refusing to allow Creel's Four Minute Men—touring patriotic exhorters—to speak in his theater.[155] The following year, H. J. Paradis—manager of the Oasis theater of Wilson, North Carolina—was likewise "investigated" for refusing to allow the Four Minute Men to speak on the far less inflammatory grounds that "it would disarrange his program."[156] Though Paradis was eventually acquitted, it is clear that rejection of government propaganda (or political advertising) was a dangerous choice that could arouse both cultural and governmental retribution.[157]

In an atmosphere in which public condemnation and even loss of one's theater were plausible outcomes, it is not surprising that exhibitors accepted the intrusion of political advertising on their screens. The film press helped to ease exhibitor hesitation by heaping praise on theater men as leaders of their communities. As early as mid-1914, W. Stephen Bush declared that the professional exhibitor was to be praised not for being a showman, but because "the great forces which to-day are working for the good of mankind are coming after the exhibitor to enlist his aid" through the screening of Safety First and Department of Health slide messages. Bush—relying on the notion of spectator captivity that would become common among cinema-advertising proponents during the 1910s—described the cinema as the best way to "reach all the public" because unlike print pages, which could be skipped, "you cannot escape the screen." The door opened by advertising slides—or, as Bush would have it, "the space which the cigarette makers could not buy at any price and which few exhibitors sell at any price for any advertisement"—became the avenue for the exhibitor to flex his social conscience, as it became the exhibitor's job to "mentally and morally" improve his community.[158] The coerced exhibitor could at least bask in the glow of public praise while he struggled to organize a pleasurable show around government slides, patriotic films, and the Creel Committee's mandatory political speakers.

Regardless of exhibitor consent, however, these political and philanthropic slides—shown largely from 1914 to the end of World War I—obliterated any advertiser, slide maker, and even exhibitor hesitation about the effectiveness of slides as an advertising medium. While some (perhaps even a majority of) exhibitors may have continued to harbor reservations about the intrusion of advertising onto their screens, there could be no doubt after the war that the site was an effective means of reaching the public. In 1914 and 1915, the pages of *Moving Picture World* clearly indicate a growing use of slides for these philanthropic and political purposes.[159] The campaign period of late 1916 witnessed substantial use of slide advertising for drives as disparate as voter registration in "a large Southern city," preservation of Cincinnati's Zoological Gardens, and road improvement in Battle Creek, Michigan.[160] As often as not, such slides were, in an echo of the bygone song slides, indirect advertising for major manufacturers, such as the "anti-fly" slides circulated by the International Harvester Company and the Detroit Brick Manufacturers and Dealers Association's fireproofing campaign.[161]

Most common of all was the political campaign slide featuring either the face of a candidate for office or an endorsement for a ballot issue.[162] As political tensions increased, the quantity of campaign slides escalated. Indeed, many of these slides were justified (i.e., not seen as an imposition or as patently offensive to the audience) when they became more openly self-serving. Countless theaters took up slide campaigns opposing motion-picture censorship and Sunday closings.[163] Exhibitors in the state of Illinois went so far as to mandate that any candidate who desired to run a campaign slide in a theater must first publicly oppose legal censorship of motion pictures.[164] *Moving Picture World* itself circulated anti-censorship slides as early as February of 1915, even taking ad agency N. W. Ayer & Son's old slogan, "Keeping Everlastingly at It Brings Success," as its own.[165] Renowned film director D. W. Griffith himself circulated slides, at his own expense, supporting the reelection of New York Governor Charles S. Whitman, who had vetoed a state censorship bill in his first term. Whitman won reelection.[166] In 1917, theater manager Joseph L. Steurle used cinema-advertising slides to come within 158 votes of the Democratic nomination for city auditor of Louisville, despite being a political unknown.[167] Though many exhibitors did not consider this a form of intrusive advertising, campaign slides were, like any other advertising, generally screened for a fee; "practically every theater in the city" of Louisville was attaining a "good price . . . for this service" in 1915.[168] With three distinct benefits—profit, furthering anti-censorship, and the integration of the theater into the modern information web—it is understandable why so many exhibitors would have found ways to integrate them into the program.

Even openly self-serving advertisements for consumer goods were acceptable to certain theaters. For example, some theaters offered to run slides advertising local papers in order to encourage them to have larger film sections.[169] As the theatrical self-advertising slide pushed traditional advertising slides further and further out of the program, a few consumer-goods producers found clever means to disguise advertising slides as announcement slides, indicating the class and quality of the theater. In exchange for a price break, the company that provided one's fire extinguishers or air purifiers would also give the exhibitor a slide indicating that their equipment was a primary reason why the theater was a safe and healthful environment.[170]

Postwar histories of the moment, however, would give virtually all credit for the success of political and cultural advertising in motion-picture theaters to the Liberty Loan and other related Creel Committee slides.[171] Indeed, the US government put a massive amount of money into slide advertising for wartime funding. Two New York companies—the Novelty Slide Company and the Unique Slide Company—received multiple payments for services rendered to the Departments of Food and Fuel Conservation during the war, some as high as four digits. For example, Novelty—whose president Joseph F. Coufal was part of Hollywood's War Cooperation Committee—received $7,811.76 on October 23, 1917.[172] The Excelsior Illustrating Company received $490 for "Safe Coal" slides on June 27, 1918, and the Unique Slide Company received $1,860 in two installments from the Department of Fuel Conservation on June 22 and August 31, 1918.[173] The war also brought with it the first definite attention in the historical record that slide advertising received from major ad agencies; the food conservation campaign was being handled, free of charge, by powerhouse ad agency J. Walter Thompson.[174] Wartime advertising dollars and the tacit blessing of a mainstream agency may therefore have stabilized the oligarchy of quality slide producers that had been developing prior to the war in the wake of price-cutting. It would be an extreme coincidence if wartime dollars and prestige did not aid Joseph Coufal's 1919 combine of slide manufacturers in which roughly half of the founding members of the 1916 New York association officially became a single company: the Standard Slide Corporation.[175]

After philanthropic and compulsory wartime propaganda had legitimized the presence of advertising in theaters on the grounds that it was a public good, it remained only for commercial advertisers to reclaim the site. Over the course of the war, several changes, problematic for advertising slides, had become common across the exhibition community. The integration of a second projector, so as to eliminate reel-change breaks, had become the mode of exhibition in most theaters.[176] The construction of picture palaces and establishment of studio-owned chains of theaters had solidified both a class divide and a split between urban and rural viewing. In the cities and/or in large theaters, overt class consciousness was, as often as anything else, tied to an explicit rejection of screen advertising. "Roxy" Rothapfel himself made the distinction, in an article from July 1916, when he declared that "in the cities [advertising] will not be tolerated at all in the best houses, while in the smaller towns it is taken rather as a matter of course and a part of the program."[177] Additionally, the commercial trailer (see chap. 2) had grown to prominence and was in competition for the same program space. As such, the lantern slide never regained the cinematic prominence of the early 1910s, though it did make a permanent reentrance after the war.

Likely as a result of the excess profits tax—which could be dodged by a company funneling ever-larger dollars into their advertising appropriation—ad slides were vigorously readopted by postwar companies spending ballooning appropriations on every medium imaginable. The new concept of the cross-media advertising blitz pulled lantern slides into the postwar mantra of "reiteration"—pushing the same advertising into all formats simultaneously.[178] As early as 1921, it was clear that the spending bubble had heavily impacted the glass slide. According to a history of advertising slides in *Moving Picture Age*, "During the post-war years slides came to be used in practically every line of business. *The tendency was to advertise through every possible medium*, and the dealers used all channels of help to continue the prosperous times. This abnormal period was so protracted as to allow commercial slides to become firmly entrenched as a successful advertising medium, not because the unusual situation encouraged products which had no merit, but because dealers used commercial slides and found that the investment yielded definite results."[179] As such, slide acceptance went hand in hand with advertising convergence and proliferation in the postwar boom. The wartime competition for space—which could easily have been the final straw for the direct advertising slide—became little more than a speed bump thanks to the postwar flood of advertising dollars.

Though slide dollars tapered off with the continuing growth of trailer advertising and the repeal of the excess profits tax in 1921, "slide-vertising"—as the Standard Slide Corporation became fond of calling it—had attained a level of acceptance that it would never truly relinquish.[180] A slowly dwindling number of entrenched companies would continue for decades to produce slides that were acceptable and desirable to national manufacturers, local distributors, and theater managers alike. In an almost triumphant note, the Standard Slide Corporation estimated that in 1921, "more than 8,000 theaters in the United States . . . and many more abroad" were open to slide advertising—a number that could have accommodated upward of five million slides per year.[181] Though estimates vary and these 8,000 were made up entirely of the lower-class houses, this would have accounted for roughly half of the active theaters in the United States at the time—an astonishing level of integration for a form of advertising that, a few short years earlier, was considered by many to be naturally offensive to film patrons.[182]

The slide had also made inroads with the mainstream advertising community. At least one prominent slide maker—the Advertising Slide Company of St. Louis—had developed a presence in its local advertising association.[183] By 1920, the Standard Slide Corporation—Joseph Coufal's New York conglomerate—was attending the yearly convention of the Associated Advertising Clubs of the World and openly solicited established advertising agencies by offering a special "Agency Rate Card."[184] Slides were deemed a safe-enough investment that mainstream manufacturers were, by the 1920s, generally having custom slides made; as *Moving Picture Age* somewhat inaccurately declared in 1921, "stock slides are practically a thing of the past," as the notion of cross-media advertising reiteration took firm hold.[185] Philanthropic advertising continued to act as a bulwark; its existence offered a convenient way to defend slide advertising as a valuable information service to the American public; for example, the American Humane Education Society circulated free slides for Be Kind to Animals Week in 1921.[186] The lantern slide—and its commercialized variant, the advertisement slide—had become an accepted adjunct to the film industry as a whole, and its progeny extend, though in increasingly circumscribed placement, all the way to the digital projectors of the present day.

SLIDE-VERTISING AND THE HAPPY CAPTIVE

The rhetorical debate over lantern slides, the first widely used form of direct advertising in motion-picture theaters, occurred in a relative vacuum and established the parameters for the debates to come. Supportive and antagonist rhetoric about advertising slides opened up debate on three fronts: the psychology produced by the cinematic space, whether or not low costs were outweighed by other problems, and the promise and problems of a fleeting advertisement in a public space. In every case, the debates seem to have deadlocked, resulting in the sharp downturns and slow growth that are very obvious in the history section above.

Figure 1.5. A complete Radio-Mat slide kit for typewriter slides. As indicated in the instructions, the user was to simply feed the entire paper sheet (lower left) through a typewriter, type onto the exposed red tissue paper in the center, and then tape the finished message in between two of the provided pieces of clear glass. Author's personal collection.

With its status as the forerunner of a movement, the slide could take advantage of some broad rhetorical claims that seem, in hindsight, wildly misplaced. Lantern slides were, of course, already a very old technology, and full-motion film advertisements had been made as early as 1910. By mid-decade, trailer makers would frequently critique slides for being out of place in an environment dedicated to moving pictures. Despite this, from 1908 to 1914, slides were regularly described as an "up-to-date" medium of advertising.[187] In line with historian Pamela

Walker Laird's argument that novelty is an important factor in the selection of advertising methods, the Harold Ives Company even called slides one of "this year's styles" in advertising, declaring that advertising is akin to fashion: "You can't hold your trade by last year's methods."[188] At worst, slides had not yet worn out their welcome with the public and should be adopted because "in many towns . . . [they] have not been overworked."[189] At times, the stillness of the slide even provided the implicit link to old media; the Lee Lash Company called slide advertising the "Front Cover Medium," effectively arguing that the cinema was the perfection of the magazine model—a medium in which one's standard advertising designs could have pride of place in the most eye-catching location imaginable.[190] These notions that in-cinema advertising via the glass slide was novel, stylish, and forward-thinking were important elements in the rhetoric for its adoption. For a small number of years in the early 1910s, the lantern slide was the hot new novelty in advertising.

Of course, with novelty comes unpredictability. In order to more clearly define the value of the cinema space to an advertiser, most slide proponents immediately leapt to the notion of "captivity." It is virtually impossible to find a single argument for the use of slides as an advertising medium that does not make some mention of slides being a 100 percent medium due to the assumption that "folks, in the darkened hall, must concentrate upon the screen."[191] As early as 1912, the Thornton Advertising Company claimed that slides were "the only medium which *guarantees* a reading of the advertiser's message."[192] Frank Farrington, the most vocal advocate of slide advertising in the first half of the 1910s, claimed that slides in cinemas had "no waste circulation" because "every man, woman, and child there sees the advertisement, and if it is given fair display and . . . allowed to remain long enough to be read, every man, woman, and child will read it and know what is advertised."[193] Standard Slide Corporation employee D. H. Harris even declared that audiences could "see nothing else, read nothing else, and *think* nothing else" while a slide advertisement was onscreen.[194] This was, of course, no more true for slide advertising than any other form of advertising in any other medium, but advocates of onscreen advertising preferred to ignore the fact that the room, even when dark, could not entirely compel. An unsigned article in the March 1921 issue of *Moving Picture Age* was as close as ad-slide proponents would get, in the transitional era, to acknowledging viewer empowerment, as the author made the marginally more hesitant assertion that the slide "is in front of [the viewer] and he has to look at it *or close his eyes*. With an attractively gotten up slide, preferably in color, he does not close his eyes."[195] The advertising-slide industry wanted advertisers to see the cinema theater as a site of audience passivity—where messages could be inserted into open eyes with no waste.

This notion of captivity became so rapidly assumed that most arguments segued directly from it to an argument about consequences. In the early 1900s, the expanding advertising industry was undergoing a turn toward medium-specific psychology, as everything from magazines to novelty records was marketed on the grounds that its form (the state of mind correlated to the way in which it was experienced) improved its ability to function.[196] For those whose livelihood depended on the sale of advertising slides, there was a uniform turn to a mythically receptive cinema viewer. If spectators had no choice but to read your advertisement, one would hope that they would not do so with hatred in their hearts. Thankfully, as far as slide makers and proponents were concerned, the motion-picture theater was a zone of uniformly happy people. Farrington noted that "no other form [of advertising] . . . is received in so favorable a frame of mind."[197] *Moving Picture Age* asserted that the motion-picture theater was a perfectly comfortable environment in which "every body [was] relaxed to enjoy the exhibition" and "every mind [was] alert to receive impressions."[198] The Harold Ives Company assured the advertiser that "the psychological moment to offer your sales arguments is when your listener is in an agreeable frame of mind"—a frame of mind only attainable by advertising during "pleasant, leisure hours."[199] The Levi Company even went so far as to assert that its slides were "Good for Sore Eyes" and were therefore "a distinct relief to the monotony of the film."[200]

It was at this point of presupposed happiness that opposition to screen advertising first crested. For opponents of slide advertising, the salient feature of a theater was not that movies were fun and made people happy, but that advertising was "an imposition upon their time." Regular *Moving Picture World* columnist Epes Winthrop Sargent declared: "The screen advertisement . . . is thrust upon the patron. He *must* read it whether he wishes to or not. There is no alternative. It is thrust into his face. . . . There is no objection to a few house slides, but the foreign advertisement has no place on the screen."[201]

Thus, slide opponents did not take issue with the assumption of compulsory attention. On the contrary, they reveled in it, arguing instead that the compulsory nature of the ads was, itself, what destroyed the receptive mood of a theater audience. Contrasting slides with magazine advertising, Roy D. Mock argued in 1916 that involuntary advertising "forced to his attention" would not leave the viewer in "a very satisfactory frame of mind" and would instead result in a backfire. Rather than "being inclined toward the advertiser . . . [viewers would] become biased against him."[202] Ernest Dench explicitly linked this hostility to a breach of the American social contract, calling compulsory methods "detestable to the people of this democratic country."[203]

Clearly indicating that the dispute was between definitions of the audience as active or passive, George M. Rittelmeyer argued in 1913 that "a few nights ago . . . I looked around the house to see how many people were reading the slides that were being shown. I counted probably a dozen people in an audience of about one hundred and fifty. The balance of the crowd was passing the time away the best they could, waiting patiently for the ads to cease." The disinterest was so obvious that he professed to see life return to the "bored, tired" faces of the crowd when the first reel finally came on.[204] For the opposition, screen advertising via slides was a worst-case scenario for the cinema; they were the opposite of pleasure.

Provided a potential slide advertiser was still optimistic despite these weighty concerns, adoption of the medium could still collapse through a cost-benefit analysis. Most of the arguments for the use of slide advertising specifically were connected to its cheapness (as opposed to the expense of producing an advertising film or even the expense of a print campaign). As Quality Slide and Photo Makers bluntly claimed, a slide "Reaches More People At a Smaller Cost Than Any Other Advertising Medium."[205] Though estimates of the cost of a motion picture were extremely variable and determined as much by selection of production company as by length of the final product that one was after, by World War I, a custom-made glass slide would generally cost about a dollar—shipping included—and sometimes significantly less. The Kansas City Slide Company was still charging seventy-five cents for stock slides as late as 1927. Even custom slides were only $1.25 at that late date, if the advertiser included their own artwork.[206] In 1920, the *Furniture Worker* estimated a price of seventy-five cents to one dollar for a custom slide, given that the illustration was provided by the advertiser and not designed by the slide manufacturer's staff.[207] This was undeniably cheaper than all but the smallest print display advertisement.

Additionally, the cost for running a slide in a given theater was typically low. Although we must remember Dench's assertion that "there are really no standard rates" for exhibition, as "each exhibitor has his own ideas in regard to the value of the location and size of his theater," we do have some indication of the range of prices at the time.[208] From the exhibitor's perspective, the income—based on quantity of slides and the amount the house was able to charge—could be as high as four digits; the Bijou Theater of Mt. Clemens, Michigan, claimed to be making $800 per year on the date that it abandoned advertising slides (on principle) in 1915.[209] From an advertiser's perspective, Farrington claimed that the absolute minimum cost was twenty-five cents per week for small houses where they ran films three nights a week.[210] An upper estimate would have to be that of the two top-flight theaters in Louisville, which were pulling down ten dollars per week, per slide in 1915.[211] The Keeshen Advertising Agency claimed, also in 1915, to be able to guarantee a minimum of four showings every day in five first-run Oklahoma City theaters for eighty dollars per month—an average weekly screening cost of only four dollars per theater.[212] Ernest Dench, despite being very hesitant about standards, offered a (very wide) estimate of five to ten dollars per theater, given a six-month contract. The latest estimate, from 1920, was "from fifty cents to two or three dollars, depending on the locality."[213] That said, some public-service advertisers, like libraries, for example, were often capable of getting theaters to screen their advertising slides for free, as if they were a charitable organization.[214] As such, although there was at least one assertion that a slide campaign would bear no fruit if it lasted less than three months, the total outlay for slide advertising was generally assumed to be much lower than it was for any other form of mass advertising.[215]

The cheapness of the medium was not simply a generalized positive. Specific value arguments were made. First, it was cheap enough to allow individual dealers to use it quickly to "couple up their name with products which are continually advertised in the magazines and newspapers."[216] Though an individual store may not have had much of a budget for advertising, the fact that they dealt in nationally recognized brands, especially if those national brands distributed glass slides for free as a selling "help," could allow the local store to piggyback on widely recognized advertising campaigns. As such, a very small outlay for a local store could effectively allow them to receive massive collateral advertising from newspapers, magazines, and billboards hawking national products.[217] Additionally, with the commonness of exclusive advertising contracts (no competing products or sellers allowed to advertise in the same theater at the same time), the appearance of having a monopoly on a national brand could make cinema advertising seem like very cheap advertising indeed for a local merchant, compared to the benefits it offered.

Thirdly, cheap slide advertising allowed for rapid, even constant, change in copy with minimal cost. A change of slides did not add any work for the exhibitor, and the easy availability of stock slides rendered the transition simple for the advertiser. As such, one could change slides at will. Additionally, the wide availability of extremely cheap home-typed or handwritten slides—purchased blank, in bulk, at an average rate of one penny per finished slide—allowed one to slip in a quick update when desired, letting regular customers know of a sale or special event.[218] Provided one had been advertising regularly in the theater and the sale announcement was seen as beneficial information, the audience would likely not take too unkindly to the general ugliness of a homemade slide.

Despite the obvious cheapness of the method, slide-advertising opponents pinpointed significant areas of concern—any of which could catastrophically increase the cost of slide usage if efforts were made to deal with them. Some writers tied audience irritation directly to ticket cost, asserting that not only was the audience being annoyed, but they were being forced to pay for the privilege. Indeed, in 1909, a "good many picture theater managers . . . declare[d] . . . that the exhibitor ha[d] neither the right to expect continued patronage nor the right to collect admission fees" if showing ads.[219] An unsigned article in 1915 voiced the still commonly heard opinion that advertising was incompatible with ticket costs, as "passing a dime into the box office makes one the proprietor of the screen . . . and anything that is shown without contributing to the amusement of the audience . . . is going to be frowned upon." The result was bound to be "hisses on the part of a good many people in the theater."[220] As such, arguments about advertising as an unwelcome imposition carried significant weight with a particular crowd that considered not just entertainment, but *paid* entertainment, as a zone where commercial exhortation should not intrude. Although it is probable that, as noted earlier, hissing and booing were more likely tied to slide and projection quality and not the concept of advertising itself, this argument raised some thorny issues. If the only way to avoid antagonism was to pay for part or all of the ticket cost, the price for slide advertising increased considerably.

Of course, the receptivity of the audience was only half of the equation. An advertiser likewise had little reason to trust that their slides would receive a warm reception from the exhibitor himself. Despite persistent comments about limiting advertising slides to a comfortably small number (probably twelve) in any given program, exhibitors could and did often engage in behavior that was actively destructive of viewer pleasure and therefore of the value of slide advertising to the advertiser. Rittelmeyer, likely with a bit of overstatement, declared that a theater not only ran slides in the middle of a two-reel film, but ran them "for five or ten minutes."[221] This clearly would have consisted of more than three ads and would understandably have felt like overkill, as the slides would have been nearly equal in duration to the entertainment. A collected list of humorous advice for projectionists, published in early 1916—effectively a summary of poor exhibition practices at the time—included "catch[ing] up on your sleep" during the ad slides as one of its suggestions, assuring the projectionist that the audience would "talk to the Lord about you for teaching them the gentle lesson of patience."[222]

Even if duration were not the problem, quantity could still be a source of concern. Ernest A. Dench mentions the persistence of the problem of the "slide dodge," a term for when the exhibitor would run the slides for which he had contracted, up to thirty or more at any one time, all in a rapid burst at the end of the program, rather than scattering them throughout the program and leaving them onscreen for a reasonable reading time.[223] The appeal of the dodge to the exhibitor was undeniable. Flipping through thirty slides in a minute could have allowed the exhibitor to keep the advertising dollars and also keep the most valuable screen time for coming-attraction slides and other announcements that were more directly beneficial to the theater.

If the exhibitor wanted to dodge his slides while leaving the audience unaware, he might elect to show the coming-attractions slides before the advertising slides; the coming attractions generally indicated that the program was over and would have largely cleared the theater of spectators before ads had run.[224] Alternatively, the exhibitor might take the money and simply not show the slide at all. As such, anyone booking a single slide for screening in a theater, without having developed a long-standing relationship with the exhibitor, had to double-check that they were being screened, and screened properly—a difficult procedure considering the business model of a motion-picture theater. Whereas evidence that a magazine advertisement was printed could be confirmed by picking up a single issue, checking up on slide projection required someone to be present all day, every day, at every theater.[225] This would likewise have been a vast additional expense.

Even if both the philosophy and the cost of slide advertising were considered acceptable, the debate could turn to the equally thorny issue of converting impressions into actual dollars. Popularity and influence would have meant little if the people receiving the message could not be relied on to spend money on the goods advertised. As such, the notion of the motion-picture theater as a site of potential consumers—stressing, regardless of class, their possession of and willingness to spend cash—was also common. Farrington asserted that advertising in cinema theaters could "reach a class of people whom it is often hard to reach in other ways [including] . . . the transient population . . . the lower middle classes . . . [and] the poorer class. It reaches many people who do not read newspapers. It takes in all nationalities."[226] The Thornton Advertising Company went so far as to assert that the slide "gives you a circulation that reaches *every* class."[227] An unsigned article in *The Furniture Worker*, in 1920, also asserted that "the people who attend the moving pictures are the ones who are on the street and ready to spend money, and it pays any man with goods or services to sell to get his name before these crowds."[228] In fact, all writers except Ernest A. Dench—who, without any stated reason, declared that lower-class theaters should be avoided—thought that the existence of a ticket price indicated that all cinemagoers, regardless of class, possessed spending money that advertisers should court.[229] This notion of motion pictures opening advertising up to lower-class spending was important, as contrary to magazines, cinema was described as a medium for the masses. An aggregate of small purchases by film fans was part of its "all classes" advertising philosophy, and those who adopted it were therefore acting on a theory of advertising that was mass rather than class oriented.[230]

Motion pictures weren't simply attended by people willing and able to spend money, however. They offered a type of audience selection that was rare in print media. As opposed to newspapers (which generally targeted everyone in the city) and magazines (which targeted everyone in the country, limited only by magazine topic), the motion-picture theater was "sectional" and represented a stable local audience. Much like direct mail (which might be thrown out, unread) or billposting (which could be ignored or torn down), slide advertising reached a massive proportion of local inhabitants.[231] This was especially true of neighborhood theaters—as opposed to the scattered circulation of downtown theaters—and it was these neighborhood theaters that were most likely to accept advertising.[232] As such, the cinema theater was, it was argued, ideal for advertising because it had the broad mass appeal—even attracting the illiterate—of newspapers but the targeted appeal of a local clientele. As such, one could advertise to very particular audiences in a way impossible in other media. Farrington even suggested an early variant of niche marketing when he argued that one could put on an advertisement in a foreign language at a theater that catered to a largely immigrant population—an action that would have been implausible in all but the smallest-circulation newspapers or magazines, as large-circulation print materials did not give price breaks to advertising that was not geared to general readers. Such immigrant-targeted advertising in the citywide or national press would have been phenomenally wasteful—nowhere near "100 percent circulation."[233] As such, though mass appeal was still the goal, cinema-slide advertising allowed for local advertising as an element of mass campaigns.

The dearth of opposition to these claims indicates that, in general, it was accepted that motion pictures reached an audience unlike any other medium. Where debate arose was over whether or not reaching this audience could be useful. The issue of temporal structure of daily life became a primary concern. Unlike print media, which had a real-world solidity and could be picked up and carried around at any time of day, a screen advertisement could occur only at the moment the viewer was in the theater. In short, the fleeting nature of screen advertising—soon to become a major concern in broadcasting—was also a conundrum for cinema advertisers. For example, Neosho Slide Company owner G. R. Lowe asserted that motion-picture viewers—who were already out of their home and on the town—would see screen advertising at the same time of day that certain stores were open (in Lowe's argument, it was drug stores). As such, they could "go right from the show to the store" while the advertising compulsion was fresh. Lowe encouraged druggists—and by extension any business with hours of operation similar to a theater—to use slide advertising on the grounds that it could be reasonably assumed to have the least lag time between seeing the ad and shopping.[234] For Lowe, then, cinema advertising was fleeting but in a positive way: it may have been brief and ephemeral, but it occurred geographically as near as possible to the point of sale—something only in-store advertising could otherwise reasonably promise. Predictably, an opponent of slide advertising argued exactly the opposite. Rittelmeyer, in his previously cited article, claimed that no matter where the audience viewed the advertising, its position within the flow of a film program meant that it would be forgotten before the viewer even left the theater.[235] As troubling as the venue may have been to some advertisers—in terms of both its psychology and its possible hidden costs—the new condition of ephemerality in advertising was likely the most befuddling.

In sum, the rhetoric surrounding slide advertising was as important as physical and historical conditions in the advent of the medium. The particular debates waged set the terms for all cinema advertising and revealed and determined the horizon of expectations for the slide as a form. Captivity, receptivity, low cost (in both production and exhibition), new demographics, and temporal and geographic nearness to the point of sale all became common positive reference points for cinema advertising. Meanwhile, hidden dangers and hidden costs (combative audiences, slide dodges, etc.) and ephemerality became the standard concerns. As new methods arise and enter the conversation in future chapters, these rhetorical touchstones will be very apparent as foundational assumptions.

CASE STUDY: SERVICE AND SPECTACLE IN THE TECHNOLOGICAL SLIDE

The history of slides is the history of an uphill battle. With perpetual antagonism from nearly all quarters of the motion-picture industry, the average lantern slide purveyor's primary goal was to

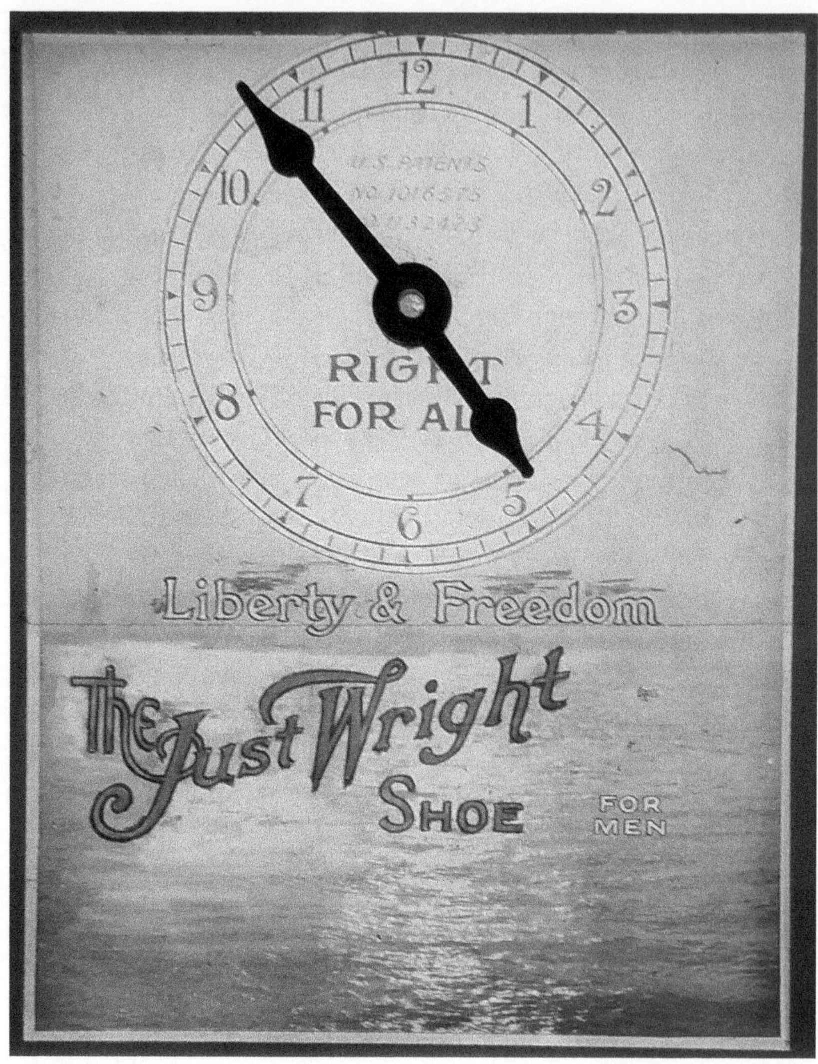

Figure 1.6. A clock slide from the Perfection Slide Company, with custom art for Just Wright Shoes. The dial includes the official patent number, which would have been visible upon projection—a clear indication of the ongoing patent war over clock slides. Note: It is not clear why the aspect ratio of this slide is so abnormal. It is likely that the water and Just Wright logo were clumsily added beneath a wartime "Liberty and Freedom" image originally designed to stand alone. Author's personal collection.

differentiate their product from the norm—attempting to find a format that could defuse the litany of complaints. In an implicit acknowledgment that the low-tech style of slides was viewed, even within the slide industry, as a problem, and echoing the film industry's then-current fascination with patent control, the most common approach was technological manipulation. Foreshadowing developments in future realms of cinema advertising (see chaps. 2 and 3), slide makers attempted to both modernize and dominate their field through two key ideas: the reluctance-defusing power of "usefulness" and the eye appeal of spectacle.

In the early 1910s, offering a public service as a means to defuse audience hostility was an increasingly common idea. The billposting industry, to name just one, had begun to attempt improving its public image through a broad public-service campaign in which unsold space would be filled with educational or informational material.[236] Numerous examples of such "useful" advertising exist in the early years of the slide industry; advertisers frequently attempted to dodge both exhibitor and audience reluctance by turning standard exhibition announcement slides into advertising slides. In 1913, Calumet Baking Powder offered to add phrases like "Another fine picture coming up next" as the text portion of a slide otherwise dominated by an advertising image.[237] By 1914, the Fisk Rubber Company made a popular "Good Night" announcement slide (to be shown at the end of the last show of the night) that contained the company logo and the witticism "Time to Re-Tire," alongside a picture of a weary child holding a Fisk Tire.[238] Neosho's G. R. Lowe likewise suggested that doctors might get free advertising by asking the exhibitor to call them to the telephone or the lobby in an emergency via the use of a slide that displayed their name to patrons. Such a slide could be shown free, as it was a service to the exhibitor (no need to stop the show to call the doctor), and it would get across the doctor's name more clearly than an announcement while also implying that he was in demand.[239] As slide makers sought an endlessly reusable method of public-service slide advertising, many hit on a single concept: the clock slide.

The history of the clock slide is convoluted. Prior to the creation of a patented version, many exhibitors apparently acquired (or made) slides with blank clockfaces, simply painting in the hands any time they wished to display the correct time.[240] The first technological version of the clock slide was filed for patent on September 12, 1911, by Hans A. Meinhardt and Thomas J. Urell of Pittsfield, Massachusetts; the patent was for a simple concoction in which metal clock hands, set into the glass of a standard slide, were accessible for manual adjustment by the projectionist.[241]

Although the invention was rapidly deemed a failure by Meinhardt and Urell, due to struggles in their local market, it ran through the slide industry like wildfire.[242] As early as December 1911—only three months after Meinhardt's patent filing—Epes Winthrop Sargent, advertising columnist for *Moving Picture World*, published a do-it-yourself method for pirating the concept. Sargent suggested simply boring a hole in a blank slide with a rattail file and buying clock hands from a jeweler.[243] Over the next few years, knock-off clock slides would spring up everywhere, with at least eight different companies entering the field. The Kansas City Slide Company was creating "Correct Time" slides no later than February 1912.[244] It was apparently Kansas City Slide's version that first captured significant business attention, as it reportedly caused quite a stir when shown at a 1912 cinema trade show.[245] The American Slide & Poster Company (Chicago) offered brass clock slides in May of 1913, though with no mention of advertising content (cut metals were typically chosen for permanence, not advertising).[246] The Novelty Slide Company (New York City) offered a combined brass and glass version in May of the same year, with the glass portion serving as a space for custom content.[247] That same month, the Levi Company (New York City; soon to become the Perfection Slide Company) purchased the rights to the original Meinhardt and Urell patent and began selling the slide with dozens of stock versions available.[248] By the middle of 1913, the *Exhibitors' Times* was even offering a clock slide free with a one-year subscription, describing it as something "every exhibitor should have."[249] The Best Slide Company (Kansas City), in an undated catalog (plausibly from 1915), included four clock-slide designs.[250] In April 1916, Fred G. Rockwell (Rochester, NY) became the seventh known to offer a clock slide, selling all-brass (and thus, advertising-free) versions.[251] In August of that same year, the Greater New York Slide Company (New York City) began offering a brass and mica version that, much like Novelty's old brass and glass model, could include custom content in the exposed mica portions.[252] As the Best Slide example clearly indicates, there may have been many companies that never mentioned clock slides in the trades but were nonetheless selling their own versions through catalogs.

The appeal of the clock slide was ubiquitous, and for good reason. In an industry where audience reticence was the default assumption, clock slides provided a tangible benefit—easy access to the time for women, who generally did not wear watches, and for men, who had trouble seeing their watches in the darkness of the theater.[253] As Meinhardt's original patent declared, the clock slide would hold "the attention of the audience . . . in an agreeable manner."[254] The Perfection Slide Company described clocks as a means to "remed[y] . . . the suspicion of rudeness"—in other words, the audience's assumption that their attention was being abused. With Epes Winthrop Sargent considering the idea so valuable that it was worth pirating and Perfection indicating that in order to avoid even the minor effort of home construction, a "good percentage of . . . theatres display them gratis," it is clear that the clock slide was, by and large, a successful means of circumventing reluctance.[255]

However, despite becoming a commonly used technology, the clock slide did not become the market-dominating technology any company or advertiser hoped it would be. Patent control failed utterly to hold it. Meinhardt and Urell, through disinterest, let the concept slip away. By the time the Levi Company purchased the patent rights and attempted retroactive patent control, it was too late. Levi, under both original company president Joseph Levi and later head Fred A. Apfelbaum, was clearly attempting to set itself up as a slide-industry version of the Motion Picture Patents Company. The company either filed or acquired multiple patents in the early 1910s, including those for a spotlight slide (song slides that included a gap in the border to quickly and efficiently throw a spotlight on the singer) and two motion slides (described below).[256] The acquisition of the Meinhardt patent and failed attempt to pursue infringement cases against other companies serve as an example of the many patent conflicts across the slide industry, which fizzled quickly due to rampant infringement and already-diminishing interest in the form.[257] Multiple examples from the above seven competitors were still being advertised years after Levi's assertion of patent rights.

Additionally, price-cutting was as problematic with clock slides as it had been with standard advertising slides. In the trade advertisements noted above, one can see a clear line of descent in prices. Kansas City Slide offered clock slides for $1.25 standard and $1.50 with custom text. American Slide & Poster offered clocks for seventy-five cents. Novelty offered their brass and glass slides for only fifty cents, plus "a small charge" for custom inclusions. The Best Slide Company, competing primarily with its neighbors at Kansas City Slide, offered stock clocks for seventy-five cents and custom for one dollar. Only Rockwell's 1916 model, postdating the slide industry's price war nadir, shows a return to normalcy with its $1.50 price tag. Although no clear fallout from price-cutting is evident, the early battles did establish one paradigm that effectively minimized the value of the form as an advertising proposition: the multiplicity of cut-metal options allowed theaters that liked the idea to adopt it without breaking the advertising taboo.

Although usefulness, via the clock slide, did create an opening for advertising slides through technological improvement, much more typical was a turn to spectacle. The notion was common that greater eye appeal would necessarily result in more productive advertising. For most, this was simply a reason for better or more creative visuals. Any company, from the Novelty Slide Company, to the Kansas City Slide Company, to the Levi Company, would make assertions that their imagery had greater drawing power than their competitors. The Levi Company, for example, claimed that "there is no other Slide made that grips the attention of the audience and holds it as ours do. They are . . . dazzling in their variety, full of humor and surprises . . . [and] will be found to be a source of unqualified delight."[258] Though the direct mention of humor was somewhat anomalous—comedy was, at this time, typically seen as unsuited to the seriousness of business—such claims about artistic quality and eye appeal were otherwise common and almost always referenced the superior creative powers of the company hawking their wares.[259] Several American companies, however, took the concept of eye appeal in the direction of technology, patenting upgrades to the old concept of the slipper slide—an early nineteenth-century format in which a secondary slide element could be slid into place during projection, resulting in rudimentary motion.[260]

Between 1910 and 1915, at least six inventors or companies attempted some form of spectacular motion through slides, typically with the clear intent of automating the motion (as a projectionist could not be expected to expend any effort on advertising slides).[261] The Enterprise Optical Manufacturing Company, the Illinois Motion Picture Advertising Corporation, and the Genre Transparency Company all dealt in motion slides of one make or another, while the Spiegel Motion Slide (a version of barrier grid animation) was licensed to the Levi Company.[262] Levi, after its rebranding as the Perfection Slide Company, offered an additional spiral design in which a central shaft would spin an interior element of the slide like a record.[263] Despite the wide variety of options on the market, moving slides typically required the purchase of a special projector or slide carrier or manual adjustment by the projectionist—impositions that kept theatrical adoption low. A non-motion, automatic variant was the Florida Photographic Concern's Color-Changing Chameleon Slide, which would fade "from green to reddish-brown" due to exposure to the heat of the projector lamp.[264]

Within this small movement of spectacularly mutating slides, the clear leader was the Vitaslide Company of San Francisco. As early as January 1913—the date of his first patent—Earl L. Gilmore, president of Vitaslide, had conceived of a fully functioning moving-picture slide that required neither manual nor mechanical assistance. The Vitaslide contained a fluid-filled chamber that housed a moving portion of the design on a separate, floating piece. When not in use, the slide was to be stored right side up, so that the moving element would sink to the bottom. During projection—which, due to the construction idiosyncrasies of lantern slide projectors, occurred with the slide positioned upside down—the moving part would appear to slowly rise in the image as it began, within the projector itself, to sink through the fluid chamber. The presence of the fluid chamber was disguised by design, so the appearance of motion had no clear cause. With the apparent direction of motion being clearly upward rather than down, a Vitaslide included not only motion, but also an element of mystery: How could such motion, in defiance of gravity, have been achieved?

The visible interaction between the stationary and moving parts of the image could create a variety of onscreen effects. Gilmore described three types of motion in the patents. The simplest included a diagonal trench so that, for example, an image of a car could appear to drive uphill. A more complicated design included a "Merry Christmas" message where the words were broken into two collections of apparently meaningless scratches; as the bottom half of the image rose to meet the top half, the scratches would align and render the message readable. In the most complicated iteration of the method—a variation of the standard "Ladies, Please Remove Your Hats" announcement slide—the moving part rotated rather than moving upward. In this concept, the lady's hat was attached to one end of a pivot; at the other end was an image of an usher connected to the hat by a line. As the hat was made of heavier material, it would "sink" upward in the image during projection, rotating the tilting portion and making it appear as though the tiny usher had flipped the hat skyward by jumping on the other end of the shaft. As if this weren't complicated enough, this slide also used the message-forming scratches to spell out the announcement.[265]

With these various approaches possible—angled, straight, and rotating motion—Vitaslide could create eye-catching advertisements unlike any other slides on display in the theater. The company developed ads that were more interesting and therefore more memorable than the stationary ads and also avoided the potential problem of a still slide being disruptive in an environment dedicated to moving pictures. Vitaslide motion was so unexpected, when compared to other advertising slides, that it was reportedly able to "create the remarkable situation of a theater audience applauding an advertisement."[266] Indeed, the surprise was part of the sales pitch; moving slides capitalized not on blending in with the flow of moving pictures, but on a surprising return to life from a space with an expectation of stillness. Motion slides thus preserved the concept of the advertising break while simultaneously providing a triumphant return to motion.

Despite the time it took to create working designs (Vitaslide's early announcement slides were released one per week beginning in April 1914), frequent reports from 1914 to 1915 indicate that the company was effectively an overnight success.[267] Bernard Wolf's cross-country sales trip from San Francisco to New York City (stopping at all major cities along the way) resulted in slides "being ordered extensively by business men for advertising purposes," including a single order from New York City that accounted for a hundred slides all by itself.[268] Considering they sold for three dollars each—approximately three times the cost of a regular slide and twice that of the most expensive clock slide—adoption represented a relatively large expense for advertisers. George Breck, Gilmore's partner and a well-known West Coast purveyor of projection equipment, was circulating Vitaslides to such great success in the latter half of the 1910s that the company was able to focus entirely on yearly service contracts rather than single orders. A yearly contract consisted of a new slide every two weeks—a minimum of twenty-six slides per year.[269] Of course, if the slides were looked on as both pleasing and entertaining, they would have defused the common critique of viewer displeasure without having to resort to outright comedy.

The Vitaslide was, it should be remembered, only a transitional form and had a somewhat predictably brief life span. Shortly after reports of the company being behind on orders, an article in *Camera Craft* magazine was already describing the slides as primarily good for advertising in shop windows, as only small-town theaters were still amenable to slide advertising on the screen.[270] With the decreasing fortunes across the board in the slide industry, Vitaslide appears to have been unable to weather the death of George Breck in 1924; though the company was listed in the 1925 San Francisco City Directory, with Breck's widow Ella now identified as owner of the company, all involved parties dispersed by the 1926 edition.[271]

Despite the struggles of even the most notable, the qualified success of motion slides as a format, especially prior to the widespread adoption of syndicate trailers (see chap. 2), indicates an early hunger in cinema advertising for the creation of motion. Though still decidedly less impressive than real film, these slides could enter more comfortably into the flow of film exhibition, appealing to the same interest in motion pictures while simultaneously standing out as something special as they were (hopefully) compared favorably to other slides, rather than being compared unfavorably to the films. It elevated the slide via spectacular effects in an attempt to be the most likely slide remembered. The minor industry that emerged around expensive technological novelty slides indicates another way in which the slide industry, when backed into a corner, attempted to evade long-standing critiques by shifting the very terms of the debate; rather than attempting to sway the audience through usefulness, motion slides attempted to rally support through an assertion that even advertising could produce pleasure. The brevity of their appearance in the historical record, however, also provides evidence that spectacular motion was unlikely, at this date, to function as a long-term solution. Indeed, it likely hastened the turn to the use of actual motion via trailers.

These two types of technological slides were both noteworthy attempts to soothe the irritation caused by compulsory attention—clock slides through practical use value, and motion slides through pleasurable spectacle. In all examples, however, the advertising was rendered palatable by its seemingly secondary status. As a precursor of the later notion of sponsorship, the advertisers seemed to be providing a service or a form of entertainment and merely declaring their philanthropy openly. Indeed, both ideas fit clearly into the trajectory of twentieth-century advertising. The clock slide is an obvious precursor to broadcasting's Bulova time signal—an advertisement for Bulova watches that integrated the current time as part of the content of the ad.[272] Spectacular motion fits into a much larger history, as it is part of the advertising appeal of animation (which will be discussed in more detail in chap. 2). As such, these types of slides are indicative of the struggles of the slide industry to fully integrate with motion pictures and the tactics that would continue to be adopted as advertisers attempted to integrate with future media. Direct advertising needed a little boost in order to get over the

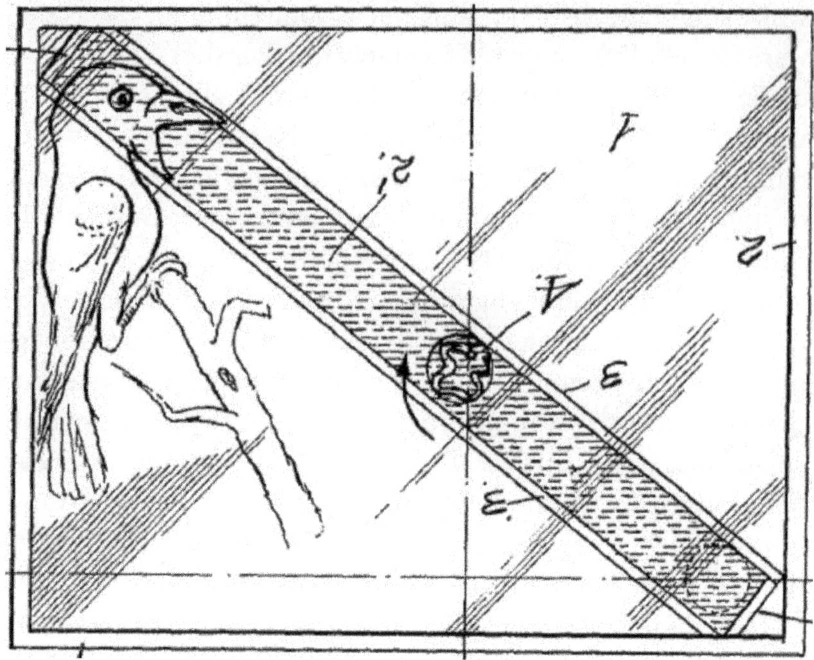

Figure 1.7. A drawing of a Vitaslide design from Earl L. Gilmore's patent (#1,083,679). In this layout, a diagonal fluid-filled trench was to be used to send a floating image of a worm into the mouth of the bird, disappearing behind the head.

footlights, as it were. The impending advertising-trailer revolution was, from a certain angle, simply another technological step in this process.

SEEDS AND WEEDS

From their plausible inception in motion-picture theaters in 1908 to their solid, but class-stratified 1920s integration, advertising slides developed a stable, profitable, largely unquestioned, but decidedly marginal presence in motion-picture theaters. This presence set the tone for the other advertising concepts that would arise and develop over roughly the same time period, as lantern slides were the first to encounter and negotiate the thorny problems of exhibitor and spectator reluctance. Through experimentation with various business models, slide manufacturers taught the advertising industry that filmgoers would accept the intrusion of commercial messages into entertainment for which they had paid under the express conditions that it be presented in a form that was not cut-rate and in a quantity that did not dominate the proceedings. If the slides could include elements of entertainment (spectacular motion) or some element of public service (the current time), so much the better.

The perceived failings of slides either added weight to the adoption or directly inspired the creation of other models of in-cinema advertising. In an implicit extension of the creation of motion technologies, the push for advertising trailers (chap. 2) was a clear attempt to defuse irritation with spectacle. The creation of off-screen technologies, many of them advertising clocks (chap. 3), were likewise an extension of the practicality theories underpinning clock slides; the advertising clock was, in a very real sense, simply a clock slide moved onto the wall. Indeed, although indirect advertising will not be discussed in this book, even the minor boom in industrial films and product placement were indebted to the slide era; as assumptions grew about the implausibility of direct advertising in the cinema space, industrial film and product placement were an admission of defeat via a return to trickery and concealment.

With the lantern slide, then, the typical motion-picture theater opened its doors—hesitantly—to consumer-goods advertising. Though long-standing assumptions about audience displeasure would cause direct sales messages to slowly decrease in favor of sneakier advertising like product placement, the American cinema would never again be entirely devoid of advertising. Slide advertising successfully navigated its early troubles, maintaining a place for itself in cinema theaters and tacitly supporting further investigation of the venue. Slides proved the logic that the captive audience of the theater—though perhaps more psychologically complex than hoped—was in truth a profitable and desirable community. Their flaws only encouraged national advertisers to further experiment with the best way to profitably draw this community's attention.

In fundamentally changing the dynamic of the silent cinema from an exclusively entertainment- and information-oriented venue to one in which advertising was plausible, slides also set the stage for the debates to come. The regular advertising caesura became a central element of the developing discourse around broadcasting in the following decade. Although it would take a few years for American advertisers to forget the harsh lessons of slide advertising and again attempt the broadscale insertion of commercial breaks into a popular medium, the history of electric media advertising breaks—broadcast radio, television, and even web video (with its occasional forced pauses)—is incomplete without an acknowledgment of the developmental years of the lantern slide.

NOTES

1. "Cinema Slides," *Screenvision.com,* accessed March 15, 2013, http://www.screenvision.com/advertise-with-us/cinema-slides. Archive.org's last access date for this page, through the Wayback Machine, is February 6, 2016.

2. "Screenings," *North Tonawanda Evening News,* December 15, 1917.

3. Lara Cain Gray, "Magic Moments: Contextualising Cinema Advertising Slides from the Queensland Museum Collection," *Queensland Review* 18, no. 1 (2011): 73–84.

4. Cynthia B. Meyers, "From Sponsorship to Spots: Advertising and the Development of Electronic Media," in *Media Industries: History, Theory, and Method,* ed. Jennifer Holt and Alisa Perren (Malden, MA: Wiley-Blackwell, 2009), 73.

5. In 1909, slide historian C. K. Larson wrote with surprise that, rather than destroying the slide business, "the moving picture houses ha[d] actually increased the demand for lantern slides." C. K. Larson, "History of Slide Making in America," *Nickelodeon,* March 25, 1911, 330.

6. "How to Use Ad Slides," *MPA*, May 1921, 19; Display Ad, *MPW*, November 29, 1913, 1006; and "Some Slides for Advertising in the Moving Picture Show," Box 4, KCS, 82.

7. Frank B. Howe, "Commercial Lantern Slides," *CC*, February 1917, 69.

8. Display Ad, *MPW*, February 14, 1914, 826; Display Ad, *MPW*, January 6, 1912, 52; and "Projection Department: An Announcement Slide Scheme," *MPW*, May 10, 1913, 591.

9. The Kansas City Slide Company offered photographic reproduction at twice the cost of drawn slides: $1.50 per slide in 1913. "Some Slides for Advertising in the Moving Picture Show," Box 4, KCS, 5.

10. Thomas P. Mason, "Commercial Slide Making," *CC*, August 1917, 315. See also Howe, "Commercial Lantern Slides," 66; and "Some Slides for Advertising in the Moving Picture Show," Box 4, KCS, 1.

11. Pamela Walker Laird, *Advertising Progress: American Business and the Rise of Consumer Marketing* (Baltimore, MD: Johns Hopkins University Press, 1998), 69.

12. The three terms (*stock*, *billboard*, and *special*) come from Kansas City Slide Company catalogs. Though there was slight variation in terminology, all slide companies differentiated their products into these three lines.

13. "Picturization" and a decrease in written content (such as limiting headlines to three words) were two elements of the "aesthetics of speed" and distraction, then a common approach to distracted readers and temporal limitations. Catherine Gudis, *Buyways: Billboards, Automobiles, and the American Landscape* (New York: Routledge, 2004), 66–68.

14. G. R. Lowe, "Slide Advertising for the Retail Druggist," *American Druggist and Pharmaceutical Record*, April 1914, 44. See also "Use Slides to Advertise," *Furniture Worker*, May 1920, 178; and D. H. Harris, "Making 'Slidevertising' Pay," *The Advertising Yearbook for 1921–1922*, ed. Noble T. Praigg (Garden City, NY: Doubleday, Page, 1922), 211–212.

15. Frank Farrington, "Advertising in Moving-Picture Shows," *Bulletin of Pharmacy*, June 1913, 250; and *Slide News*, May 1922, Box 4, Folder "KC Slide Co—Flyers 'Slide News,'" KCS, 4.

16. Farrington, "Practical Talks with the Shop Butcher," *National Provisioner*, December 27, 1913, 40.

17. "How to Use Ad Slides," *MPA*, May 1921, 19; and "Screen Advertising with Slides and Films," *MPA*, January 1921, 24.

18. *Slide News*, May 1922, Box 4, Folder "KC Slide Co—Flyers 'Slide News,'" KCS, 4.

19. KC Process: Cauger, Patent 1,142,143; and Display Ad, *PI*, December 4, 1913, 89.

20. An operator, working at peak efficiency, could make "five hundred slides in a working day of eight hours." David E. Ardley, "Commercial Slide Making," *CC*, October 1920, 317.

21. Standard sizes were different around the globe. Britain, for example, used a three-and-a-quarter-inch square.

22. Although I have encountered no evidence of color photography being used, such was technically possible as early as 1915. "Natural Color Slides Are Startling," *MPW*, August 7, 1915, 1035.

23. "Some Slides for Advertising in the Moving Picture Show," Box 4, KCS, 7.

24. Meyers, "From Sponsorship to Spots," 71.

25. Charles Musser, *The Emergence of Cinema: The American Screen to 1907* (New York: Charles Scribner's Sons, 1990), 20, 38.

26. Musser and Carol S. Nelson, *High-Class Moving Pictures: Lyman H. Howe and the Forgotten Era of Traveling Exhibition, 1880–1920* (Princeton, NJ: Princeton University Press, 1991).

27. Musser, *The Emergence of Cinema*, 42. See also Gray, "Magic Moments," 82.

28. Musser, *The Emergence of Cinema*, 258.

29. Musser, "American Vitagraph, 1897–1901," *Cinema Journal* 22, no. 3 (Spring 1983): 4–46; "Fred A. Clark Goes to Edison," *MPW*, November 22, 1913, 870; and F. H. Richardson, "Operators' Column," *MPW*, August 13, 1910, 355.

30. "Dealers' Advertising," *Edison Phonograph Monthly*, January 1904, 13. This experimentation was global. In late 1904, stage theaters in London began integrating lantern slides into "the interval between acts," rather than using the standard advertising curtain: Theodore Brown, "From the Editor's Pen," *Optical Lantern and Cinematograph Journal* (November 1904): 2.

31. Display Ad, *New York Clipper*, December 31, 1904, 1072.

32. Lee Lash, *Theatre Curtain Advertising* (Philadelphia: George H. Buchanan, 1909).

33. David Bordwell, Janet Staiger, and Kristin Thompson, *The Classical Hollywood Cinema: Film Style & Mode of Production to 1960* (New York: Columbia University Press, 1985), 115; and Richard Abel, *The Red Rooster Scare: Making Cinema American, 1900–1910* (Berkeley: University of California Press, 1999), 36, 48.

34. Richard Butsch, *The Making of American Audiences: From Stage to Television, 1750–1990* (Cambridge: Cambridge University Press, 2000),

150; Eileen Bowser, "1907: Movies and the Expansion of the Audience," in *American Cinema 1890–1909: Themes and Variations*, ed. André Gaudreault (New Brunswick, NJ: Rutgers University Press, 2009), 179; and Robert F. Bruner and Sean D. Carr, *The Panic of 1907: Lessons Learned from the Market's Perfect Storm* (Hoboken, NJ: John Wiley & Sons, 2007), 142–143, 175.

35. The song slide was already being described as past its prime by 1909. It is plausible, therefore, that slide makers were caught in a boom-and-bust bubble and hit on the advertising slide as a replacement for lost income. A Song Slide Maker, "The Value of Lantern Slides as Advertisements for Sheet Music," *MPW*, May 15, 1909, 633. The music video, via small companies like Cinema Concepts and Concert Cinema, likewise helped ease the transition to Screenvision and NCM in the early 1980s. Kim B. Rotzoll, "The Captive Audience," 77, 80.

36. John W. Ripley, "All Join in the Chorus," *American Heritage Magazine* 10, no. 4 (June 1959).

37. Richard Abel, "That Most American of Attractions, The Illustrated Song," in *The Sounds of Early Cinema*, ed. Richard Abel and Rick Altman (Bloomington: Indiana University Press, 2001), 145, 149.

38. Display Ad, *Billboard*, December 26, 1908, 35.

39. Howe, "Commercial Lantern Slides," 66. See also Roy D. Mock, "Fundamental Principles of the Telephone Business," *Telephony*, December 9, 1916, 43.

40. Quentin J. Schultze, "Manufacturers' Views of National Consumer Advertising, 1910–1915," *Journalism Quarterly* 60, no. 1 (1983): 10–15.

41. Schultze, "Legislating Morality: The Progressive Response to American Outdoor Advertising, 1900–1917," *Journal of Popular Culture* 17, no. 4 (1984): 37–44.

42. "The Brayton Baby Show Scheme," *MPW*, May 15, 1909, 632; Display Ads, *MPW*, June 26, 1909, 877; and "The Baby Show as a Summer Attraction," *MPW*, June 26, 1909, 869.

43. "Among the Lantern Slide Makers," *MPW*, July 4, 1908, 9.

44. Display Ad, *MPW*, April 11, 1908, 329.

45. Young was almost certainly contracting for slides, as a "new" idea, rather than curtains. "Ads with Moving Pictures," *MPW*, July 25, 1908, 63. See also "Motion Pictures as an Advertising Proposition," *MPW*, July 18, 1908, 43.

46. "Among the Slide Makers," *MPW*, November 7, 1908, 357.

47. This count does not include companies offering slide-making kits for home-made slides. The companies advertising in the *World* included

Preston Lombard, Ohio Transparency, Wells Enterprises, Brayton, Premo Co., J. E. Naylor, Wm. H. Swanson, Levi, Novelty Slide, Curtainyline, Economy Slide Depot, National Song Slide, Neosho Slide, North American Slide, Genre Transparency, R. Naylor and Company, Three Star Slide, Niagara Slide, Paris Slide, Metropolitan Slide, Erker Bros. Optical, Excelsior Slide, and Specialty Slide Makers.

48. Display Ad, *MPW*, May 15, 1909, 649.

49. "A Progressive Slide Concern," *MPW*, June 12, 1909, 793.

50. Musser, *The Emergence of Cinema*, 36–37. Advertising-slide production occurred predominantly in the established national advertising hub cities of Chicago and New York. Those two cities alone account for 44 of the 104 known advertising-slide manufacturers. Only five were in the other major advertising city: Philadelphia. Each hub city also appears to have its own subtly different culture; for example, New Yorkers were far more concerned with technological innovation and patent control than their counterparts in Chicago.

51. A "more geographically centralized location" was the overt reason given by the Alexander Film Company for moving its business from Washington state to Colorado. "Alexander Film Co.: Behind the Scenes" pamphlet, unpaginated [3], AIR.

52. Untitled News Note, *MPW*, May 29, 1909, 714.

53. Thomas Bedding, "Propagandry and the Picture House," *MPW*, February 18, 1911, 347.

54. "Former Neosho Boy Makes Good," *Neosho Daily Democrat*, April 20, 1912, 2; Timothy S. Susanin, *Walt Before Mickey: Disney's Early Years, 1919–1928* (Jackson: University Press of Mississippi, 2011), 11; and Brian Burnes, Robert W. Butler, and Dan Viets, *Walt Disney's Missouri: The Roots of a Creative Genius* (Kansas City: Kansas City Star Books, 2002), 88.

55. "A Progressive Slide Concern," *MPW*, June 12, 1909, 793; *'Some' Comic Slides*, Box 3, KCS, 135; and *Third Industrial Directory of Pennsylvania, 1919* (Harrisburg, PA: J. L. L. Kuhn, 1920), 965. North American Slide Company had the same number of employees on page 1305 of the 1916 volume of this same directory (see following note for full citation).

56. *Second Industrial Directory of Pennsylvania, 1916* (Harrisburg, PA: Wm. Stanley Ray, 1916), 1304. No-Destructo was no longer active by the 1919 directory.

57. "To Our Readers," *MPW*, May 15, 1909, 633; and "The Marshaw Slide Co.," *MPW*, May 29, 1909, 710. A second, persistent act of bad faith in the early slide business was F. H. Richardson's regular recommendation,

in his *Moving Picture World* column, of the "Make 'Em Yourself" slide kit from the Utility Transparency Company. Richardson owned Utility but never revealed that information in his column. See Richardson, "Projection Department," *MPW*, September 2, 1911, 622; November 18, 1911, 546; December 30, 1911, 1069; August 10, 191,: 550; March 22, 1913, 1216; and March 29, 1913, 1334.

58. Howe, "Commercial Lantern Slides," 66.

59. T. Stanley Curtis, "Lantern Slide Making," *Motography*, November 1911, 217. See also "Among the Slide Makers," *MPW*, November 21, 1908, 401.

60. Display Ad, *MPW*, March 6, 1909, 272.

61. Display Ad, *MPW*, August 5, 1911, 316.

62. Display Ad, *Billboard*, December 26, 1908, 43.

63. Display Ad, *MPW*, March 27, 1909, 354.

64. Display Ad, *Billboard*, September 11, 1909, 40.

65. Display Ad, *MPW*, June 8, 1912, 969.

66. Classified Ad, *MPW*, January 27, 1912, 314.

67. Display Ad, *PI*, December 25, 1913, 91. Emphasis in original.

68. International Shoe Company Contract, Folder 3, CTP.

69. Howe, "Commercial Lantern Slides," 67.

70. "Correspondence: Louisville," *MPW*, February 3, 1912, 406; and "Correspondence: Louisville," *MPW*, February 10, 1912, 506.

71. The third slide is recognizable from trade ads for the Columbia Slide Company of Chicago. "Some Slides for Advertising in the Moving Picture Show," Box 4, KCS, 77.

72. For a straightforward history of the professionalization of the agencies, see chapter 4 of Daniel Pope, *The Making of Modern Advertising* (New York: Basic Books, 1983).

73. Display Ad, *MPW*, May 15, 1909, 649.

74. Display Ad, *MPW*, June 12, 1909, 801.

75. Display Ad, *PI*, January 26, 1911, 91.

76. Display Ad, *PI*, May 2, 1912, 16. Thirty-year-old Bert Samuel Presba had by this point spent eight years with the Mahin Advertising Agency in Chicago and had developed a reputation for his work with Gold Dust, Carnation Milk, and Welch's Grape Juice. "B. S. Presba with Thornton Adv. Co.," *PI*, May 2, 1912, 47.

77. Display Ad, *Simmons' Spice Mill*, July 1913, 686; and August 1913, 790.

78. Compare this to the 1913 price-cutting era, when the Mica Lantern Slide Company explained its decrease in prices as solely the result of negotiating a lower price for mica. See "Philadelphia Notes," *Exhibitors' Times*,

May 24, 1913, 8; and *Slide News*, March 1922, Box 4, Folder "KC Slide Co—Flyers 'Slide News,'" KCS, 4.

79. "Some Slides for Advertising in the Moving Picture Show," Box 4, KCS, 1; and Display Ad, *MPW*, November 7, 1908, 363. As with any study of advertising, one can never entirely trust labels. The "first edition" implied in the Levi ad may have been sleight of hand akin to the agency name N. W. Ayer & Son (which the son named after his father in order to add an impression of stability to the young business of a young man). See Ralph M. Hower, *The History of an Advertising Agency* (Cambridge, MA: Harvard University Press, 1939), 34.

80. Display Ad (Brayton), *MPW*, March 5, 1910, 345; Display Ad (Scott and Van Altena), *MPW*, June 1, 1912, 848; Display Ad (Niagara), *MPW*, June 8, 1912, 955; Display Ad (Erker), *MPW*, June 8, 1912, 969; and Display Ad (Burden and Salisbury), *Simmons' Spice Mill*, April 1913, 379.

81. Thomas P. Mason, "Commercial Slide Making," *CC*, August 1917, 315.

82. Display Ad, *PI*, May 9, 1912, 96; and Display Ad, *PI*, January 14, 1915, 104.

83. Pope, *The Making of Modern Advertising*, 113–117.

84. The Auerbach agency claimed to "represent thirty of the best photo-play houses in Montana." See Display Ad, *A&S*, February 1913, 79. The Motion Picture Advertising Company claimed "500 motion picture theaters throughout the Eastern States." See Display Ad, *PI*, December 12, 1912, 97. The Keeshen Advertising Agency claimed to have guaranteed screenings in five "first run" theaters in Oklahoma City in August of 1915, though it did not claim exclusivity. See Display Ad, *PI*, August 26, 1915, 88. Though I have found no evidence for the typical duration and cost of an exclusive cinema theater contract, the Lee Lash Company signed ten-year and five-year contracts with stage theaters in 1902 and 1908 respectively. See "Lee Lash Co. v. White," *District Reports of Cases Decided in All the Judicial Districts of the State of Pennsylvania During the Year 1907* (Philadelphia: Howard W. Page, 1907), 393–397; and "Nixon & Zimmerman Amusement Co. v. Lee Lash Company, Appellant," *Pennsylvania Superior Court Reports, Volume 46* (New York: Banks Law, 1915), 89–93.

85. "Lee Lash Co. v. Northwestern Consol. Mining Co.," *Federal Reporter with Key-Number Annotations, Volume 218* (St. Paul, MN: West, 1915), 910–911. Lee Lash had a track record of significant space brokering, having placed ads for American Chicle chewing gum on the curtains of 550 stage theaters in 1917. "How the American Chicle Company Sold Its Salesmen on New Campaign," *PI*, January 25, 1917, 61.

86. Display Ad, *PI*, May 2, 1912, 16.

87. Display Ad, *A&S*, June 1913, 45; Display Ad, *Boot and Shoe Recorder*, November 1, 1911, 125; and Display Ad, *PI*, June 20, 1912, 81.

88. Display Ad, *PI*, June 20, 1912, 81.

89. "'Some' Comic Slides," Box 3, KCS, 132.

90. Harris, "Making 'Slidevertising' Pay," 212.

91. Display Ad, *PI*, December 11, 1913, 79; and Display Ad, *MPW*, January 25, 1913, 393.

92. The company also claimed to have "sold Sunkist their first slides and have been honored with their business ever since." Portfolio, Folder 4, CTP.

93. Display Ad, *PI*, June 20, 1912, 81; and Display Ad, *A&S*, February 1913, 77.

94. Display Ad, *PI*, May 2, 1912, 16.

95. Here, as in all chapters to follow, it is valuable to compare cinema advertisers' quest for national contracts to the development of advertising in other forms. As Richard Ohmann has found, mass magazine advertising quickly became dominated by national advertising campaigns. See Ohmann, *Selling Culture: Magazines, Markets, and Class at the Turn of the Century* (London: Verso, 1996), 83–84. The failure of cinema to be a venue of national use is a key differentiating factor in comparing it to other forms. See also Pope, *The Making of Modern Advertising*, 8–9, 42–46; and Laird, *Advertising Progress*, 15.

96. Howe, "Commercial Lantern Slides," 67.

97. Epes Winthrop Sargent, "Advertising for Exhibitors," *MPW*, June 21, 1913, 1244.

98. "Correspondence: Louisville," *MPW*, May 25, 1912, 744.

99. R. J. Edenfield, "On the Job from Eight to Eleven," *Motography*, April 29, 1916, 971.

100. "Graded License Fees," *MPW*, August 21, 1915, 1341.

101. William M. Flynn, "An Anti-Advertising Slide Bill," *MPW*, February 5, 1916, 754–755.

102. Display Ad, *MPW*, January 14, 1911, 110.

103. "Letters to the Editors," *MPW*, January 7, 1911, 37. This request dates to slightly before the full turn to publicizing actors' names. See Richard deCordova, *Picture Personalities: The Emergence of the Star System in America* (Urbana: University of Illinois Press, 1990).

104. Display Ad, *MPW*, July 6, 1912, 65; and Display Ad, *MPW*, July 20, 1912, 212.

105. Display Ad, *ET*, June 14, 1913, back cover.

106. Display Ad, *ET,* May 31, 1913, 32; Display Ad, *Variety,* November 9, 1912, 36; and Display Ad, *ET,* June 7, 1913, 10.

107. At each program change, the operator would place the new film list between a reusable pair of clear mica plates. See Display Ad, *ET,* May 31, 1913, 5; and "Advertising the Picture," *ET,* June 7, 1913, 10.

108. "Baltimore Notes," *ET,* May 31, 1913, 6.

109. "Exhibitors' Slides," *ET,* June 21, 1913, 29.

110. Flynn mentioned that by 1916, theaters were split between a model in which slides were shown "at intermission . . . or between reels." See Flynn, "An Anti-Advertising Slide Bill," *MPW,* February 5, 1916, 755. The use of a second projector was "steadily on the increase" in the middle of 1912. See "Facts and Comments," *MPW,* June 1, 1912, 805. The notion that an intermission occurred between turns, not in the middle of the program, comes from John B. Rathbun, "Motion Picture Making and Exhibiting," *Motography,* August 9, 1913, 95.

111. Ernest A. Dench, *Advertising by Motion Pictures,* 195. George M. Rittelmeyer declared "the increasing number of advertising slides" to be the biggest problem. See Rittelmeyer, "Slide Advertising," *MPW,* September 13, 1913, 1178.

112. "How to Use Ad Slides," *MPA,* February 1921, 17.

113. Rittelmeyer, "Slide Advertising," 1178.

114. The truth in advertising movement and the attempts to inaugurate college-level advertising education were both branding tactics designed to combat the "humbug" problem (association of advertising with the misleading tactics of P. T. Barnum and patent medicines). See Laird, *Advertising Progress,* 241–242; and Schultze, "An Honorable Place."

115. Curtis, "Lantern Slide Making," *Motography,* November 1911, 217.

116. Howe, "Commercial Lantern Slides," 70; and "Some Slides for Advertising in the Moving Picture Show," Box 4, KCS, 5.

117. Display Ad, *MPW,* January 11, 1913, 197.

118. Lowe, "Slide Advertising for the Retail Druggist," 44. Two years earlier, Philadelphia's North American Slide Company similarly claimed "the quality of our slides is remembered long after the price is forgotten." See Display Ad, *PI,* October 24, 1912, 83.

119. "Lee Lash Co. v. Northwestern Consol. Mining Co.," 910.

120. Display Ad, *Illustrated Milliner,* April 1914, 45.

121. C. E. Livengood, *The Tuner's Magazine,* January 1915, 29–30; and *The Best Booster,* November 1915, Box 4, Folder "Best Slide Co—Catalogs 1915," KCS, 10.

122. Howe, "Commercial Lantern Slides," 70. Imagery implies that the two were Kansas City Slide and Novelty Slide. The Kansas City Slide Company's catalog was even quoted directly in this article as stating: "Poor, cheap slides are hurting the business. Time will change this, as the tendency is to give more attention to the matter of better slides." A form of this claim was being printed in Kansas City Slide Company catalogs as early as 1913; see "Some Slides for Advertising in the Moving Picture Show," Box 4, KCS.

123. Thomas P. Mason, "Commercial Slide Making," *CC*, August 1917, 321.

124. "Chicago Letter," *ET*, July 12, 1913, 15–16.

125. "Combine of Slide Manufacturers," *Billboard*, October 3, 1914, 52.

126. "Film Chiefs Meet in Chicago," *Motography*, November 11, 1916, 1056.

127. "Slide Manufacturers Organize," *Motography*, November 25, 1916, 1160; and "Film Chiefs Meet in Chicago," *Motography*, November 11, 1916, 1056.

128. An alternative list was published in *Motography* two weeks earlier, from which the Perfection Slide Company and Long and Heller were omitted, with Scott and Van Altena and the Economy Slide Company included instead. Seven of the nine mentioned had known connections to advertising slides. See "Film Chiefs Meet in Chicago," *Motography*, November 11, 1916, 1056.

129. Ardley, "Commercial Slide Making," *CC*, October 1920, 317.

130. Dench, *Advertising by Motion Pictures*, 195, 197; Lowe, "Slide Advertising for the Retail Druggist," 44; *Best Booster*, December 1915, Folder "Best Slide Co—Catalogs 1915," KCS, 4; and Farrington, "Advertising in Moving-Picture Shows," 249.

131. Harris, "Making 'Slidevertising' Pay," 213.

132. For those advertisers who were concerned by the increased cost, slide proponents suggested signing contracts with multiple theaters, allowing each slide to be used for one week *per theater*. See "Use Slides to Advertise," *Furniture Worker*, May 1920, 178.

133. An 1893 article in *Iron Age* directly attacked the "clutter" of merchant areas papered liberally with "gaudy and senseless placards" and suggested that the use of advertising lithographs was only acceptable if they were exceptionally attractive and limited in number. Laird, *Advertising Progress*, 219.

134. Charles A. Young, "Among the Chicago Houses," *MPW*, November 25, 1911, 624; and "Exhibitors' News: In the Southwest," *MPW*, April 25, 1914, 545.

135. William T. Braun, "Problems of the Operating Room," *Motography*, November 1911, 228.

136. John B. Rathbun, "Motion Picture Making and Exhibiting," *Motography*, August 9, 1913, 96.

137. Dench, *Advertising by Motion Pictures*, 201.

138. S. L. Rothapfel, "First Aid to Theater Men," *Motography*, July 8, 1916, 77.

139. Chalmers L. Pancoast, "Picture Slides as Business Getters," *A&S*, February 1913, 77.

140. "The Soda Fountain," *American Druggist and Pharmaceutical Record*, November 1914, 50.

141. There were only two dissenting letters, both from George W. Allen of the Consumers' Gas Company of Toronto. Both were merely vague assertions that slides were not dignified or profitable for gas companies. See the following issues, all from 1914, for the conversation: April, 276; May, 373; June, 459; and July, 561. Allen's letters appeared in April and July.

142. Display Ad, *PI*, October 29, 1914, 85.

143. St. Louis was the earliest to definitely use the plan; see "St. Louis Theater Men Meet," *Motography*, January 27, 1917, 162. Ohio did so two years later—see "Black Chosen President of Exhibitors' League," *Billboard*, July 5, 1919, 81—though it was under discussion as early as 1914; see James S. McQuade, "Fourth Annual Convention of Ohio," *MPW*, February 7, 1914, 681. Michigan was also using the plan in 1920; see Display Ad, *PI*, May 27, 1920, 203.

144. One thin critique simply asserted that a high-class theater should "keep them out just as far as possible" and mentioned "some" patrons in Chicago theaters walking out when ad slides were shown. Rothapfel, "First Aid to Theater Men," 129. A slightly harsher critique from April 1917 called ad slides and films "perennial like iron weed in a farmer's garden. They systematically rob good soil and give no return." Untitled Editorial Note, *MPW*, April 14, 1917, 241. I have found no arguments critical of slides after this point.

145. Stephen Fox, *The Mirror Makers: A History of American Advertising and Its Creators* (New York: William Morrow, 1984), 76–77; and Roland Marchand, *Advertising the American Dream: Making Way for Modernity, 1920–1940* (Berkeley: University of California Press, 1985), 6.

146. "Facts and Comments," *MPW*, May 26, 1917, 1253.

147. Thornton Fisher, "Grinding the Crank," *MPW*, March 2, 1918, 1227.

148. The first and second Liberty Loans used 30,000 and 70,000 slides. There was also an unknown quantity in the third and fourth, and countless

Red Cross, fuel conservation, and military recruitment slides screened free of charge. See "McAdoo Writes Letter to Industry," *MPW*, June 30, 1917, 2108; "Theaters Furnished with Slides," *Motography*, October 13, 1917, 746; "Secretary McAdoo Writes to Exhibitors," *MPW*, February 9, 1918, 834; and "Exhibitors Protest Lightless Nights," *MPW*, January 5, 1918, 120.

149. Display Ad, *MPW*, June 23, 1917, 2001; Display Ad, *MPW*, May 12, 1917, 1031; and Display Ad, *MPW*, June 2, 1917, 1477.

150. See, for example, Marcus Loew's assertion that "nothing [including the Four Minute Men] should be included in the show except what the patrons expected to find when they paid the admission." Hanford C. Judson, "Marcus Loew, a Real Showman," *MPW*, October 6, 1917, 78.

151. "Facts and Comments," *MPW*, June 5, 1915, 1575. San Francisco exhibitors got particularly annoyed with tuberculosis slides; see "Opposed to Free Slides," *MPW*, June 5, 1915, 1646.

152. Joseph McGuire, "Does It Pay to Lend Theaters to Politicians," *MPW*, November 11, 1916, 891.

153. The "refusal to pay," though not commonly a critique of slides, was the primary criticism of product placement.

154. "Exhibitors Organizing to Aid U.S.," *Motography*, September 8, 1917, 485.

155. "Remark Causes License Loss," *Motography*, November 10, 1917, 1004.

156. "Investigating H. J. Paradis," *MPW*, June 29, 1918, 1879.

157. "Paradis Acquitted of Unpatriotic Action," *MPW*, July 27, 1918, 585.

158. W. Stephen Bush, "The Exhibitor and the Public," *MPW*, May 30, 1914, 1223.

159. "Exhibitors News: Detroit," *MPW*, December 12, 1914, 1552; Florence Margolies, "Promoting Public Health," *MPW*, December 5, 1914, 1359; "Exhibitors News: Kansas," *MPW*, December 12, 1914, 1550; and "Exhibitors News: St. Louis," *MPW*, November 21, 1914, 1101.

160. The road issue was technically self-serving; the quality of roads into the city was a determining factor in rural film-fan attendance at urban theaters. "Facts and Comments," *MPW*, November 25, 1916, 1137; Jas. S. McQuade, "Chicago News Letter," *MPW*, November 18, 1916, 891; and "Film Men Benefit by Good Roads," *MPW*, November 25, 1916, 1206.

161. Fly-swatting pest-control campaigns were common at the time. "Snap Shots at Showmanship in Illinois," *MPW*, June 26, 1915, 2123; and "Exhibitors News: Detroit," *MPW*, November 28, 1914, 1260.

162. Michigan eventually banned them entirely as in excess of the state's size restrictions on "campaign cuts for advertising purposes." "Exhibitors

News: Detroit," *MPW*, August 29, 1914, 1256. The Kansas City Slide Company's Slide News for July 1924 included three pages of campaign slide designs, clearly indicating wide usage; see *Slide News* July 1924, Box 4, Folder "KC Slide Co—Flyers 'Slide News,'" KCS, 3–5.

163. Oregon exhibitors distributed 1,000 slides to help repeal Sunday closing laws. "Portland's Curfew Rings Again," *MPW*, October 28, 1916, 590; and "Oregon Blue Law Repealed," *MPW*, December 2, 1916, 1370.

164. "Political Power of the Screen," *MPW*, October 7, 1916, 78.

165. "Facts and Comments," *MPW*, February 27, 1915, 1259; Display Ad, *MPW*, April 3, 1915, 142; and "No Compromise with Censorship," *MPW*, March 20, 1915, 1743. Philadelphia exhibitors had their own variant known as "Liberty Bell Slides"; see "'Liberty Bell' Slides," *MPW*, April 17, 1915, 420. Ayer had been using this slogan since 1886; see Laird, *Advertising Progress*, 161. I have found no evidence that Ayer was involved in the anti-censorship campaign.

166. "Griffith Film, 'A Day with Governor Whitman,'" *MPW*, November 4, 1916, 722. Watterson R. Rothacker, industrial and advertising film producer from Chicago, took similar action when he encouraged all Chicago theaters to run an ad slide for Captain Louis A. Boening (vocally anti-censorship) free of charge. Jas. S. McQuade, "Chicago News Letter," *MPW*, February 19, 1916, 1109.

167. "Screens Helped J. L. Steurle Pile Up Votes," *MPW*, September 1, 1917, 1415. See also "Candidates," *Kentucky Irish American*, May 12, 1917, 1; "Democrats," *Kentucky Irish American*, June 30, 1917, 1; and "Politicians," *Kentucky Irish American*, August 11, 1917, 1.

168. "Profit From Politics," *MPW*, August 21, 1915, 1339. *Moving Picture World*'s "man about town" was clearly incorrect in his 1913 prediction that campaign slides would soon be banned for causing disturbances in theaters. "Observations by Our Man About Town," *MPW*, November 15, 1913, 723.

169. "Getting Co-Operation of Local Newspapers," *MPW*, October 14, 1916, 278.

170. Display Ad, *MPW*, October 21, 1916, 463; and Display Ad, *MPW*, January 10, 1914, 210.

171. "How to Use Ad Slides," *MPA*, March 1921, 35.

172. "Leaders of 'Movie' Industry Confer with Officials on War Program for Film World," *Official Bulletin* 1, no. 53 (July 12, 1917): 8; and *United States Food Administration Report for the Year 1917* (Washington, DC: Government Printing Office, 1918), 111. Also see page 119 for a payment to the American Slide Company. Novelty was central to government slide work

from the earliest days of the war, as the company produced the Navy's first wave of recruitment slides. "Navy Offers Free Recruiting Slides," *MPW*, May 12, 1917, 993.

173. *Final Report of the Business Manager to H. A. Garfield, United States Fuel Administrator* (Washington, DC: Government Printing Office, 1920), 48; and George Edwin Howes, ed., *Report of the Administrative Division, 1917–1919: Part 1, Reports of the Bureau of State Organizations and of the Federal Fuel Administrators for the Various States and Districts* (Washington, DC: Government Printing Office, 1919), 90.

174. "Advertising in Food Control Campaign," *PI*, July 12, 1917, 66.

175. "Lantern Slide Makers Combine," *PI*, February 20, 1919, 65. The three other companies were the Greater New York Slide Company, Commercial Slide Company, and Economy Slide Company, all of which were listed as members of the 1916 association, meaning that roughly half of the original association took part in this merger. George Appel, the former owner of the Economy Slide Company, apparently regretted the decision as he returned to the slide field shortly thereafter, breaking the noncompete clause in the sale contract. *Reports of Cases Heard and Determined in the Appellate Division of the Supreme Court of the State of New York* (Albany, NY: J. B. Lyon Company, 1920), 799–801.

176. Rick Altman dates the transition to the theater "building boom" between 1912 and 1915. We can assume that the percentage of two-projector theaters began to outweigh that of single-projector theaters around 1914 or 1915. Altman, *Silent Film Sound* (New York: Columbia University Press, 2005), 250.

177. Rothapfel, "First Aid to Theater Men," 77. In these same years, there are countless additional news reports, especially in *Moving Picture World*, of the leading theaters of various towns rejecting advertising as a matter of principle.

178. "How to Use Ad Slides," *MPA*, March 1921, 35. See also O. B. Carson, "A Campaign That Gives 'Business Insurance' Against Irresponsible Competition," *PI*, January 14, 1915, 31; and Portfolio, Folder 4, CTP.

179. "How to Use Ad Slides," *MPA*, June 1921, 21. Emphasis added.

180. Ibid.

181. Display Ad, *PIM*, March 1920, 84; eight thousand theaters using twelve new advertising slides per week would result in 4,992,000 slides per year.

182. See the following estimates: 18,000—*Crain's Market Data Book and Directory of Class, Trade and Technical Publications* (Chicago: G. D.

Crain Jr., 1920), 321; 14,000—Frank Leroy Blanchard, *The Essentials of Advertising* (New York: McGraw-Hill, 1921), 241; 15,000—"Movie Director Hays Favors Express," *Express Gazette Journal* (March 1922): 75.

183. George E. Gayou was secretary through 1922. See "Ad Folks' News," *Fourth Estate*, October 14, 1916, 21; and "Weisenburger Heads Ad Club," *United States Investor*, October 21, 1922, 140.

184. Display Ad, *PIM*, May 1920, 107. By 1921, the Associated Advertising Clubs of the World convention included a "Screen Advertisers" section, including both film and slide makers, featuring a presentation from the Standard Slide Corporation. See "Let's Go—Step on the Gas, Keynote of AACW Convention," *Editor & Publisher*, May 21, 1921, 16, 35.

185. "How to Use Ad Slides," *MPA*, February 1921, 17.

186. "How to Use Ad Slides," *MPA*, April 1921, 19.

187. Display Ad, *PI*, November 21, 1912, 103; and Display Ad, *Billboard*, December 12, 1908, 25.

188. Laird, *Advertising Progress*, 72, 211; and Display Ad, *PI*, October 2, 1913, 69.

189. Display Ad, *PI*, November 6, 1913, 56. See also "Moving Picture Advertising for Druggists," *American Druggist and Pharmaceutical Record*, April 1914, 84.

190. Display Ad, *PI*, December 29, 1910, 63; and January 26, 1911, 91.

191. Dench, *Advertising by Motion Pictures*, 196, 198. See also the Brite Lite Film Advertising Company's display ad for the phrase "100% Efficient Advertising" as a business slogan (*PI*, April 25, 1918, 162).

192. Display Ad, *PI*, May 2, 1912, 16. Emphasis in original.

193. Farrington, "Advertising in Moving-Picture Shows," 249.

194. Harris, "Making 'Slidevertising' Pay," 211. Emphasis added.

195. "How to Use Ad Slides," *MPA*, March 1921, 35. Emphasis added.

196. Countless examples could be offered. See, for example, the psychological turn made by the magazine *Cosmopolitan* in 1902, when it claimed that the power of popular magazines for advertising rested in their status as "peculiarly the companion of leisure hours, when the mind is free to accept new impressions"; John Brisben Walker, "Beauty in Advertising Illustration," *The Cosmopolitan* 33, no. 5 (September 1902): 491. In 1915, Shredded Wheat publicity director Truman A. DeWeese defended newsprint as the preeminent advertising medium on the grounds that "it is peculiarly a home institution and sustains an intimate relation to the family circle"; DeWeese, "The Lazy Dollar and How to Put It to Work," *A&S*, December 1915, 49. In 1916, the Emerson Advertising Record (a novelty for use with phonograph

disc players) was marketed on the appeal of a psychology of technological infatuation, as the listener would "preserve . . . indefinitely and repeat . . . over and over again" their interaction with the advertisement and even share it excitedly with their friends; Display Ad, *PI*, August 3, 1916, 97. In 1917, Strauss Theatre Programs asserted that the live theater was the best venue for advertising, as the foregrounding of acting made it the site of an "Emulative Attitude of Mind"; Display Ad, *PI*, February 8, 1917, 40.

197. Farrington, "Advertising in Moving-Picture Shows," 249.

198. "How to Use Ad Slides," *MPA*, June 1921, 21.

199. Display Ad, *PI*, August 7, 1913, 30. Same ad also published in *A&S*, August 1913, 52.

200. Display Ad, *Billboard*, November 28, 1908, 25. This phrase was reworded as "Good for Tired Eyes" for the ad in *Moving Picture World* on the same day (427). Display Ad, *MPW*, January 16, 1909, 70. By the time of the Levi Company's assertion, this was an old belief regarding the "flicker show." The first issue of *The Optical Lantern and Cinematograph Journal*, published in 1904, declared "no one will deny . . . that after watching a long series of animated pictures . . . an ordinary slide comes as a welcome pause, and . . . a source of restfulness to the eye"; Theodore Brown, "From the Editor's Pen," *Optical Lantern and Cinematograph Journal* (November 1904): 2.

201. Sargent, "Advertising for Exhibitors," *MPW*, August 7, 1915, 987.

202. Roy D. Mock, "Fundamental Principles of the Telephone Business," *Telephony*, December 9, 1916, 43.

203. Dench, "Slide Hints for the Motion Picture Advertiser," *American Stationer and Office Outfitter*, January 8, 1918, 36.

204. Rittelmeyer, "Slide Advertising," 1178.

205. Display Ad, *PIM*, April 1921, 113.

206. "1927 Red Book of Advertising Slides," Box 3, KCS, inside back cover.

207. "Use Slides to Advertise," *Furniture Worker*, May 1920, 178.

208. Dench, *Advertising by Motion Pictures*, 197.

209. "No More Advertising Slides," *MPW*, March 20, 1915, 1798.

210. Farrington, "Practical Talks with the Shop Butcher," 40.

211. "Free Picture Show with Ads," *MPW*, June 5, 1915, 1647.

212. Display Ad, *PI*, August 26, 1915, 88.

213. Dench, *Advertising by Motion Pictures*, 201.

214. The Carnegie Library of Mitchell, South Dakota, claims to have had its slides run for free in the town theater; see "News From the Field," *South Dakota Library Bulletin*, June 1926, 42.

215. "Tips to 'Movie' Advertisers," *Jewelers' Circular—Weekly*, September 26, 1917, 108.

216. Chalmers L. Pancoast, "Picture Slides as Business Getters," *A&S*, February 1913, 78.

217. Farrington, "Practical Talks with the Shop Butcher," 40.

218. See, for example, the "Make 'Em Yourself" slides, offered by the Utility Transparency Company, for three to four dollars. Included in the price were twenty-four sheets of cover glass and enough colored gelatin to make "300 to 400 slides." Display Ad, *MPW*, February 14, 1914, 826.

219. "Advertising Slides," *Nickelodeon*, July 1909, 3.

220. "Publicity for Plumbers," *Domestic Engineering*, December 11, 1915, 337.

221. Rittelmeyer, "Slide Advertising," 1178.

222. "Helpful Hunches for Operators," *Motography*, April 15, 1916, 855.

223. Dench, *Advertising by Motion Pictures*, 209.

224. Ibid., 210.

225. Ibid., 207–8.

226. Farrington, "Advertising in Moving-Picture Shows," 249.

227. Display Ad, *PI*, May 2, 1912, 16. Emphasis added.

228. "Use Slides to Advertise," *Furniture Worker*, May 1920, 178.

229. Dench, *Advertising by Motion Pictures*, 200.

230. Richard Ohmann has found that few agencies asserted the value of aiming for the lower classes. Calkins and Holden was an exception, however, asserting that although the "uneducated and credulous class" would generally "buy only the most inexpensive things . . . large numbers of them do buy." Ohmann, *Selling Culture*, 113.

231. "How to Use Ad Slides," *MPA*, March 1921, 35.

232. Dench, *Advertising by Motion Pictures*, 196, 199.

233. Farrington, "Advertising in Moving-Picture Shows," 249.

234. Lowe, "Slide Advertising for the Retail Druggist," 44.

235. Rittelmeyer, "Slide Advertising," 1178.

236. Gudis, *Buyways*, 29–30.

237. Chalmers L. Pancoast, "Picture Slides as Business Getters," *A&S*, February 1913, 77–78.

238. Display Ad, *MPW*, January 17, 1914, 326.

239. Lowe, "Slide Advertising for the Retail Druggist," 44. See also Untitled Article, *MPW*, February 8, 1913, 575.

240. Sargent, "A Clock Slide," *MPW*, December 30, 1911, 1060.

241. H. A. Meinhardt, Patent 1,016,575.

242. "The Meinhardt Clock Slide," *MPW*, May 17, 1913, 714.

243. Sargent, "A Clock Slide," 1060.

244. Display Ad, *Billboard*, February 3, 1912, 57. By 1913, they insisted that they were "the originators of this slide" and had "sold thousands"; see "Some Slides for Advertising in the Moving Picture Show," Box 4, KCS, 80.

245. "Of Interest to the Trade," *Motography*, August 31, 1912, 183.

246. Display Ad, *MPW*, April 26, 1913, 430.

247. Display Ad, *Billboard*, May 10, 1913, 53; and "The First International Exposition," *MPW*, July 19, 1913, 324.

248. Display Ad, *MovPN*, May 24, 1913, 26; and Display Ad, *R&S*, May 1919, 33.

249. One of many incentives offered in a broad subscription drive; a full-page display ad was published in every issue from July 5 to August 23, 1913. See the inside back cover on the latter date. No maker was listed, and the design does not match any known.

250. *The Slider*, Box 4, Folder "Best Slide Co—Catalogs 1915," KCS, unpaginated.

251. Display Ad, *MPW*, April 8, 1916, 339.

252. "Greater New York Slide Company Issues Forty-Eight Page Catalog," *MPN*, August 5, 1916, 812.

253. "Advertising Slides for Moving-Picture Shows," *Electrical World*, October 25, 1913, 847; and Display Ad, *PI*, December 25, 1913, 81.

254. Meinhardt, Patent 1,016,575.

255. Display Ad, *R&S*, May 1919,: 33.

256. "Levi Spot-Light Slides," *MPW*, December 23, 1911, 995.

257. "The Meinhardt Clock Slide," *MovPN*, May 10, 1913, 21; and *MPW*, May 17, 1913, 714. This was self-serving. Levi/Perfection was as culpable as anyone for the slide industry's disinterest in patents and copyrights. In 1910, the company was caught copying imagery from De Witt C. Wheeler. See Display Ad, *Film Index*, September 10, 1910, 32; and Display Ad, *Film Index*, September 17, 1910, 30.

258. Display Ad, *Billboard*, December 5, 1908, 94.

259. As early as 1903, ad-industry powerhouse J. Walter Thompson refused to use humor in advertising. *The J.W.T. Book: A Series of Talks on Advertising*, Box 25, Folder "Addresses and Published Materials by J.W.T. Personnel 1908–1927," JWT, Chicago Office Records, 45–46.

260. Gray, "Magic Moments," 75.

261. Again, a global parallel is evident. Ernest Dench indicates that an unnamed British company was also experimenting with motion slides, as

a slide on which a dog could be seen lapping up beer is described in detail. Dench, *Advertising by Motion Pictures*, 176.

262. The inventor is Alexander S. Spiegel, who popularized barrier grid-animation in the United States. See "The Motiograph Machine for 1912," *Motography*, October 1911, 172; "To Handle Advertising Slides," *Motography*, June 12, 1915, 961; and Display Ad, *MPW*, March 5, 1910, 343; "Levi Company Purchases Patent Rights," *MPW*, January 13, 1912, 127. Relevant Spiegel patents include 957,119 (filed 1908), 946,407 (1909), 1,066,766 (1911), and 1,088,177 (1913).

263. F. A. Apfelbaum, Patent 1,116,201.

264. Howe, "Commercial Lantern Slides," 70.

265. E. L. Gilmore, Patents 1,083,679 and 1,113,610.

266. "At the Golden Gate," *MPW*, May 29, 1915, 1406–1407.

267. Display Ad, *MPW*, April 11, 1914, 273; Display Ad, *MPW*, April 18, 1914, 433; and Display Ad, *MPW*, May 9, 1914, 896.

268. "Exhibitors News: San Francisco," *MPW*, May 30, 1914, 1280; and "Exhibitors News: San Francisco," *MPW*, June 20, 1914, 1711.

269. Breck was the West Coast agent for Edison projectors and Radium Gold Fibre Screens and was briefly famous for installing the first permanent film projector on the West Coast; see "George Breck Reminiscent," *MPW*, July 10, 1915, 241. See also "Other San Francisco Notes," *MPW*, January 2, 1915, 99; "Other San Francisco Notes," *MPW*, March 20, 1915, 1791; Display Ad, *MPW*, June 13, 1914, 1611; and "Vitaslide Newest Ad Novelty on the Market," *R&S*, June 1919, 37.

270. Howe, "Commercial Lantern Slides," 69.

271. "San Francisco," *MPN*, April 12, 1924, 1672; and Crocker-Langley San Francisco City Directory 1925 (San Francisco: R. L. Polk & Co.), 1868.

272. Alexander Russo, *Points on the Dial: Golden Age Radio Beyond the Networks* (Durham, NC: Duke University Press, 2010), 115–116.

TWO

SCREEN SUGAR PILLS

The Advertising Trailer and the Commercialized Intermission

> It was felt by advertisers that the lantern slide had had its run. People yawned at the still picture on the screen. Some method of knocking them down and dragging them out had to be devised. The little ad-plays turned the trick.
>
> —Jonas Howard (December 1919)

IN THE FIRST QUARTER OF 1938, J. Walter Thompson's Fred Fidler encouraged the company to experiment with motion-picture trailer advertising—roughly one-minute-long direct advertisements designed for circulation in movie theaters. Fidler, in a tone of preemptive vigilance, made the suggestion on the grounds that trailer work would "provide invaluable preparatory experience against the time when commercial public television arrive[d] and demonstration share[d] description's importance as an advertising technique."[1] After forty years of "agency apathy" toward cinema advertising and more than a decade as a major player in radio, J. Walter Thompson finally gave serious consideration to the moving picture.[2] Years of experimentation and improvement, as well as a persistence that had purportedly developed "an appreciative tolerance" of advertising in the cinemagoing public, finally drew the approving glance of a mainstream advertising agency toward the cinema.[3] Tellingly, J. Walter Thompson—on the cusp of the development of television's participating sponsorship model—was interested in the cinema trailer as a parallel to the radio spot (then still largely restricted to daytime programming).[4] Fidler and the J. Walter Thompson Company's analyses throw into sharp relief a key underacknowledged element of cinema-advertising history: the motion-picture advertising trailer—itself the descendent of the glass slide—is the direct ancestor of the televisual sixty-second spot.

The commercial trailer rose to prominence shortly after the advertising slide and would slowly usurp, over the course of two decades, much of the position of its technologically simplistic sibling in motion-picture theaters. Indeed, commentators of the time saw the trailer as a direct replacement for the outdated lantern slide, which "had had its run."[5] The most common response to the promising but faltering concept of advertising slides was to criticize the stillness of the slide, leading numerous cinema-advertising producers to develop the advertising trailer as a better means of capturing and captivating the audience. The trailer revolution spawned a wave of new companies that saw themselves as the direct competitors and successors of the struggling slide makers. This transition was not simply a broad industrial change, however; at times it occurred within the walls of slide companies themselves—the Kansas City Slide Company, to name just one example, attempted to integrate trailers into its line of wares around 1920. Company President A. V. Cauger trained his young artists Walt Disney and Ubbe Iwerks—originally hired to produce cartoon and wash drawings for advertising slides—to produce advertising trailers. Disney, who was to make himself a household name in the field of animation, thus discovered cartooning largely due to cinema-advertising trends as the slide lost ground to the commercial trailer.[6]

Trailers, like slides before them, were designed to be inserted into an entertainment sequence in the gaps in the program, perpetuating the developing commercial break model but without the jarring transition from full-motion images to stills. The rise of this more technologically suitable form correlated, however, to a historical moment when pauses for advertising were diminishing in programs rather than growing, due to the rise of two-projector theaters (which did not need to pause during a reel change). Trailers, despite their suitability for use at the end of each reel, commonly wound up strung together on a reel of their own and used as a form of intermission between turns of the program. It is in the marginalization of the trailer that screen advertising found its stable form—unbroken feature films (and, to a decreasing degree, shorts) surrounded, in lower-end theaters, by an intermission buffer zone of advertising clips. Despite this stability, the advent of the trailer also correlates to an acceleration of a hierarchical organization of American theaters. As the commercial intermission became common, it also took on the same association with commoners that had begun to plague the slide in its latter days; the move toward palatial cinemas and the social-climbing nature of the motion-picture industry doubly marginalized the trailer, pushing it into the intermission and lower-class theaters simultaneously.

MINUTE MOVIES

Referred to variously as "minute movies," "photoplaylets," and "visualized publicity telegrams," trailers were very short advertising filmstrips that played out like temporally, rather than spatially, organized slides.[7] Most often they were made, like lantern slides, to promote generic products, with a dealer identified in the concluding moments of the film. Trailers could—and did—promote national brands but even then would almost invariably include a local dealer name and address in the final seconds. Commonly, the running length of an individual trailer advertisement was roughly forty-five feet for the story and fifteen feet for the name

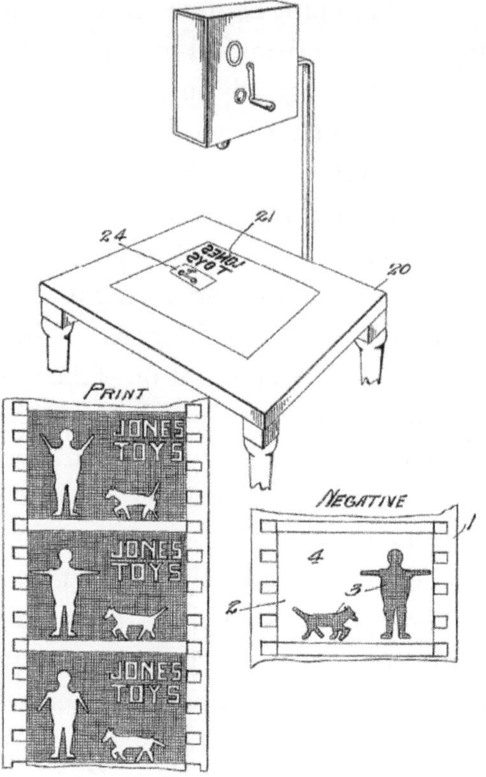

Figure 2.1. A depiction of the camera and the two stages of the Artfilm Studios animation process, from Reginald V. Stambaugh's patent (#1,226,135). In stage one, a film strip of the boy and dog, with copious blank space at the margins, would be created in black figure and added to the Artfilm Studios library. In stage two, a print of the strip created in stage one, laid on top of a strip of blank film, would be run through the camera a second time in order to film custom advertising copy. The result would be a white-figure film featuring a stock cartoon alongside custom copy.

and address of a local business where the product could be purchased. Due to the variability of projection speeds in the silent era, the actual viewing of an advertising trailer may have taken much less than the commonly presumed one-minute running time of sixty feet of film. Roughly one minute was, however, the standard estimate, if not the standard experience.

At their inception in the early 1910s, trailers were circulated individually. As the name would imply, trailers were intended to be appended to the ends of entertainment reels that ran a bit shorter than the typical one thousand feet. Research conducted by the J. Walter Thompson agency in 1929 found that mainstream films of this era could run "as short as 650–700 feet," causing exhibitors to "look with a good deal of favor on film novelties running about 50–250 feet . . . which could be patched onto the ends of short reels when it was desirable to lengthen the program, or left off when it was preferable."[8] Although trailers could be circulated in blocks on their own reels, which became more common as the method matured toward the early 1920s, the duration of a trailer was consciously chosen for mobility, as it allowed the local exhibitor to position it in the program as he or she saw fit.

As with slides, trailers could be had in either stock or custom formats. Custom trailers were usually made to order and purchased outright, with circulation left as a responsibility of the advertiser. The typical cost for a custom trailer was between fifty cents and one dollar per foot, or about thirty to sixty dollars per trailer.[9] As with custom slides, a custom trailer typically had significant input from the advertiser on the visual and copy decisions. A common form of custom trailer was a full-motion version of a well-known brand logo or trade character—for example, "the 'Gold-Dust' twins scamper[ing] around the kitchen and . . . turn[ing] black pots into shiny ones."[10]

Although custom trailers persisted throughout the life of the form, trailers, like slides before them, were predominantly of the "stock" or "syndicate" variety—generic trailers selected from a catalog for merchants in particular lines of business. For example, the growing industry of automotive accessories and repair work accounted for a vast percentage of trailer rentals (with one official estimate placing the auto industry at over ten percent of the business).[11] As such, virtually any trailer company would have had a large collection of stock trailers geared specifically toward this group. Stock trailers had a wide variation in cost—ranging from four to twelve dollars—depending on whether they were rented or purchased outright, with a typical rental price in the vicinity of five dollars.[12] In the mature trailer period, any given trailer producer would offer both custom and stock trailers simultaneously.

Surprisingly, trailers even had their own version of the billboard in which custom text was integrated into stock imagery. The Rothacker Film Manufacturing Company, in an attempt to leave copy decisions in the hands of the advertisers, offered to integrate all text via intertitles. Paired with suitably generic action, this could have resulted in significant fine-tuning of the advertising message, though in practice the copy was often minimal, as it was difficult to integrate more than one or two intertitles in under a minute.[13] By contrast, Artfilm Studios performed technological gymnastics to try to put stock animation and custom copy on the same frame. Artfilm left open spaces in the frame designed to accommodate custom dialogue and then developed a complicated dual-threading process in which two pieces of film (a shooting negative and a completed animation positive) would be passed through the camera simultaneously, rerecording the action at the same time that the copy was recorded. Artfilm's patent for this technology—filed by company head Reginald V. Stambaugh—provides clear reasoning for why so few companies attempted this partially stock method of production. Stambaugh's list of the many ways in which image "wobbling" could arise at the joint is lengthy and dissuasive.[14] Customized-stock trailers could thus vary widely from producer to producer and could be technically compromised in various ways, though the goal of these companies was the same: to provide preconceived story imagery with flexible copy.

Despite the vast differences in cost and production style between custom, stock, and customized-stock trailers, their form and content (what the cinemagoer actually saw onscreen) had little variation. Custom production was a means to more completely integrate the brand, not a way to create an ad of higher formal quality or more densely informative copy. Few types of persuasive appeal were considered plausible in a running time so brief. As Yvonne Zimmerman has said, "the length of commercials . . . affects scope and pace, rhetoric and audience address" such that brevity has a streamlining and flattening effect. Only two rhetorical tactics were regularly attempted: humor and comparison.[15]

Slides had begun the transition to a positive association between humor and advertising. Although he was, like many advertising men of his time, a firm believer that "business talk is more effective . . . when presented in business form," slide theorist Frank Farrington asserted as early as 1913 that "a lighter, brighter form of advertising can be used . . . in a place of amusement than . . . in the newspapers. A little humor carefully handled is not out of place at such a time . . . though it would act as a boomerang in the printed medium."[16] Although slide advertising had adopted humor sparingly, the content of trailers was frequently comic and reliant on soft sell strategies "linking . . . the brand name with . . . favorable and memorable associations."[17] Commonly, however, these jokes were distributed across a brief dramatic narrative that was almost always structured as a comparison: life with and without the product.[18] Jonas Howard described this narrative structure of playlets as providing "a sort of object lesson, negative or positive," in order to persuade the viewer of "the necessity for new shoes or a safety razor."[19] These object lessons could be either rational or emotional appeals—either "reason why" or "impressionistic" copy. Providing a perfect example of all of the above, Howard described a corset film in which the near indestructibility of a corset was put on display when two rambunctious children used it to play tug-of-war before soaking it in a tub. The quality of the corset was assured by a narrative claiming it neither tears nor rusts easily, implying superiority to a lower-quality model. Though the argument is rational, the behavior of the children provides a comic and impressionistic edge to the film.[20] Howard likewise provided an example of a more clearly emotional, impressionistic comparative: a shoe advertisement linked the quality of a man's shoes to his romantic appeal, having an onscreen love interest refuse to marry the romantic lead until after he had purchased a new pair of shoes. Such binary arguments are the structuring motif of virtually every published example of the form, whether comic, dramatic, or a mixture of both.[21]

Most variation in style was thus not copy related but confined to minor aesthetic differences. A multitude of aesthetic possibilities, largely determined by the technology developed by a given company, were available. Trailers could be made in live-action, hand-drawn animation, or cut-out puppetry (the latter was seemingly the most common method). The Rowntree Process of the Scenic Film Company was designed to backlight cardboard "figures . . . cut out in the fashion of paper dolls."[22] The Kansas City Slide Company used a similar method; Walt Disney once described his work there as the manipulation of "little puppet things" with joints.[23] The Federal Development Company, as revealed in a self-advertisement, used hand-drawn animation highly reminiscent, due to color inversion (black marks registering white onscreen), of the chalkboard style of Emile Cohl's famous film *Fantasmagorie* (1908).[24] The Rothacker Film Manufacturing Company preferred to deal in live-action and expressed a weakness for "pretty girls."[25]

Unlike lantern slide makers, who, for several reasons (see chap. 1), developed a propensity for white figures on black backgrounds extremely early, trailer animators commonly operated in both white-on-black and black-on-white styles. The future of the form was in black figure, as developments in mainstream entertainment animation (Winsor McCay and Bray Productions) eventually rendered black-figure animation the standard. Numerous early trailer producers were ahead of the curve, working in black-figure immediately. The Scenic Film Company described its animation as consisting of "silhouette and manikin effects" and reproduced several black silhouette images in a 1916 article in a local newspaper.[26] (See fig. 2.5 on p. 138.) Sample images in the display ads for the Dra-Ko Film Company also reveal black-figure production.[27] B. F. Goodrich circulated early animated trailers in black figure as well.[28] In contrast, Artfilm Studios' Reginald V. Stambaugh not only made white-figure animation, but strongly asserted that a white background "contrasts uncomfortably with the usual background of motion picture plays . . . [by] produc[ing] a high light that is out of place."[29] The previously cited chalk-like imagery from the Federal Development Company was also obviously white-figure production.[30] It is possible that the decision was initially either technologically or financially determined; certain methods may have simply produced better or cheaper product in one or the other form. It is also probable that black backgrounds were more common with those who continued the hand-coloring practices of slide production; black backgrounds allowed for easier "slopping" of color across a space, as the background would hide the color that fell outside the lines. For companies concerned about heavy usage, however, the black backgrounds of white-figure work would have been more susceptible to visible streaking as a print deteriorated.

At the point of screening, those exhibitors who accepted trailers were almost always paid for the screening time—either by the merchant who had paid for the film (directly, if placing the film himself, or indirectly, if he hired a space broker to produce the trailer) or by the consumer-goods manufacturer (if it was a national campaign). Any given film was guaranteed, as far as possible, to be screened according to contract, either by sending a man to check up on the exhibitor or by developing long-standing, mutually respectful relationships with exhibitors through space brokering. As such, commercial advertising trailers—though not as common as lantern slides in the years between 1910 and

Figure 2.2. Two employees of the Alexander Film Company at work on advertising trailers in Spokane, Washington, in 1923. Courtesy of Special Collections, Pikes Peak Library District, 056-10296.

1913—would have been seen by many film patrons as a normal piece of the program. An advertising trailer hawking either a national product like Coca-Cola or a local one like Jones's Toys was unlikely to be seen by viewers just once; instead, it was part of a larger pattern witnessed every time they went to their favorite theater.

A "CINEMA OF ATTRACTION" FOR THE NICKELODEON AGE

There were instances of proto-trailers prior to their institutionalization as a form in the 1910s, just as there were with slides. *Washing Day in Switzerland* (1896, Sunlight Soap) and *Admiral Cigarettes* (1897) are two of the best-known examples.[31] The number of examples from the period of cinema as an attraction, however, is vast. To name just one, J. Stuart Blackton (future animation pioneer) and Albert E. Smith formed the Commercial Advertising Bureau in 1898 and screened short advertising films (for everything from Columbia Bicycles to Dewar's Scotch Whiskey) on canvases at busy New York City intersections.[32] Though it is important not to oversell the comparison, most early commercial films were much like mature commercial trailers, as the jokes and last-second slogans were integrated into a (then common) running length of roughly one minute.

As film expanded, however—both in terms of celluloid running length and national audience—between 1900 and 1914, advertising films expanded apace, relegating the extremely brief advertising film to the rubbish bin as an outdated form. Large film producers continued to make commissioned films stylistically parallel to their entertainment fare. Charles Musser, in the most detailed study of advertising in the pre-nickelodeon era, asserts that American Biograph was so heavily engaged in producing commissioned advertising and public-announcement films that "of the 653 films [it] made from 1 May 1903 to 1 May 1904, more than 120 were sponsored by large corporations or the United States government," including films for "Shredded Wheat Biscuits, Mellin's Baby Food, and the Gold Dust Twins."[33] Vitagraph—Blackton and Smith's second film venture—experimented with product placement and was able to extract fabulous sums from advertisers for the service; it was eventually sued for commissions on these contracts, which included $25,000 from American Tobacco for a hanging sign during the Johnson–Jeffries fight and $15,000 from Wrigley for a close-up of a girl unwrapping a piece of gum.[34] The National Cash Register Company was also using film at the St. Louis Expo in 1904.[35] As such, advertising film—via one-reel shorts and product placement—was everywhere. It was likely to be screened in every plausible American venue prior to the establishment of the nickelodeon, from Edison's kinetoscope parlors, to vaudeville performances, to general public celebrations of modern technology at fairs and expositions.

With the stabilization of exhibition practices in nickelodeon theaters, however, advertising motion pictures began losing ground. As the industrial advertising short and tourism-boosting travelogue fought for integration into cinema programs between 1908 and 1913, the roughly fifteen-minute duration of a standard reel became a problem. Once film had lost its status as inherently spectacular, advertising annoyed patrons at the length of a full reel. More and more advertising in motion pictures was camouflaged with a veil of human interest or educational content and reduced to an indirect integration of trademarks into otherwise educational or pleasurable narratives.[36] As the advertising component of a reel became less noticeable, the fantastic costs of making such films—reaching as high as $5,000 apiece—became less attractive.[37] Slides, on the other hand, could be picked from a catalog, ordered for a dollar, and taken to every local motion-picture theater until some exhibitor agreed to run them. The cost of failure with film, therefore, was dissuasively high. With the success of advertising slides prior to 1910, numerous articles dreaming of a future for the advertising film were published, but attempts at full-reel production were impressing neither the clients nor the public.[38] By 1913—after significant efforts from industrial film producers like Watterson Rothacker, Arthur N. Smallwood, and the industrial division of Essanay—the advertising film appeared to be destined for a life of nontheatrical exhibition.[39] The expensive indirect approach found few adherents when forced to compete with direct advertising via cheap slides.

By this same date, however, even the direct advertising slide was struggling through a wave of negative publicity, as a price war was resulting in an avalanche of ugly cut-rate slides. By 1913, exhibitor elimination of advertising slides was in full swing (see chap. 1). The American advertising industry was, however, going through significant expansion in this period; Quentin J.

Schultze points to the era between 1910 and 1915 as a period of "rapid growth" in national advertising in the United States.[40] As such, the mass rebellion against industrial reels and advertising slides, in an era when the desire to advertise was expanding rather than contracting, opened a clear space for a new kind of film advertising to fill the vacuum. Enter the trailer film, appended to the ends of film reels or distributed as a short reel of one-minute-long advertisements, which began its rise in 1914.

Over the course of the following two years, trailer producers and advocates commonly described the trailer as the logical replacement for the faltering lantern slide. The earliest known trailer producer—Houston's Southern Film Service—directly declared, in its 1914 self-advertising, that its films were "not to be compared with the ordinary slides."[41] The Fort Wayne and Northern Indiana Traction Company justified its use of trailer footage that same year on the grounds that it involved neither the pause nor the resentment inherent in slides.[42] Atlanta's Scenic Film Company used simple derisive metaphors to critique the impertinence of using still slides in moving-picture theaters, claiming "even a piece of paper, blown by the breeze across a screen, will attract attention and would be watched by anyone, when something still may stand unnoticed for a long time."[43]

Although slide usage continued (and continues) in American motion-picture theaters, the 1913 backlash against slides was a necessary prerequisite for the boom in advertising film. It not only inspired the creation of short, cheap, and direct advertising film (rather than the subtle camouflaging tactics of product placement and "educational" reels), but also opened up a simple rhetorical argument for adoption: upgrade your slides with the more captivating and pleasurable moving advertisement. In short, the trailer industry was a parasite on the slide industry, pushing condemnation of still advertising in favor of its own full-motion product.[44]

The trailer method arose independently in at least three places: Houston, Atlanta, and New England.[45] In Houston, the Southern

Film Service Inc. began offering "mysterious writing" advertising films, designed "to be attached to your daily film." Using the slogan "An unseen hand in letters white on a darkened screen appears to write," the ads were nothing more than stop-motion writing projected in negative to achieve a white-figure effect.[46] Atlanta cameraman Carl B. Rowntree, of the Scenic Film Company, produced a more complicated practice of cardboard puppet animation, claiming to have invented his process for producing short animated ads in the middle of 1914.[47] By early 1915, he had filed his animation technique with the United States Patent Office and was regularly soliciting the business of Atlanta merchants and manufacturers. He, too, declared that his cartoon films were to be used "by attaching them to the end of regular moving picture reels."[48] Meanwhile, also in the latter half of 1914, New England's National Advertising Motion Picture Weekly Inc. contracted with sixteen nearby theaters to run a weekly five-minute reel containing five distinct advertising films, though nothing more is known about their aesthetic style.[49] In short, multiple aesthetic approaches, as well as both plausible business models—the appended trailer and the reel of trailers—were in use in the United States by the end of 1914. The idea would spread remarkably quickly, with at least seven further companies adopting the form by the end of 1915.[50] A total of at least thirty-three trailer producers were, or had been, in operation by 1921, including Tilford & Tilford, a Chicago company that made trailers exclusively for segregated black theaters.[51]

While it is not entirely clear where the idea came from, there are several plausible origins for the thinking. The term *trailer*, as the inverse of the term *leader*, was in use no later than 1910 to describe the short strips of informational film at the end of a reel—company logos, "The End" tags, and censor board approvals. At times, the production of such material was even outsourced to companies that specialized in the form.[52] It would not have been a great leap for such a company to branch out into sales messages, as they were effectively acting as film branding agents already. A secondary influence may have been split-reel and newsreel releases. In split reels, two films—neither of which was a full reel in length—were released together as a single product. By 1914, one half-reel film, *Fireproofing Children,* was said to be "released as a trailer," indicating that the line between a split-reel film and a trailer was breaking down.[53] Newsreels were similar to split reels in that they strung together largely unrelated footage, which could be shuffled or dropped at will, on a single reel.[54] The fact that advertisers continually attempted to get brief footage into newsreels—culminating in the Ford Motor Company producing newsreels of its own from 1914 to 1921—indicates early interest in the placement of short advertising strips onto larger reels of unrelated material.[55] Newsreels, split reels, and informational trailer footage were all common practices in entertainment cinema that in hindsight were logical precursors to the advertising trailer concept.

There is also evidence that the commercial advertising film industry had long been fascinated by brevity. Attempts at getting advertising into newsreels were but one piece of a much larger interest in the powers of very short advertising footage. A January 1913 article reveals that advertising films intended for theatrical release and those intended for use by salesmen were being distinguished by the term "regulation lengths" for the former and "short lengths" for the latter.[56] It is possible, then, that the creation of full-reel advertising films was always seen as a formal imposition and an unnecessary expense. If salesmen could make do with less, why couldn't the consuming public? The same article provides a practical example of a one-reel advertising film in which the most popular and influential piece was a quasi-trailer magic trick at the end of the film. *The Story of the Fountain Pen* (Waterman Pens, presumably 1912) was believed to be successful largely for its animated ending in which pieces of rubber and gold assembled themselves into a pen and then drew pictures that were made to "come to life." Audiences loved this part of the film, which was described as "about a minute" in duration.[57] At a time in which impressionistic copy was already making inroads into mainstream advertising, it is not implausible that the Waterman company, along with other businesses, would have begun to wonder if the roughly 900 feet of film prior to this novelty animated section was entirely superfluous. The appeal of the animated attraction vastly outweighed that of slow description.

SPECTACLE, SPEED, AND SALESMANSHIP

Even if *The Story of the Fountain Pen* had no direct bearing on trailer development, it serves as a perfect transitional moment, due not only to the duration and placement of the sequence, but also to its reliance on animated effects. Sharply highlighting just how much the cinema-advertising industry could differ in opinion from the print agencies, early trailer producers embraced entertainment and pleasure and made their advertisements almost exclusively as humorous animated cartoons.[58] Between 1914 and 1916, animation wasn't simply the most common form of trailer; it was so predominant as to render live-action trailers a decided anomaly. Aside from proto-coming-attractions trailers, the only live-action trailers of which I am aware in these early years were one-time efforts: the Fort Wayne and Northern Indiana Traction Company's electrification footage in late 1914, the Raymond Anderson Company's early 1915 commercial using local children, and the trailer used to advertise the 1915 Portland Rose Festival.[59]

Although the history of drawn advertising art implies continuity from lithography to slides to trailers (drawings come to life), the appeal of animated advertising was not continuity but novelty. Popular animation was in a very early stage of development at this point: Bray Productions, the largest early animation house, did not release its first cartoon (*The Artist's Dream*) until June 12, 1913, and was still seeking a wide audience for its work at mid-decade.

Winsor McCay did not begin screening his highly influential third animated short, *Gertie the Dinosaur,* until February 8, 1914.[60] As such, from mid-1914 to mid-1916, it is likely that animation did not just dominate the trailer business; the trailer business also dominated animation. In at least one city—Atlanta—a local newspaper effectively stated as much; the *Atlanta Constitution,* in an article on animation, asserted "you have seen it—if you're a picture play-goer—queer little cartoon-like characters that perform all manner of intricate antics . . . *in exploitation of the merits of this trade shop or that.*"[61] In short, the novelty of animation was a core element in the successful circulation of early trailers.

The focus on animation had two practical benefits—it helped convince advertisers that the form had value and defused exhibitor reluctance to screen the films. For advertisers, the need to produce recognizable sales copy (i.e., written persuasive claims) in a medium of motion virtually required that letters be kinetic. Early trailer producers almost universally promoted "moving" or "mysteriously appearing" letters as their primary asset.[62] Although advertising animators believed that minimizing written content produced better ads, all advertising films had to include a small amount of written copy, at the very least providing a dealer's name and address.[63] One could use stop-action and animation to do this with flair in many ways—letters that appeared in a place previously occupied by another object, that flew around the screen and formed words, or that seemed to write themselves without a visible hand, to name just three examples. Simple stop-motion tricks could render the onscreen reproduction of words a dynamic experience. Likely emerging from pre-narrative trailer practice in which an abstract visual was made to reveal a product or merchant name—like the Scenic Film Company's ad for Nunnally's chocolates, in which the letters appeared out of an exploding heart—the persistent need to include written advertising copy kept animated letters at the forefront of trailer practice in the early years.[64] Animation was, therefore, a means to inject spectacle not just into the action of the film, but into even the most mundane of content.

Animation also had a direct appeal to exhibitors and audiences. It used spectacle to create a mentally engaged spectator. Early commentators remarked on the "unusual interest" the audience expressed in animated trailers and proposed that this may have been a result of the audience "try[ing] to figure out how [it was] done."[65] Add in the fact that trailer producers also oriented their scripts toward pleasure—the Dra-Ko Film Company went so far as to hire Frank A. Nankivell, famous for his work in the humor magazine *Puck*, to head its art department—and the animated trailer had distinct appeals across the board: directness and cheapness for advertisers, brevity and humor for audiences, and cash for exhibitors.[66]

The establishment of the sixty-second running time, also easy to ignore as a holdover from slide and print antecedents, was no less consciously chosen than the turn to animation. Although brevity was intentional, one minute was neither a technological nor exhibitor-mandated maximum.[67] In fact, over the course of roughly a year, the typical running time slowly but perceptibly increased in published accounts from thirty seconds to one minute. In mid-1915, the Raymond Anderson Company was producing trailers with a uniform running length of thirty-five feet.[68] A general article on the form from the end of 1915 declared that one could succeed with a cartoon trailer using "not more than twenty or thirty feet of film."[69] The Scenic Film Company, in early 1916, though offering durations ranging anywhere from twenty-five feet to multiple reels, asserted that thirty-five to fifty feet was the norm.[70] By September of 1916, Harvey F. Morris, advertising manager for the Hickey-Freeman Company, claimed that sixty to seventy feet was the norm for a trailer film.[71] By 1919, however, there had been no further change, as two of the most prominent trailer-producing companies—the Rothacker Manufacturing Company and the Alexander Film Company—were continuing the practice of one- to one-and-a-half-minute-long advertising trailers. This duration would remain constant throughout the 1920s.[72] By 1921, the phrase *minute movies* had even become acceptable shorthand.[73] It appears, then, that the roughly one-minute running time developed as a standard between 1914 and 1916 partly as a compromise: it was long enough to integrate rudimentary narrative but short enough to fit onto a film reel that was only slightly below full.

Of course, cost control likely also had some impact on running time. In 1916, Ernest Dench declared that the average price per foot for a trailer film was fifty cents, resulting in a cost of thirty dollars for a one-minute trailer—a drastic increase over the typical one-dollar cost of a lantern slide.[74] The Scenic Film Company quoted the same price that year, though the price would double to one dollar per foot if the advertiser wanted to handle the bookings himself.[75] Therefore, even at durations under one minute, trailers were a financial burden to merchants with small advertising budgets. This cost issue rapidly led to the development of the syndicate or stock catalog trailer to cut rates further to the more affordable price of four to five dollars. Copying the idea of a stock slide selected from a catalog with a specific dealer name appended eventually shifted the trailer business from a purchase to a rental structure, resolving at least two cost problems. First, it distributed first-copy costs across unrelated businesses. Second, as with entertainment fiction before them, it allowed trailers to "be made in a central location and on a predictable basis," reducing idle labor and travel expenses.[76] It also added to the profitability of the form, as exceptionally popular copy could produce nearly unlimited profits. The Alexander Film Company, for example, worked exclusively on a rental system for its stock trailers, as revealed in its 1921 sales manual. As such, sixty-foot lengths, stock products, and generic narratives—all in their infancy in 1917 but standard by 1921—pulled costs down to that of little more than a high-end slide.[77] This was a perfect price point for a parasitical relationship.

The developmental period of trailer advertising, then, was a two-year-long attempt to find a compromise between quality and cost. The result was experimentation with three modes of production: custom, stock, and "partially stock" (stock imagery with gaps for custom text). The fully stock model, which would eventually become the dominant model, was not necessarily superior, nor can we presume that its users believed it to be. The American advertising film industry intentionally sacrificed elements of message delivery, like product specificity and advertiser-written copy, to cost considerations. In the absence of an easy way to fund and nationally circulate trailers for specific brands, trailer producers targeted merchants by producing the cheapest possible variant. The other two modes of production (custom and partial-stock) shifted into the background due entirely to cost and circulation problems, not technological inefficiency or aesthetic dislike. Trailer producers, like slide producers, became cinema-advertising agencies at a very early date out of necessity, providing copy-writing services and circulation assistance; production was generally too expensive if the producer allowed advertiser input.

THE VANISHING SPACE AND THE RISE OF THE BROKER

Despite the marked difference in public approval (slides were largely derided, while trailers were frequently enjoyed as bite-sized entertainment), the years 1916 to 1918 provided nearly identical problems and benefits for trailers as they had for slides. Wartime propaganda, alongside film industry changes, simultaneously entrenched the concept while usurping much of the available screen time.

Competition from the film industry itself emerged alongside the rise of cinema self-defense and self-advertising in 1916. Industry defense announcements were common in this era of expanding film censorship; Balboa, for example, was circulating an

Figure 2.3. Four nonconsecutive frames from the Alexander Film Company's dealer strip for jeweler J. B. Gilmore of Kennewick, Washington. A custom dealer strip, appended after a short stock-advertising cartoon, was the sole custom element of almost all Alexander trailers. Note also the production company name clearly indicated beneath the dealer—a declaration of authorship uncommon in the advertising industry. Box 2, Folder 4, Alexander Industries Records, MSS0056, Special Collections, Pikes Peak Library District.

anti-censorship trailer in the first quarter of 1916.[78] In short order, however, the most prominent trailer format was the coming-attraction snippet. During the transition of the motion-picture industry from the early decade dominance of the patents company to the vertically integrated independent studios, competition for viewership increased. In an effort to guarantee profitability in an environment of increased competition and increased expense (due to the production of features, which the industry believed required individual marketing), film promotion by the studios increased.[79] By September of 1916, Famous Players "issue[d] an advance strip" to promote the upcoming film *The Quest of Life*.[80] The following month, the Triangle Film Corporation—with the assertion that "the screen . . . is a most powerful advertising medium . . . that was not being taken full advantage of"—began circulating coming-attraction trailers for its own products.[81] By July of 1917, *Moving Picture World* declared that such trailers had "come into use extensively of late" and reported that Selznick as well had adopted the form.[82] Rather than the issue of multiple projectors closing off the open spaces in the program, then, the first major crisis in the trailer industry was competition from studios themselves over the established space.[83]

What space was not being claimed for film industry self-promotion was being adapted for wartime use. As early as 1914, Universal (typically the quickest to engage with new advertising theories) had already adopted the direct advertising trailer model for philanthropic exhortation, with the company attaching a thirty-foot leader to every film release encouraging spectators to "buy a bale of cotton"—a response to the overstock of cotton caused by the closing of European markets during the early hostilities of World War I.[84] By 1917, both the US government, through the propaganda campaign of the Creel Committee, and the public, through growing patriotic sentiment, pressured exhibitors to integrate this sort of political advertising into film programs.

While the trailer form was adopted frequently for war work, the Liberty Loan was again the watershed.[85] The Creel Committee, not surprisingly, circulated official Liberty Loan trailers.[86] The movement was bolstered by a few motion-picture studios, like Kalem and Selig-Polyscope, who, eager to display their patriotism, produced Liberty Loan trailers of their own.[87] Wartime patriotic trailers unaffiliated with the Liberty Loan drives were circulated as well, most notably the American Bioscope Company's "Your Flag and Mine," which was offered interminably in the pages of *Moving Picture World*.[88] By March of 1918, patriotic messages were so ingrained in American exhibition culture that *Moving Picture World* columnist Walter K. Hill was able to propose, without seeming to wildly overstep the bounds of taste, that *all* feature films should include a leader or trailer in which "the star of the piece be posed . . . holding a sign" extolling the virtues of purchasing war stamps.[89] The proliferation of patriotic appeals on the screen solidified or expanded the presence of advertising copy in even the highest-class theaters and likely helped to develop the "appreciative tolerance" for direct appeals in between film reels that the J. Walter Thompson agency would remark on years later.

With the adoption of the form for both film industry messaging and politics, the first two years of trailer development were followed by roughly three years of transitioning business models. As the circulation of government and announcement trailers increased, exhibitors were faced with a decision: devote a larger percentage of the program to trailers of all kinds, decrease their use of commercial trailers, or decline to use the (free) self-advertising sent out by the studios in favor of commerce. With the increasing dominance—even ownership—of exhibition sites by production companies, the exhibitor's ability to decline decreased; exhibition was becoming a national business, not a local one. In hindsight, it is obvious that the commercial trailer was likely to be the loser in that equation.

Unlike slide makers, who fought the circulation battle under a cloud of bad practices, trailer producers did not fight back through assertions of artistry or printing long testimonial lists of national advertisers who had at one time or another used their services.[90] Trailer makers attempted to survive the competition, and the war, solely through professionalization—escalating the scale of their operations and adopting the appearance of mainstream ad agencies. Echoing the slide industry's turn to full-service production and distribution, which had occurred over the previous few years (see chap. 1), trailer producers adopted space brokering as a business model and began to actively court national advertisers. The increasing scale of contracts, both with exhibitors and advertisers, added a patina of proficiency and efficiency to trailer production, while space brokering itself guaranteed minimums of activity for any given business. All of these changes occurred between late 1916 and 1918—the same years in which the competition for space was at its heaviest.

Such space brokering, however, led to a significant change in integration practices. Rather than fight to maintain the original position of trailers as patched onto the end of short reels, the trailer industry, almost in perfect unison, opted to seek new quarters in the program sequence. Whether this was a serendipitous accident or a conscious choice in realization that the rise of feature films and dual-projector screenings was likely to eliminate the gaps anyway, most trailer producers began contracting for large blocks of space as an intermission in the program. The focus of American screen advertising was finally and irrevocably shifted from buffering a sequence of shorts for transient spectators to inhabiting a roughly ten-minute advertising break in the entertainment.[91]

Identifying the location of this intermission is difficult, though any such clarity is more semantic than practical. Trailer producers needed to convince clients that the trailers would be seen and therefore described the location of the intermission as existing between certain established pieces of the program. Jonas Howard's article on Rothacker photoplaylets, published in late 1919, declared that good trailers must be able to "hold the attention of the audience between Mary Pickford and the news weekly."[92] In 1921, the Alexander Film Company asserted that its contracted films were screened "between the comedy and the feature" in most theaters.[93] In other words, the likely placement of commercial trailers was either immediately before or after the feature, with the latter position being significantly more likely. It is clear, therefore, that trailer producers were hoping that the use of the word *between* (a vague assertion, as a looping program is an endless series of *betweens*) would obscure the fact that, for all viewers, there is an optimal moment of egress. This moment was increasingly likely to occur while the advertisements were playing. By 1921, *Printers' Ink* columnist Arthur McClure clearly indicated that this was the drift of current practice when he declared that "the day is not far off when the motion picture theater will offer its patrons a programme consisting of five or six parts entertainment and one part advertising," with the advertising reel placed where the patron may "leave the theater . . . before the advertisement is run."[94] In short, the shift in trailer practice at this time was in line with the film industry's ongoing transition from transient spectatorship (where spectators could enter or leave at any time) to scheduled entertainments. Paradoxically, what Ernest Dench once described as the "slide dodge" (running all ads in a lump when most patrons wouldn't see them) became the standard practice in the trailer industry.

Compared to the hazy history of the location of this contracted space, the rise of space brokering in the trailer industry is clear. A few trailer producers likely integrated space brokering into their business models very early.[95] These early efforts could be quite small. The Real Publicity Company had contracted with only two Kansas City theaters by mid-1915—the Benton and the Royal—to which it delivered weekly reels containing twelve ads each.[96] As the practice grew, trailer producers would typically attempt to control ever larger percentages of the theaters in their home cities and states. The Scenic Film Company controlled seventeen theaters in Atlanta as early as May 1916.[97] Nelson Motion Picture Studios claimed sixty theaters across Detroit in 1918.[98] Screen Press Inc. dominated Minneapolis and St. Paul by 1919.[99] James P. Simpson developed a stranglehold on the state of Texas by 1920.[100] Over 1916 and 1917, a secondary trend toward multistate coverage is apparent in space-brokering announcements. The Scenic Film Company attempted to expand into Boston and Philadelphia in 1916 in an effort to become an East Coast power.[101] More notable, however, was Screen Advertising Inc. and its chain of contracts with "1,000 Better Class Neighborhood Theatres" east of the Mississippi River. Organized in 1917 and contracting for only 200 feet of advertising per program in each of its theaters, Screen Advertising Inc. offered not only the selection of pre-certified theaters but also a service department to help national advertisers contact dealers and inform them of upcoming ad screenings (thereby presumably eliminating the need to append dealer information to the trailer itself). On July 5, 1917, Screen Advertising Inc. claimed the enormous vote of confidence of the Marcus Loew theaters of New York, which signed on for its service.[102] By 1921, the Alexander Film Company had transitioned from a West Coast company to a national business and was contracting theaters across the United States for a reel of between five and ten ad trailers. Alexander provides the only direct evidence of what a theater could expect to earn from such a relationship, declaring that the average theater was contracted at a hundred dollars per month.[103] It is important, however, not to overstate the strength of these early turns to space brokering. Although progress was clearly being made toward nationalizing the trailer industry, a 1929 research report for the J. Walter Thompson Company indicated that trailer producers' "promises . . . turn[ed] out to be mirages in a good many instances."[104]

In transitioning to space brokering, trailer producers abandoned the piecemeal approach of most slide producers and developed a model nearly identical to that of early magazine advertising—placing large swaths of precontracted advertising in a bookend position (the closest to an "optional" position that the screen could offer) and stressing audience selection as the form's greatest strength. Screen Advertising Inc., for example, used detailed knowledge about the clientele of particular theaters to offer advertisers various types of audiences. While Screen Advertising Inc. described all of its theaters as middle class, it offered to rent space by neighborhood, city, or zone so that the advertiser could feel confident of reaching his target audience without overpaying for valueless screenings.[105] Signing contracts in advance with the theaters guaranteed placement, enabling advertising film manufacturers to approach advertisers armed with their list of theaters and allowing the advertisers to decide for themselves how many and of what type to use. Exhibitor reluctance was cut off before the film was even produced, opening up the field to advertisers who had previously avoided film as a questionable investment that might simply "repose peacefully in [its] can" after it was made.[106]

BATTLES FOR THE BOTTOM OF THE BARREL

The ubiquitous rise of space brokering is but one element of homogenization that is apparent within the trailer industry at this time. Much of the codification of standard business practices seems directly traceable to the advent of the Advertising Film Producers Association (AFPA) in June of 1916. The AFPA was formed during a meeting of seven trailer producers—the Federal Development Company, the Kansas City Slide Company, the Scenic Film Company, the Camel Film Company, and three others that are unknown—at the Associated Advertising Clubs of the World convention in Philadelphia.[107] Although the

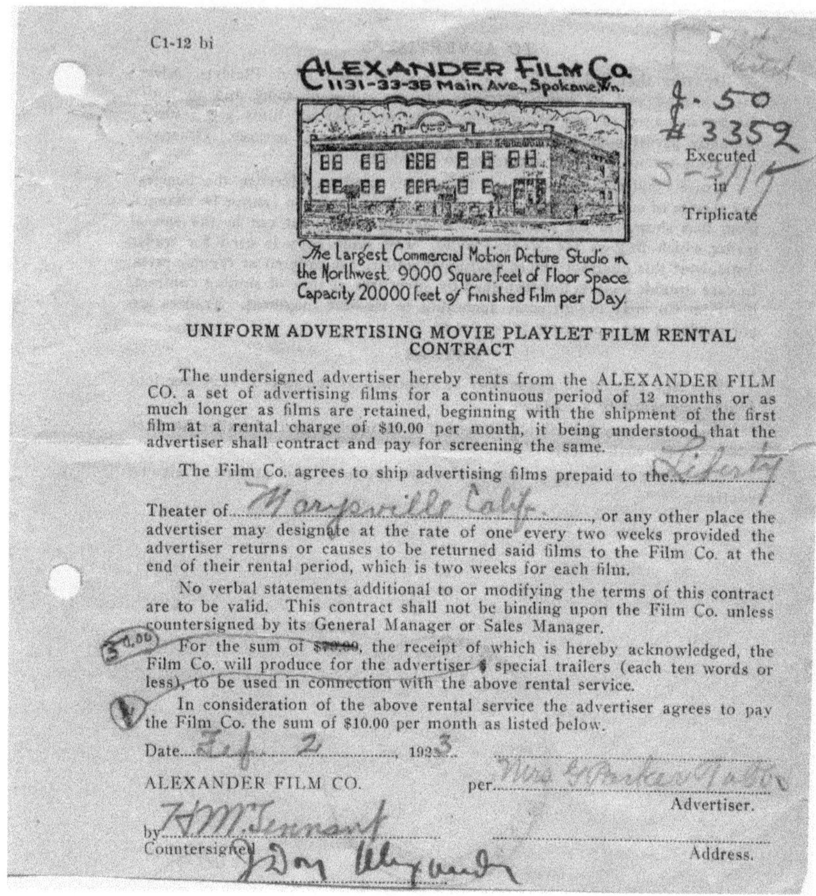
C1-12 bi

ALEXANDER FILM CO.
1131-33-35 Main Ave., Spokane, Wn.

The Largest Commercial Motion Picture Studio in the Northwest. 9000 Square Feet of Floor Space Capacity 20000 Feet of Finished Film per Day

Executed in Triplicate

UNIFORM ADVERTISING MOVIE PLAYLET FILM RENTAL CONTRACT

The undersigned advertiser hereby rents from the ALEXANDER FILM CO. a set of advertising films for a continuous period of 12 months or as much longer as films are retained, beginning with the shipment of the first film at a rental charge of $10.00 per month, it being understood that the advertiser shall contract and pay for screening the same.

The Film Co. agrees to ship advertising films prepaid to the Liberty Theater of Marysville Calif., or any other place the advertiser may designate at the rate of one every two weeks provided the advertiser returns or causes to be returned said films to the Film Co. at the end of their rental period, which is two weeks for each film.

No verbal statements additional to or modifying the terms of this contract are to be valid. This contract shall not be binding upon the Film Co. unless countersigned by its General Manager or Sales Manager.

For the sum of ~~$10.00~~ 5.00, the receipt of which is hereby acknowledged, the Film Co. will produce for the advertiser ~~$~~ special trailers (each ten words or less), to be used in connection with the above rental service.

In consideration of the above rental service the advertiser agrees to pay the Film Co. the sum of $10.00 per month as listed below.

Date Feb 2, 1923

ALEXANDER FILM CO. per Mrs G Parker Tubbs
Advertiser.

by H M Tennant
Countersigned J Don Alexander

Address.

Figure 2.4. A signed contract for one year of service (to be screened at the Liberty Theater in Marysville, CA) between the Alexander Film Company and Edna Tubbs, wife and office assistant of chiropractor George Parker Tubbs. Note the drawing of the company's Spokane office building in the header. Box 2, Folder 3, Alexander Industries Records, MSS0056, Special Collections, Pikes Peak Library District.

association was usurped by industrial film producers in 1917 and then rapidly collapsed, its importance lies not in its duration but in the uniformity of sales rhetoric and tactics it fostered among trailer producers.[108] For example, the exchange of information among multiple businesses allowed AFPA President W. A. Harris to make blanket, industry-wide statements in print; he could provide a general cost of trailer usage (seven dollars per film) and a range of costs for weekly screenings (a minimum of one dollar and a maximum of five).[109] The increasing predominance of stock film production may also trace to this association, as trailer producers learned tricks of the trade from their competitors. As a united bloc, the association also managed to improve business conditions in ways that would have been unattainable for small companies. For example, the AFPA claimed responsibility for making film "admissible through the United States mails," allowing for the shipment of film "in three days by parcel post," as opposed to requiring special transit arrangements.[110]

In the shift to stand-alone reels of multiple trailers rented for standard prices from stock film lists, circulated regularly to contracted theaters, and sometimes containing national advertising messages, the model had largely completed its development. The years after the war (in this study, 1918 to 1922) can be defined quite accurately as an era of stabilization, as trailers increasingly became the replacement for slides. Former slide manufacturers—like the Manhattan Slide and Film Company (1917), the Brite-Lite Film Advertising Company (1918), and the Perfection Slide and Film Company (1919), all from New York—joined the transition and began to offer animated trailers as a second line of business.[111] Leaping into the fray, auto manufacturer Dodge shifted to the "minute movie" model in 1921, producing a trio of cartoons that it rented to dealers at the rate of fifteen dollars for the three.[112] In the years after the war, the trade presses for various industries clearly indicate the slowly widening adoption of a relatively stable form.

Two particular points of contention, however, kept growth more sluggish than it might otherwise have been. The first was industry infighting. Though the viability of the trailer format was no longer in contention after the war, significant debate arose over which mode of trailer production was best suited to advertising. After inaugurating the form with a spectacular flourish, animation came under direct attack from producers of live-action trailers as they attempted to elevate trailer advertising to the level of sober, dignified discourse preferred by the mainstream advertising industry. In an implicit echo of the J. Walter Thompson Company's 1903 claim that "we don't believe in funny advertising," H. H. Dewey, of the Rothacker Company, declared that "the animated cartoon . . . would get a laugh at the expense of dignity." Though he claimed that even "the better grades of [cartoon trailers] . . . failed to place the [quality and beauty of] the merchant's goods . . . upon the counter of the silver screen," Dewey's examples of his own work otherwise varied in no noticeable way from the work of others. A short comedy about a girl turning down a suitor because her current boyfriend buys her ice cream and a nostalgic story about a husband and wife remaining in lifelong bliss through the aid of boxes of chocolates can, at best, be said to be more "dignified" than the work of others by stressing romance.[113] While nothing really came of the critique—the dominant company of the 1920s was an animation house, the Alexander Film Company—such industry infighting placed sectional gains above the trailer industry as a whole at a time when the space formerly occupied by propaganda was once again up for grabs.[114]

Second, and more importantly, the film industry's class stratification was widening, with cinema advertising still caught in the middle.[115] "Roxy" Rothapfel, in a 1916 article full of advice for exhibitors, was already able to confidently assert that advertising "will not be tolerated at all in the best house" in major urban centers, though "in the smaller towns it is taken . . . as a matter of course and a part of the program."[116] In 1918 and 1919, a survey of clothing stores indicated that usage of motion-picture advertising of any kind was almost nonexistent in cities with a population greater than 40,000. In 1918, the survey turned up eighty-two stores using cinema advertising in towns of less than 40,000 people, compared to only eight in larger cities. In 1919, the ratio was slightly worse: 105 to 10. Though the researchers seem unaware of the reasons, it is clear in hindsight that stores in larger cities were steering clear of motion-picture advertising not by choice but by necessity; there was simply nowhere to have such advertising screened.[117] By 1921, this split between urban and small-town theaters was so entrenched that Francis T. Kimball, in an article in *Moving Picture Age,* described the trailer as a mode of advertising exclusively for "the thousands of cities and towns and hamlets of the United States which are not among the leading few." First-run downtown theaters in large cities "will not put even the most sugar-coated trailer on their screens."[118] By the late 1950s, this long-standing cultural hierarchy remained so entrenched that the J. Walter Thompson Company simply omitted the eight largest cities in the United States from a research report on trailer advertising so as not to create errors in the data.[119] In sum, the postwar years, though an era of stabilization across vast swaths of the United States, were a time of widening distinctions between urban and small-town advertising.

Where such advertising was accepted, competition was fierce. But for those companies winning hearts and minds, trailer advertising was, at the national scale, big business. By the early 1920s, the Alexander Film Company was reporting astonishingly high commission rates for salesmen. A "Mr. Morris" earned $23,757.54 in one year.[120] (This would translate to a $325,000 salary in 2021.) Two other employees, extrapolating from strong sales rates in brief windows (less than a year) of time, were earning at the rate of $10,000 and $40,000 per year in 1920 and 1921 respectively.[121] W. A. Rice made $1,117.60 in June of 1924; Jack Woltz make $1,098.35 in his first twenty-two days.[122] Generally promising commissions as high as 35 percent, Alexander was clearly turning a large profit even in its earliest years and offered a profit split to its salesmen, which kept the best men interested in selling Alexander trailers.[123] Clients, too, were loyal; one "ladies' and children's shop in Green River, Wyo[ming]" used Alexander trailer films unceasingly for eleven years (from 1923 to 1933).[124] In the bulk of the country, even though trailers had been pushed into isolation in an intermission, the business was stable and worth fighting for.

After 1920, then, the history of direct advertising in cinema theaters is largely a history of the entrenchment of the trailer model. By 1922, the commercial trailer was the predominant mode of cinematic advertising but had, through a confluence of events, been relegated to a doubly marginalized position: a bookend location in the program and rural and low-end theaters geographically. Despite this ostracism, decades before television, the cinema had developed its own "magazine format" consisting of multiple small advertisements created and placed by a space broker and restricted to an advertising section at either the beginning or the end of the content (depending on if one arrived early or left late), much like the wraparound advertising in early nineteenth-century magazines. As such, the cinema had abandoned the pulsing sequence of slide advertising and developed a spatially influenced structure in a temporal program, with advertising placed regularly but in the only position where patrons could readily ignore it.

THE BATTERING RAM OF PLEASURE

Trailers were the clear replacement for slides, in the minds of most at the time, and the rhetoric surrounding them was predominantly an expansion of the slide conversation; there were clearer buzzwords and better data, but the focus was on nearly identical issues. The value of the cinema space, the financial and hidden costs of trailers as opposed to other advertising methods, and concerns about the predictability of audience behavior remained the key topics of concern. Despite the increasingly professional-sounding arguments and a clearly diminishing quantity of hostile critiques in the trades, trailer support faltered in ways almost identical to that of slides. The opposition, though quieter, retained a number of questions and concerns that trailer advocates, like their slide brethren, were not able to fully assuage.

Audience captivity and receptivity remained at the forefront of the dialogue, but the engagement took on a more polarized tone. The concept of captivity was reduced to yet another variant of one of the advertising industry's most abused phrases: 100 percent circulation. W. A. Harris of Screen Advertising Inc., among numerous others, took to referring to the cinema as a "100% medium."[125] This is not to say that there was a complete disappearance of articles laying out, in long hand, the value of the screen for advertising purposes. For example, a 1916 issue of the trade journal *Clothier and Furnisher* rhetorically asked: "Can you imagine how more ideal conditions could possibly be devised than to assemble your audience in a darkened theatre, all waiting to see what's next—and then flash your story on the screen before their eyes?" But for most, 100 percent was enough. Being the center of attention, having exclusive contracts (no competing products advertised alongside yours), large audiences waiting for input—all were implied in the phrase *100 percent*.[126] The near perfect replication of the concerns of slide proponents is evident in the way both groups gravitated to the print metaphor; the Alexander Film Company described trailers as the equivalent of buying "the whole front page" of a magazine—the same description that the Lee Lash Company had used for lantern slides roughly a decade earlier.[127] As such, the starting point for every argument in support of trailer advertising was nearly identical to that of slides: cinema patrons could not help but see your advertisement, exclusive not only of the surrounding environs but also the competitive market.

It was, again, the idea of connecting captivity to receptivity that trailer proponents argued most strenuously and creatively. The possibility of ill will and the vanishing audience were as visible in debates about full-motion advertising as they had been in slide rhetoric. As early as 1911, the Motion Picture Patents Company

Figure 2.5. A sampling of the visual comedy of the Scenic Film Company, as printed in Britt Craig's 1916 article in the *Atlanta Constitution,* using its patented black-figure shadow style. Scenic Film Company shadow cartoons were produced by placing cardboard puppets on a glass stage and lighting them from below.

had gone so far as to ban the circulation of all advertising films in its theaters on the grounds that their inclusion "would inevitably and rapidly degrade the business" by chasing away patrons.[128] As late as 1931, an advertiser with film experience still asserted "the screen . . . is dedicated to the duty of entertaining those who pay their admission at the box office. Therefore it can offer nothing but entertainment if it is to keep faith with the public."[129] Moving the advertising from a glass slide to a film strip was obviously not, in itself, an answer to the concerns about mixing business and pleasure. Although the 1931 example should make clear that trailer producers never effectively answered such concerns, their response to them is the key to understanding trailer advocacy. Concerns over receptivity, along with the need to differentiate trailers from slides, led to two significant additions to cinema-advertising theory: mesmerism and pleasure.

In order to press the belief that receptivity could be controlled, rather than being a natural and insurmountable problem, most trailer supporters argued that the slide, as a still image, was in some way destructive of passivity and that the trailer, in motion, restored or retained it. The argument for animated trailers, offered by the Scenic Film Company's Irvin A. Burdette in 1916, is a perfect case study for what became a common defense. Burdette asserted:

> Actions speak louder than words. . . . Animated Films are 100% action. The public is moved by Curiosity; all are wondering what the actions will develop into next. The minds are receptive and accept your point of view through the "art of suggestion." Animated Ads are "Direct," "Main Point" Evangels of Trade. . . . Cartoon ads create a feeling of personal interest and confidence in you and your product which must exist between the Buying Public and Successful Sellers. The same subconscious "Good Will" which the public have in the players.[130]

Note that the first sentence implicitly condemns the lantern slide by indicating that actions, not images, are louder than words. The following year, AFPA President W. A. Harris—presumably borrowing directly from Scenic, which was a founding member—would likewise assert "action compels attention" in his broad defense of the trailer form.[131] The Alexander Film Company persisted in this argumentation over the course of the 1920s by asserting that human beings were predisposed to attend to motion out of self-defense, variously using metaphors of predators in the bushes, snakes in boxes, and thieves throwing bricks through windows.[132] Indeed, such phrasing builds a sales pitch by exploiting the connotative slippage between cinematic action and consumer action—between a moving (in motion) picture and a moving (impactful) one.

Burdette, however, immediately turns to his own product—animation—adding the secondary claim that magical fabricated motion links directly to suggestion; an almost involuntary "curiosity" is created by "wondering what the actions will develop into next." (The notion that all of this was somehow occurring "subconsciously" was also not uncommon; by 1921, trailer proponent Francis T. Kimball would simply describe cinema audiences as "absorbent."[133]) The power of animation, for Burdette, is what would create the very "good will" that slide proponents had simply asserted as a generic quality of cinema audiences. Remarkably quickly, then, Burdette moves from implicitly questioning receptivity to implying a restoration of it via both motion and magic before finally scaling the heights to the perfection of appeal via funny and lovable characters.

It is Burdette's turn to those final tactics that is the most meaningful. In the field of cinema advertising, entertainment and humor had been broached with much hesitation. Humor had, after all, long been considered inappropriate in the serious business talk of advertising. For trailer producers, especially animators, the cinema was a venue of entertainment, and their product was described as equal to the task. Indeed, a second Scenic Film Company self-advertisement turned to blunt pronouncement that its animated trailers would work "whether [the audience was] in a receptive mood or not," expressing an almost gleeful disinterest in the development of a medium-specific psychology for film on the grounds that it was true of animation in any case.[134] The predominance of both animation and comedy in trailer advertising was, therefore, part of a concrete theory of audience receptivity in which the stoic, critical viewer's defenses were broken down by pleasure—usually laughter. Openly referencing the hissing and irritation that could accompany the slide, trailer producers therefore attempted to both integrate and abandon active audiences by asserting that the failure of slides had been rectified; slides were unpleasant, and trailers were fun.

Although I have focused here almost exclusively on the Scenic Film Company and its associates in the AFPA, the argument that humor was the ultimate panacea was extremely common in pro-trailer rhetoric. The Dra-Ko Film Company declared that animated cartoon trailers were a form of advertising in which "fun predominates."[135] The Alexander Film Company offered trailers with "Punch and Ginger and usually humor."[136] Trade presses interested in the form repeatedly asserted that amusement was the way in which one kept the audience docile.[137] This attempt to promote fun as a counter to active audiences could result in descriptions uncomfortably close to outright manipulation; for example, Jonas

Howard, in typical fashion, asserted that Rothacker Company photoplays were "snappy" and had "laugh and a punch" but concluded that the style was "calculated to draw the unwary movie goer into a spending mood."[138] The power of "fun" was even at times promoted by admen who, in all other articles, adopted the philosophy of separating humor and business. *Printers' Ink*'s unidentified "Little Schoolmaster" was forced to declare, in early 1918, that his "poor opinion of the short, comic moving-picture" ad was incorrect, as "the right kind of a comic goes big, even with very sedate business men."[139] By 1921, the ethos of pleasure was so ingrained in trailer theory that Francis T. Kimball described the typical trailer via the euphemism "screen sugar pill" and included two entire paragraphs likening the pleasure of trailers to the sweet taste that convinces children to take medicine.[140] The pleasures of comedy, therefore, were central to arguments about the appeal of trailers that opted not to trade on the assumption of universal captivation.

By the end of the period under study, the two arguments—captivation and screen sugar—had become a united front, as trailer advertisements, through the aid of humor, were described like an injection or photograph of information directly onto the brain. The aforementioned Francis T. Kimball used both metaphors in the space of only two sentences, in 1921, asserting both that fun resulted in messages being "subtly and . . . irrevocably injected into the receptivity of little Willie Audience" and that trailers resulted in "the dealer's advertisement get[ting] . . . 'fixed' as surely in the mind of the spectator as it is in the emulsion of the film."[141] The Monache Theatre Company Inc., in a 1923 testimonial letter on behalf of the Alexander Film Company, called film advertising "a sort of photographic process registered permanently in the brain cells of the prospective customer."[142] Even when integrating the critique of slides ("hissing," for example) into their rhetoric, then, trailer advertisers persisted in describing cinema viewers' minds as blank photographic plates that would register whatever message the advertiser could compel them to see.

DANCING THROUGH THE MINEFIELD

Of course, early debates about the adoption of new mediums are always rife with disagreement. By the time the trailer had reached a level of maturity and prominence, the humor and fun elements, which had been central to the most successful trailer producers, were questioned from within. As mentioned in the history above, in 1920, H. H. Dewey, of the Rothacker Company (a screen advertising company of significant age but mostly associated with educational and nontheatrical product), attempted market differentiation for Rothacker trailers partly through an appeal to "dignity."[143] Accusing both comic and animated trailers of being degrading or improper for business use and negatively impacting the sales message even as they drew the eye and the mind, Dewey effectively reclaimed the long-standing prohibition on "funny advertising." The return of such concerns from the pen of a major advocate of cinema advertising indicates the persistent struggle for legitimacy that America's first pleasurable advertising medium faced at the time. The advertising industry would take decades to be fully swayed from long-standing assumptions about the seriousness of business.

In the realm of financial, rather than theoretical, matters, despite the need to differentiate from slides, the bulk of historical rhetoric is more familiar. What was not argued in detail was cost efficiency or even use value, the two elements for which the slide industry had argued most often and strenuously. Typically the cost efficiency of trailers was simply asserted. Sometimes such assertions were vague, like Manhattan Slide and Film's description of trailers being of "reasonable cost" or the National Builders' Bureau's assertion that cost was "nominal."[144] Other times, direct dollar amounts, such as the four to five dollars Dench claimed for trailers or Rothacker's twelve-dollar price were cited, along with a declaration that such a cost was "cheap enough for merchants."[145] Likewise, it was rare to assert, through concrete data, that trailer advertising boosted sales. Even vague claims of this nature have only arisen once in my research—an article on a particular Goodrich Tire ad included a smattering of dealers declaring that the trailer had "increased my sales at least ten percent" or resulted in the need to "put on another man" to handle the business boost.[146] These were persuasive battles presumably already won by their predecessors in the slide industry.

Detailed argumentation was reserved for enumerating the various ways in which trailer usage was a more efficient use of one's advertising appropriation than other methods. In the early years, cost comparisons were predictably aimed at slide makers. Despite the 500 percent (or more) increase in cost over slides, trailers were described as *cheaper* than slides. In some cases, one sees an assertion that exhibitors might run trailers for less than they'd charge for slides; as trailers were asserted to provide entertainment, exhibitors, seeking the most entertaining program for the least cost, would gladly run trailers—sometimes even for free.[147] Such argumentation was, of course, quite shallow and reliant on assumptions rather than data. Regardless, such attempts were clearly geared toward minimizing the difference between the cost of slide and trailer adoption—the one arena in which slides had a clear advantage.

Toward the early 1920s, as the competition from slides became less pressing, financial arguments began to focus on print. Indicating the significantly greater strength of the opponent, much more detailed numerical claims were marshaled to show that the cost per prospect of trailer advertising was actually superior to magazine and newspaper advertising. Francis T. Kimball, for example, argued that "the cost of one page in one issue is about three-tenths of a cent [per] possible prospect. And the 'possible' is used advisedly, because it is far from certain that every individual in the total circulation is going to get the message. . . . [Meanwhile] the trailer costs the manufacturer about six-one-hundredths of a cent a prospect—and here the 'possible' is advisedly omitted, since in a motion picture theater there is but one attention focus!"[148] Even if one removed the familiar "100 percent attention" rhetoric Kimball used, the comparison of circulation figures clearly gave motion pictures the edge. In 1921, the Alexander Film Company explicitly compared its yearly contracts to full-page ads in magazines; while the latter cost seventy-five dollars and only ran once, an advertiser could receive six months of biweekly service on theater screens for only slightly more (eighty-six dollars).[149] By 1924, Alexander had adopted Kimball's argumentative tactic and declared that film's cost per prospect was "one-tenth to one-fifth of a cent"—much higher than Kimball's figure but still superior to the cost of print advertising.[150]

Not surprisingly, the same reliability concerns that had plagued slides were voiced about trailers. New Orleans film journalist George M. Cheney was scathing in his mid-1916 indictment of New Orleans theaters for simply transferring bad slide practices into the realm of trailers. Cheney asserted that "there are exhibitors who are running it into the ground as they did the still slides" by running such ads for "ten to twenty minutes"—the length of a full reel—and using the trailers for consecutive days, rendering them repetitious and "exceedingly boresome to an audience used to a daily change."[151] The notion that screen advertising, either by its nature or by excessive quantity, was an act of bad faith clearly remained a primary factor in exhibitor thinking throughout the silent era, even in the realm of the tiny trailer advertisement. The reliability of the exhibitor and the potentially enormous cost of double-checking that a paid advertisement had been screened in an acceptable way remained troubling issues. But the system adopted to increase trust between exhibitors and trailer producers—space brokering—actually served to exacerbate the other problem; space brokers typically provided all trailers to the theater on a single reel, resulting in a "boresome" ten-minute flood of advertising. It was a vicious circle in which a solution to one problem exacerbated the other.

When discussing the value of the venue, once again we see that trailer producers were elevating and improving the rhetorical defense already used for slides while struggling with the exact same issues: Were the patrons worth reaching, and did a fleeting screen advertisement have enough memorability to be of any use? Regarding the patrons, one can see exactly the same arguments, with some claiming that lower-class theaters could be diligently weeded out through selection of venue but most claiming that a cross-class audience was actually beneficial. As mentioned above, Screen Advertising Inc., in an attempt to elevate the ad industry's perception of the class reached by its trailer service (and downplay the fact that the larger urban palaces were still off-limits to advertisers), offered to its customers the ability to select the theaters from its already-selective collection of "high-class theaters," which included "no nickel shows" and therefore reached only "the great middle class—the buying class—the class that is most responsive to good advertising."[152] Screen Advertising Inc., however, was anomalous. Most chose to assert that film, with its broad audience base, reached the "representative families" of a community without any further selective effort on the part of the advertiser or the space broker; among the typical cinema crowds were "a splendidly high percentage of just the people Mr. Dealer wants to be known to and patronized by."[153] The Alexander Film Company went even further; explicitly attacking notions that even a minor amount of the film audience was "waste circulation," Alexander defended film as a means to reach the *lower* classes. Attacking the typical American ad agency's focus on the affluent, Alexander asserted that even though a person may be the type "that spend[s] nearly all they make," that did not mean they wouldn't "spend some with you" if enticed.[154]

In a perhaps unsurprising turn, trailer makers connected their audience value openly to illiteracy. Trailers were, after all, the first form of advertising in which reading, due to action and brand logos, could be rendered virtually unnecessary. Anti-reading rhetoric was presaged in a late 1916 article on trailers in the *Clothier and Furnisher,* in which the following (probably apocryphal) conversation between advertising men was reported:

> "Why does not advertising in the magazines bring the results it used to?" Various answers were suggested . . . until finally one man summed it up in a way which left nothing further to be said. This man's explanation was in effect as follows: "In former times the whole family used to sit around the library table in the Winter time or out on the porch in the Summer and read magazines from cover to cover. . . . Nowadays, in all stations of life, it's 'Let's go to the movies.' I tell you we advertising men have got to go to the movies, too. We've got to advertise where the people are!"[155]

Fears that the birth of the film medium had resulted in a shift in the advertising values of old media were encouraged widely by film advertising producers. In 1921, both the National Builders Bureau ("Break Away from Old-Time Methods") and Francis T. Kimball ("the majority . . . never read much of anything at all") voiced variants of the death knell of reading as a reason to transition at least a percentage of one's advertising budget to trailer advertising.[156] As late as 1927, the Alexander Film Company was still asserting that print was inferior to film, as the former required "the effort of reading"—described as an unreasonable requirement because "the mind is naturally lazy."[157] As such, the cinema as an advertising venue was not simply a means to access previously unreachable class and ethnic groups; through adoption of the trailer form, an advertiser could escape even the limitations of intellect. A trailer could address, quite literally, everyone at once: male and female, rich and poor, young and old, educated and illiterate.

Where it all fell down was, again, in arguments about the fleeting nature of a screen advertisement. In a simple inversion of G. R. Lowe's assertion about the value of slides for druggists, an extremely early (July 1915) tirade against cartoon trailers by a Chippewa Falls newspaperman criticized trailers as a "little frill" that would generally be seen at "night when your business is closed."[158] It is clear that, for this particular ad man, the problem of making an advertisement "sticky" in a fleeting medium remained an overwhelming (and possibly unanswerable) concern. Again, the permanence of print media and the possibility that print ads would be re-referenced and even carried about while shopping were significant points of contention for screen advertising. As print-centric agencies continued to dominate the industry, advertisers undoubtedly had (and were encouraged to have) doubts about the fleeting impression of an ephemeral, experiential medium.[159] Such claims—self-serving though they may have been, for the agencies—were likely repeated often in verbal exchanges and may have been a major factor in advertiser reluctance to use the form.

In short, trailer rhetoric is almost wholly predictable. Trailer advocates effectively reused the best arguments, polished and tightened after a few years of open debate over the cinema as an advertising venue, of slide proponents. Meanwhile, they cleverly adopted anti-cinema arguments only to defuse them as a problem solely for slides. The passive audience did not naturally exist, but trailers could produce it. Film was admittedly expensive but was cheaper per prospect than any other form. The cinema contained a large number of poor spectators, but cumulatively they were a lucrative market. As such, the trailer proponent's take on screen advertising seemed to agree with everything an advertiser had ever heard—both positive and negative—while still producing a sense that the new form had dealt with the most pressing issues.

It is in this reclamation of oppositional rhetoric as a positive that we see both the greatest difference between slide and trailer rhetoric and perhaps its greatest failing. At least one company—the Alexander Film Company—recommended, in its training manual for salesmen, a delicate response to criticism in which the salesman was never to disagree with a critique of the screen as a site. Even if the critique was aimed at trailers themselves, the salesman was not to disagree; rather, he was instructed to concur and then overwhelm the critique with tangentially related positive claims. For example, if the prospect says that onscreen ads make people angry, the salesman should respond, "That is good evidence . . . that they see the ad, otherwise it would not make them mad."[160] While this massaging of the advertiser's ego was likely a very successful approach to sales, it encouraged erroneous preconceptions about film advertising in the name of boosting Alexander's bottom line. In this particular exchange, the salesman was to avoid the very persuasive rhetoric about the powers of both animation and comedy and admit that onscreen advertising angered patrons. (No advice was offered for the obvious follow-up question: What keeps an angry audience from forming ill will rather than good will toward the product?) In the same training manual, Alexander also encouraged salesmen to "stay as far away from advertising agencies as possible."[161] While there are numerous likely reasons for this encouragement, particularly Alexander's avoidance of pricing standards and preference for haggling over every contract, in the short run it closed the door to perhaps the greatest avenue for growth. Agencies were the most powerful pro-advertising community in the country; winning their favor, though it would have been difficult, would have been a net asset even if it took a bite out of the profit from each commission.

Alexander, then, not only held back from defending trailers, it even implicitly attacked its own medium in the name of ascending to the top of the industry. The critiques of the form in public discourse were therefore likely exacerbated by the sales behavior of trailer makers themselves. As such, the greatest strength of trailer rhetoric was also its greatest weakness. The "honesty" of admitting to criticisms did not necessarily defuse them; the criticisms

Figure 2.6. This humorous chart of increasing cash flow shows Alexander's explosive 1,000 percent growth over its first five years. Alexander would remain the preeminent producer of cinema-advertising trailers through the 1950s. Box 11, Alexander Industries Records, MSS0056, Special Collections, Pikes Peak Library District, 108.

were allowed to remain in the public consciousness. It is not surprising that this kept discussion optimistic but growth slow.

CASE STUDY: AIMING FOR "CLASS" AT THE ALEXANDER FILM COMPANY

Unlike the slide industry, which found itself in a struggle for legitimacy from which it never truly recovered, the trailer industry descended almost immediately into a class war. Many theaters across the country were amenable to advertising trailers, which would provide revenue, entertain, and fill empty space simultaneously. But just as many transferred their developed antipathy to slides to the new form. For trailer makers, the battle was not about modernization in the face of mounting losses, but professionalization in order to defuse hierarchical thinking and class-based hostility. As such, a case study on the Alexander Film Company—a flagship trailer producer that professionalized both itself and its industry before becoming a major player in early television commercial production—reveals useful specifics about how a trailer producer could navigate the troubles of its own industry.

Opened for business in January 1919 by brothers J. Don and Don M. Alexander in Spokane, Washington, the Alexander Film Company, which moved to Colorado for a "more geographically central location" in 1923, represents the culmination of the cinematic trailer advertisement.[162] Its growth between 1919 and 1923, likely at the expense of numerous other small companies nationwide, was meteoric. According to internal figures, business increased roughly 1,000 percent over these first five years.[163] By 1923, the company was already circulating trailers regularly in forty-two states and had approximately 150 employees.[164] By the end of the 1920s, it was circulating trailers to 2,400 theaters and was receiving over 60 percent of the trailer business in the United States.[165] By the middle of the twentieth century, Alexander's circulation had swelled to include 16,000 theaters.[166]

Although Alexander's dominance is in and of itself deserving of study, for the purposes of this book its key trait is its role as a leader in the professionalization of the trailer business. Alexander took a leading role in the development of national standards in the trailer community—the very role the AFPA had hoped to serve in 1916. By the end of the 1920s, the national reach of agency-created radio advertising had thrown into sharp relief the major problem with cinema trailer circulation: there was no simple way to show a single trailer in all available theaters. Such a screening plan would have required days of contractual negotiations with a multitude of trailer companies. Alexander helped to restructure the trailer-producing community to meet the demands of national advertisers. In negotiating a contract for national advertising with Chevrolet in 1929, Alexander was instrumental in creating the National Film Advertising Bureau, allowing simultaneous access to the space-brokering contracts of multiple companies. The bureau made it easy for national advertisers to place advertising, with one purchase, in over 5,000 theaters across the country—a uniformity of distribution that had been lacking in cinema advertising since the beginning. As Alexander was by far the dominant partner (controlling over half the available theaters), this effectively opened up even non-Alexander theaters to Alexander service.[167] By 1938, ad industry powerhouse the J. Walter Thompson Company singled out Alexander's "library service" of stock trailers as the paragon of the form.[168] The work of the Alexander Film Company thus represents the perfection of the stock animated trailer and the height of exhibition penetration prior to the development of Screenvision and NCM in the latter decades of the twentieth century.

In many ways, Alexander looked like any other trailer producer in its formative years. The company's theory of cinema spectatorship invoked the common "captive audience" and "receptive mood" concepts and described the effects of film advertising as "a photographic process registered permanently in the brain cells," likening advertising to the chiseling of cavemen "carv[ing] creases in the memories of . . . prospects with pictures."[169] The form of Alexander trailers was also in line with previous standards, running roughly one minute and stressing humor, with the final 25 percent of the running time devoted to the dealer name, which maintained interest through motion and font choice.[170] Alexander, then, is indicative of the standards that had developed in the field before the company was born.

What stands out about Alexander is the ways in which the company streamlined its product and business model in order to push those standards even further. Alexander's strengths were twofold. First, it provided extremely polished trailers, focusing more on subtle pleasurable effects than spectacle. Second, as a business, the company operated almost everywhere in the country simultaneously using complex information systems, modern transportation, and adaptable contracts to please both locally and nationally focused advertisers.

At the risk of implying that business success is a meritocracy, any discussion of Alexander's developing success must begin with the polish the company brought to its trailer work. General high-quality production elements are apparent, including filming in negative (in order to retain "half tones and fine details") and repairing or retiring prints before damage became visible in projection.[171] Compared to, for example, the Scenic Film Company (which attempted to minimize irritation by moving heat distortion artifacts to the beginning of the film, rather than eliminating them), Alexander's choices indicate perfectionism and concern with a high-class image, both for its clients and itself. More important, however, was the company's desire to stress leisure and pleasure even in the high-pressure style of direct advertising. Focusing on viewer pleasure as much as copy punch, Alexander developed a more leisurely pace for the merchant's business card at the end of the trailer, a highly restricted notion of word use, fade transitions for consecutive advertisements, and a mood-based theory of color usage. Each idea was clearly laid out as business policy in the company's November 1921 handbook for its traveling salesmen.

Their sense of written content was perhaps the most obvious difference between Alexander ads and trailers from another company. While the company followed the standard industry maxim of three-quarters of a foot per word as a reading pace, Alexander mandated fifteen feet for a ten-word dealer strip, with an extra foot per word thereafter. As the bulk of trailer producers allowed only ten feet for the dealer strip, Alexander was allowing for significantly more leisurely reading even at maximum word counts.[172] The company went further, however. By early 1925, Don M. Alexander penned an article for the company's house organ, the *Alexander Cooperator,* in which he asserted that four words should be the target, as short copy was "dignified" and brevity was not only "the soul of wit . . . [but] the soul of advertising." Offering three examples ("Chesterfield Cigarettes—They Satisfy"; "Ivory Soap—It Floats"; and Alexander's own "J. B. Gilmore—The Jeweler"), Don M. asserted in the strongest possible terms that limited copy was the best copy in the medium of trailer advertising.[173] Stress-free reading at a leisurely pace was one of the primary selling points of trailer advertising conceived by the Alexander Film Company.

As the literal trailer had, prior to 1919, given way to a reel of consecutively screened trailer-length advertisements, Alexander also took pains (and running time) to keep transitions from jarring the spectator during the projection of the advertising reel. As its contracted theaters would run "from 5 to 10" trailers in a row, Alexander made sure that the exhortations had room to breathe. The company not only used fade-ins and fade-outs to comfortably ease the spectators into and out of an advertisement, it added "a couple of seconds" of solid black footage in between, extending any given reel by ten to twenty seconds rather than fostering irritation through abrasive jumps from trailer to trailer.

Alexander's use of color overtly combined this sense of viewer comfort with theories of impressionistic copy. Declaring that green was a good color for a picnic "not only to show that the grass is green but to utilize the restful effect of green as a color," the company was deeply concerned with the control of the spectator's mood. Simple color-wheel concepts, like red for excitement and blue for cold, were foundational to Alexander productions. In addition, however, the company would use color tinting to polish and perfect the display of products. In one telling example, sepia toning was proposed for bread advertising, as it would give the crust a pleasing and realistic brown color while leaving the loaf "a little more white and pure than any loaf of bread could ever be."[174] As such, Alexander's conception of not irritating the spectator with an avalanche of words or a jarring transition and its use of color for both pleasure and product gloss were all designed to create a subtle and overwhelming minute of advertising—an advertising environment in which every element of the trailer registered the dignity, comfort, and perfection of the product for sale, regardless of whether the copy was humorous or serious.[175]

The willingness of the Alexander Film Company to spare no expense to get the mood correct was apparent in its inauguration of weekly screen tests for new work. Before any trailer would be shipped out for theatrical usage, it needed to receive a positive verdict from the "super-critical audience" of Alexander employees, who would meet in the company screening room every Wednesday at the end of the working day. If a positive response could not be attained through editing out or replacing elements of the footage, an entire film would be "throw[n] . . . in the junk pile."[176] Although the notion of a preview screening was not new in the film industry by this time—the Motion Picture Patents Company and the Mutual Film Corporation had experimented with it as early as 1909 and 1914, respectively—the existence of the practice at Alexander is another mark of the care it took in sending out only work of which it was proud.[177]

The consistently high quality of production was designed to appeal to any potential client, no matter how large their advertising appropriation. For Alexander, the goal was always to produce the highest-quality trailers on the market. This allowed the company to produce a form that was priced for local merchants and yet appealed to national advertisers. Contracting with theater chains and national brands as often as possible, requiring six-month or one-year contracts in any case, maintaining detailed records for trailer circulation, and even pioneering the use of private aircraft for its sales force, Alexander created a business model that was amenable to both the largest and the smallest possible contracts, allowing for both windfall profits and the steady accumulation of small sales.

In contracting with theaters, the company allowed for the exhibitor's own sense of worth to dictate the value of the space. Although its generic sales pitch was to suggest that theaters "may average $100.00 or more per month" from screen advertising, significantly larger contracts were signed. Two theaters in Billings, Montana (the Regent and the Strand), were charging twenty dollars per month per advertiser in 1920 and were offering to carry between seven and ten ads at any one time.[178] A full contract at either theater could have resulted in twice the average profit. In 1921, large West Coast theaters were receiving "as much as $150 per month from each advertiser or about $20,000 per year for a full screen."[179] This represents a rate approximately fifteen times greater than the standard offer of one hundred dollars per month. While these theaters were certainly outliers—especially the West Coast contract—they are indicative of the fact that Alexander, as a space broker, was willing and able to pay fantastically high rates for desirable theaters. The goal was always to increase the available space, regardless of price variation. California's circuit of T&D Theatres, various state exhibitor associations, and even the Fox theaters across the Midwest all signed contracts for Alexander service at one point.[180] For the most part, the theaters needed to do no more than screen and return the reels and cash checks; Alexander would solicit all business, negotiate all contracts, and send the preconstructed reels each week. Aside from the potential continuation of audience disapproval, it is obvious why exhibitors would have appreciated the Alexander model; it was effectively an agreement to listen to a small number of patron complaints in exchange for $1,000 or more per year.

Contracts with advertisers were equally open to negotiation. In exchange for the guarantee of multiple months of usage, Alexander gave its salesmen the right to haggle over the cost of service.

The sales manual only listed "Minimum Prices of Playlet Service" under which there would be no profit for the company; anything above the minimum was up to the skill of the salesman.[181] For example, the minimum cost for a year of biweekly service was ten dollars per week with twenty dollars for the dealer strip.[182] However, an archived contract from 1923 indicates that the salesman, while contracting service at the minimum rate of ten dollars per month, talked the advertiser into paying fifty dollars for the dealer strip.[183] The target for salesmen was, therefore, not a dollar amount, but the signing of one contract per day at whatever rate they could achieve.[184] In their six- or twelve-month contracts, merchants would select their preferred advertisements by looking through a catalog and choosing the numbered ads that appealed to them. Alexander data tracking would double-check that none of these trailers had screened in that particular town before, as the company had a standing rule that "the same animation [would] not appear twice in the same town."[185] The advertiser would also select whether they wanted a weekly or biweekly change, so that any given advertisement would not get stale. In all other ways, Alexander operated like any trailer advertising company, offering exclusivity (no ads for competing products in the same program) and regular screening checkups.

Thus able to suck up as many dollars as local merchants were willing to pay to get on their local screens, Alexander provided itself with a business model that could turn a profit on an aggregate of extremely small contracts. Large contracts, in contrast, would provide occasional massive boosts to the cash flow. In 1920, for example, Alexander signed a contract to produce a custom series of thirteen films (equivalent to six months of biweekly service) for the National Builder's Bureau. Alexander contracted for one hundred prints—which the National Builders Bureau was responsible for circulating to dealers—at a price of between three and four thousand dollars. By January of 1921, eighty-nine dealers had signed on, plausibly guaranteeing Alexander additional profit from the creation of dealer strips to match the hundred prints for each trailer advertisement.[186] While such national campaigns were undoubtedly a minority of Alexander's product, they were actively sought.

The result of the business model was a bewilderingly large output. While data does not exist for the years before 1924 and an average likely skews the number upward in early years, between 1924 and 1931, Alexander produced 8,771 different trailer advertisements—an average of just over 90 per month.[187] That is not the number of rentals; it represents only the number of newly produced playlets that could then start generating a profit through years of national circulation. As such, Alexander's business model was clearly resulting in massive cash flow. Substantial quantities of trailers were produced regularly over the course of a dozen years, and the company would remain in business deep into the television era.

Perhaps the most important element of Alexander's business model—certainly the most intriguing—is the fact that in 1925, the company began manufacturing and selling airplanes to its salesmen. As "bad roads and poor train schedules used up lots of time" in nonproductive travel, in the early twentieth century, Alexander gambled that its best salesmen would leap at the chance to cheaply purchase an airplane to simultaneously expand their zone of influence while reducing the cost of travel to established areas.[188] Selling what it named the Eaglerock, a two-seat plane, for $2,475 to salesmen (who were making roughly $10,000 per year in commissions) provided Alexander with a second revenue stream and allowed the company to profit further from the greater reach of its best men.[189] Thirty salesmen had ordered planes before a single aircraft left the assembly line.[190] With the Eaglerock, Alexander's already broad national reach expanded even further.

In this assembly of a national distribution and sales system for a fundamentally local advertising medium, the Alexander Film Company became, and remained, the largest company in

Figure 2.7. The Englewood, Colorado, offices of the Alexander Film Company as depicted on company letterhead. This building was the home of Alexander from 1923 until 1928, when it was destroyed by fire. Author's personal collection.

the field. Using economies of scale to simultaneously increase quality and minimize costs, Alexander perfected the stock trailer, opened itself up to income from custom trailers, and maintained strong working relationships with all involved parties, from small-town toy stores to major goods manufacturers, from mom-and-pop theaters in small Midwestern towns to multistate chains in the densely populated coasts. The Alexander Film Company nationalized a trailer industry threatened with stagnation and dominated output for the next several decades.

LYING IN WAIT

The introduction and standardization of trailer advertising over the latter half of the 1910s are emblematic of a rapidly codifying theory of advertising in moving media. The form was a specifically cinematic one in its aesthetics and tone, as pleasurable and humorous content was used to create direct advertising without overtly rational argumentation. Tied to the national shift away from "reason why" advertising and toward modern electric hyperactivity, trailer ads were emotional more often than cerebral, mobile rather than stable, and so pleasing as to be a form of entertainment in themselves. As such, the sense that advertising must not only occur onscreen, but be made as a motion picture, was accepted by the bulk of the cinema-aware public, as the notion of the passive audience (or pacified audience, as animation proponents would have it) led most advertisers to obsess over onscreen placement of advertising. A captive audience receiving pleasurable commercial stimulation via moving pictures thus seemed like the perfection of the form originally proposed with slides. As an industry grew around this form of production, it developed cost-effective methods for producing spectacularly brief and kinetic images of dancing products and jumbling copy, producing the model for broadcasting and the online video spot of the future.

However, the nearly simultaneous increase in film length, the corresponding decrease in gaps in the program, and a continuing cultural discomfort with integrating advertising into a temporal medium forced this impressive form into a buffer zone at the intermission between turns of the program. As such, the commercial spot—effectively a form of participating sponsorship funding local exhibitors rather than national broadcasters—was born and streamlined predominantly in motion-picture theaters of the latter half of the 1910s. In their eventual onscreen but marginal position, cinema playlets helped to define the classical motion-picture experience, including the establishment of a time-based entry model, and reinforced the idea that commercialism was an outsider to the cinema, to be inserted only in clearly labeled and unobtrusive areas. As radio became the new playground, the trailer was effectively abandoned in this margin for decades.

With early broadcasting's focus on big network programs and broadcast historians' traditional and justifiable focus on the same, the long but marginal history of the pre-commercial spot has remained on the sidelines.[191] Unlike nationally broadcast radio and television, cinema theaters were local entities. Even chain theaters were managed to meet local tastes, reediting newsreels to boost local value and constructing musical accompaniment to suit the house musicians' skill set and popular styles. Trailer advertising was likewise seen as local advertising, with national branding typically subservient to the names and addresses of local dealers. By the time the minute movie attained a place of prominence in national brand advertising in 1950s television, its origin as a locally oriented and "low-class" concept in the cinema went largely unremarked.

NOTES

1. Fred Fidler, "A Discussion of the Current Status and Future Possibilities of Commercial Motion Pictures," January 8, 1938, Box 7, Folder "1937 Nov. 9–1938 Oct. 25," JWT, Staff Meeting Minutes, 2.

2. Mr. Kimball, "Industrial Film Facts as of March 12, 1929," Box 1, Folder 7 "1929 Jan 4–April 17," JWT, Staff Meeting Minutes, 10. J. Walter Thompson kept cinema at a distance despite heavy engagement with the Creel Committee's wartime advertising (which was itself heavily engaged with cinema) and having famously manipulated Hollywood into giving large-scale testimonial advertising for Lux Soap. For agencies, the bugbear had always been national circulation. Even when the desired circulation could be acquired, it was impossible to pre-estimate attendance figures for any given advertising film, as there were too many variables. Even post-release attendance figures could be very unreliable. The increasingly data-conscious advertising industry was thus very wary of the seemingly unsettled nature of cinema advertising. See Kimball, "Industrial Film Facts," 5, 9; "Advertising in Food Control Campaign," *PI*, July 12, 1917, 66; and Jane Gaines, "From Elephants to Lux Soap: The Programming and 'Flow' of Early Motion Picture Exploitation," *Velvet Light Trap* 25 (Spring 1990): 29–43.

3. Kimball, "Industrial Film Facts," 3. Fred Fidler and Wallace Boren, "Commercial Movies," February 1, 1938, Box 7, Folder "1937 Nov. 9–1938 Oct. 25," JWT, Staff Meeting Minutes, 3, 5.

4. Cynthia B. Meyers, "From Sponsorship to Spots," in *Media Industries: History, Theory, and Method*, ed. Jennifer Holt and Alisa Perren (Malden, MA: Wiley-Blackwell, 2009), 73. See also Michele Hilmes, "Conclusion: Terms of Preferment," *Radio Voices: American Broadcasting, 1922–1952* (Minneapolis: University of Minnesota Press, 1997), 271–290; and Alexander Russo, *Points on the Dial: Golden Age Radio Beyond the Networks* (Durham, NC: Duke University Press, 2010).

5. Jonas Howard, "Sodas or Shaves," *Photoplay*, December 1919, 112. See also "Little Schoolmaster's Classroom," *PI*, September 2, 1915, 94; "Publicity for Plumbers," *Domestic Engineering*, December 11, 1915, 337; "The Newest Kind of Store Publicity," *Clothier and Furnisher*, September 1916, 98; and "How to Make a 'Movie' for Straw Hat Day," *American Hatter*, April 1917, 69. The trailer was occasionally described as an alternative to industrial films, which by this point had proven far easier to make than to screen. The bulk were left little used or isolated in nontheatrical screenings. As such, the trailer, to a small degree, built its business model on frustrations caused by indirect advertising experiments.

6. On the strength of his previous work in commercial illustration for local art studio Pesman-Rubin and his fledgling independent venture Iwerks-Disney, Walt was hired to create advertising slides for use in motion-picture theaters. Ubbe Iwerks joined Kansas City Slide months later. Only five months after Disney was hired (May of 1920), he claimed, in a letter to a friend, to "draw cartoons for . . . advertiser films." Though his hiring was for slide work, his transition to animation was rapid. Disney later specifically claimed to have been trained in stop-motion filming by Kansas City Slide Company employee George E. "Jimmy" Lowerre. See Timothy S. Susanin, *Walt Before Mickey: Disney's Early Years, 1919–1928* (Jackson: University Press of Mississippi, 2011), 10, 12, 16; and Neal Gabler, *Walt Disney: The Triumph of the American Imagination* (New York: Vintage Books, 2006), 49.

7. "Used-Car Sales Promotion Work," *Automobile Topics*, October 8, 1921, 639; Fidler, "A Discussion of the Current Status," 5–6; H. H. Dewey, "Movies Are Moving Goods Over the Counter," *Confectioners Gazette*, March 10, 1920, 24–25; and Display Ad, *A&S*, January 1917, 46.

8. Kimball, "Industrial Film Facts," 3. See also Francis T. Kimball's earlier assertion that a trailer "is hitched on to the last and slightly shorter reel of one of the features." Kimball, "The Film Trailer and What It Will Do," *MPA*, February 1921, 11.

9. Carl B. Rowntree, "A Business Producing Idea That Compels Attention," *Refrigeration*, April 1916, 34; and Ernest A. Dench, "Motion Picture Photography," *The Camera*, September 1916, 520.

10. Rowntree, "A Business Producing Idea," 34. See also Watterson R. Rothacker, "Advertising with Moving Pictures," *Library of Advertising*, ed. A. P. Johnson (Chicago: Cree Publishing, 1911), 246.

11. W. A. Harris, "Movie Film Becoming Big Car Sales Feature," *Motor World*, January 17, 1917, 65. The quantity of automobile-related material in the Alexander Film Company scrapbook indicates that this predominance

continued at least into the 1920s. For examples, see "Alexander Film Company—Scrapbook, 1919–1923," Box 11, AIR, 36, 41.

12. Dench, "Motion Picture Photography," 520. In 1921, the Alexander Film Company's minimum price per film was $4.25 ($17 per month for weekly change), and its maximum was $5.50 ($11 per month for biweekly change). "Sales Manual," Box 5, AIR, 80–81.

13. "One-Minute 'Ad' Playlets," *Optical Journal and Review of Optometry*, March 25, 1920, 953.

14. Reginald V. Stambaugh, Patent 1,226,135.

15. Yvonne Zimmerman, "Advertising and Film: A Topological Approach," in *Films That Sell: Moving Pictures and Advertising*, ed. Bo Florin, Nico de Klerk, and Patrick Vonderau (London: British Film Institute, 2016), 29.

16. Frank Farrington, "Practical Talks With the Shop Butcher," *National Provisioner*, December 27, 1913, 40; and Frank Farrington, "Advertising in Moving-Picture Shows," *Bulletin of Pharmacy*, June 1913, 249.

17. Juliann Sivulka, *Soap, Sex, and Cigarettes: A Cultural History of American Advertising* (Boston: Wadsworth Cengage Learning, 1998), 55.

18. Lynne Kirby, "Gender and Advertising in American Silent Film: From Early Cinema to the Crowd," *Discourse* 13, no. 2 (Spring/Summer 1991): 3–20.

19. Howard, "Sodas or Shaves," 112.

20. "Little Schoolmaster's Classroom," *PI* 7, March 1918, 142.

21. For other clear examples, see H. A. Shaw's monthly column, "A Few of Last Month's Productions," in the house organ, the *Alexander Cooperator*, Box 8, Folder 1, AIR. Other plot descriptions are scattered throughout the trade press of the time. See "Publicity for Plumbers," *Domestic Engineering*, December 11, 1915, 337–338; "Kansas City Trade," *Black Diamond*, February 3, 1917, 101; Kimball, "The Film Trailer," 11; and "Used-Car Sales Promotion Work," 639.

22. Britt Craig, "What Makes the Animated Movie Ads Move?: How the 'Go-Fans' Go on a Picture Screen," *Atlanta Constitution*, April 2, 1916, D3.

23. In later reminiscence, Disney claims to have personally experimented with hand-drawn animation but failed to convince Slide Company president A. V. Cauger to adopt it. Susanin, *Walt Before Mickey*, 11, 15–16.

24. Display Ad, *Simmons' Spice Mill*, January 1917, 78.

25. Howard, "Sodas or Shaves," 112.

26. Display Ad, *Refrigeration*, January 1916, 54. Craig, "What Makes the Animated Movie Ads Move?," D3. Vast stretches of white, in black figure animation, could be avoided in other ways; see, for example, the extant

1921 short *The First Circus*, which uses a combination of scenery and irises to reduce unnecessary white space.

27. Display Ad, *MPW*, March 25, 1916, 2078.

28. Kimball, "The Film Trailer," 11.

29. Stambaugh, Patent 1,226,135.

30. Display Ad, *Simmons' Spice Mill*, January 1917, 78. The extant wartime propaganda trailer from B-D-F Films, known as *W.S.S. Thriftettes* (1918), was also white-figure.

31. Jay Newell, Charles T. Salmon, and Susan Chang, "The Hidden History of Product Placement," *Journal of Broadcasting and Electronic Media* 50, no. 4 (December 2006): 575–594.

32. Charles Musser is the best source of information on this movement, specifically indicating that there was a site at Herald Square and giving concrete dates for certain productions. Kerry Segrave provides the list of advertisers but otherwise offers less detailed information. Musser, "American Vitagraph, 1897–1901," *Cinema Journal* 22, no. 3 (Spring 1983): 4–46; Musser, *The Emergence of Cinema: The American Screen to 1907* (New York: Charles Scribner's Sons, 1990), 169, 253; and Segrave, *Product Placement in Hollywood Films: A History* (Jefferson, NC: McFarland, 2004), 5.

33. Musser, *The Emergence of Cinema*, 359–369. Kathryn H. Fuller additionally points to Vitagraph, Selig, Essanay, and Edison as companies that experimented with advertising and industrial films. Fuller, *At the Picture Show: Small Town Audiences and the Creation of Movie Fan Culture* (Washington, DC: Smithsonian Institution Press, 1996), 79–81. See also Kirby, "Gender and Advertising in American Silent Film," 3; and Musser, "Early Advertising and Promotional Films, 1893–1900: Edison Motion Pictures as a Case Study," in *Films That Sell*, Florin et al., 83–90.

34. Julius Legett, the man who claimed to have negotiated the contracts, was seeking $26,000 in commissions, implying that there were several very large contracts with Vitagraph prior to the Patents Company banning the practice. Typical commissions for advertising agencies at this time were roughly 15 percent. If Legett was seeking the same percentage, Vitagraph's contracts amounted to $173,000. The Goat Man, "On the Outside Looking In," *Motography*, June 1912, 252.

35. James H. Collins, "Advertising via the Moving Picture," *PI*, February 23, 1910, 24. For more on the rise of full-reel corporate advertising films, see Gregory A. Waller, "International Harvester, *Business Screen*, and the History of Advertising Film," in *Films That Sell*, Florin et al., 40–53.

36. Watterson R. Rothacker, "Motion Pictures that Really Advertise," *Nickelodeon*, February 11, 1911, 161; and "System in Motion Picture Advertising," *Motography*, May 1911, 71. See also, among countless others, Collins, "Advertising via the Moving Picture," 24; and "The Newest Kind of Store Publicity," *Clothier and Furnisher*, September 1916, 99.

37. Collins, "Advertising via the Moving Picture," 28.

38. See Collins, "Advertising via the Moving Picture," 422–423; H. F. Hoffman, "From the Cradle to the Grave," *MPW*, May 28, 1910, 877; and Horatio F. Stoll, "Value of the Moving Pictures for Advertising," *MPW*, March 11, 1911, 519.

39. By 1912, even Watterson Rothacker was calling theatrical release a noisy but ineffective "blunderbuss" tactic and had turned his attention to films for traveling salesmen. Watterson Rothacker, "Pictures as an Advertising Force," *Motography*, February 1912, 71. For further references to Rothacker's work, see Mack Sennett, *King of Comedy* (Lincoln, NE: iUniverse, 2000), 122; Fuller, *At the Picture Show*, 83–84; and Nanna Verhoef, *The West in Early Cinema: After the Beginning* (Amsterdam: Amsterdam University Press, 2006), 313–314.

40. Quentin J. Schultze, "Manufacturers' Views of National Consumer Advertising, 1910–1915," *Journalism Quarterly* 60, no. 1 (1983): 10–15.

41. Display Ad, *MPW*, March 7, 1914, 1330.

42. "Advertising Tailpieces," *Motography*, October 10, 1914, 498.

43. Rowntree, "A Business Producing Idea," 34.

44. Anti-slide rhetoric remained a useful persuasive angle for trailer producers at least as late as 1921. The Alexander Film Company made a habit of slide derision, made evident in its 1921 comparison in which a slide was described as a valueless window shopper and a trailer was a man throwing a brick through the glass. Strand Theater, Billings, MT, to "All Advertisers and Prospective Advertisers on the Strand Screen," January 1, 1920, "Alexander Film Company—Scrapbook, 1919–1923," Box 11, AIR, 23; and "Sales Manual," Box 5, AIR, 32, 58, 61, 62, 81.

45. It is possible that it was likewise invented in Chicago and New York around this time. Donald Crafton mentions, without citation, that Watterson Rothacker's Industrial Moving Picture Company was making animated advertisements prior to 1915. As for New York, Giannalberto Bendazzi asserts, again without citation, that Raoul Barré and William C. Nolan were making animated advertisements as early as 1912. Though neither is directly described as a "trailer," animation would have been used in very short bursts at this early date. Crafton, *Before Mickey: The Animated*

Film, 1898–1928 (Chicago: University of Chicago Press, 1993), 260; and Bendazzi, *Cartoons: One Hundred Years of Cinema Animation* (Bloomington: Indiana University Press, 1994), 18.

46. Display Ad, *MPW,* March 7, 1914, 1330.

47. Craig, "What Makes the Animated Movie Ads Move?," D3.

48. Rowntree, Patent 1,227,075; and Display Ad, *Atlanta Constitution,* August 8, 1915, B5. Quote from Rowntree, "A Business Producing Idea," 34. By June 1915, there was already a waiting list for their services. "Ads That Entertain," *MPW,* June 5, 1915, 1650.

49. "Plans to Check Film Circulation," *PI,* October 29, 1914, 28.

50. Fort Wayne and Northern Indiana Traction Company, "Advertising Tailpieces," *Motography,* October 10, 1914, 498; Triograph Film Manufacturing Company, Display Ad, *Atlanta Constitution,* June 20, 1915, 11; Effankay Film Company, Display Ad, *MPW,* July 24, 1915, 745; Raymond Anderson Company, "Comic Advertising Films," *MPW,* July 31, 1915, 850; Real Publicity Company, "Local Film Ad Men Meet," *MPW,* October 23, 1915, 649; Pacific Coast Film Advertising Company, "New Concern Enters Field," *MPW,* November 13, 1915, 1345; and Ray, Classified Ad, *MPW,* November 20, 1915, 1563.

51. "A New Enterprise," *Chicago Defender,* February 14, 1920, 19.

52. Gunby Bros., Display Ad, *MPW,* August 27, 1910, 489; and General Data, "Just a Moment Please," *Motography,* November 29, 1913, 384.

53. "Fireproofing Children," *MPW,* November 21, 1914, 1090.

54. "Roxy" Rothapfel, in particular, would edit together material "from up to four different newsreel services to create his in-house newsreel program." Ross Melnick, *American Showman: Samuel "Roxy" Rothafel and the Birth of the Entertainment Industry* (New York: Columbia University Press, 2012), 17.

55. An even earlier example is the Hunton-Fell-Elliott agency's 1912 offer to aid manufacturers in producing their "own illustrated daily news bulletin carrying your exclusive advertisement projected on the screens of the better and larger Moving Picture Theatres." Display Ad, *PI,* October 17, 1912, 61; and Lee Grieveson, "The Work of Film in the Age of Fordist Mechanization," *Cinema Journal* 51, no. 3 (Spring 2012): 25–51.

56. A. Rowden King, "The Commercial 'Movies': How the Manufacturer is Using the Moving Pictures to Help Business," *A&S,* January 1913, 52.

57. Ibid., 54.

58. Roland Marchand describes the chagrin of some agency men over their growing association, over the 1920s and early 1930s, with "frivolous entertainment," which they saw as a debasement of the advertising

industry. See his material on the adoption of comic strips for advertising in the early 1930s. Marchand, *Advertising the American Dream: Making Way for Modernity, 1920–1940* (Berkeley: University of California Press, 1985), 115; Dench, "Motion Picture Photography," 520; and Howard, "Sodas or Shaves," 112.

59. Fort Wayne, "Advertising Tailpieces," *Motography,* October 10, 1914, 498; Raymond Anderson, "Comic Advertising Films," *MPW,* July 31, 1915, 850; and Portland, "McDowell Puts Over Another," *Motography,* April 17, 1915, 614.

60. Crafton, *Before Mickey,* 110, 143.

61. Emphasis added. Craig, "What Makes the Animated Movie Ads Move?," D3.

62. Southern Film Service, Display Ad, *MPW,* March 7, 1914, 1330; Effankay Film Company, Display Ad, *MPW,* July 24, 1915, 745; Ray, Classified Ad, *MPW,* November 20, 1915, 1563; Susanin, *Walt Before Mickey,* 11; and Scenic Film Company, Display Ad, *Refrigeration,* January 1916, 54. There is evidence of the same appeal of animated letters in Germany around this time, as an American consul station in Breslau remarked on a Dorndorf Shoes ad that was "a kind of puzzle picture in which the letters . . . were made to appear in irregular order, but each letter, after more or less confusion, finally arranged itself in place." Harry G. Seltzer, "Motion-Picture Advertising in Germany," *A&S,* January 1916, 76.

63. Don M. Alexander, "Advertising Words, Cut Them Out," *Alexander Cooperator,* April 1925, Box 8, Folder 1, AIR, 4.

64. By the 1920s, an example of a jeweler's merchant strip shows that the Alexander Film Company was attempting to surround letters with moving objects, rather than make the letters themselves move. In this particular strip, an undulating string of pearls surrounded the otherwise immobile merchant name. Sample Images from Jeweler Trailer, Box 2, Folder 4, AIR.

65. "Kansas City Trade," *Black Diamond,* February 3, 1917, 101. See also Display Ad, *MPW,* March 7, 1914, 1330; and W. A. Harris, "History, Future, and Possibilities of the Advertising Film Industry," *Simmons' Spice Mill,* March 1917, 357.

66. Display Ad, *MPW,* May 6, 1916, 1033.

67. The only known mention of technological problems impacting duration comes from the Scenic Film Company. The company filmed all of its product in reverse in order to avoid having the brand logo or dealer name marred by heat distortion. Rowntree, Patent 1,227,075.

68. "Comic Advertising Films," *MPW,* July 31, 1915, 850.

69. "Publicity for Plumbers," *Domestic Engineering*, December 11, 1915, 337.

70. Rowntree, "A Business Producing Idea," 34.

71. "The Newest Kind of Store Publicity," *The Clothier and Furnisher*, September 1916, 98.

72. Howard, "Sodas or Shaves," 112; and "Sales Manual," Box 5, AIR, 18. The running time started to recede in mid-century to a new standard of roughly forty seconds. This may have been simply an artifact of the increased projection speed in the sound era. The same sixty-foot strip that ran for one minute on silent projectors would have taken exactly forty seconds to screen at twenty-four frames per second on a sound-era projector. If clients were billed in feet rather than minutes, forty seconds would maintain the status quo. "What Are Alexander Movie Ads?" pamphlet, Box 10, Folder 2, AIR.

73. "Used-Car Sales Promotion Work," 639.

74. Ernest Dench mentions one dollar as a stock slide price in 1916. By 1920, even custom slides could be had for this price. Dench, "Motion Picture Photography," 520; and "Use Slides to Advertise," *Furniture Worker*, May 1920, 178.

75. Rowntree, "A Business Producing Idea," 34.

76. David Bordwell, Janet Staiger, and Kristin Thompson, *The Classical Hollywood Cinema: Film Style & Mode of Production to 1960* (New York: Columbia University Press, 1985), 113.

77. In January 1917, even stock films were described by the Federal Development Company's W. A. Harris as having been sold "outright" to dealers, "becom[ing] his property" for the cost of seven dollars. By 1921, Kimball had no sense of purchased trailers and claimed that the entire industry worked on a rental model. Harris, "Movie Film Becoming Big Car Sales Feature," 65; and Kimball, "The Film Trailer," 11.

78. "Brevities," *MPW*, March 4, 1916, 1480.

79. Janet Staiger, "Announcing Wares, Winning Patrons, Voicing Ideals: Thinking About the History and Theory of Film Advertising," *Cinema Journal* 29, no. 3 (Spring 1990): 3–31. Coming-attractions announcements began as an independent business before becoming an in-house product of major studios. The Indiana Curtain Advertising Company pioneered coming-attractions trailers with simple ten-foot footage of stars and titles, made by commission for theaters, in 1915, the same year that serials began to use edited footage as teasers for the next episode. "Chicago Film Brevities," *MPW*, August 28, 1915, 1464; and Margaret I. MacDonald, "'Exploits of Elaine,' Episode 14," *MPW*, April 10, 1915, 246.

80. "Famous Players Issue Advance Film," *MPW*, September 30, 1916, 2094.

81. *Motography* called this a new idea, making it very likely that Triangle was the first entertainment producer to regularly circulate its own coming-attractions trailers. "New Advertising Idea," *Motography*, October 28, 1916, 970.

82. "Selznick Has Clever Trailer," *MPW*, July 28, 1917, 663.

83. At least one group, the association of exhibitors in St. Louis, even legitimized the inclusion of advertising trailers without shifting to self-advertising or political material. At the same meeting at which they decided to accept the screening of a slide as sufficient to cover member dues (see chap. 1), they allowed a trailer film to serve the same purpose. "St. Louis Theater Men Meet," *Motography*, January 27, 1917, 162.

84. "Universal Boosting 'Buy a Bale,'" *MPW*, October 31, 1914, 619. I presented a fuller study of the Buy-a-Bale movement at the 2013 SCMS conference under the title: "Engines and Anchors: The National and the Local in Atlanta's *Buy a Bale of Cotton*, 1914."

85. Navy recruitment trailer, "Associated Advertisers 'Doing Their Bit,'" *MPW*, April 7, 1917, 73. Food commission trailer against hoarding, "Hoover Trailers On Paralta Plays," *MPW*, February 16, 1918, 979.

86. Joseph A. McGuire, "Buffalo Screens to Boost Liberty Bonds," *MPW*, June 9, 1917, 1645.

87. Creel, "Films to Boom Liberty Bond Buying," *MPW*, June 16, 1917, 1761; and Kalem (with image), "Industry to Back Liberty Loan," *MPW*, June 9, 1917, 1617. See also "Kalem Aids Liberty Loan," *Motography*, October 27, 1917, 863. Second Kalem trailer (with image), "Kalem Uses Animated Liberty Trailer," *MPW*, October 20, 1917, 483; and Selig (with image), "Selig Has Liberty Bond Trailer," *MPW*, June 16, 1917, 1765. Further solidifying the power of animation, the first liberty loan trailer was apparently a cartoon. See "McAdoo Writes Letter to Industry," *MPW*, June 30, 1917, 2108.

88. See Display Ad, *MPW*, May 12, 1917, 1031.

89. Walter K. Hill, "Rambles Round Filmtown: 'Weeklies' Hold the Palm," *MPW*, March 2, 1918, 1243.

90. Recognizable national brands have only appeared twice in my research into trailers: the Camel Film Company illustrated one ad with a strip of film featuring the Firestone name; and Triograph used the Coca-Cola brand as a testimonial from February to May of 1917. Firestone, Display Ad, *MPW*, June 17, 1916, 2109; and Coca-Cola, Display Ad, *PI*, February 1, 1917, 111.

91. Stephen Bottomore, "Rediscovering Early Non-Fiction Film," *Film History* 13, no. 2 (2001): 160–173; Ben Singer, "Feature Films, Variety Programs, and the Crisis of the Small Exhibitor," in *American Cinema's Transitional Era: Audiences, Institutions, Practices*, ed. Charlie Keil and Shelley Stamp (Berkeley: University of California Press, 2004), 85, 95; Eileen Bowser, *The Transformation of Cinema, 1907–1915* (New York: Charles Scribner's Sons, 1990), 167; Richard Koszarski, *An Evening's Entertainment: The Age of the Silent Feature Picture, 1915–1928* (New York: Charles Scribner's Sons, 1990), 48, 53–54, 163; and Michael Quinn, "Distribution, the Transient Audiences, and the Transition to the Feature Film," *Cinema Journal* 40, no. 2 (Winter 2001): 35–56.

92. Howard, "Sodas or Shaves," 112.

93. "Sales Manual," Box 5, AIR, 22, 58.

94. Arthur McClure, "Advertising Stories Told in the Movies," *PIM*, February 1921, 31.

95. See National Advertisers' Motion Picture Weekly Inc., Display Ad, *MPW*, September 5, 1914, 1441.

96. If these reels were full—one thousand total feet—the average ad would have been roughly eighty-three feet long. Despite the uniformity of the reel, the two contracted theaters received wildly different income—$200 per month for the Royal, but only $50 per month for the Benton—though Real Publicity charged advertisers the same price: $30 per month for each theater. "Local Film Ad Men Meet," *MPW*, October 23, 1915, 649.

97. The seventeen local theaters included the Criterion, New Piedmont, Georgian, Victoria, Alpha, Bonita, Strand, Bijou, Alsha, Regent, Bonheur, Park, Bellwood, Fulton, Euclid, and "the two largest negro theaters." The last nine were described as neighborhood theaters. Scenic, Display Ad, *Atlanta Constitution*, May 21, 1916, C8.

98. Classified Ad, *MPW*, March 30, 1918, 1877.

99. Display Ad, *PI*, September 11, 1919, 236.

100. Display Ad, *A&S*, April 10, 1920, 39.

101. A July 30, 1916, article asserted that 126 theaters in Philadelphia and 150 in Boston and surrounding territories had signed contracts and that D. D. Marcus had been appointed as the company's Philadelphia-based representative to "the eastern territory." By August, *Moving Picture World* corroborated Marcus's appointment but did not mention the number of contracts. "The Scenic Film Co. Appoints Eastern Agt.," *The Atlanta Constitution*, July 30, 1916, B6; and "Atlanta Notes," *MPW*, August 19, 1916, 1285.

102. Two-Page Display Ad, *PI*, March 29, 1917, 82–83; and Display Ad, *PI*, April 12, 1917, 111. Screen Advertising was one of the first trailer producers to focus almost exclusively on national product advertising, and it pushed the boundaries of the trailer in other ways. For example, its tendency was to use up its entire 200 feet of contracted space on a single long trailer. See "Louis Geleng Takes Up Advertising Work," *MPW*, May 12, 1917, 934.

103. Alexander, "Feeding Ambition with Gold" pamphlet, Box 5, AIR, 6.

104. Kimball, "Industrial Film Facts," 5, 9.

105. Display Ad (city, state, and region), *PI*, June 15, 1916, 64; Display Ad (class), *PI*, April 26, 1917, 92; and Display Ad (zones), *PI*, April 19, 1917, 104.

106. "Plans to Check Film Circulation," *PI*, October 29, 1914, 28.

107. The first elected officers were President W. A. Harris (Federal Development Company),Vice President A. V. Cauger (Kansas City Slide Company), Secretary Carl B. Rowntree (Scenic Film Company), and Treasurer Fred C. Laflin (Camel Film Company). For information on the seven original members, see "Advertising Film Producers Organize," *PI*, July 13, 1916, 35. For officer affiliations, see Harris, "Movie Film Becoming Big Car Sales Feature," 65.

108. Industrial film powerhouse Watterson Rothacker became increasingly important (often holding AFPA meetings at his Chicago factory), while Camilla Donworth (then with industrial film producer E. I. S.) encouraged a focus on training films due to wartime employee turnover. The presence of the AFPA at the AACW convention of June 1917 was announced by a constant screening not of trailers but of industrial films. For reasons that are not clear, the association disappears from search results after December 1917; neither the original name, nor the proposed new name—Moving Picture Advertising Association of the World—have turned up any further results. A distributors' association, called the Advertising Film Service Association of America and also featuring Cauger and Laflin on its board, arose in 1917 and suffered the same rapid disappearance in the historical record. See "Chicago Film Brevities," *MPW*, September 1, 1917, 1379, and October 6, 1917, 64; "Urges 'Movies' to Train New Salesmen," *Associated Advertising*, July 1917, 44; "Movie Men Show Great Variety of Films," *Associated Advertising* (July 1917): 44; and "Advertising Films Organization," *MPW*, April 14, 1917, 310.

109. Harris, "Movie Film Becoming Big Car Sales Feature," 65.

110. Ibid.; and Harris, "History, Future, and Possibilities," 356–357.

111. Display Ad, *PI*, August 30, 1917, 113; Display Ad, *PI*, April 25, 1918, 162; and "Perfection Short Ad Films," *R&S*, March 1919, 32.

112. "Used-Car Sales Promotion Work," 639.

113. *The J. W. T. Book: A Series of Talks on Advertising*, Box 25, Folder "Addresses and Published Materials by J. W. T. Personnel 1908–1927," JWT, Chicago Office Records, 45–46; and H. H. Dewey, "Movies Are Moving Goods Over the Counter," *Confectioners Gazette*, March 10, 1920, 24.

114. Compare this to Kathy M. Newman's assertion that product advertising on radio could, by implying that competing products were harmful, sow suspicion of their own. See Newman, *Radio Active: Advertising and Consumer Activism, 1935–1947* (Berkeley: University of California Press, 2004), 17–18.

115. Fuller, *At the Picture Show*.

116. S. L. Rothapfel, "First Aid to Theater Men," *Motography*, July 8, 1916, 78.

117. Northwestern University School of Commerce Bureau of Business Research, *Costs, Merchandising Practices, Advertising and Sales in the Retail Distribution of Clothing*, vol. 4 (New York: Prentice-Hall, 1921), 284, 328, 363–369, 377.

118. Kimball, "The Film Trailer," 11.

119. J. Walter Thompson Media Research, "Report on Theatre Advertising, Revised March, 1959," Box 24, Folder "No. 64G," JWT, Information Center Records, T-49. See also Fidler and Boren, "Commercial Movies," 9.

120. As the manual was published in November of 1921 and the company opened for business in 1919, the year was likely 1920. "Sales Manual," Box 5, AIR, 3, 11.

121. The two figures quoted here were written on internal correspondence, as evidence of the strength of these particular salesmen. As such, the prorated calculation was the way Alexander chose to speak to everyone, including themselves. J. F. Jokeman to Mr. Alexander, March 19, 1920, and Walter Morris to Mr. Alexander, January 30, 1921, both in "Alexander Film Company—Scrapbook, 1919–1923," Box 11, AIR, 9, 25.

122. "Feeding Ambition with Gold," 1.

123. Ibid., 3.

124. "Oldest Customer Renews Contract," *Weekly Animator* 6, no. 8 (February 27, 1933), Box 7, AIR, Colorado Springs, 1. As this was reported in 1933, it's possible that the store continued to use the Alexander service for many additional years. Also, as record keeping was hazy in the early years of Alexander's operation, it's possible that this same store had been a client for even longer than the company knew.

125. Harris, "History, Future, and Possibilities," 356; Screen Advertising Inc. Multipage Display Ad, *PI*, March 29, 1917, 82–83; Brite-Lite, Display Ad, *PI*, April 25, 1918, 162; National Builder's Bureau, Display Ad, *Helping*

'Em Build, January 1921, 2, in "Alexander Film Company—Scrapbook, 1919–1923," Box 11, AIR, 59; and "Sales Manual," Box 5, AIR, 32, 62.

126. "The Newest Kind of Store Publicity," *Clothier and Furnisher,* September 1916, 98; Strand Theater, Billings, MT, to "All Advertisers and Prospective Advertisers on the Strand Screen," "Alexander Film Company—Scrapbook, 1919–1923," Box 11, AIR, 23; and "Sales Manual," Box 5, AIR, 81.

127. "Sales Manual," Box 5, AIR, 35, 62.

128. Joseph B. Baker, "Examples of Motion Picture Advertising," *Motography,* June 1911, 133.

129. "Six Advertising 'Talkies' Get Talked About," *PI,* March 26, 1931, 75.

130. Display Ad, *The Atlanta Constitution,* August 27, 1916, E3. Burdette's claim seems to presage the later claim by a European reporter that "the very process . . . [of animation] is extremely interesting and spurs viewers to reflection. . . . The audience . . . cannot help but ask itself how this image was recorded." As quoted in Michael Cowan, "Advertising and Animation: From the Invisible Hand to Attention Management," in *Films That Sell,* Florin et al., 94.

131. Harris, "Movie Film Becoming Big Car Sales Feature," 65.

132. "Opportunity Knocks" pamphlet, Box 10, Folder 2, AIR, 11; and "Sales Manual," Box 5, AIR, 61–62.

133. Kimball, "The Film Trailer," 18.

134. Display Ad, *Refrigeration,* April 1916, 61.

135. Display Ad, *MPW,* May 6, 1916, 1033.

136. "Sales Manual," Box 5, AIR, 32.

137. "Publicity for Plumbers," *Domestic Engineering,* December 11, 1915, 337; and "The Newest Kind of Store Publicity," *Clothier and Furnisher,* September 1916, 99.

138. Howard, "Sodas or Shaves," 112.

139. "Little Schoolmaster's Classroom," *PI* 7, March 1918, 142.

140. Kimball, "The Film Trailer," 11. Note that for Kimball, a sugar pill was a flavored and palatable drug, not a placebo as in current parlance.

141. Ibid., 18.

142. Monache Theatre Co. Inc. to "To Whom It May Concern," February 16, 1923, "Alexander Film Company—Scrapbook, 1919–1923," 33, Box 11, AIR, 33.

143. H. H. Dewey, "Movies Are Moving Goods Over the Counter," *Confectioners Gazette,* March 10, 1920, 24.

144. Manhattan Slide and Film, Display Ad, *PI,* September 6, 1917, 145; and National Builders' Bureau, Display Ad, *Helping 'Em Build,* January 1921, 2, in "Alexander Film Company—Scrapbook, 1919–1923," Box 11, AIR, 59.

145. Dench, "Motion Picture Photography," 520; and Howard, "Sodas or Shaves," 112.

146. Kimball, "The Film Trailer," 19.

147. "The Newest Kind of Store Publicity," *Clothier and Furnisher*, September 1916, 99; "Sales Manual," Box 5, AIR, 81; and Kimball, "The Film Trailer," 19.

148. Kimball, "The Film Trailer," 18.

149. "Sales Manual," Box 5, AIR, 63, 80.

150. "Feeding Ambition with Gold," 4.

151. George M. Cheney, "Do Screen Ads Pay?," *MPW*, July 8, 1916, 282.

152. Display Ad, *PI*, April 26, 1917, 92.

153. Kimball, "The Film Trailer," 18. Similar assertions of the cross-class value of advertising audiences can be found in Don Herold, "Moving Pictures and Advertising Pictures," *The Printing Art*, September 1915, 33; and "The Cinema as a Medium for Making Sales," *Simmons' Spice Mill*, April 1919, 468. The National Builders' Bureau went so far as to assert that "ninety per cent of the inhabitants of the average community" attend the local motion-picture performances, implying that cinema was not only cheap but reached, quite literally, virtually everyone in the area. Display Ad, *Helping 'Em Build*, January 1921, 2, in "Alexander Film Company—Scrapbook, 1919–1923," Box 11, AIR, 59.

154. "Sales Manual," Box 5, AIR, 54.

155. "The Newest Kind of Store Publicity," *Clothier and Furnisher*, September 1916, 98. This article is dominated by an "interview" with the advertising manager for the Hickey-Freeman Company and as such was likely placed or suggested either by Hickey-Freeman itself or by the company to whom it outsourced production of its trailers.

156. Display Ad, *Helping 'Em Build*, September 1920, 2, in "Alexander Film Company—Scrapbook, 1919–1923," Box 11, AIR, 54; and Kimball, "The Film Trailer," 11. Kimball correlates this to a US Commissioner of Education statement that "seventy-five million folks in this country never read a book of any kind."

157. "Opportunity Knocks" pamphlet, Box 10, Folder 2, AIR, 12.

158. G. R. Lowe, "Slide Advertising for the Retail Druggist," *American Druggist and Pharmaceutical Record*, April 1914, 44; and George M. Rittelmeyer, "Slide Advertising," *MPW*, September 13, 1913, 1178. "Do Local Pictures Pay?," *MPW*, July 31, 1915, 846.

159. The cinema was one element of a larger cultural turn to temporal awareness in advertising. American billboarding was dealing with the

development of an aesthetics of speed at this time, as automotive transit grew. Similarly, electronic billboards in cities—particularly the work of Oscar Gude in New York—began transitioning to temporal sequencing through electronically controlled lights, in a variant of the motion-picture model. Catherine Gudis, *Buyways: Billboards, Automobiles, and the American Landscape* (New York: Routledge, 2004), 66–70; and Darcy Tell, *Times Square Spectacular: Lighting Up Broadway* (New York: Smithsonian Books, 2007), 34–46.

160. "Sales Manual," Box 5, AIR, 52.

161. Ibid., 121.

162. "Alexander Film Co.: Behind the Scenes" pamphlet, AIR.

163. "Alexander Film Company—Scrapbook, 1919–1923," Box 11, AIR, 108.

164. Liberty Strand Theatres (Fresno, CA) to Alexander Film Co., March 5, 1923, in "Alexander Film Company—Scrapbook, 1919–1923," Box 11, AIR, 42; and J. Don Alexander to "Friends," February 1, 1924, in "Alexander Film Company—Scrapbook, 1919–1923," Box 11, AIR, 129.

165. Kimball, "Industrial Film Facts," 3; and "Over 10,000,000 Extra Revenue for Theatres" pamphlet, Box 10, Folder 2, AIR. Alexander's internal figures indicated that between 1923 and 1932, an average of 2,000 theaters per year had screened its service. "Treasurer Gives Interesting Facts," *Weekly Animator* 6, no. 1 (January 7, 1933), Box 7, AIR, 6. An undated pamphlet, probably from 1923 or 1924, provides a figure of "over 1,800 theaters." "Opportunity Knocks" pamphlet, Box 10, Folder 2, AIR, 15.

166. An undated pamphlet declares that by some point in the mid-twentieth century, Alexander was circulating its service to 16,000 theaters in the forty-eight states. (The pamphlet is probably from the late 1940s, as it does not mention television. Alaska became the forty-ninth state in 1959.) Although the average running time for trailers had decreased to approximately forty seconds and the average number per program had dropped from "five to ten" to three or four, Alexander continued to dominate. By this point, the company's business model had also grown to include published weekly rates for all theaters, with the focus on haggling apparently abandoned. See "What Are Alexander Movie Ads" pamphlet, Box 10, Folder 2, AIR.

167. *Alexander Cooperator*, October 1929, Box 8, Folder 1, AIR, 5.

168. Fidler, "A Discussion of the Current Status," 5–6; and Fidler and Boren, "Commercial Movies," 7–8.

169. "Sales Manual," Box 5, AIR, 55, 61–62; Monache Theatre Co. Inc. to "To Whom It May Concern," February 16, 1923, "Alexander Film

Company—Scrapbook, 1919–1923," Box 11, AIR, 33; and "Opportunity Knocks" pamphlet, Box 10, Folder 2, AIR, p. 3, 6–7.

170. "Sales Manual," Box 5, AIR, 25–29.

171. "Sales Manual," Box 5, AIR, 25–29, 51. These pages are a laundry list of why Alexander's films are superior to those of its competitors.

172. "Sales Manual," Box 5, AIR, 18.

173. Don M. Alexander, "Advertising Words, Cut Them Out," *Alexander Cooperator*, April 1925, Box 8, Folder 1, AIR, 4. As with word limitations in slides, the correlation between brevity and limitations on the reader's time has important parallels in billboard copy developments. See Gudis, *Buyways*, 66–68.

174. "Sales Manual," Box 5, AIR, 20.

175. This is not to say that all of its trailers were "calming" in terms of their copy. Indeed, Alexander advertisements evince some of the earliest use of "scare copy" in motion-picture advertising. For example, the hand of life literally dealing out horrible cards labeled "sickness," "permanent disability," and "death" was used in an advertisement for insurance. The trailers were designed to make consumption of advertising easy and palatable, regardless of the positive or negative emotions the copy itself played upon. H. A. Shaw, "A Few of Last Month's Productions," *Alexander Cooperator*, February 1925, Box 8, Folder 1, AIR, p. 14–15.

176. "Sales Manual," Box 5, AIR, 24.

177. Bordwell et al., *The Classical Hollywood Cinema*, 104, 152.

178. "Alexander Film Company—Scrapbook, 1919–1923," Box 11, AIR, 4, 23.

179. "Sales Manual," Box 5, AIR, 98.

180. "Sales Manual," Box 5, AIR, 42; J. Don Alexander (Letter from the President), *Alexander Cooperator*, January 1925, Box 8, Folder 1, AIR, 2; "Alexander Acquires Fox Houses in Missouri, Kansas, Illinois and Colorado," *Weekly Animator*, January 1933, Box 7, AIR, 2.

181. Alexander never, to my knowledge, directly explained how it financially covered the higher prices of some screens. It seems most likely the company had worked out a generic minimum to cover all costs. If so, Alexander would have been selling space at a top-flight theater at a 90 percent or greater loss, with that loss being covered by comparative overcharges elsewhere.

182. "Sales Manual," Box 5, AIR, 80–81.

183. Liberty Theater (Marysville, CA) Contract, Box 2, Folder 3, AIR. The first film was #3352 of the then-current catalog.

184. Webb Garrison, "Hash a la Comment," *Weekly Animator,* May 15, 1925, Box 7, AIR, 8.

185. "Natural Color Films," Box 2, Folder 3, AIR.

186. "Alexander Film Company—Scrapbook, 1919–1923," Box 11, AIR, 1, 8, 57, 59.

187. In early January of 1933, Alexander reported that 2,374 playlets had been produced in 1932 and that 11,145 playlets had been produced in the previous nine years combined. The caveat about inflating the numbers of early years is rendered clear by the jarring difference between the average yearly rate (1,096) and the 1932 rate (more than twice as high despite being called a "tragic" year). R. A. Duncan, "Proof of Progress," and C. J. Shaw, "1933—The Year to Work and Build," in *Weekly Animator* 6, no. 1 (January 7, 1933), Box 7, AIR, 1, 9, 11.

188. J. Don Alexander (Letter from the President) and "The Era of Airplanes," both in *Alexander Cooperator,* July 1925, Box 8, Folder 1, AIR, 2, 7.

189. Display Ad, *Alexander Cooperator* 2, no. 4 (September 1925), Box 8, Folder 1, AIR, back cover; "Feeding Ambition With Gold"; and "Alexander Film Company—Scrapbook, 1919–1923," Box 5, AIR, 9, 25.

190. J. Don Alexander (Letter from the President), *Alexander Cooperator* (July 1925), Box 8, Folder 1, AIR, 2.

191. For a study of the history of spot advertising in early radio, see Russo, *Points on the Dial.*

THREE

WATCH THIS SPACE

Peripheral Advertising through Technologies

> You Must Invest Thousands to Make the Front of the Chair a Profit Producer; You Need Invest a Few Hundred to Make the Back of the Chair Bring You in as Great, if Not Greater Profits.
>
> —Inter-state Vending Company (1914)

IN AUGUST OF 1915, PROMPTED by a letter from an exhibitor, *Moving Picture World* columnist Epes Winthrop Sargent—resident expert on advertising for film shows—let loose with yet another of the many published examples of institutional hostility to screen advertising. Sargent's response was predictable: screen advertising is bad practice because it is "thrust upon the patron . . . whether he wishes [it] or not." His choice of counter example, however, was unique and raises the specter of an obvious alternative to onscreen advertising that has been almost entirely forgotten. Opting to compare the cinema not to magazines but to the stage theater, Sargent declared that "a manager, if he wishes, may plaster his walls with advertisements and fill up his program with them until it becomes valueless to himself or anyone else, but the screen is his stage. He should not permit the advertising slide any more than a dramatic theater should permit a sandwich man to walk on and spoil the realism of a performance."[1] Sargent's comparison of the advertising slide to a sandwich board on a theater stage is interesting for multiple reasons, not least of which is the conundrum of whether this would be compulsory or more like product placement and why exactly sandwich men advertising real-world products did not qualify, in Sargent's mind, as "realism."[2] More important for the present discussion, however, is his telling revelation of the specific spatial relations of the theater. The screen was indeed not the same as the wall, but they did reach the same crowd.

By the mid-1910s, though filmed advertisements were still developing, the positives and negatives of onscreen advertising seemed relatively clear to many in the film industry. Such ads provided a small amount of income that could be inflated further by trading in monopoly contracts and keeping the total number of ads small, but they could annoy patrons and, if inserted into the program in larger quantities, diminish the amount of time that could be devoted to entertainment. From the advertisers' perspective, onscreen advertising was also problematically fleeting and required extremely memorable copy in order to make a lasting impression in its few seconds of visibility. It was a conceptual environment conducive to broad rethinking. A few dedicated individuals fought to maintain the integration of cinema and advertising while disposing of almost all of the rationale of onscreen placement.

Playing with long-standing concepts in advertising at the margins, numerous tinkerers (many of them not otherwise associated with either cinema or advertising) and a few small advertising companies concocted techniques and technologies that allowed an entire collection of advertisements to crowd around the motion picture without landing on the screen itself—tactics to make, among other things, "the back of the chair bring you . . . profits."[3] Peripheral advertising, which was indebted to the lantern slide advertising tactic of running roughly a dozen ads easily and inexpensively in a contracted space, represented a relatively simple shift in thinking from object to venue, but the shift required an entirely new philosophical definition of advertising. For peripheral advertisers, the theater was no longer a single window through which one viewed an unceasing flow of images, but a media center capable of housing multiple entertainments and distractions. Abandoning the hypodermic theory of cinema spectatorship altogether, peripheral-advertising proponents reconceived the theater as a site of active audiences: people who (like the target audiences of magazines and billposters) perused or ignored the ads at their own discretion.

Between 1912 and 1920, cinema-oriented tinkerers devised a variety of offscreen technologies. Calculated specifically to blend into modern American cinema spaces, peripheral technologies were a flashy window into a world of consumption, bringing consumer goods into the theater just as display windows brought them onto the streets—encased in spectacular designs of glass and electric light.[4] These concepts ranged from alternative magic-lantern placements, to stacks of glowing advertisements flanking the screen, to complex advertising clocks, all in an attempt to compel without compelling (much like the slide and the minute movie attempted to take up time without taking too much time). However, as with slides and trailers, the peripheral advertisement too was pushed slowly out; the growing fetish of opulence, along with a troubling propensity for technological errors, took a rapid toll on most businesses.[5] Peripheral advertising was thus both the most chaotic and the shortest-lived field of silent cinema advertising.

PERIPHERAL VISIONS

At the outset, it is important to note that peripheral advertising has left the fewest historical traces. It is difficult to know just how many of these technologies were put into use and if the technologies that actually were adopted were widely used nationally, regionally, or even locally. Indeed, the historical traces of such technologies are often grotesquely unhelpful; witness the following trade press report, reproduced in its entirety: "Central City, Neb.—The Donelson theater has recently installed an advertising machine."[6] For the historian of such material, this is a frustrating tease. What type of machine? What did it do and when? Although this is an extreme example, significant portions of the analysis in this chapter have been extrapolated from primary documents only marginally more helpful—patents with no connection to actual usage, trade materials (such as business cards) that contain little more content than a slogan, or brief published condemnations from *Moving Picture World* exhibition columnist F. H. Richardson.

The obvious conclusion in the face of such minimal mention of offscreen technologies in the national trade press is that peripheral-advertising businesses were, by and large, locally focused. After all, why would the national press care specifically which machine the Donelson Theater installed if the machine was only available in eastern Nebraska? Although early slide makers (for example, the high school boys from Sandusky, OH) and trailer producers (Atlanta's Scenic Film Company) began as local businesses, national companies rapidly dominated both fields. By contrast, very few national trendsetters appeared for peripheral advertising. The haphazard nature of the field makes life difficult for the scholar attempting to trace a coherent history of the form.

What is clear is that peripheral advertising in the 1910s was dominated by a single idea: installing lit advertising on the walls, predominantly near the screen. Despite precedents (see below), other possible regions—seat backs, floors, trash receptacles—were ignored in 1910s peripheral-advertising circles.[7] It is likely that this attentiveness to the walls, particularly the front wall, was driven by a common structural motif of early theaters now little remembered. Unlike twenty-first-century multiplex screens, which stretch nearly wall to wall, early exhibition commonly featured a relatively small screen. Even as the size of theaters ballooned at mid-decade, screen size remained relatively small, often resulting in screens surrounded by decorative emplacements, enormous quantities of black masking, or vast tracts of bare wall.[8] In a 1916 manual for exhibitors, Frank Rembusch indicated a sixteen-foot width as a near maximum regardless of the size of the theater, while F. H. Richardson offered a slightly more generous eighteen feet; within this manual, all estimated screen widths were less than half of the auditorium width.[9] A concrete example of such a ratio is visible in a 1914 letter from an exhibitor in Wichita, Kansas, to the "Hallberg Helps" column of the *Motion Picture News*; within this letter, the writer reveals that his screen was only fourteen feet wide, while the front row of seats was thirty-one feet wide.[10] Early cinema theaters would therefore typically provide relatively large quantities of desirable and seemingly unused space on the front wall. This space became unrelentingly attractive to early peripheral advertisers.

Although the distinction is imperfect, these wall-based technologies fragment into two relatively clear camps: technologies that simply provided a means to integrate advertising into the space with no further efforts at self-justification and technologies that were concerned with appearing useful. I term the former *frame technologies*, as the most common method was the creation of lighted advertising signs that bordered the theater screen on one or more sides, like a picture frame. The latter, *public-service technologies*, would be placed slightly farther from the screen, as the advertising was crowded around a secondary object, rather than the projected film. In this era, public-service technologies were exclusively clocks, both projected and backlit, with advertising integrated within or near the dial.[11]

At least five versions of the standard frame concept were filed for patent in the United States between 1912 and 1920, with many other versions suggested or sold without patent protection. Effectively, frame advertisements were a combination of the poster and the lantern slide: rectangular imagery usually physically hung on the wall but also lit in a darkened spectatorial space. Production style varied based on the means of illumination. At least three different approaches are evident: light diffusers, light boxes, and projection.

Light diffusers create soft and less obtrusive light by shielding a bulb from view and reflecting the light back into the room off of a surface. Light diffusion is a method designed to disperse light for ambiance, rather than focus it. At the time, it was commonly used in theatrical lighting to reduce both glare and eye strain.[12] Advertising diffusers were therefore typically sold as a means to illuminate a theatrical space. The advertising was simply described as a cost-deferral scheme—or, in the words of inventor Gloss H. Fowler, an addition that made the lighting "both useful and profitable." Light-diffusing frame technologies would thus have provided rectangular spaces into which the theater operator could insert advertising posters, diffusing the light off of paid signage rather than bare walls or ceilings. Both Gloss H. Fowler (sign painter of Tacoma, Washington) and Frank C. Thomas (New Yorker of unknown trade) are known to have patented advertising diffuser arrays and offered them for sale.[13]

By contrast, light boxes conceal the source of light behind a foreground object, calling attention to the source of the light by creating a blockage. Light boxes are effectively the opposite of diffusion; they trap the light and focus it exclusively onto a point of revelation. With light boxes, then, any illumination of the room would have been secondary and accidental, as the target was the creation of focal points. Light-box advertisers would have blocked the light with lettered and pictographic advertising printed on semitransparent paper or cut into opaque sheets. Often these sheets would have been sandwiched between two pieces of glass to keep the advertisement firm and upright, creating the appearance of an enormous glass slide. Only Minneapolis inventors

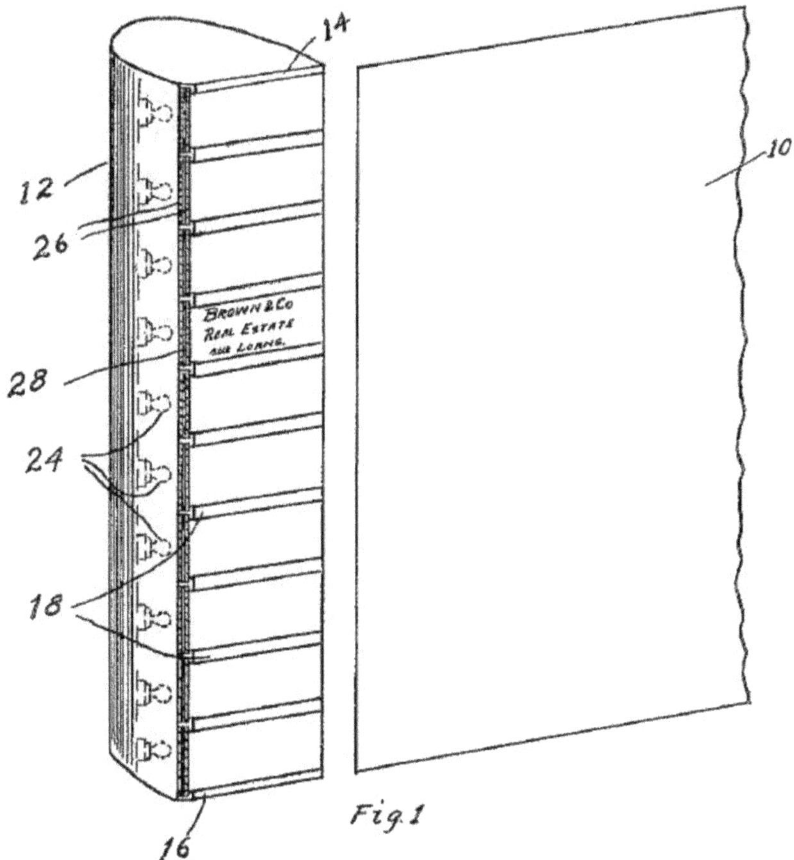

Figure 3.1. Harry Verran and Alfred R. Groetz's light-box advertising system, as depicted in their patent (#1,321,863).

Harry Verran (advertising manager for a local paper called the *South Side Booster*) and Alfred R. Groetz (trade unknown) are known to have patented such a device, although others appear unclaimed in the historical record.[14]

The above two methods would have required the installation of purpose-built contraptions—metal structures designed to hold the advertising and lights in place. Some inventors opted to instead harness the projection booth. Most either adopted preexisting projectors that were readily available on the market or designed a similar device; these dedicated advertising-slide projectors would then have been operated simultaneously with the film projector. Standard projectors would simply have been trained on the wall near the screen, creating a secondary square of imagery alongside the film.[15] Alternatively, specially designed slides (suggested by the operator of Denver's New Isis Theater) or projectors (patented by cigar maker Henry A. Miedreich of Evansville, Illinois) were created to overlap with the projection of the film so that the slide advertising was projected in a perfect frame around the edges of the motion-picture screen itself.[16] One inventor—Los Angeles film director T. Hayes Hunter—went even farther, patenting a method to print advertising messages onto the edges of the film itself.[17]

Despite the existence of multiple patent drawings, a deeper aesthetic study of these frame technologies is impossible. The few known examples of such devices actually in use were so minimally described that visual design and copy choices are not clear; often all we know is that the messages were in white or red letters. What seems certain is that the bulk of frame devices, as exclusively local and regional technologies, did not feature the common slide and trailer distinction between custom, stock, and partially stock advertising. Without national circulation of such devices, there would have been little reason to concoct an array of stock imagery to be endlessly resold. Most of this signage would likely have been custom painted or custom cut to match the advertiser's copy suggestions. For example, Gloss Fowler's light diffusers were sold through the Fowler Sign Company very likely as a means to increase demand for his custom sign-painting services. The only likely outliers in this focus on custom work would have been those frame proponents who used variations on the traditional magic-lantern slide projector—Henry Miedreich, most notably. As such, stock imagery would have entered into the equation only when a completely separate entity was responsible for the creation of the ads themselves.

As implied above, the most pronounced issue with frame technologies was their encroachment on the screen without the addition of anything of value to the film experience aside from moving the advertising off the screen. For those viewers and exhibitors who were concerned with more than simply eliminating compulsory pauses, practices that were less intrusive and more justifiable were required. Public-service technologies were therefore invented to provide the advertising with a patina of practical-use value. As mentioned in the discussion of clock slides (see chap. 1), claiming "public service" was a venerable technique for preempting audience hostility. Consider, for example, the practice of describing industrial films as "educational"; it was simply a means of slipping advertising through by asserting that the content was edifying. In the case of public-service technologies, the audience was to consider the advertising to be a necessary prerequisite to an experiential improvement—in this case, a clock or clock-like device.[18] Such technologies, in order to stress utility over advertising, were typically placed slightly farther from the screen than frames, though they too were on the front wall.

Responding to an ostensibly common problem in a darkened theater—that a patron could not see their watch face, assuming they wore a watch at all (the same problem that the clock slide was designed to address)—clock makers built and sold numerous illuminated advertising clocks specifically to be installed in darkened movie theaters. Some of the clocks were very basic: illuminated faces with light boxes installed below them—like that sold by the Standard Manufacturing Company of New York City—operating like a clock frame rather than a screen frame.[19] More commonly, clock purveyors like the Publicity Clock Company designed complex projecting devices that included a functioning clock dial alongside an automatically rotating wheel of advertising slides.[20] Manufacturers would piggyback the slide wheel onto the clock's timing mechanism so that the slides would click through the clock automatically, typically every thirty seconds.

Although the quantity of slots for slides was variable, by far the most common designs were eight- and twelve-slot models.

Unlike frame purveyors, the sellers of clocks—due to their rudimentary national marketing and their often-unique slide shapes—frequently acted as agencies, producing the advertising slides themselves and brokering the space for the exhibitor. Extant examples of Publicity Clock Company slide work differ little from other glass slide designs of the time, with stock copy and images being used. Some of the company's slides display very basic white-figure drawings of chickens, shoes, and moving vans to advertise the purveyors of those products; one particular slide design (held in a private collection) clearly shows cut cardboard (with a stock image of a truck and the phrase "Local or Long Distance Moving") appended in the center of custom phone and address information for "O. Gara."[21] As the general slide industry had by this point long established stock copy as standard practice, it is reasonable to assume that Publicity's approach was normative rather than anomalous. The description of slide-printing practices from chapter 1 is thus applicable here, although practical elements of shape and design would alter these practices slightly.

Interestingly, time-keeping patents were not always for clocks. A unique patent was for paper-mill laborer Norman T. Whitaker's elapsed-time tracker.[22] Rather than informing spectators of the actual hour, Whitaker's device would track the duration of each turn of the program, periodically indicating both the elapsed and remaining time of any given reel by scrolling a secondary reel of perforated paper past a light source; as per the patent drawing, it revealed messages like "6000 FOOT PLAY; 6000 FEET NOW SHOWN." (An odd example, as one would think that the film ending would be sufficient evidence for the viewer that the film was over.) In the interim moments, one could scroll other messages in front of the audience, like the patent's example of "EAT SMITH'S GOOD EATS."[23] As Whitaker's device required both the length indicators and the advertisements to be included on

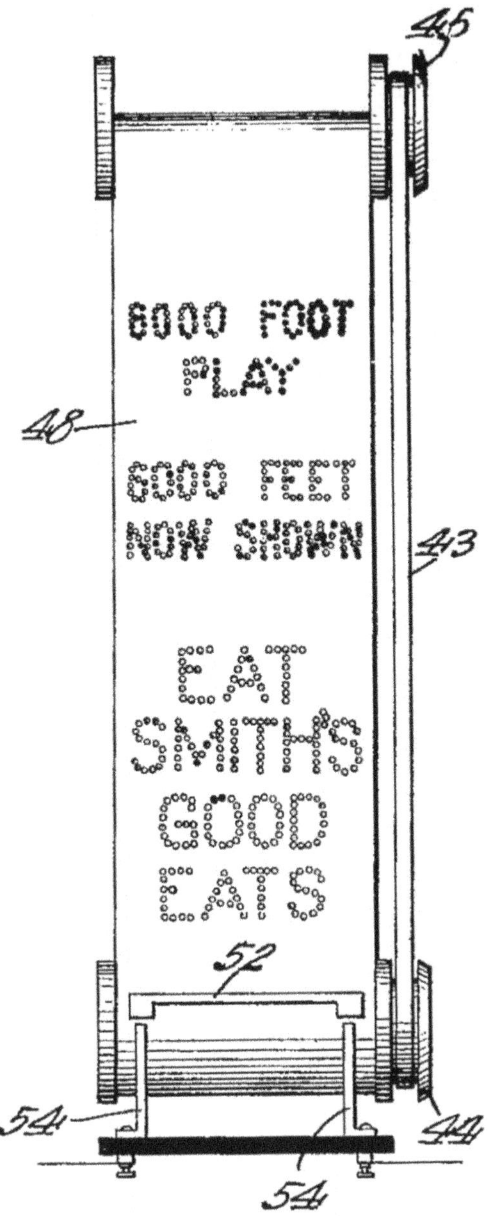

Figure 3.2. A drawing of the perforated paper strip, featuring both screening information and consumer-goods advertising, designed to run through Norman T. Whitaker's elapsed-time tracker (patent #1,329,216).

the same paper strip, it would likewise have required that the seller of the equipment also operate as an advertising agent.

In sum, peripheral advertising through both frames and clocks (and clock-like devices) was a means of harnessing unused space in the audience's peripheral vision, rather than hijacking the screen. Although any given technique could have been more or less attuned to a patron's desire to feel repaid for their attention, the range of placement was relatively narrow, with very few advertisements placed anywhere other than the front wall. The field of peripheral advertising was thus very different from that of slide or trailer advertising. Many purveyors were more interested in selling accoutrements that were capable of including advertising, rather than selling the advertisements themselves. Peripheral advertising was also most commonly sold in the immediate vicinity of the inventor's home. With a few notable anomalies, then, this is a field of eccentric inventors, not advertising agents, who were designing techniques inspired by and attuned to conditions in their own hometowns.

TINKERERS, TRIFLES, AND "CRAZY-QUILT" SUMMERS

As with all cinema-advertising techniques, peripheral-advertising technologies have a developmental history that predates the period under study. While slide advertising developed from earlier lantern usage (particularly the illustrated song) and drop-curtain advertising, and trailers were an extrapolation from both advertising slides and motion-picture formalities like credit leaders, peripheral advertising finds its origin in techniques designed to maximize the profit potential of the visual field in auditoriums and stage theaters. A brief history of theatrical advertising from beyond the stage, therefore, provides essential background.

In the years before electrical lighting became the standard in theatrical spaces, stage lighting could have been harnessed to call attention to advertising that did not rise out of view (along with the curtain) while the performance was in progress. For example, advertising wing and proscenium curtains, purchased and installed with an advertising drop curtain, would have been in use in some theaters. Theatrical advertising, however, seems to have more frequently focused on items that the audience members would approach, touch, and use. Printed playbills had long contained paid advertising in a form that was comprehensible and attractive in an era when newsprint and magazine advertising was the standard.[24] More permanent installations, though less common, were also available. In the first decade of the twentieth century, seat backs were harnessed for advertising purposes in numerous patents, as inventors appended advertising emplacements to everything from flip-up writing desks, to hat hangers, to vanity mirrors.[25] One inventor even designed an advertising card holder that was installed entirely alone, with no other useful device attached, presumably to offer commercial information as reading material while the spectator waited for the show to commence.[26] Minneapolis's Samuel W. Van Nostran was probably the most successful seat-back advertising man in the country at this time; as the operator of a theatrical supply company, Van Nostran sold advertising (acting as a space broker and splitting the revenue with the theater) on his own patented seats in at least four known theaters: three in Minneapolis (the Metropolitan, Bijou, and Lyceum) and one in New York (the Knickerbocker).[27] Waste receptacles with space for advertising content were also invented in this period, although no evidence of their actual use in theatrical venues has yet come to light.[28] Any number of these, whether lit or unlit, could have been installed near the exits of a suitably designed theater.

Just prior to the Nickelodeon theater boom, new peripheral-advertising devices were invented to take advantage of the increasing prevalence of electricity in daily life. A key idea was the illuminated or projecting clock. By April 1905, an early wave of projecting clocks had developed, with at least two functional and filed for patent. Both of these first-wave clocks used complex

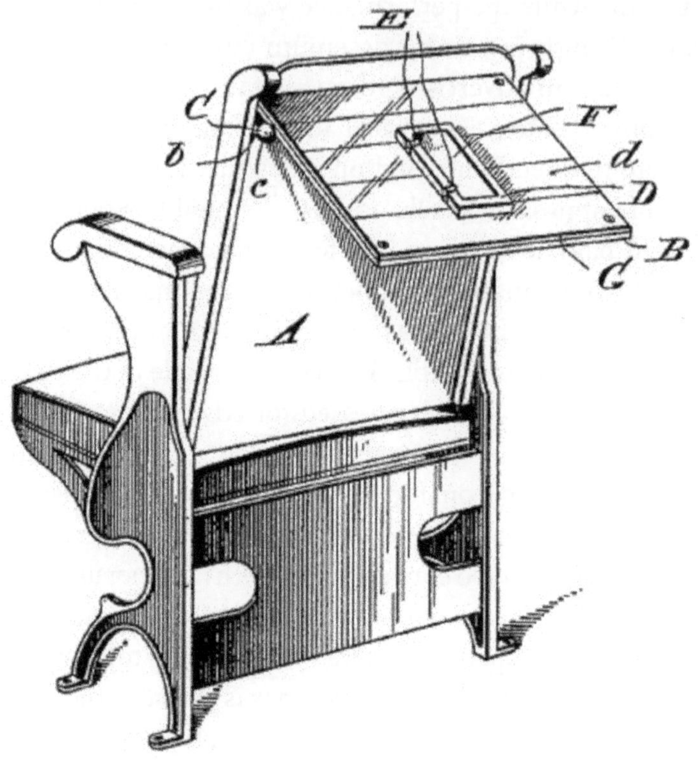

Figure 3.3. Harry L. Broad and Frederick H. Orcutt's theater seat with vanity mirror emplacement, designed to be surrounded by advertising cards, as portrayed in their patent (#901,065).

design work to insert custom advertising within the wheel of the clockface. One adapted the concept of the magic lantern to project a sequence of six advertisements (on round slides) that would rotate automatically through the clock.[29] The other scrolled messages past the light like a ticker tape via "a plurality of . . . belts."[30] As with the waste receptacles, no known adoption by theaters exists for either of these clocks; however, both would have been functionally appropriate within such a space.

Although known usage is far too minimal to draw any broad-scale conclusions about these devices, it is clear that the concept of peripheral advertising—and even the placement that would be adopted by nickelodeons—was in an advanced stage of development before the 1908 boom in permanent motion-picture theaters. Also, though this may be an artifact of research gaps, a disconnect between the East Coast and the Western states was also already apparent. Both of the known clock patents were filed in New York. Almost everything else was patented or adopted for use in states west of the Appalachians (with Minneapolis functioning as a surprising early hub of activity).[31] This split was to remain, as clocks would continue to be dominated by New York City companies with dreams of national circulation, while other types of peripheral advertising occurred predominantly west of the Appalachians in the vicinity of the inventors' own homes.

As motion-picture projection became increasingly common, the slow adoption of these established ideas in peripheral advertising by the fringes of the exhibition industry began. Although it remains possible that permanent theaters were experimenting with established items like chairs or clocks, it appears that the film industry's initial foray into peripheral advertising occurred via summer airdomes—outdoor vaudeville and projection spaces enclosed with a basic fence or wall. Such temporary exhibition spaces would often have had their rudimentary architecture covered with cheap advertising posters. By the beginning of the 1911 spring season, a correspondent to *Moving Picture World* noted that "most of the airdomes we have noticed up to the present time look more like billboards than they do like theatres. It seems to be the fashion to reserve a small section of the enclosure for an entrance and turn the remainder over to the bill-poster and sign-painter, who decorate it in their usual crazy-quilt fashion . . . inside and outside."[32]

By 1913, noted advertising expert Epes Winthrop Sargent's only criticism, when confronted with the idea, was that "the space nearest the entrance should be held for the house to the extent of the width of six sheets on each side."[33] This idea of using

Figure 3.4. View of the Delmar Air Dome in St. Louis, which featured an outer wall composed entirely of four large billboards. Courtesy of the Missouri Historical Society, St. Louis (https://mohistory.org/collections/item/resource:143550).

advertising as wallpaper was clearly still drifting intermittently through the exhibition industry as late as 1915, when the Empire Theater (on "Bank Street" in an unknown city) installed advertising cards all over the side walls "more or less like . . . a streetcar."[34] Problematically, the posters and cards would have been unlit. Indeed, none of these objects would have been readily visible with the house lights down, and in the era of transient spectatorship—films playing continuously with patrons entering and exiting at times of their own choosing—the lights were nearly always down.[35] However, the key point is that watching films while surrounded by advertising was a lived reality for some summertime cinemagoers in these early years.[36]

SEND IN THE CLOWNS

Within a year after the trades began discussing the "crazy-quilt fashion" in the airdome field, and just as the slide industry was approaching the low ebb of its public image, a clear turn to garish, electric signage for permanent theaters is evident. In January of 1912, Gloss H. Fowler (proprietor of the Fowler Sign Company) of Tacoma, Washington, filed for patent an electric (and less crazy) version of the wall advertisement. Fowler's very basic lighting design used advertising cards as the reflective surfaces for an array of light diffusers placed at regular intervals along the left and right house walls. Indicating clear hesitation about placing advertising within the cinema, Fowler's patent was focused on the lighting needs of the theater (with a full paragraph on the history of theatrical lighting) and included drawings that placed the diffusers unobtrusively at the outer reaches of the space. Fowler thus became the first known individual in the United States to attempt a large-scale reassessment of peripheral advertising as it could apply specifically to the cinema space, even suggesting, hesitantly, the notion of a proscenium frame (noting that it "can [alternatively] be used to form a border or frame about the screen").[37] Despite his pioneering status, Fowler's unexpected death only two years later, at the age of thirty-six, likely cut short the life span of not only the inventor, but also the invention. No evidence of its widespread adoption is apparent in the historical record.[38]

In the spring and summer of 1912, *Moving Picture World* columnist F. H. Richardson accidentally spurred the development of peripheral advertising with two key bits of printed matter. In April, Richardson proposed that exhibitors preempt the growing concerns about "overcranking" (speeding the projection in order to fit more showings into a single operating day) by installing clocks in plain view of the audience so that they could see that a promised one-hour program was delivered.[39] In July, Richardson printed a letter from the operator of the New Isis Theater in Denver in which the exhibitor proposed the use of overlapping projection to create "a border around the picture, announcing the big features." The writer suggested that such an effect might be achieved by simply creating a lantern slide with

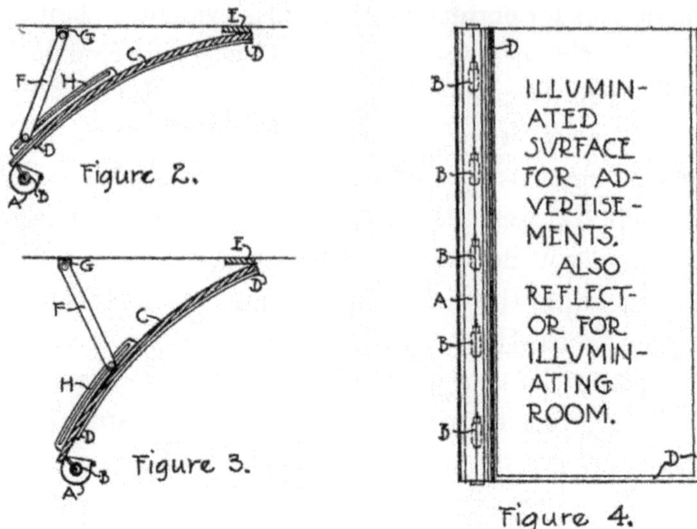

Figure 3.5. One of Gloss H. Fowler's light diffusers, designed for advertising unobtrusively along the left and right walls of a theater, as portrayed in his patent (#1,054,759).

a large dark square in the middle and projecting the film into the gap.[40] Although in the former case Richardson did not even imply the inclusion of advertising and in the latter he directly condemned the idea ("I do not believe I would like that very well"), these two published documents were the first appearance in the national trade press of the two ideas—clocks and frames—that would dominate peripheral cinema advertising for the rest of the decade.

The former idea was rapidly adopted by cinema advertisers, perhaps due to Richardson himself, thanks to the promotional phrasing. One year, almost to the day, after Richardson's spontaneous remark, the first newly developed advertising clock in eight years was announced for sale in the pages of *Moving Picture World*.[41] From 1913 to 1915, a sudden rise of a second wave of advertising clocks is evident; six different companies—all but one from New York City—filed advertising clocks for patent. The extant material clearly indicates a rapidly standardizing field and suggests relatively widespread adoption in some quarters.

The first second-wave clock indicates a lack of any standards in the early going. Offered for sale in April 1913 by J. H. Genter (a thirty-year-old theater-supply dealer from Newburgh, New York) and filed for patent the following month, Genter's Announceoscope was the first known attempt to bring a slide-based advertising clock, designed specifically for motion-picture theaters, to the market in the mature nickelodeon era. Genter's model offered ten slots, used American standard-sized slides, and simply projected them to overlay the lower half of the dial and the space below.[42] As Genter's Mirroroide Screen continued to dominate the company's trade advertising while the Announceoscope slowly slipped away, it is clear that Genter was either unable to get the machine to work reliably (all trade advertisements listed it as "coming soon") or unable to drum up significant interest in the invention.[43]

By August, a second short-lived company would try its hand at the form when Pittsburgh's General Sales Company of America offered a device dubbed the Wonder Clock. We can presume that General Sales's clock also had a rotating slide mechanism of some sort, as the clock was said to "caus[e] considerable conjecture . . . as to the working arrangement of the device," although the quantity of slide slots is not known.[44] General Sales's reuse of a 1905 concept—inserting round advertisements into the center of the clock dial—was the first move toward aesthetic standardization in the field.[45] While General Sales claimed to have installed "hundreds" of them across the United States, with more than thirty-five in New York City, the company abandoned its clock by the end of 1914, offering the purportedly $125 timepiece for a clearance price of $35.[46] It is not clear exactly why the clock was abandoned; in two different ads, General Sales asserted both that wartime export problems left the company with too much stock and that it was shifting its focus to a more recent invention.[47]

By the end of 1913, then, standards were shaky but developing; two of four projecting clocks (dating back to the first wave in 1905) included the advertising on a round slide within the dial, while all four included some mechanism for automatic rotation through a sequence of advertisements. Between May 1914 and October 1915, four more companies would firm up these standards even further, as in-dial placement reached near ubiquity and slide-slot counts of eight (for cheaper models) and twelve (for expensive models) became common across all manufacturers. New York City spawned three of these producers: the Publicity Clock Company had sold seventeen clocks by August 1915 (clock patented in 1914), the Wonder Clock Company (no apparent relation to the previous clock of the same name) had filed articles of incorporation by August as well, and the Standard Manufacturing Company began nationally advertising its clock by October 1915.[48] In July 1915, Chicago's Kineto Machine Company released the only known competing model manufactured outside of New York.[49] By early 1917, a couple of stragglers appeared on the already-congested scene. In February, the Kalck Safety Specialty Company, of Amityville, New York, patented and released an eight-slot advertising clock.[50] In April, Norman T. Whitaker filed the patent for his elapsed-time tracker mentioned above—effectively a clock that did everything except tell the time.

Indicating the rapidity of standardization of the form, three of the five actual clocks patented between 1914 and 1917 were, operationally, nearly indistinguishable. Kineto, Publicity, and Kalck all offered machines that placed round ads, projected from a rotating internal "petal" wheel, in the center of the clock dial, as General Sales had done previously. All three likewise offered standard slot counts with automatic rotation.[51] The only outliers were Standard Manufacturing, which used rectangular slides (like J. H. Genter) projected beneath the clock and had an anomalous slide load (six), and the second Wonder Clock, which had no rotation mechanism at all, allowing "but one product at a time [to] take advantage of th[eir] service".[52] Likewise, a price of approximately one hundred dollars for an entry-level model had been established; both the Kineto and Publicity eight-slot versions were listed for roughly this price (ninety-five and one hundred dollars, respectively).[53] Only Standard Manufacturing, which produced a significantly less complicated clock, offered its machine for an anomalous price: thirty-five dollars.

Less clear is whether or not standards had developed for the distribution of clocks. As the bulk of clocks were advertised for a price, there is some indication that exhibitors were being asked to bear this cost burden themselves in hopes of eventually turning a profit. Alternatives are clearly visible, however. The Wonder Clock Advertising Company, with only one space per clock to sell, attempted to maximize profits by acting as an agent; without a rotation mechanism, Wonder Clock focused on an early version of roadblocking—renting all of its space "in 75 leading moving picture houses" in New York at the same time to a single advertiser.[54] At least one company (Publicity) was offering its clocks to regional dealers, indicating that local middlemen, behaving as space brokers, may have been the more common target.[55] John C. Green's (manager of the Temple Theater in Galt, Ontario) purchase of distribution rights for clocks for his entire province is a clear indicator that Kineto was likewise seeking local agents.[56] Proto-franchising may have been the most common method of installation outside of the hubs of New York City and Chicago.

Regardless of the identity of the investor, profit similar to that of slide and trailer advertising was promised. The two companies using standard-sized rectangular slides offered identical estimates: Genter promised "anywhere from 20 to 50 dollars weekly" in his 1913 ad (a per-slot estimate of $2 to $5); Standard Manufacturing suggested exactly the same price ("$2 to $5 weekly" per slot) in 1915.[57] Profit at that level would have paid off either device in mere weeks, if not days. Although no other estimates from the 1910s are known, Publicity Clock contracts from the 1930s indicate that the company was continuing to sell space in Brooklyn theaters for between $1.25 and $1.50 per week, with contracts lasting between three and six months.[58] Even if purchased by a theater itself, therefore, these clocks were intended to be seen as a gravy train; it was akin to buying one's own medium to place within a cinema venue that, once the device was paid off, would print money unfettered into a golden future.

In February of 1916, F. H. Richardson explicitly gave his blessing to this advertising variant of his original proposal of clocks in theaters; he declared that such a device was "*the* way" to integrate advertising into the cinema theater, as "several theater managers" had installed them and communicated a favorable impression.[59] With all of these clocks on the market and even the notoriously cranky Richardson giving his approval, it should not be surprising that the years 1915 to 1917 were the peak for advertising clocks in the historical record. In 1916, the Empire Theater of Auburn, Indiana, installed an eight-slot model of unknown manufacture, while Redmon's Majestic of St. Louis installed a Kineto clock.[60] The Wonder Clock Advertising Company, of course, claimed to have seventy-five clocks scattered throughout New York in 1917.[61] Kineto filed suit over a broken contract that had initially called for the purchase of 242 clocks to cover a single state, also in 1917; tellingly, that state was Minnesota, long a bastion of peripheral advertising.[62] Though the flurry of activity at mid-decade appears to have fizzled quickly, two companies developed strong-enough market positions to persist for years. Kineto was selling advertising clocks until at least 1925, likely making it the dominant player in the West.[63] The Publicity Clock Company, as indicated by the above contracts, persisted at least into the late 1930s and had a stranglehold on New York City. The weight of scant evidence implies that the advertising clock was a significant fad at mid-decade and that it found a comfortable niche in a small subset of theaters thereafter.

Studying the trade press in isolation, one may come away with the impression that advertising clocks were the only peripheral-advertising tactic in use between 1915 and 1917. This is a mirage, an artifact of the national pretensions of numerous clock companies in major hubs of advertising activity. Historical evidence for frame advertising also peaks in roughly this period, with most information occurring between 1915 and 1918 (and exhibiting, in line with pre-cinematic peripheral advertising, a continuing predominance of Midwestern invention). Although the reasons for this boom are unclear, a growing crowd of frame techniques arose in these years almost entirely off the radar of the trade press.

It is likely that the wartime competition for onscreen space (see chaps. 1 and 2) was one key motivating factor. Indeed, it is telling that one inventor—Hollywood director T. Hayes Hunter—used "Buy War Saving Stamps" as the sample advertising copy in his patent.[64] However, a secondary and more likely motivation is the fact that frames were a remarkably easy form to experiment with. In low-end theaters in which ornamentation did not obscure the front wall, there was nothing aside from expectations and personal feelings of shame to keep the exhibitor from simply switching on his slide projector while the film was running and pointing it at an empty space on the wall. Indeed, by 1917, "most of the houses" in Topeka, Kansas, had done exactly this.[65] Considering that the idea could reach epidemic proportions in a single city, it is likely that many theaters nationwide were operating a slide projector in exactly this manner at some point during the 1910s—creating a one-at-a-time proto-frame constructed entirely from materials and devices already on hand.

In spite, or perhaps because, of the existence of such simplistic frame devices, more complicated technologies were designed and sold over the latter half of the decade. During the boom period of 1915 to 1917, numerous devices are known to have existed, though few remain linked in the historical record to an inventor or a selling company. In November of 1915, Frank C. Thomas of New

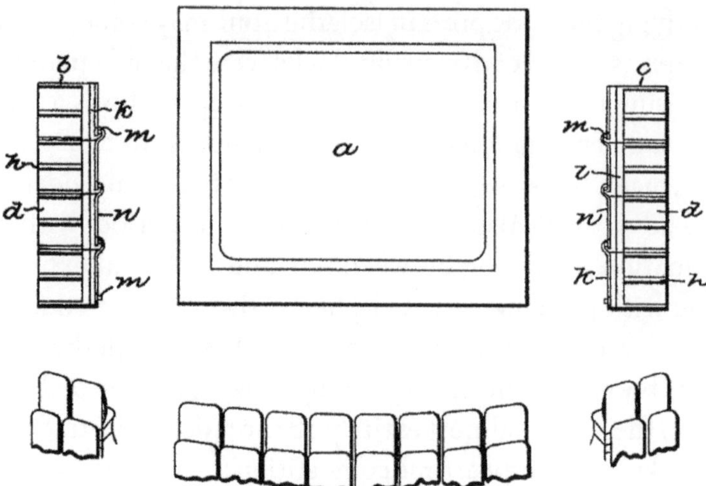

Figure 3.6. Frank C. Thomas's light-diffuser array, designed to surround the screen with lighted advertising signs, as depicted in his patent (#1,252,629).

York City adapted the concept of light diffusion and described its function in relation to the needs of theatrical lighting ("a sufficient but not brilliant" ambient light). However, unlike his predecessor Gloss Fowler, Thomas was more audacious; he was interested exclusively in building frame towers along each side of the screen, with eight slots per side in an average setup, turning theater lighting into spot lighting.[66] Indicating his intention to push the device as far as it would go, Thomas assigned his patent rights to George C. Vedder, who at the time had enough clout as a member of the trade press (via the journal *Export American Industries*) that he earned an invitation to a 1915 Nicholas Power business luncheon (where, coincidentally, he sat directly across the table from F. H. Richardson).[67]

By July of the following year, Lester Nichols, of the Gem Theater in Petersborough, New Hampshire, suggested placing lighted picture frames on the theater's side walls, indicating that reticence about angry patrons had not (yet) left the frame field entirely. Although Nichols's concept left the front wall unmolested, its use of light and mass quantities gave it similar functionality. Epes Winthrop Sargent, whose column had printed the letter, proposed to add even greater deference to the audience via the addition of a switch so that the sign could be illuminated only when the pictures stopped ("the flashing into sight will attract attention where the constantly lighted sign soon becomes a part of the surroundings").[68]

By April of 1917, F. H. Richardson discovered two theaters (Nashville's Strand and New Orleans' Pearce's Tudor) placing alongside the screen "an advertising announcement board with . . . five or six lines of letters in white lights."[69] Later that month, Richardson found a "'shadow box' of light colored advertising cards" surrounding the screen at the Orpheum in Centerville, Iowa.[70] By early 1918, Chicago's Crystal Theater was using a frame in which "several bright lettered illuminated signs advertis[ed] future programs . . . on the wall not far from the screen."[71] Although it is unclear who owned the rights or installed any of these machines, it is apparent that numerous machines of wildly divergent styles were available throughout the United States.

Although information on standards, prices, companies, and individuals is more scant for frames than their clock counterparts, they too appear to have hit their stride via the direct blessing, in 1916, of a prominent voice in exhibition theory. In early July of that year, exhibition giant "Roxy" Rothapfel, in his regular column in the trade journal *Motography*, proposed that exhibitors deal with spectator irritation at onscreen advertising by "establishing a regular billboard" around the screen.[72] Although Rothapfel did not suggest a clear method, endorse a particular company, or even claim to have established such a billboard in one of his own theaters, this statement undoubtedly carried as much weight as Richardson's February pronouncement about clocks—perhaps more so, as Rothapfel was, unlike Richardson, a practicing exhibitor. Indeed, the sheer quantity of "announcement boards" discovered by Richardson in 1917 and 1918 may indicate the direct impact of Rothapfel's claim.

"DISTINCTLY OBJECTIONABLE"

These Richardson discoveries, however, do not simply provide evidence of the commonness of frame devices at the time. They are also the clearest known evidence for the rising tensions that likely pushed the bulk of clock and frame purveyors into oblivion. As Richardson embarked on what was a nationwide tour of theaters over the course of 1917 in an effort to see firsthand the state of exhibition in America, his standard approach was to identify each theater by name in his published account and either praise or condemn it for the quality of exhibition he found within. Over the course of his updates from the road, projection problems caused by peripheral advertising were a regular refrain, with clocks and frames receiving similar treatment. "Smear[s] of white light" were reported three times in April—in New Orleans (Pearce's Tudor and the Globe Theater) and Mobile, Alabama (Empire Theater)—with the smear at the Tudor bad enough that it actually went across the screen itself.[73] Pearce's Tudor came in for particularly heavy condemnation for also including green illuminated letters below a clock ("presumably advertising the jeweler who supplied [it]"), the above mentioned advertising billboard, and six other inexplicable red lights. Richardson walked out over the theater's attempt to "murder the picture."[74] Light leakage, though not particularly common in Richardson's reports, was of major concern when it occurred.

More commonly Richardson discovered illuminated letters and signs and simply declared them "distracting immensely" or, when he was feeling more verbose and aggressive, "very, very bad . . . from the projection point of view." Some such complaints were leveled at clocks, like the one found at the Graphic in Bangor, Maine, which featured "two or three [brightly illuminated]

Figure 3.7. A cropped section of Fred Gildersleeve's photo of the interior of the Hippodrome Theater in Waco, Texas, which clearly reveals the presence of five advertising cards above the left-hand exit doors at the front of the theater. Five more advertisements were hung above the corresponding door on the right. The Texas Collection, Baylor University, Waco, Texas.

advertisements beneath its dial."[75] Others were directed at slide projectors, shadow boxes, and even exit signs.[76] By the end of his tour, Richardson had been frustrated by peripheral advertising and other offscreen signage often enough that he declared the billboard at Chicago's Crystal Theater "not good practice" without feeling the need to provide any specific reason.[77]

Although it is impossible to determine whether or not Richardson's published complaints had any measurable impact on the decline of frame technologies, his tour is conspicuously situated in the historical record. Published just as patented technologies were cresting, these missives from the field indicate significant problems, both technological (shoddy workmanship) and cultural (an affront to quality exhibition). Importantly, in the wake of Richardson's tour, very little evidence exists of continued adoption. Only the continuing existence of Publicity and Kineto and the filing of a few further patent technologies (none of which is known to have been implemented) indicate any further activity in the peripheral-advertising field after 1918. From that point forward, the trade press ignores the form almost completely. It seems likely, therefore, that many of the active companies failed on strictly technical grounds; a company regularly producing "smears of light" was not likely to continue drumming up business, especially if its zone of activity was severely limited (to a single region or even a single city). At minimum, it seems safe to assume that only Publicity and Kineto were capable of producing peripheral devices that met an acceptable standard, as their competitors disappeared quickly.

In the absence of further data, it must be concluded that peripheral advertising, like its screen advertising siblings, was pushed into lower-end theaters and then slowly died out, to be replaced eventually by alternative concepts like branded paper cups and other concession-oriented techniques. Indeed, evidence for this assertion is implicit in Richardson's tour. Of the seven offending theaters Richardson identified by name, nearly all were smaller, older theaters. Take, for example, the Graphic Theater of Bangor, Maine—a 750-seat theater just down the block from a competitor (the Park) nearly twice its size.[78] The only exception I have found is Chicago's Crystal Theater, which was a newly built, 2,000-seat theater when it experimented with peripheral signage.[79] It would appear, then, that even during peripheral advertising's zenith, it was adopted almost exclusively by small or struggling theaters in an effort to recover sagging profits.

It is also reasonable to assume that, even where quality construction did not lead to light leakage and angry patrons, peripheral-advertising techniques were incompatible with the theatrical beautification tactics being pursued as the picture palace trend took hold. Indeed, even the 1915 side-wall signage at the Empire Theater was critiqued at its first appearance as failing to "harmonize with the decorations of the theater."[80] As with all elements of modern palatial theaters, the front wall had seen growing use over the previous years as the rise of the feature film was paralleled by increasingly opulent surroundings. By the latter half of the 1910s, even smaller theaters were attempting to emulate palatial architecture as convincingly as their operating budgets would allow. As William Paul has noted, the concept of the "picture setting"—stage dressing designed to attractively frame the projected image—had become common enough by 1916 that the "window in the garden" motif had become a basic template. By 1920, one could find ads in the trade presses from companies whose primary product was picture settings.[81]

Even in theaters without picture settings, a shifting consensus in proper projection likely reduced the available space by a significant margin. Over the course of the 1910s, exhibition manuals began to clearly suggest the placement of black masking around the screen as a cheap and effective means to boost the perceived brightness of the projected image. Richardson himself, in his 1916 revision of the *Motion Picture Handbook,* had mandated "at least a two-foot band of dead black"[82] around the screen. (Even a cursory comparison of patent drawings to Richardson's example photo indicates that frame technologies were typically intended to encroach much closer than two feet. Only Thomas's drawing, which includes a scale drawing of both screen and masking, leaves a significant gap.) Even if such a buffer zone did not preclude peripheral advertising completely, Richardson's additional claims that one must beware of "interfering light," including that caused by "light shaded from the screen but glaring directly into the eyes of the audience,"[83] indicate clear concern regarding the placement of any additional light sources on the front wall. For Richardson, even placing lights on the side walls was considered "distinctly objectionable."[84]

In fact, "glaring directly into the eyes" would be a serviceable description of even a properly functioning light-box sign. In response to feature filmmaking and accelerating standards of a quality show, the front wall had undergone a multiform process of reclamation from exactly the tactics that formed the foundation of peripheral advertising.

It is perhaps not surprising that no evidence has been found indicating the adoption of any of the frame devices patented after 1918. Not only were these technologies entering a rapidly contracting field, they also reflect a remarkable upswing in audacity. Light boxes were clearly on the rise. Indeed, Richardson's descriptions above indicate that some of the signage he encountered in 1917 was of the light-box variety. In 1919, Minneapolis inventors Harry Verran and Alfred R. Groetz filed the only known patent for the approach, designing light-box towers with ten slots per side of the screen.[85]

Later that year, as though peripheral advertisers had learned nothing from the experiences of others, two inventors even began to encroach on the screen itself, negating what had been the key appeal of such advertising. Film director T. Hayes Hunter, already working in Hollywood for Samuel Goldwyn by the date of his invention, filed for patent an intriguing technology that integrated a frame at the moment of production rather than exhibition. Hunter's design would have printed the film with an oval mask, creating a permanent iris on the image that would have kept the edges of the negative from registering on the positive print. Running the film through the printer a second time, one could then have appended "a still picture or scene in the border or corner of the motion picture, which w[ould] persist unchanged in the vision of the spectators . . . without breaking into the thread of the drama."[86] The result would have been an oval shaped entertainment film with from one to four advertising messages perpetually hanging from the corners. In a model that blurred the lines between peripheral advertising and product placement, Hunter

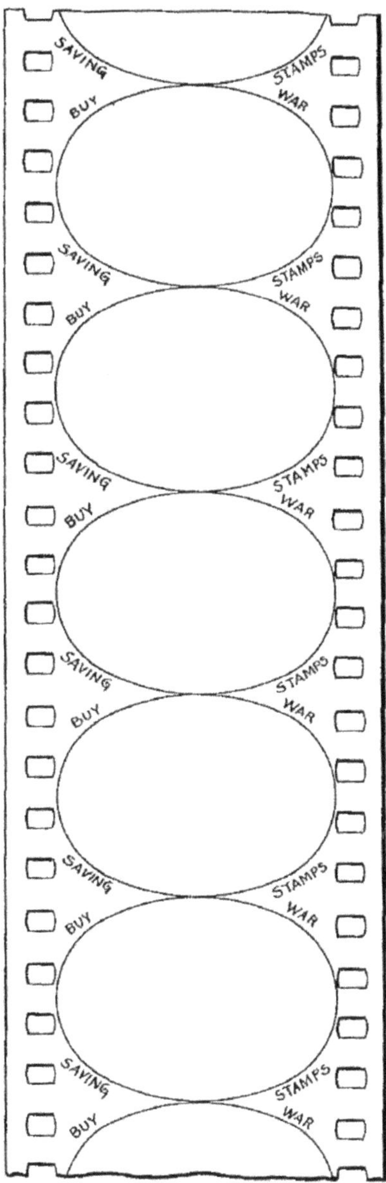

Figure 3.8. T. Hayes Hunter's advertising iris, which would have appended advertising messages to the four corners of a film during the printing process, as depicted in his patent (#1,426,567).

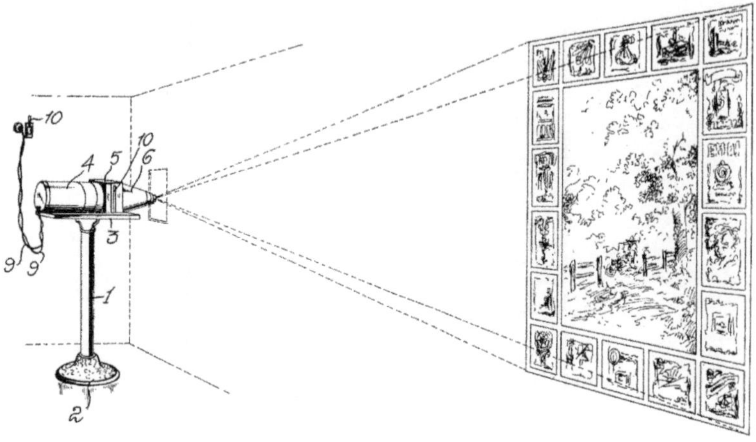

Figure 3.9. Henry A. Miedreich's Advertising Stereopticon, which electrically replicated the drop-curtain aesthetic of a central scene surrounded by advertising cards, as drawn in his patent (#1,362,274).

effectively created the earliest version of what we now know as the television advertising "bug." Unsurprisingly, no evidence exists of Hunter's patent ever being used.

In 1920, Henry A. Miedreich, of Evansville, Indiana, patented an equally problematic Advertising Stereopticon that also attempted to claim the edges of the screen.[87] Effectively, Miedreich invented a bulky, clumsy magic lantern that was little more than an overly complicated variant of the 1912 single-slide concept proposed by the manager of the New Isis Theater. Miedreich's device would have projected approximately twenty independent advertising slides simultaneously around the film. In the center of the array was a gap in which the film would unspool otherwise unmolested.[88] Miedreich assigned half of the value of his patent to Herbert W. Becker, a twenty-five-year-old projectionist in the motion-picture industry of Evansville, but there is a predictable lack of evidence for the machine's adoption.[89]

Despite the avalanche of peripheral-advertising devices available and in use in the latter 1910s, therefore, the form appears to have suffered rapid contraction and decline in the immediate postwar years. Although I cannot say for certain that the industry as a whole did not maintain a low level of activity off the radar of the trade press, very little evidence of peripheral advertising exists after 1918. Even patent records rapidly sputtered out; after the three late frame patents, the only known peripheral-advertising technology filed with the US patent office is a seat-back patent from 1927 filed by Francis T. Hayes, of Richmond Hill, New York.[90] Designed primarily to replace the need for ushers, Hayes's concept used advertisements in luminous paint both to indicate empty seats and advertise to the occupants.[91] However, nothing in Hayes's patent indicates a particularly healthy market for peripheral advertising at that date. Indeed, Hayes's New York location (in Queens) can be interpreted as further evidence that the Publicity Clock Company was effectively the only peripheral advertiser in operation at the time.

In 1926, cinema analyst Siegfried Kracauer provided a theoretical interpretation of modern American cinema architecture that also serves as a reasonable concluding statement on the history of peripheral advertising. Kracauer argued that the opulence of palatial theaters produced an atmosphere of distraction that, rather than allowing for critical thinking, overwhelmed the viewer with an overload of imagery. For Kracauer, "the stimulations of the senses succeed each other with such rapidity that there is no room left for even the slightest contemplation to squeeze in between them."[92] If Kracauer was correct, or if the drift of industry sentiment would have agreed with him, then peripheral advertising required attention in an environment that was sliding relentlessly toward an anti-intellectual aestheticism. Peripheral advertising, already suffering from the emerging hierarchy between beautification and commercialization, was relegated, in Kracauer's terms, to the realm of theoretical impossibility—a fitting end to a method that never quite fit into American exhibition culture.

BROWSING THE OPTIONS

The multiplicity of peripheral-advertising techniques—resulting in permanently visible but optionally viewable advertising—provided the point of entry for the first of two significant departures from the developing theory of cinema advertising. At the same time that trailer advocates were describing concerns about audience passivity as a problem exclusive to lantern slides, peripheral advertisers were arguing what most film studios and exhibitors had believed all along: passivity is a fantasy; there is only pleasure and the avoidance of its opposite. Peripheral advertising functioned by rigorously dividing advertising content from the entertainment (rather than trying to "slip it through") and then justifying its presence as a service or an alternative diversion. As such, these early twentieth-century inventors described viewers who were subject to their own tastes and whims and whose motivations and interpretations were therefore individual. Operating under a definition of the cinema environment as competitive rather than compulsive, the rhetorical arguments in support of peripheral advertising were radically different from those of screen advertising, despite dealing with the same topics: theory of venue, cost of adoption, and concerns about reliability.

In the same way that trailer advocates opened with an admission that slide critiques had validity (see chap. 2), peripheral advertisers concurred with the prevailing belief that onscreen advertising was "a source of more or less dissatisfaction to your patrons."[93] However, this recognizable act of market differentiation led peripheral advertisers down a much different path. Unlike slide and trailer proponents, who could move quickly from platitudes about captivity to a discussion of entertainment and receptive moods, peripheral proponents were forced to first argue that attention was merit-based. For offscreen advertisers—whose services were designed to compete, rather than blend in, with the onscreen entertainment—captivation itself was a rhetorical enemy. If the advertisers believed that the audience could not look away from the screen, that advertiser was bound, rationally, to be deeply skeptical of peripheral placement.

In order to make their products plausible, peripheral advertisers were the only cinema-oriented admen to encourage advertisers to believe that a motion-picture audience might become bored or irritated by the very films they had paid to see. Frank C. Thomas, for example, defended the usefulness of his invention by bluntly asserting that "the pictures being displayed upon the screen [might] fail to interest anyone in the audience," thus leaving plenty of opportunity for the patron's gaze to wander elsewhere.[94] Harry Verran and Alfred R. Groetz used very similar wording, claiming that the audience might voluntarily look away from the screen if "any particular portion of the picture exhibition [did] not prove of interest."[95] In short, active audiences served, for peripheral advertisers, nearly the same rhetorical function that "stillness" had served for trailer producers; it was the fundamental flaw against which their products were framed. Peripheral-advertising proponents therefore attempted to reach a theory of receptivity through an inversion: if attention was something that even an entertainment film could lose, it was not the job of the advertiser to live up to the standard set by the screen; rather, the task was to exceed the quality of the screen at its weakest moments.

However, this turn from compulsion to voluntary reading put peripheral advertisers in a precarious position; it required an admission that an audience was likely to be unhappy, thus dismantling the core assumption in all previous arguments about receptivity. Peripheral advertisers attempted to restore faith in receptivity by turning to a surprising assumption that the audience would be well aware of the possible approaches to cinema advertising and, as advertising was apparently inevitable in some form, would appreciate that peripheral advertising allowed freedom of choice. In short, audiences would recognize in peripheral advertising specifically what it did not do. Frank C. Thomas, for example, argued that his technology would create "advertising... so associated with the main screen that... the illuminated display [could not] fail to attract the eye" at some point during the show while simultaneously dispelling the belief that the audience had been "tricked into reading advertising matter when expecting other things."[96] Verran and Groetz again made nearly identical claims; they asserted that their device would avoid "the unfavorable impression... produced by having the advertisements forced upon [patrons] to the exclusion of the pictures" before launching into a list of the possible moments when a patron might choose to look at the ads (during a reel change, after having seen the entire program, while looking away to relieve eye fatigue, or when bored by the films).[97] Similar implications are obvious in the patents of Hunter ("without breaking... the thread of the drama") and Miedreich ("without interfering in the least with the moving picture").[98] In short, the rhetoric of peripheral advertisers subtly shifted the terms of debate: what was to be avoided was the compulsory viewing of something that the viewer did not enjoy—a label that could be applied to the films as well as the advertising. The increase in freedom of choice would purportedly have been noted and appreciated regardless of the advertising content.

As such, rather than implicitly arguing that the cinema was the best medium for advertising due to inherent benefits found in images and motion, peripheral advertisers saw the cinema as little more than an architectural version of print. For these inventors, the cinema was simply another medium in which the content (screen imagery rather than text) was surrounded by advertising in the margins.

It is from within this print parallel that one can see just how far peripheral advertisers were challenging established advertising theory. Frank Thomas's patent reads like a willful misinterpretation of the contemporaneous theory of psychologist Hugo Münsterberg, who declared that integrating content and advertising on the same page of a magazine produced a "sermon of bewilderment and scramble"—an uncomfortable lurching back and forth between pleasure and business, which could only lead to a "feeling of irritation."[99] Thomas, in a move Münsterberg may have approved of, asserted that the temporal integration of advertisements (slides and trailers) required this jarring change of mindset as well: it would "caus[e] one naturally to resent the drawing of one's attention so abruptly to advertising matter."[100] For both Thomas and Münsterberg, resentment was the product of psychological wrenching caused by direct juxtaposition of content and advertising. However, Münsterberg was explicitly offering a critique of multiple-address—peripheral, rather than sequential—advertising in its original print application. His concern was with the shift in the magazine industry from placing advertising in a bookend position to integrating it throughout each issue. Thomas, by contrast, left the concept of marginalia out of the equation and argued that bewilderment was a concern solely for temporal advertising. For Thomas, multiple-address advertising, at least in the cinema, was freedom of choice, not "scramble." In short, Thomas defended multiple address by recourse to exactly the same ideas that academic psychology was using to critique it.

Provided the prospect could be convinced of this radically different theory of cinema psychology, issues of practicality would again rise to prominence. Attempts to assuage cost concerns were common across these patents. Such concerns are clearest in the patents sold primarily as light fixtures. Gloss H. Fowler's light-diffuser patent provided examples of both advertiser- and exhibitor-oriented arguments. For exhibitors, the technology would lower the lighting costs of a theater, providing soft ambient light (so the theater was not "uninviting for the timid, particularly women and children") in a method that required "less electric current than the common dark shaded fixture" and offset even those costs through advertising sales. For advertisers, the appeal of cinema-advertising experimentation was the comparatively low cost per prospect; the panels were angled intentionally to be visible from almost every seat in the theater—a design decision geared entirely toward increasing the advertising value of the panels.[101] Francis T. Hayes took a similar approach to the sale of his glowing seat backs in the late 1920s, asserting that the signage would replace the cost of ushers with a profit-generating advertising device; as the signs would allow the patron to find a seat without assistance, marvelous savings could be realized by installing advertising signs made with radium paint.[102] (For obvious reasons—one sign per seat—Hayes made no claims about the cost per prospect.)

As with other forms, however, concerns about hidden costs were just as relevant to discussions of peripheral advertising. Note, for example, the frequent discussions about shoddy workmanship described in the history above. On at least seven occasions, F. H. Richardson pinpointed light leakage and other "bad practices," in one case condemning the bulk of an entire town (Topeka, Kansas). Not even lighted clocks, of which he was publicly supportive in his column, received any positive words during Richardson's long 1917 tour. Although badly made or damaged slides and trailers could draw strong condemnation, their poor quality was isolated, impacting only the advertisement itself and only for the duration that it was shown. By contrast, malfunctioning peripheral advertising offended throughout the entire show with smears of light or distracting imagery rotations. Whether or not the frequency of Richardson's public condemnation of offscreen technology influenced the decision-making of exhibitors, concerns about the operation of the object itself—whether it would break down, require frequent repairs, or need to be removed quickly after its installation—and how such issues might impact the advertiser or exhibitor were undoubtedly part of the conversation.

Beyond cost concerns, questions of reliability of the audience were as noteworthy for peripheral advertising as they were for all other methods. Indeed, questions of reliability took on much heavier importance with the breakdown of assumptions of receptivity. It is noteworthy that the above claims about being bored by the films were made by frame designers who, despite arguing for a spatial meritocracy, remained pessimistic about advertising's ability to draw attention on its own merits. As numerous inventors implied, the advertising needed, at the very least, to be associated with the main screen in order to be considered viable; as such, the positioning of the technology, even if the screen was off-limits, still implied that the audience needed to be nearly, if not entirely, forced to read advertising.

Although no further thinking along these lines is evident in the historical record, questions about the mental state of a cinema audience would have led into progressively deeper waters. As mentioned above, peripheral-advertising inventors typically avoided questions of receptivity, choosing instead to discuss the audience's plausible feeling of relief that the advertising was off-screen rather than on. However, if the ads were being perused at moments when the audience was bored or disappointed in the films on the program—so bored that they were more interested in their surroundings than the show—how would the advertising have been received? If the uniform happiness of the cinema audience could no longer be assumed, thus eliminating the theoretical "receptive mood," was there even any value to advertising in the cinema? If the best one could hope for was to harness a sense of relief, how impactful would the advertising truly be? Without the fantasy of receptivity, desire for the space may have been minimal.

Less abstract were questions about the caliber of audience that could be reached. Debates over the suitability of advertising in a medium with upper-class pretensions were already impacting the ability of onscreen advertising (both slide and trailer) to make inroads into high-end theaters. In addition to such abstract theories of what was appropriate for certain classes of audience, peripheral advertisers had to contend with actual physical limitations. The increasingly lavish design of massive first-run theaters, then cresting with the rise of the first "picture palaces," was steadily replacing bare or curtained walls with sumptuous architectural flourishes. To quote a criticism of the time, movie theaters were becoming "gaudy horrors . . . [that] stink with class."[103] The industry-wide encouragement to include such architectural flourishes even carried an implicit condemnation of direct advertising. Consider, for example, the advice of a 1918 vaudeville theater construction manual: "A theatre should represent to the less favored of its patrons something finer and more desirable than their ordinary surroundings; and to the better class, it should never present itself as inferior to the environment to which such persons are accustomed."[104]

Advertising was not a type of content one would expect in high-class environments; rather, it was the purview of commercial settings, democratic thoroughfares, and the popular press. The type of active audience then being solicited by the film industry was one that would appreciate ornamental curlicues and faux Grecian columns and turn up its collective nose at the common advertising sign. As such, peripheral advertising was also out of step with the standard-bearers of exhibition; the periphery was becoming the venue of ostentation and beautification rather than technological gimmickry.

On the rare occasion that advocates attempted to deal with such concerns in print, most responded with clunky or specious arguments about the appeal of their inventions. Frank C. Thomas, possibly in an attempt to overcome the cynicism of the rest of his patent, included an overzealous claim about the appeal of quality advertising, arguing that patrons could "look at the advertisement several times . . . [and] thoroughly assimilate the idea" if they found the ad particularly interesting or amusing.[105] Kineto and General Sales even went so far as to imply that their projecting clocks were attractive enough to draw business on their own. Kineto called its clock "a decided and distinct attraction" for the theater opting to use it. General Sales called its Wonder Clock a "crowd puller" and praised its "startling," looming size as a novelty that would, itself, attract a crowd.[106] In a surprising turn, Kineto head George Willens even adopted "compulsion" as a key description of his clock, claiming that his invention "compels one to see an advertisement when looking at the time on [the] clock."[107] One can make interesting theoretical extrapolations from this claim: Perhaps compulsion via a useful object was forgivable? Willens, however, provided no theorizing beyond the tantalizing use of the word.

In sum, patent inventors took a wholly different approach to the debate—not just defending cinema audiences as desirable and reachable, but defending advertising as being a part of the modern entertainment environment that could enter a venue without necessarily being prejudged as an unwanted intrusion. The choice to rigidly separate the theatrical sites of art and commerce into screen and margin paradoxically allowed these men to describe the two in fundamentally similar experiential terms. The advertisements at the margins became potential alternative diversions—something else to see if one was inclined to appreciate one's surroundings or if the screen failed to entertain. Implicitly conceiving of cinema advertising not in the temporal terms assumed by others, but as a venue designed around personal selection, these inventors had a notion that cinema was experientially parallel to magazines and billboards. They argued that, though one may not have any control over the progress of the main entertainment (no ability to turn the page or, in a vehicle metaphor, skip past the less beautiful pieces of landscape), one could at least look to the advertising for alternative material.

Though they struggled to defend this idea on a practical level, they provide evidence of the breadth of theorizing about cinema advertising in the wake of slides and purportedly captive audiences.

CASE STUDY: THE PERSISTENCE OF TIME AND THE PUBLICITY CLOCK COMPANY

In the arena of offscreen technologies, the topic of greatest historical concern is not modernization, professionalization, or any other shift in response to struggles. There are virtually no known companies that successfully navigated industrial challenges. In fact, so little information exists after 1918 that it is reasonable to assume that peripheral advertising, as a whole, was effectively stillborn. As such, the most useful question to ask with a case study is how and why a particular company avoided the ubiquitous problem of nearly instant collapse. With that goal in mind, the Publicity Clock Company, which had a far longer life span than any other known peripheral-advertising company, is the only reasonable choice.

Publicity Clock was the earliest of the third wave of advertising clock makers. Opening for business in 1914, Publicity was one of numerous small companies formed by New Yorker John Upton Barr specifically to sell a device he had invented (alongside such companies as the Handy Pail Company and the Locking-Chain Corporation).[108] Publicity survived into the 1930s, offering its services in various locations and under various names, including the Sidewalk Ad Service and the Ad-Traction Phantom Clock. Despite this long life, Publicity had a complicated birth, no notable early successes, and a dysfunctional relationship behind the scenes. Publicity's first two years are a humorous and shocking odyssey through stock options, infighting, and untimely death.

The company was formed by Barr (president) and his financial backer Charles Rose (treasurer) in 1914; original secretary Fred

Weiss (a local attorney) was replaced later that year by Leo J. Wertheimer (previous line of work unknown), who purchased Weiss's one-third of the company.[109] Neither Barr nor Rose appears to have had much interest in day-to-day operations, as the entire company was up for sale by mid-1915. In early August, sixty-four-year-old Louis Neuberger (a recent widower, wealthy business owner, and stock trader whose interest in the company is difficult to fathom) purchased the stakes of both Barr and Rose and took over the positions of both president and treasurer.[110] It is unclear whether either of the founders retained any financial stake in the company or a position on the board of directors.

The acquisition of the bulk of the company by Neuberger led rapidly to messy infighting between Neuberger and continuing secretary Wertheimer. A hilarious flurry of official memos documents their deteriorating relationship. On August 24, 1915, Neuberger, as president, addressed a letter to the company rescinding his consent for the payment of Wertheimer's salary; as Neuberger was also the treasurer, this was effectively a unilateral firing of Wertheimer from his position.[111] Four days later, at the end of the business week, Wertheimer sent an official letter to the treasurer (Neuberger) demanding his week's pay and declaring the communication from the president (also Neuberger) unofficial and illegal.[112] That same day, in a delightful tit for tat, Wertheimer (as stockholder) wrote a letter to the company likewise rescinding his consent for the payment of *Neuberger's* salary. Wertheimer followed this with a third letter (as secretary) addressed to Neuberger (as employee) informing him that his "employment by the Company . . . is hereby terminated." In short, Wertheimer, whose status as secretary gave his letter official weight, unilaterally fired Neuberger as well.[113]

By this point, technically neither Neuberger nor Wertheimer, representing the company's entire upper management, had official consent to receive their weekly pay. Although Neuberger appears to have won this battle with access to the checkbook,

Wertheimer, as late as September 7, was still demanding pay for the week (having reduced his demand to include only Monday and Tuesday, apparently accepting that, for at least Wednesday through Saturday, he had been well and truly fired).[114] At some point during these two weeks, the dispute went public; Neuberger, in a letter to potential investor H. B. Hale, described Wertheimer as "a partner who has neither ability nor principle."[115] Hale's response to this is unknown, though his decision not to purchase a stake in the company is telling.

As neither could completely fire the other, the two men spent ten days—September first through tenth—exchanging buyout offers.[116] The negotiations culminated with a meeting of the board of directors and a furious letter from Wertheimer in which he described Neuberger—in a letter addressed to Neuberger—as "a very questionable and doubtful character" who "has . . . [not familiarized] himself with such [technical] details of the business as would qualify him to take charge."[117] By the end of the day, Wertheimer admitted defeat, presumably having agreed to sell his stock, and submitted letters turning over his company key and multiple pieces of mechanical equipment.[118] The split remained ugly, however. In late October, Neuberger was still sending threatening letters to Wertheimer; the $2,000 worth of preferred stock still held as collateral against Wertheimer's promissory note were to be sent to auction unless immediate payment was received.[119] Wertheimer, apparently disinterested in further association with the company, allowed the threat to be consummated. The auction went as laughably as one might expect at this point. The entire lot of twenty shares sold for fifteen dollars—less than 1 percent of the estimated value.[120]

However, with Wertheimer ejected from the company, misfortune did not abate. In December, salesman Harry Smith was hired and almost immediately began embezzling; when his case went to court, Smith was found guilty of not only theft but also, unexpectedly, of desertion of the US Army. In the beginning of

February, Smith's history of malfeasance resulted in the petty crime becoming front-page news in the *New York Daily Sun*.[121] Less than two weeks later, Louis Neuberger died of heart failure. Whether or not this was brought on by recent stress is unknown, but the end result was that the company wound up in the hands of his twenty-five-year-old son, Leslie L. Neuberger—a man who apparently had not spent a day with the company prior to his father's death.[122] After a tumultuous first two years, one would be forgiven for expecting the young Neuberger to set fire to the company storeroom or get swallowed up by a freak sinkhole. However, in a turn of events perhaps even more shocking, he appears to have piloted the company capably for the next twenty years.[123] Leslie's much more successful brother, Roy (a stock trader and art patron of great repute), remembered Leslie as a man who "for quite a while . . . earned a very good living running an early advertising firm our father had purchased."[124]

Louis Neuberger's prior wealth notwithstanding, then, it is difficult to claim that Publicity survived because it was filled with especially competent or congenial businessmen. There is no evidence other than persistence to indicate that business went well in the company's early days. We must therefore look for other elements to explain Publicity's success. To my mind, there are six elements of note—four of them productive (though not necessarily ethical) business decisions and two simply fortuitous. On the business side, the type, quality, and price of the company's materials were all as good as or better than those of its contemporaries, and its status as a patent holder was leveraged as a market tactic. On the fortuitous side, its location and a particular trade press article both boosted its chances of success.

After a discussion of the company's many internal failings, it is only fair to begin with the elements over which it had control. For starters, the machine itself was in no way anomalous for the time; just as most of the third-wave clocks did, it used a round projected image with the advertisement contained within the dial of the clock and an automatically moving magazine of eight or twelve slides with a rotation every thirty seconds.[125] The hands of the clock were attached to the outer ring, rather than poking out from a central location (as they do in a standard clock), and the integration of clockface and advertisement was pleasantly free of conflict and obstruction. In addition, the machine was compact and easy to install; weighing ten pounds, in a box of twelve by twenty by seven and one-eighth inches, it was intended to be placed on a shelf high up one wall, plugged in, and left alone for days on end.[126] Although I have neither the physical artifacts nor the technical knowledge with which to determine, by comparison, if the product was in any way superior, it at the very least did not suffer from anomalous problems like the Wonder Clock (which could hold only one advertisement) or Wetzler and Ornstein's clock (which had a complicated belt system). In short, the device was in line with practical and popular design sensibilities.

Cost and profit estimates would also have allowed for market positioning equal to or better than the company's competitors. Although Publicity's hundred-dollar sale price falls on the high end of known values, its fifteen-dollar manufacturing cost would have allowed for significant price-cutting without selling at a loss.[127] An estimated dealer profit of fifteen dollars per week indicates a minimum slot rate slightly below the two-dollar price suggested by others (presuming the dealer was entitled to most or all of the income from a clock purchased outright).[128] This pricing also appears to have been a comfortable overcharge, as the slots were still being rented profitably twenty years later at roughly the same rate: $1.25 per week per slot.[129] As such, both the product and the financials either equaled or exceeded what the company's peers could offer, with room for further price breaks.

The slides themselves also provide some evidence for why Publicity may have succeeded where competitors faltered. Publicity's slides had a unique flower-petal shape designed to allow the clock dial to project around the advertisement without

Figure 3.10. An advertising trade card portraying the suggested positioning and appearance of a Publicity Clock. The increasing class consciousness of the developing theater field is implied by portraying a Publicity Clock in a mid-tier nickelodeon theater (minimal musical accompaniment via a piano trio, minimal decor, and showing a generic Western) rather than an urban palace. Author's personal collection.

obstruction from either clips or the slide's own rough edgework. A contract would thus have guaranteed not simply that the space on a clock would be filled, but also that the advertiser would be purchasing their slide directly from Publicity itself—a secondary revenue stream with no third-party competition. Aesthetically, its copy work replicated many of the ideas popular in magic-lantern advertising—predominantly white figure work with "brilliant colors" added after printing and minimal word counts designed for quick impact.[130] Using an image that was often generic (removed and reused from design to design) and typically placing merchant address information at the bottom, Publicity would have been able to quickly convince advertisers already comfortable with lantern slides that its clock was capable of doing exactly the same work in exactly the same way—with cheap, catalog-selected slides containing brief custom copy and the only difference being projection on the wall rather than on the screen. Aside from Publicity slides' roundness, their aesthetic was likewise normative.

Publicity's success may be due, in part, to aggressive patent control. As an experienced professional inventor, Barr was conscious of the financial importance of his patents. He once filed suit against the enormous American Tobacco Company for infringement of his design for tobacco cans, seeking either $20,000 or $20,000,000 in damages, depending on which report you believe (the former being the most likely).[131] The entirety of Publicity's (minor) national advertising was geared toward patent control. In August and September of 1915, as other third-wave clock competitors were arising, Publicity took out two small advertisements in *Moving Picture World* declaring "WARNING: The Publicity Clock Company . . . are the sole patentees and owners of the Automatic Advertising Clock. . . . Exhibitors and others are hereby cautioned against the use of devices infringing our patent rights."[132] The New York City market was absolutely central to the advertising clock; nearly every known device was invented and sold from that location. As such, if Publicity's patent pressure had any impact, all but one of its competitors (the Chicago-based Kineto Machine Company) would have been under direct attack on their home soil. Additionally, any dealer or theater ordering a clock would have been almost certain to be ordering it from New

York City anyway; if patent claims held sway, a buyer may not have bothered risking an order from a different company.

This attempt at patent control leads us to the first of the two elements of chance that likely boosted the coffers of the company. Success is, at times, a result of a market grown on the backs of one's competitors. Even if Publicity did not actively steal the business of its competitors with these patent claims, it is reasonable to assume that the New York location offered more opportunities for quick sales than any other location in the country. With numerous competitors all selling projecting clocks in the region, a New York exhibitor was less likely to ask why than to ask which one. Indeed, Roy R. Neuberger's remembrance, though likely slanted by firsthand knowledge of his brother Leslie's business, is telling; projecting clocks were "an advertising medium with a raison d'être at that time in history: all the theaters had clocks that were lit up in the darkness."[133] New York City may have been the most competitive environment, but the quantity of clocks visible on the market likely helped to develop healthier conditions, less hostile exhibitors, and more receptive audiences.

Finally, and perhaps most importantly, F. H. Richardson, whether intentionally or not, gave Publicity a boost in early 1916. Richardson's article on February 5 in favor of advertising clocks ("where the theater manager desires to show advertisements of local merchants [an advertising clock] is *the* way to do it") was titled "Publicity Clocks."[134] Although he mentioned no clock makers by name within the body of the article, Publicity was the only company that ever described its product with the phrase that gave the article its title. Thus, any exhibitor whose interest had been piqued by the article would likely have sought and discovered the Publicity Clock Company first. Even the date of the article was a stroke of luck, arriving just under two weeks before Leslie Neuberger inherited the company. Richardson's testimonial—whether paid, friendly, or unintentional—would have been a business booster timed nearly to the day of the new boss's arrival.

In the absence of further archival material, additional assertions about the latter years and continuing strengths of the Publicity Clock Company are impossible to make. However, with the long-term success of Publicity, advertising clocks, like slides and trailers, persisted in cinema theaters long past the transitional era and were, for some filmgoers (at least in the state of New York), a recognizable and regular element of their cinema experiences. Thus, although purveyors of peripheral technologies fared worse as a group than nearly all other cinema advertisers during the silent era, such products and theories were culturally significant and continued to influence cinema-advertising debates in New York City, the most prominent of locations, throughout the first half of the twentieth century.

IN THE WINGS

Despite minimal historical evidence about the actual use of the objects, the concept of peripheral advertising is vital to our understanding of silent-era advertising debates. It provides our only direct evidence of attempts to respond to concerns about commercial breaks in ways other than simply removing all consumer-goods advertising from the theater and provides us with the most tantalizingly unfulfilled glimpses of how the cinema experience might have been different. The motion-picture theater, still connected to (at least the perception of) lower-class and immigrant audiences, could have metamorphosed into a circus-like riot of lighted entertainment and advertising elements—a technological rather than architectural wonderland—with the film itself privileged only by its central placement. The decision to pursue a high-class ambiance foreclosed this possibility just as it was being conceived. However, the existence of the idea and the implication that it was incompatible with high-class cinema reveal that "class" and "advertising" were drifting more firmly into separate spheres in early twentieth-century American media.

Peripheral advertising also adds to our growing understanding of the regional volatility of exhibition practices. Although the possibility remains open that peripheral advertising was more uniform that we know, the evidence presented in this chapter indicates that these concepts were nearly ubiquitous in some areas and unknown in others. The states of New York and Minnesota and the city of Topeka were heavily invested in peripheral advertising for a time; most 1910s cinemagoers in those regions would have considered peripheral advertising to be either normal or a decidedly high-profile exhibition fad. In cities with a prominent inventor, like Evansville or Tacoma, the idea might have taken on the appearance of an interesting local novelty. Meanwhile, there is virtually no evidence of such clocks and signs in the American southeast.

In short, peripheral advertising was simultaneously awkwardly unfashionable (immobile and literally left of center) and progressive. It would take decades for the active audience to become second nature in media and advertising research. The first twenty years of internet-era advertising harbors numerous echoes of these early practices, from framing via banners and long-tail stacks of web links to the advertising bugs on digital television and the advertisements rising out of an elapsed-time bar on YouTube (as if the ghost of Whitaker were still happily telling us to "Eat Smith's Good Eats"). Its existence vividly displays the subtlety of American advertising thinking in the early silent era—and, by extension, in the formative years of all media. While there were significant historical barriers to its adoption, including the cultural pretensions of the film studios and the swelling opposition to cinema advertising caused by onscreen methods, peripheral-advertising techniques provide evidence of the complexity of theorizing advertising in the wings, whether in movie theaters or the media of the future.

NOTES

1. Epes Winthrop Sargent, "Advertising for Exhibitors: Advertising Slides," *MPW*, August 7, 1915, 987.

2. Indeed, it is worth noting that offscreen advertising theory is the space in which the history of indirect advertising has the clearerst influence on the development of direct-advertising tactics. For a staunch opponent of all forms of onscreen advertising, the concept of screen hijacking provided a convenient means for Sargent, and others, to critique both indirect and direct advertising simultaneously. Offscreen advertisers were thus providing an alternative not only to slides and trailers, but also to product placement and industrial film.

3. Two-Page Display Ad, *Motography*, May 2, 1914, 30–31. This advertisement was actually for an automated candy machine installed on chair backs; though this bit of rhetoric perfectly suits the discussion in this chapter, the object itself begs for a study of the history of theater concessions and marketing decisions. See also Display Ad, *MPW*, February 4, 1911, 226.

4. See chapter 2 of William Leach, *Land of Desire: Merchants, Power, and the Rise of a New American Culture* (New York: Vintage Books, 1993).

5. It is also plausible that wartime materials shortages and restrictions had deleterious effects on the production and installation of these devices. Although demand vastly outstripped supply for resources like iron, steel, and lead, it is impossible to estimate whether or not priorities decisions by the War Industries Board had any impact at the individual level. According to all published accounts of the board's activities, the reduction of available materials was reportedly offset by requiring large manufacturers to radically reduce the number of models of each product (thereby reducing the amount of idle material used in showroom models). See John Maurice Clark, *The Costs of the World War to the American People* (New Haven, CT: Yale University Press, 1931); Bernard M. Baruch, *American Industry in the War: A Report of the War Industries Board* (New York: Prentice-Hall, 1941); and Robert D. Cuff, *The War Industries Board: Business-Government Relations During World War I* (Baltimore, MD: Johns Hopkins University Press, 1973), 201–204.

6. "Interesting Nebraska Theater Jottings," *MPW*, March 17, 1917, 1811.

7. It is plausible that seat-back advertising was in use during the 1910s. However, I have turned up no evidence of this between 1908 and 1926.

8. William Paul, *When Movies Were Theater: Architecture, Exhibition, and the Evolution of American Film* (New York: Columbia University Press, 2016), 232, 248–249.

9. F. H. Richardson, *Motion Picture Handbook: A Guide for Managers and Operators of Motion Picture Theatres*, 3rd ed. (New York City: World Photographic, 1916), 183.

10. "Kind of Screen to Use," *MPN*, August 28, 1915, 120.

11. There is a surprisingly narrow distinction between these two approaches. In both cases, one visual object surrounded another: for frames, advertising surrounded the movie screen; for clocks (usually), the clock dial surrounded the advertising. With the integration of the ads into the dial and the obliteration of any potential boundary lines between dial and advertisement, most clock advertisements functioned in a way similar to product placement; the advertisement was part of the focal point, but one did not necessarily need it to comprehend the scene. Frame technologies, which always had visible dividing lines, did not link the advertising as clearly to the scene on the screen.

12. Richardson, *Motion Picture Handbook*, 635–637.

13. Gloss H. Fowler, Patent 1,054,759. Frank C. Thomas, Patent 1,252,629 and 1,200,399.

14. Harry Verran and Alfred R. Groetz, Patent 1,321,863; "Richardson Visits Chicago and St. Louis," *MPW*, May 25, 1918, 1147; and US Draft, Minnesota, Minneapolis, September 12, 1918, Serial Number 985.

15. "Richardson Riding Eastward," *MPW*, July 14, 1917, 246.

16. F. H. Richardson, "Projection Department: From Denver," *MPW*, July 27, 1912, 348; Henry A. Miedreich, Patent 1,362,274; and US Bureau of the Census, Thirteenth Census of the United States, 1910, Indiana, Vandeburg, Evansville City, Sheet 4B, Line 51.

17. T. Hayes Hunter, Patent 1,426,567.

18. The concept persists as one of the most common ways to advertise or market without seeming pushy. See, for example, the online long-tail concept in which each product page includes a list of links to products "also of interest." Chris Anderson, *The Long Tail: Why the Future of Business Is Selling Less of More* (New York: Hyperion, 2006).

19. Display Ad, *MPW*, October 9, 1915, 354. See also "Richardson Crosses Pine Tree State," *MPW*, October 13, 1917, 223.

20. Richard B. Smith, Patent 813,836; John U. Barr, Patent 1,146,839; A. J. Thereault, Patent 1,275,791; and George Willens, Patent 1,292,196.

21. Little Acorns Antiques, "Spotlight on an Object," accessed December 16, 2017, https://web.archive.org/web/20150214091632/http://www.littleacornsantiques.com/spotlight-on-an-object.html.

22. US Bureau of the Census, Thirteenth Census of the United States, 1910, New York, Ulster, Saugerties Township, Sheet 8B, Line 84.

23. Norman T. Whitaker, Patent 1,329,216. Although there is no evidence that Whitaker ever sold a single apparatus, it is likely that he would have mass-produced stock strips for one-reel, two-reel, and five-reel films, perforating them again later to add advertising.

24. See, among many examples, Catherine Parsons Smith, *Making Music in Los Angeles: Transforming the Popular* (Berkeley: University of California Press, 2007), 76.

25. Harry L. Broad and Frederick H. Orcutt, Patent 901,065; Samuel W. Van Nostran, Patent 741,004; Jerome W. May, Patent 769,868; and Van Nostran, Patent 785,987.

26. John A. Olson and Perry D. Sherwin, Patent 784,590.

27. S. W. Van Nostran Co., *Davison's Minneapolis City Directory* (Minneapolis: Minneapolis Directory Co., 1906): 1921. Untitled News Note, *PI*, August 17, 1904, 35.

28. See Samuel Leveen, Patent 757,403; and Eugene B. Cooke and Chauncey O. Lewis, Patent 1,108,066. New Yorker George J. Richardson was a one-man avalanche of trash-can patents in the early twentieth century; see Patent 1,364,209 (filed September 3, 1919) among many others.

29. Smith, Patent 813,836.

30. Ferdinand Wetzler and Max Ornstein, Patent 812,105.

31. Minneapolis featured three seat-back patents (Olson and Sherwin and a pair from Van Notran). Another seat back was from Alpena, Michigan (Broad and Orcutt). Leveen's waste receptacle was from Anderson, Indiana.

32. "The Airdome Season," *MPW*, April 29, 1911, 934.

33. Sargent, "Advertising for Exhibitors: Plenty of Poster Space," *MPW*, June 7, 1913, 1022.

34. "Puts Ads on Walls," *MPW*, January 23, 1915, 550. It is plausible that this was actually the Imperial Theater in Ottawa, Canada.

35. Michael Quinn, "Distribution, the Transient Audiences, and the Transition to the Feature Film," *Cinema Journal* 40, no. 2 (Winter 2001): 35–56.

36. For further information, see Maggie Valentine, *The Show Starts on the Sidewalk: An Architectural History of the Movie Theatre* (New Haven, CT: Yale University Press, 1994), 23–24.

37. Fowler, Patent 1,054,759.

38. "Deaths," *Tacoma Times*, February 11, 1914, 8.

39. F. H. Richardson, "Projection Department," *MPW*, April 6, 1912, 44.

40. F. H. Richardson, "Projection Department: From Denver," *MPW*, July 27, 1912, 348. Automatically rotating slide projectors for advertising

were already available; at least three were patented between 1910 and 1917. Bert C. Ferguson, Patent 946,500; Jacob W. Haag, Patent 1,004,163; and John W. Billings, Patent 1,321,003.

41. Display Ad, *MPW*, April 12, 1913, 197.

42. Display Ad, *MPW*, April 12, 1913, 197; Jacob H. Genter, Patents 1,101,429 and 1,147,501; and US Bureau of the Census, Thirteenth Census of the United States, 1910, New York, Orange, 1st District, Sheet 16B, Line 79.

43. See the following additional display ads for the Announceoscope's slow drift from prominent product to "Also ask about our Announceoscope": *MPW*, April 19, 1913, 297; *MPW*, May3, 1913, 513; *MPW*, May 10, 1913, 631; *MPW*, May 17, 1913, 747; *MPW*, May 31, 1913, 972; *MPW*, June 7, 1913, 1073; *MPW*, June 14, 1913, 1171; *MPW*, June 21, 1913, 1307; *MovPN*, July 5, 1913, 42; *ET*, July 12, 1913, 26; and *MovPN*, July 12, 1913, 33.

44. "A Picture Theater Timepiece," *MPW*, January 31, 1914, 554.

45. Display Ad, *MPW*, August 23, 1913, 867.

46. "The 'Wonder' Clock," *MPN*, December 27, 1913, 24.

47. Display Ad, *MPW*, November 21, 1914, 1161; and Display Ad, *MPW*, December 5, 1914, 1413.

48. Display Ad (Publicity Clock), *MPW*, August 14, 1915, 1246; Leo J. Wertheimer to Jerome L. Danzig, August 2, 1915, private collection; Barr, Patent 1,146,839; *R. L. Polk & Co's 1915 Trow New York Copartnership and Corporation Directory Boroughs of Manhattan and Bronx* 63 (New York: R. L. Polk/Trow, August 1915), 1125; Display Ad (Standard), *MPW*, October 9, 1915, 354; and Harry Miller, Patent 1,137,512 (probable Wonder Clock patent).

49. Display Ad, *MPW*, July 24, 1915, 748; and Abraham Steinberg, Patent 1,172,844.

50. Thereault, Patent 1,275,791; and *Motography*, March 17, 1917, 560.

51. Display Ad (Kineto eight-slot version), *MPW*, July 24, 1915, 748; Willens, Patent 1,292,196 (Kineto twelve-slot version); "The Publicity Clock" pamphlet (eight-slot version), PBC; "New Publicity Clock Placed on Market for Picture Theaters," *Billboard*, November 18, 1916, 51; and Thereault, Patent 1,275,791 (Kalck eight-slot version).

52. Display Ad, *MPW*, October 9, 1915, 354; and Display Ad, *PI*, February 1, 1917, 102.

53. "Kineto Mach. Co. v. Ugland," *Northwestern Reporter* 177 (St. Paul, MN: West Publishing, 1920), 1018–1019. Louis Neuberger to H. B. Hale (undated 1915), private collection.

54. Display Ad, *PI*, February 1, 1917, 102.

55. The ad offered an estimate of $75 weekly profit from a $500 investment, indicating that Publicity expected each clock to pull in approximately $15 per week for the dealer alone. Classified Ad, *Cosmopolitan* (July 1919): 165.

56. "Advertising Clocks in Ontario," *MPW*, January 13, 1917, 261.

57. Display Ads, *MPW*, April 12, 1913, 197; and *MPW*, October 9, 1915, 354.

58. On March 2, 1932, a Brooklyn drugstore signed a contract for a year of service at the Graham Theater at $1.25 per week. On April 6, 1938, the Glen Morris Meat Market signed a contract for sixteen weeks of service at the Farrell Theater for $1.50 per week. On September 8, 1938, J. Barker signed a contract for twenty-eight weeks of service at the Echo Theater, also at the rate of $1.50 per week. All in author's private collection.

59. F. H. Richardson, "Projection Department: Publicity Clock," *MPW*, February 5, 1916, 774.

60. "Indiana Notes," *MPW*, March 4, 1916, 1515; and Display Ad, *MPW*, July 15, 1916, 550.

61. Display Ad, *PI*, February 1, 1917, 102.

62. "Kineto Mach. Co. v. Ugland," 1018–1019.

63. "Theater Equipment Directory: Clocks, Advertising and Screen," *Exhibitors Trade Review* 26 (December 1925): 128.

64. Hunter, Patent 1,426,567.

65. "Richardson Riding Eastward," *MPW*, July 14, 1917, 246.

66. Thomas, Patent 1,252,629 and 1,200,399.

67. "Thirty-Seven Guests of Nicholas Power Company," *MPN*, September 18, 1915, 139. Vedder formed the United Exhibitors' Advertising Corporation of Wilmington, Delaware, specifically to sell the device, though no actual sales are known. *Standard Corporation Service, July 1916* (New York: Standard Statistics Co, 1916), 104; and *Directory of Directors in the City of New York, 1917–1918* (New York: Directory of Directors Co, 1917), 753.

68. Sargent, "Advertising for Exhibitors: Lighted Announcements," *MPW*, July 22, 1916, 629.

69. "Richardson Lets Out a Link," *MPW*, April 21, 1917, 415; and "Richardson Going Strong," *MPW*, April 28, 1917, 596–597. As these two descriptions are similar and geographically near to one another, I assume they are both examples of a single as-yet-unknown product from the region.

70. "Richardson Reaches Old Home Town," *MPW*, July 28, 1917, 650.

71. "Richardson Visits Chicago and St. Louis," *MPW*, May 25, 1918, 1147.

72. S. L. Rothapfel, "First Aid to Theater Men," *Motography*, July 8, 1916, 77–78.

73. "Richardson Going Strong," *MPW*, April 28, 1917, 595–597.

74. Ibid., 596–597.

75. "Richardson Crosses Pine Tree State," *MPW*, October 13, 1917, 223.

76. "Richardson Lets Out a Link," 415; "Richardson Riding Eastward," 246; and "Richardson Reaches Old Home Town," 650.

77. "Richardson Visits Chicago and St. Louis," 1147.

78. "Richardson Crosses Pine Tree State," 223.

79. "Richardson Visits Chicago and St. Louis," 1147.

80. "Puts Ads on Walls," *MPW*, January 23, 1915, 550.

81. Paul, *When Movies Were Theater*, 202, 210.

82. Richardson, *Motion Picture Handbook*, 180.

83. Ibid., 169–170.

84. Ibid., 639. See also Paul, *When Movies Were Theater*, 87.

85. Verran and Groetz, Patent 1,321,863.

86. Hunter, Patent 1,426,567.

87. US Bureau of the Census, Thirteenth Census of the United States, 1910, Indiana, Vandeburg, Evansville City, Sheet 4B, Line 51.

88. Miedreich, Patent 1,362,274.

89. US Draft, Indiana, Evansville, June 5, 1917, Number 155. At the time of the draft, Herbert W. Becker was working for Cook's Electric Park Theater, though it is unclear if he remained there in 1920.

90. Though difficult to corroborate, Francis was likely the twenty-four-year-old son of a lifelong billposter named Dennis Hayes. US Bureau of the Census, Fifteenth Census of the United States, 1930, New York, Queens, Richmond Hill, Sheet 6A, Line 3.

91. Hayes, Patent 1,728,731. Hayes's phosphorous ad tactic—or a knockoff—was put into use at least once, with disastrous results. Hal Hodes, on behalf of the Thayer Advertising Agency, signed two-year contracts with theaters resulting in a total of 225,323 seats in 1928, at the rate of one dollar per seat per year. Hodes asserted that Thayer had erroneously claimed to have contracts with multiple national advertisers—including the Coca-Cola Company, the Wrigley Chewing Gum Company, and the Ward Baking Company—in hand and won a suit for unpaid commission: $104,900 for $450,000 worth of contracted space. "Judgment of $104,900 Against Agency," *Fourth Estate*, March 5, 1932, 42; and Kerry Segrave, *Product Placement in Hollywood Films: A History* (Jefferson, NC: McFarland, 2004), 11–12.

92. Siegfried Kracauer, "Cult of Distraction: On Berlin's Picture Palaces," trans. Tom Levin, *New German Critique* 40 (Winter 1987), 91–96.

93. "The Publicity Clock."

94. Thomas, Patent 1,252,629.

95. Verran and Groetz, Patent 1,321,863.

96. Thomas, Patent 1,252,629.

97. Verran and Groetz, Patent 1,321,863.

98. Miedreich, Patent 1,362,274; and Hunter, Patent 1,426,567.

99. Hugo Münsterberg, "Social Sins in Advertising," in *Psychology and Social Sanity* (Garden City, NY: Doubleday, Page, 1914), 243–244.

100. Thomas, Patent 1,252,629.

101. Fowler, Patent 1,054,759.

102. Hayes, Patent 1,728,731.

103. Valentine, *The Show Starts on the Sidewalk,* 41.

104. Ibid., 21.

105. Thomas, Patent 1,252,629.

106. Display Ad, *MPW,* July 24, 1915, 748; and Display Ad, *MPW,* August 23, 1913, 867.

107. Willens, Patent 1,218,607.

108. Barr, Patent 1,146,839; Fred Weiss to Publicity Clock Co. Inc., August 17, 1914; Display Ad, *MPW,* August 14, 1915, 1246; and *Directory of Directors in the City of New York* (New York: Directory of Directors Company, 1915), 34. In addition to Barr's inclusion in the early list of officers, his patent number is etched into an extant clock from the Publicity Clock Company, currently held by a private collector. All company papers in this section are held by private collectors, except where noted.

109. *1915 Trow General Directory of New York City Embracing the Boroughs of Manhattan and the Bronx* (New York: R. L. Polk / Trow, March 1915), 1494; *1915 Trow New York Copartnership and Corporation Directory Boroughs of Manhattan and Bronx* 63 (New York: R. L. Polk/Trow, August 1915), 839; and L. J. Wertheimer to Jerome L. Danzig, August 2, 1915.

110. L. J. Wertheimer to Jerome L. Danzig, August 2, 1915. The address in this letter is a typographical error. Jerome J. Danzig was a thirty-five-year-old New York stockbroker. "Roy R. Neuberger Dies at 107; Applied a Stock-Trader's Acumen to Art," *New York Times,* December 25, 2010, A27; and Roy R. Neuberger, *So Far, So Good: The First 94 Years* (New York: John Wiley & Sons, 1997), 3–10.

111. Louis Neuberger to Publicity Clock Co. Inc., August 24, 1915.

112. L. J. Wertheimer to Publicity Clock Co., August 28, 1915.

113. L. J. Wertheimer to Publicity Clock Co., August 28, 1915; and L. J. Wertheimer to Louis Neuberger, August 28, 1915.

114. L. J. Wertheimer to Louis Neuberger, September 7, 1915.

115. Louis Neuberger to H. B. Hale, undated 1915.

116. Louis Neuberger, signed statement, September 1, 1915; and Louis Neuberger to unknown recipient, September 10, 1915.

117. L. J. Wertheimer to Louis Neuberger, September 10, 1915.

118. Two signed statements by L. J. Wertheimer, both dated September 10, 1915.

119. Louis Neuberger to L. J. Wertheimer, October 21, 1915.

120. "Securities Sold at Auction," *New York Sun*, October 28, 1915, 10. See also *Standard Corporation Service, Daily Revised, Vol. 4, August 1 to October 31, 1915* (New York: Standard Statistics Company, 1915), 1202.

121. "Prisoner a Deserter," *New York Daily Sun*, February 2, 1916, 1.

122. "Mr. Louis Neuberger," *New York Herald*, February 13, 1916, 13. Leslie's business card lists him as president and treasurer, like his father. A December 1916 clothing bill from the Rogers Peet Company indicates that Leslie was receiving mail at the company address on this date.

123. He appears as company president and treasurer in New York City directories through 1923, the last year for which I have data; typically no other officers are listed. Leslie was still receiving mail from his insurance company at the company address as late as 1932 (Henry Sobel & Co. to Leslie L. Neuberger, August 6, 1932). In the 1940 US Census, however, he is listed as a real estate broker. Sixteenth Census of the United States, New York, Westchester, New Rochelle, Sheet 7A, Line 17.

124. R. Neuberger, *So Far, So Good*, 10.

125. Display Ad, *MPW*, August 23, 1913, 867; "The Publicity Clock"; and "New Publicity Clock Placed on Market for Picture Theaters," *Billboard*, November 18, 1916, 51.

126. "The Publicity Clock."

127. L. J. Wertheimer to Jerome L. Danzig, August 2, 1915.

128. Classified Ad, *Cosmopolitan* (July 1919): 165.

129. On March 2, 1932, a Brooklyn drugstore signed a contract for a year of service at the Graham Theater at $1.25 per week; copy of contract in author's personal collection.

130. "The Publicity Clock."

131. "Sue Tobacco Trust," *Richmond Palladium and Sun-Telegram*, February 13, 1910, 1; and "$20,000,000 Tobacco Suit Filed," *New York Tribune*, February 14, 1910, 12.

132. Display Ads, *MPW*, August 14, 1915, 1246; and *MPW*, September 11, 1915, 1899.

133. R. Neuberger, *So Far, So Good*, 10.

134. F. H. Richardson, "Publicity Clock," *MPW*, February 5, 1916, 774.

FOUR

THE CINEMA WANTS TO BE FREE

Parks, Tickets, and Advertiser-Funded Cinema

> Think of it! People will pack your house day after day, and night after night, because it costs them nothing to see your show, still you are paid cash for every admission.
>
> —The Robyn-Kander Movie Ticket Corporation (1915)

AMONG THE MANY DETAILS THAT make Ernest A. Dench's 1916 book, *Advertising by Motion Pictures,* a key resource for cinema-advertising historians is a curious little conversation with the Edison Film Company's young acting star Edward Earle. In this brief interview, Earle proposed a shocking vision of the future of advertising's relationship with moving media, asserting, "If I am not mistaken, there will spring up a chain of photoplay theaters in the large cities to which the public will be admitted free. At these 'billboard stations' short, regular photoplays will be sandwiched in between the ad. films so as to attract the folks inside." Accepting that compulsory advertising in a ticketed environment was "abhorrent to the people of this democratic country," Earle presumed that—for good or ill—the way around the moviegoer's reluctance was to do away with admission prices.[1] Earle's rational differentiation between "optional" print advertising, which one could skip past, and "compulsory" cinema advertising, which the spectator had to wait through even if disinterested, was the breaking point not for advertising but for a dual-revenue system. If the advertiser was going to hijack viewers' attention rather than ask for it, then spectators had to be paid for their time; a free show would fit the bill.[2] Earle was not alone in the belief that a free show was the answer to the problem of advertising and motion pictures. Many of the proponents of screen and in-cinema advertising declared that the problem was ticket prices.[3] For cinema advertising to function, perhaps the entire film industry needed to be freed from the burden of consumer cost.[4]

When Earle spoke in 1916, the breaking up of a sequence of film reels with advertising slides had been relatively common in movie houses across the country for several years, though it was then a waning exhibition model. The one- or two-reel advertising short was by then also well known, and the advertising trailer was in its early stages of development (Earle specifically mentions both types). Trailers, shorts, and slides all provided possible models for a pause in the entertainment—an interleaving of entertainment and advertising. It is even plausible to imagine a free cinema in which the advertisements were inserted between reels of a feature, rather than simply between short reels. Indeed, the popularity of serials had recently crested, as both *The Perils of Pauline* and *The Exploits of Elaine* were initially released in 1914. With serials, the multi-climax narrative structure, in which pauses were inserted at moments of heightened tension, was known. It is thus clear that transitional-era film theorists were able to conceive of a link between dramatic high points and the retention of viewer interest across an advertising break.[5] It is possible to see in Earle's comments a theoretical expansion of slide-and-trailer advertising into something nearly identical to later television spots: a larger narrative provided free of charge but broken up by advertising material. At the very least, Earle was willing to gamble that a variety program of shorts, fully underwritten by advertising, would have drawn urban crowds. The theory of free media through participating sponsorship is therefore nearly as old as cinema advertising itself. Indeed, it was a logical extrapolation of the relentless expansion of consumerism and commodification that defined early twentieth-century America.[6]

Although it is now clear that Earle was indeed "mistaken" about the inevitability of billboard stations, it is important to note that "free" cinema was not entirely theoretical. Earle's billboard station model was only one of many competing ideas. Others included "four-walling," merchant matinees, park screenings, and the Universal movie coupon.[7] In this, the outskirts of cinema-advertising theory, the range of behaviors was broad. Free cinema could occur in established nickelodeons, summer airdomes, touring tent shows, city parks, or on the streets themselves on the back of a truck. At times, "free" described the whole theater; at other times, it described a special ticket that allowed the holder to sit with the paying audience without having to pay. And free cinema could be funded through any of the tactics discussed in previous chapters, some combination of them, or through something entirely new—redemption coupons. The free-cinema movement, a developmental stage of what would become the nontheatrical circuit in later years, is cinema advertising at its most outlandish, swinging wildly between a utopian notion of ad-funded media and a cynical attempt to compel consumers to purchase goods.

BROUGHT TO YOU BY . . .

Much like peripheral technology, free cinema had multiple, often completely divergent models. Billboard screening really needs no introduction, as it was simply a variant of the slide and trailer models of advertising, as should be clear from the material above. Any free tent show, summer airdome, and mobile film truck could have attempted to cover costs in the same way. Whereas a ticket-funded entertainment theater was cautioned to keep slide content minimal (no more than twelve per turn of the program), a free theater funding itself via onscreen ads was expected to run as much as twenty minutes of advertising every hour. In June of 1916, the Crescent Amusement Company began using Nashville city parks for screenings on exactly this model: two-thirds entertainment and one-third "advertising matter."[8] Although this is likely the upper limit of silent-era ad content even in free theaters, it is noteworthy that this is roughly the same split found in twenty-first-century American commercial television, which typically features roughly eighteen minutes of advertising per hour. In actual practice, then, free screenings would have been quite similar to the form later adopted by commercial television.

It is worth noting that certain free screenings could have been even more slanted toward advertising content, though this pushes them outside of the scope of this book. Manufacturers would often simply rent out theaters—a practice common enough for advertising, educational, and exploitation films that it would eventually earn the industry nickname "four-walling."[9] In the absence of a theater to rent, advertisers would pay traveling film trucks or have films screened in store windows or other places of business; in 1911, for example, Chicago car manufacturer "Mr. Pool" was offering a fleet of film trucks designed exclusively to show industrial films on the streets of small towns across America.[10] Such sales-oriented screenings, though technically not an element of the current discussion, are worth noting as part of the milieu of free cinema of the time.

To return to ad-funded entertainment, when a forty/twenty ratio seemed less than ideal, one could remove the advertising partially or entirely from the screen. Peripheral advertising in a free cinema could manifest in numerous ways. The most common idea, echoing its commonality in the technology discussed in chapter 3, was a turn to the walls. Splashing the walls with local advertising posters and custom-painted signage was simply an elevation of screen framing and wall advertising to such a degree that it became omnipresent. A number of summer airdomes and touring tent shows diminished or eradicated altogether the onscreen ad by papering the walls with advertising materials. Although many airdomes and tent shows also sold tickets—thus making it difficult to determine whether or not it was possible to completely fund a show of this type with offscreen signage—the idea was, at the very least, in the air at the time.

Interestingly, even the walls were often not distant enough from the screen. The third—and by far the most common—model of free cinema removed the advertising almost entirely from the theater. The bulk of free cinema in this era was organized not through purchasing space within the site of exhibition, but by gathering up and controlling the dispersal of tickets. In a move that shifted the direct advertising out of the theater itself and into the newspapers and city streets *prior* to the screening, many consumer-goods manufacturers and merchants purchased large blocks of tickets and spent up to a month redistributing them, usually as a gift with purchase. These merchant screenings were highly variable in both the distribution of tickets and the restrictions placed on ticket usage. However, in one way all ticket schemes were identical: every merchant screening would be heavily advertised in the local newspaper, with a list of all participating merchants. Though the direct advertising was outside of the theater, it was functionally an improvement over hanging a sign on the wall. While signs and screen ads were a call in the hope of a response, free tickets were typically only available while standing among commodities.

Most free-ticket screenings blurred the line between advertising and marketing by requiring a purchase before the free ticket would be dispersed. At many merchant screenings, the tickets were circulated in exchange for whatever size purchase the merchant considered appropriate. Thus, a merchant might hand out one ticket for every fifty- or twenty-five-cent purchase in the store.[11] This common model, however, was flanked by alternatives that were either much more specific or much more open.

On the narrow end of the spectrum, some tickets were circulated gratis, but only to a particular class of patron. For example, many small-town merchants attempted to lure farm families on particular days of the week by offering a free screening solely for them; operating on faith that a trip into town would always be correlated to family shopping needs, the merchants would demand nothing specific in return.[12] Alternatively, some merchants opted to cast their net very widely and distribute tickets in fragments. Such a plan would decrease the amount that would need to be spent in any one visit (for example, one-twentieth of a ticket for every five cents spent, rather than one whole ticket for fifty cents) and increase the likelihood of repeat purchases (to complete the ticket). This loyalty-plan model was, to my knowledge, exclusively offered by the Robyn-Kander Movie Ticket Corporation (see the case study at the end of this chapter).

The use value of the tickets was also variable. Some merchant screenings were one-time events.[13] Most were once-per-week screenings at a regular time, with Tuesday and Saturday afternoons being the most common slots. A few were regularly scheduled on multiple weekday afternoons.[14] In all of these cases, however, the use value of a ticket was delimited quite heavily: typically a merchant ticket was good at only one time, on one date, in one theater, in the town where it was distributed. The more open the plan, however, the broader the use value of the tickets. Those who signed on for the Robyn-Kander service, for example, were able to offer tickets that were good at any screening at multiple (sometimes all) local theaters and could even be used in other Robyn-Kander towns.

In short, free cinema could be very circumscribed (a one-time farmers' matinee) or very broad (citywide Robyn-Kander service) and could be constructed through direct advertising onscreen, offscreen, or even outside and prior to the screening. In all cases, however, the target was the same: increase potential sales not through visible association with the film industry, but by subsidizing the movies' local existence. It was thus a form of sponsorship—of screenings, of theaters, of audiences, or of the film industry itself.

TEST PATTERNS AND PREEMPTIVE CRITIQUES

Edward Earle's comments were not an unprecedented act of wishful thinking. By the time those words were spoken, at least five years of experimentation with various models of free cinema had already occurred. Indeed, in the wake of mainstream film producers' turn away from nonfiction just before 1910, the film reform community had developed a small cottage industry of nontheatrical screenings, often in an attempt to influence the film content their patrons would consume. Church shows were a common form of this "community theater" concept—an offering of educational, religious, and eventually even mainstream studio pictures, as "ministers sought to recapture the attention of their straying parishioners . . . by adopting the movie theater's products and appeal."[15] Children's matinees (often held in legitimate cinema theaters) and school-affiliated shows were also common forms of community cinema.[16] By the early 1920s, this long history of the nontheatrical screening eventually became the permanent foster home for industrial and educational films.[17] In short, the notion of a cinematic experience with no admission fee has numerous antecedents in this period, not all of which are associated with advertising.

It is very likely that free shows for advertising purposes originated with four-walling, as manufacturers attempted to scrounge up viewers for the early industrial films they had been convinced to commission. Consumer-goods manufacturers had been toying with industrial film concepts as early as 1904 (a film for National Cash Register at the 1904 World's Fair), with advertising-film solicitors appearing by 1909.[18] Multiple examples of four-walling and other space renting by those manufacturers are evident as early as 1911.[19] A few enterprising businesses, exhibiting greater awareness of the importance of pleasure, rented out full theaters only to include a single reel of industrial footage in an otherwise normal program. See, for example, E.M.F. Automobile Company, which paid for a free show at the Grand Opera House in Fort Smith, Arkansas, in November 1911 with gratifying results.[20] In early 1912, National Cash Register pulled the same trick in Louisville, Kentucky, funding a free show for five full days and using the appeal of "colored pictures" to integrate a higher percentage of advertising into the program.[21] However, the exorbitant expense of funding an entire show by oneself—significantly higher than the cost of simply circulating a slide, trailer, or industrial short—appears to have largely crippled the single-sponsor model of free cinema. Examples after 1912 are extremely rare.[22]

As the idea of nontheatrical screenings began to solidify, the concept of four-walling took firm hold, and advertising shows would typically be just that: invitation-only performances with no regular entertainment content in the mix. Such theater renting could even become a regular feature of particular local houses. For example, under the auspices of Camilla Donworth, of the Films-of-Business Corporation, New York's Rialto Theater inaugurated a regular tradition of free morning screenings of advertising films in mid-1920. Begun on July 1 with a screening of four industrial films, showings were to occur every Tuesday and Thursday morning from 10:00 until 12:00.[23] Evidence exists for similar screenings at the Rialto as late as December 9 of that year.[24] However, as mentioned previously, the exclusive screening of advertising films at such shows makes them related but distinct from free, subsidized entertainment. Four-walling was not an attempt to fund free cinema; rather, it was an admission that industrial films were almost impossible to screen in any unpaid venue.

Participating sponsorship of cinema by local merchants, meanwhile, has a similar vintage, though it likely arose second; large businesses could rent a theater any time the fancy took hold, but accumulating a sufficient number of participating sponsors required time and coordination. Though it is plausible that participating sponsorship began as a gimmick by local exhibitors (thus leaving very few historical traces), the earliest extant evidence places participating sponsorship as a variant business model for touring shows. Touring open-air exhibitions, providing community performances through private advertising funding rather than donations or government dollars, appear in the trade press in 1911. Evidence suggests, however, that the concept predates even these extant archival examples by at least a few months. *Moving Picture World*'s resident cinema-advertising curmudgeon, F. H. Richardson, confidently asserted in late 1911 that no sane individual with experience in exhibition would attempt to completely fund a touring open-air show through advertising slides. Writing as though from real-world experience, Richardson asserted that any such attempt would be instantly beset with the following problems: "Where he . . . figures one dollar expense it would really take nearer five. The local papers would knock you. The local showman would inspire local authorities to make things unpleasant for you in the way of license holdups, etc. Bad weather could smite you. Breakdowns and delays would conspire to make life miserable for you. Railways would lose your stuff and break what they couldn't manage to lose. Verily, your joys would consist mainly of anticipating the day of your return, a chastened, sadder, and wiser man—oh yes, and a poorer one too."[25]

To hear Richardson tell the tale, free cinema had already left a trail of brokenhearted and impoverished men in its wake. At least one recent, real-world example could have inspired Richardson's account. Three months earlier, an open-air free theater in Jackson, Tennessee, had drawn the ire of two local exhibitors—Captain W. D. Ament (of the Elite) and D. L. Williamson (of the Marlow)—on the grounds that it operated without paying rent to the city for the park in which the films were shown. Ament and

Williamson asserted that the license for the free show should not have been granted on the grounds that it "permit[ted] the use of public property by individuals to the great harm of other citizens engaged in a legitimate and useful business."[26] Though it is unclear how this conflict ended, the circulation of legal ("unfair competition") and financial (bad business concept) arguments from Ament, Williamson, and Richardson in the trade press may have helped to put a stop to the practice, though only for a few years.

In the gap between Richardson's condemnation of touring free shows and their return in the historical record, the merchant matinee was developed as an alternative version of free cinema. Before the full flowering of the merchant matinee as participating sponsorship for local cinemas, it began as a national tactic for big business. A few manufacturers of bread and tobacco attempted to operate coupon schemes in isolation. In July 1912, inaugurating a brief wave of "bread tickets," the Arnold Bread Company of Reading, Pennsylvania, offered free admission to any screening at the Crescent Theater with "five labels taken from their bread."[27] In June of 1913, a second bread maker, this one from Indianapolis, attempted the same thing, in association with twenty different local theaters.[28] A third baker did so in Peoria, Illinois, in late 1914; in this instance, thirty coupons were required for free admission to the Liberty Theater.[29] From 1912 to 1913, the American Tobacco Company attempted a similar plan, circulating coupons in "a new brand" that entitled the bearer to half a cent off of their ticket price. Ten packets of cigarettes would thus get the smoker into any theater for free, presuming that the exhibitor was willing to accept the promise that American Tobacco would reimburse the nickel.[30] In 1914, one theater—E. H. Hill's Rex Theater of Arkansas City, Kansas—even adopted the idea for self-advertising; Hill offered free tickets to children who brought in one thousand dead flies—a philanthropic "advertisement" for summer pest control.[31] (It is not known how any of the involved parties were intended to transport or dispose of such large piles of insect carnage.) Although bread tickets were isolated to individual towns and the tobacco coupons were widely opposed by the film industry (on the grounds that cinema had enough reform problems already without being associated with smoking), each was, in its own way, foundational for what was to come.

THE PROFESSIONALIZERS

In 1913, as bakers and American Tobacco continued to attempt solo schemes, ticket tactics entered a second phase: group-funded merchant screenings. In March of that year, Chicago's George P. Loose filed a copyright on a specially designed "Merchant Matinee Pass" and began an early attempt to professionalize the endeavor.[32] Whether or not Loose had experience with merchant matinees prior to filing the copyright, he appears to have leapt immediately to national activity afterward; three months after the copyright, two entire operating days (Tuesdays and Fridays, 2:00 to 11:00) of the Palace Theater, in Bryan, Texas, were open for admission with a "Merchant Matinee Pass"—identical to the name of Loose's patent. In Bryan, one pass would be given by any of twenty-four local merchants for every twenty-five cents spent.[33] Although few performances can be directly connected to Loose, he appears to have remained active in the field at least through March of 1918, when a fourteen-week series of merchant matinees, directly affiliated with his name, took place in Carbondale, Illinois.[34]

By 1914, numerous once-per-week merchant matinees were inaugurated all across the Midwest. Matinees for all city residents occurred weekly in Council Grove, Kansas (Saturday afternoons; unknown cost), Macon, Missouri (Thursday afternoons for ten weeks; price varies), Atlanta, Illinois (Saturday afternoons for ten weeks; unknown cost), Chillicothe, Missouri (Wednesday afternoons; twenty-five cents per ticket), Shreveport, Louisiana

Cut out this AD keep it handy for future reference

Boost! Boost! Boost!

CARBONDALE

MERCHANTS' MATINEE YALE THEATRE

EVERY TUESDAY AFTERNOON 2 TO 5

Commencing Tuesday, March 26, and continuing the same afternoon each week for 14 weeks.

ATTEND THE YALE THEATRE EVERY TUESDAY AFTERNOON ON FREE PASSES ISSUED BY THE FOLLOWING MERCHANTS:

J. A. Patterson & Co., Clothing and Shoes. Both Stores.
Phillips Supply Co. Furniture & Hardware. Low prices and terms.
Ideal Plumbing Co. F. D. Grady prop. everything in Plumbing and Electrical
Candyland, E. B. Terpinitz, prop. New Hundley Corner. Phone 115
Central Restaurant, Meals, short orders and rooms.
D. Martin "The Great Sole Saver" 305 W. Walnut st.
J. D. Rushing General Merchandise, Phone 1010.
Joe White Groceries. Phone 497 L
Fox's Drug Store, The prescription store Biggest Busiest Best
A. F. Smith & Co. Wall paper, paints and Etc. Phone 226
Meat Market C. Tomlinson, successor to Earl Young. Phone 452.
United 10c Store, opposite the Yale Theatre.
Rude's Garage 202 West Jackson St.
H. O. Hall & Co., Coal feed and farm implements
Floyd's General merchandise
J. F. Baggett's cash grocery and meat market. Phone your order.
Campbells's Grocery Phone 210 and 1036

The above merchants will gladly give you a ticket to the Merchants' matinee; they give you a ticket with a 25c purchase. Ask for one. Patronize home merchants, and tell your friends and neighbors where they can get free tickets.

Favor those who favor you. Don't forget to Boost.
Merchants' Matinee (copyright) Geo. P. Loose, Chicago, Ill.

Figure 4.1. A George P. Loose advertisement for a 1918 series of Merchant Matinees in Carbondale, Illinois (*Daily Free Press*, March 22, 1918, 2). This particular series had a twenty-five-cent purchase boundary and seventeen participants.

(Mondays and Fridays; twenty-five cents per ticket), Minneapolis, Minnesota (Saturday matinee, once only; unknown cost), Iowa City, Iowa (every afternoon; twenty-five cents per ticket), Iola, Kansas (every night with one paid admission; unknown cost), and Winfield, Kansas (Wednesdays and Fridays; unknown cost).[35] In addition, a weekly farmers' matinee went into effect in Durant, Oklahoma (Saturdays 1:30 to 5:30; no purchase necessary).[36] Exactly how merchant matinees expanded so rapidly throughout the region is unclear. On the one hand, the somewhat uniform location of these matinees (roughly on a line between Chicago, Illinois, and Bryan, Texas) and the increasingly common announcement of one ticket per twenty-five cent expenditure indicate that Loose and his affiliates could have been the driving force for nearly all merchant matinees at this point. On the other hand, the phrase "Merchants Matinee Pass" disappears almost completely. This could represent a shift in tactics by Loose himself, but competing plans are an equally likely possibility.

By the following year, the merchant matinee concept ran wild through the Midwest and Plains states. Over the course of 1915, at least twenty known merchant matinees arose in Kansas, Louisiana, Texas, Michigan, Oklahoma, Alabama, Oregon, Missouri, and elsewhere. It is at this point that diversification becomes readily apparent. Two distinct entities appear, although neither is identified in the extant materials. The smaller, later group was likely operating out of St. Joseph, Missouri. Three Missouri towns—Oregon, Albany, and King City—all within sixty-five miles of St. Joseph, assembled what they called "Merchants' Matinee Clubs" within a stretch of two months. In all three cases, the local paper reported the onset of the matinee series using effectively the same description: a three-month series of matinees, held on Saturdays from 2:30 to 4:30 (or 2:00 to 4:00), which were free "only [to people] who live outside the corporate limits" of the city.[37] It is therefore clear that a person or persons—likely from St. Joseph, though possibly a branch salesman for George P. Loose—had begun touring the small towns in the vicinity selling a standardized "farmers' matinee" to as many theaters and merchants as possible. The St. Joseph brand, like all extant examples of farmers' matinees, required no outlay of cash in exchange for the tickets; one simply needed to show evidence that one was from out of town. (Due to a dearth of archival evidence, there is no way to know how a third party was able to make a living suggesting a plan like this. However, the uniformity of announcements indicates that it was centralized, and the absence of a uniform start date in all three towns indicates that the effort was probably not the brainchild of a small theater chain.)

Slightly earlier, a much more successful group was organized in Wisconsin (likely in the city of Stevens Point, though Green Bay is also plausible) and began setting up merchant matinees in multiple surrounding states: Wisconsin in 1915; Minnesota, Ohio, and Illinois in 1916; and even South Dakota, much later, in 1920. Once again, the uniformity of press wording implies an unnamed ringleader; in this case, the link is even clearer: the wording of all advertisements was identical. Though these too were held on Saturday afternoons, this Wisconsin group established a pattern of matinees of ten weeks' duration, open to all city residents (not just commuters), with tickets available as a gift-with-purchase of twenty-five cents or more. In their first three months, May through July of 1915, matinees were organized in Stevens Point, Rhinelander, and Sheboygan.[38] By the end of 1916, they had set up their ten-week plans in Brainerd, Minnesota, East Liverpool, Ohio, and Alton, Illinois, with the only change being a shift to Tuesday afternoons.[39] Again, their position in the Midwest indicates a plausible connection to George P. Loose, though by this point, the flowering of multiple ideas may be evidence that Loose's control was breaking down.

By early 1916, yet another merchant matinee purveyor had been organized in the region, this time in Kansas—long a hot spot for merchant matinees. Over the course of 1916, five different towns (El Dorado, Beloit, Hays, Holton, and Great Bend) all initiated a six-week series of merchant matinees. Again, common newsprint advertising links them into a coherent group. The first matinee was in El Dorado in March on Friday afternoons. The next three were all in May and took place on Saturday afternoons. The final known offering, in Great Bend, was in June and organized around

Wednesday afternoon screenings. All were at the twenty-five-cent price point.[40] As with the other two groups, there is no way to be certain that these matinees were not affiliated with George P. Loose, though the difference in print advertising copy strongly argues for independence.

Whether under the unified direction of Loose or multiple unrelated entities, then, the merchant matinee peaked—at least in the Midwest—in 1915. Indeed, by the end of that year, merchant-funded screenings had become so common across this region that in some towns, a significant percentage of the local merchants had experimented with it. For example, in tiny Monett, Missouri, a town of only 4,000 people, twenty-five different merchants had taken part in three different series of merchant screenings between 1913 and 1915—at least one-fifth of all the businesses in town.[41] Although little information has come to light, it is apparent that similar ticket plans had been offered in other regions of the United States as well. For example, numerous purveyors had descended on San Francisco in 1915 and 1916, attempting to prey on grocers.[42] Among extant examples, however, the Midwest remains the clear epicenter.

The rise and flowering of these various ticket tactics are more easily discussed in isolation, but they were not isolated. At the same moment that the merchant matinee was cresting, a perceptible return of the advertising-funded free screening—in various guises—is apparent across a similar region. It appears that the success of George P. Loose, after the visibility of bread and cigarette tickets, had a domino effect on other approaches. Between 1914 and 1917, ad-oriented free screenings—from film trucks, to park screenings, to full-blown touring shows—were announced across Illinois, Kentucky, Missouri, Tennessee, Texas, and Wisconsin.

Perhaps the first of the new generation of independently organized free shows in the area appeared in mid-1914 in the Chicago suburb of Chicago Heights. A man named Delmar Lee, presumably a teamster, was said to have been showing films "on the streets" of Chicago Heights (likely on a screen erected on the back of his own truck) and funding the screenings through merchant advertising.[43] By meandering from place to place while simultaneously remaining within the city limits, Lee inaugurated the return of the touring show with palpable hesitation, focusing on a stable cluster of local merchant advertisers rather than rotating through numerous towns and seeking fresh advertising at each stop. Although no other ad-funded film trucks are known in this period, it is unlikely that Lee was the only person attempting such exhibitions.

Within a year of Lee's minimalist touring, the ad-funded "park theater" movement began to take hold. Early rumblings are apparent in Missouri and Illinois in the summer of 1914, although the integration of advertising is difficult to gauge. The St. Louis City Park board opted to use Columbus Square, described as a public park for the immigrant "ghetto" region of the city, for free screenings of local scenes, the New York Zoo, and "American industries."[44] It is reasonable to assume that both the local and industrial footage were paid inclusions designed to cover operating costs, though the predominance of documentary and educational footage creates significant hazards to such an assumption.[45] This early effort was provocative enough that by 1917, Ed Batts of East St. Louis (the independent portion of the city across the Illinois border) persuaded the park board to allow him to show films "from one to three times a week" in five different parks (Jones, Emerson, Franklin, Virginia, and Edgemont), funding the screenings with advertising slides.[46] Both Chicago and Kansas City were said to be considering similar actions in the wake of the 1914 St. Louis decision, though no concrete evidence of adoption has come to light.[47]

By June 1915, enterprising individuals in Louisville proposed using a downtown site for "a free motion picture house," declaring that "the cost and a profit [were to be covered] by showing a number of advertising slides" in between each short subject reel; the originators of the plan even attempted to financially justify it by claiming that downtown theaters in the city earned between two and ten dollars per week from each slide screened—a price presumably high enough to completely fund the project via a manageable number of slides.[48] Despite admitting that "the plan has not proven successful in other cities" (presumably including St. Louis), Louisville's proponents were hopeful that a downtown location might work better.[49] In February 1916, the small town of McClure, Illinois, with "practically unanimous" support, got on the bandwagon and inaugurated weekly free screenings "to improve the social life of the community and the church and give merchants a chance to exploit their wares."[50] In June of 1916, free park screenings emerged in two major cities in Tennessee. In Nashville, the Crescent Amusement Company (owned by long-time local theater man Tony Sudekum) began using city parks for screenings that were two-thirds entertainment and one-third "advertising matter" and likely included industrial films, as the company had "been instructed . . . to secure . . . pictures having an educational value along with comedy and other subjects."[51] Nearby, a "main street moving picture man" from Chattanooga started a similar open-air theater in Warner Park but remained determined to fund the screenings entirely with slides, putting an embargo on "travel stuff and . . . educational pictures dealing with the manufacture of this and that."[52] The summer of 1916 also witnessed the first park screenings in Dallas, operated by local theater man Henry Putz.[53] Although the quantity (if any) of advertising in the screenings of 1916 is unclear, Dallas would continue to hold park screenings into the early 1920s, with "practically the entire expense . . . defrayed by advertising and cold drink concession privileges." Upward of one million Dallas citizens were estimated to attend these free summer screenings on a yearly basis.[54]

As street and park shows stabilized as a common form of free cinema in the region, the long-distance touring show returned to provide the same service to communities that, due either to their size or the unwillingness of their park board, were not providing regular free screenings. In 1916, an unknown Wisconsin entrepreneur formed the Open Air Dome Company of Green Bay. After "several weeks" of screenings in Green Bay, the company began a touring show with trips to West De Pere and Kaukauna—two small towns, with approximately 5,000 inhabitants each, on a line southwest of Green Bay.[55] It is unclear how long the Open Air Dome Company was in operation, whether it had any competitors in the region or the country, and how many towns it visited. Despite this, the company is evidence that in the wake of ticket schemes and ad-funded film trucks and park shows, touring shows did not remain dormant. Whether or not such screenings were successful, the billboard station (at least the touring and park-bound versions) was a reasonably common component of late 1910s Midwestern cinema.

As the two key models of free cinema (merchant matinees and park screenings) were reaching the peak of their popularity, the most interesting variant arose: the ticket fragment, circulated on a national scale. By 1915, bread tickets and tobacco coupons were a relatively distant memory, but various forms of merchant funding were successful enough to inspire dreams of nationwide campaigns anew. At the beginning of the year, the Robyn-Kander Movie Ticket Corporation reinvigorated the ticket-coupon movement with its more complicated variant. Backed by Universal, Robyn-Kander, first a Chicago and then a New York company, opened at least fourteen branches across eleven states (Pennsylvania, Delaware, Washington, New York, Ohio, Arkansas, Missouri, Illinois, Oklahoma, West Virginia, and California).[56] In addition to the previously mentioned merchant matinees, Robyn-Kander merchant tickets were offered in thirty-six known locales from 1915 to 1916, ranging from tiny towns (1,000 citizens in McHenry, Illinois) to enormous urban centers (700,000 citizens in St. Louis, Missouri). The corporation attempted to sell its ticket coupons from coast to coast, though its biggest successes were along the East Coast (including New York and Pennsylvania).

Robyn-Kander was clearly aware of its predecessors, as its brief business activity has the appearance of a composite of all previous attempts. It was mobile like a touring show (a ticket earned in Pittsburgh could be used in Kansas City) but had no travel costs and subsidized the local theaters rather than competing with them. It was stable like a park theater or a four-wall rental (theaters were contracted to accept Robyn-Kander tickets at all shows for at least a month) but did not subject the patron to advertising within the space itself. It was a predominantly merchant-centered tactic but was also able to contract with national or regional companies like tobacco manufacturers and bread makers. It allowed merchants to require purchasing, but fragmenting the ticket into pieces simultaneously reduced the minimum purchase and vastly expanded the profit potential into a loyalty program. Though short-lived—dissolving into infighting and lawsuits by early 1917—Robyn-Kander briefly nationalized and diversified the concept of the merchant-circulated ticket, indicating both the hopeful enthusiasm for free cinema at mid-decade and its rapid disappearance. (See the case study section below for a more detailed discussion of the specifics of Robyn-Kander.)

"A MENACE TO LEGITIMATE BUSINESS"

Much like peripheral technologies, then, the mass flowering of free cinema crested between 1915 and 1916, especially in the Midwest and Plains. During these years, at least two and possibly as many as seven groups were actively offering to professionally organize and operate merchant screenings: Robyn-Kander, George P. Loose, the Wisconsin group, the Missouri group, the Kansas group, the National Free Movie Ticket Company (founded in Chicago in 1915; nothing more is known), and the National Free

Moving Picture Ticket Company (founded in Dallas in 1916 and defunct roughly one year later; nothing more is known).[57] Free shows in city parks operated in at least five states, and at least one company—the Open Air Dome Company of Green Bay—was touring a free show through a sixth. In mid-1916, clever Tennessee exhibitors in both Memphis and Nashville were even adopting the scheme of free advertising-slide-supported screenings as a means to evade local Sunday blue laws.[58] In short, by 1916, free cinema was a vibrant, diverse, and common concept, at least in the Midwest.

This parallel with peripheral advertising, however, persists also into dissolution. World War I was again a crisis point. While slide and trailer purveyors struggled to contend with the massive space buying of the US government and technologies lost ground to other forms of theatrical beautification, free cinema simply began to fade away. Over 1917 and 1918—roughly corresponding with American involvement in the war—thirteen known merchant matinees were operated in the Midwest. Tellingly, of ten merchant screenings in 1917, all but one occurred in the first five months of the year (plausibly all planned before American entry into the war). The one outlier was a one-time free screening organized without the need to even visit a merchant for a ticket—it was simply a free day and was likely the theater's own PR response to a wartime attendance emergency.[59] After the dramatic falloff in the latter half of 1917, I find only three merchant matinees in 1918.[60] If we add in the one known city to inaugurate free screenings in city parks in these years—East St. Louis in 1917—we have only fourteen known examples of free cinema in the two war years. In sum, there were fewer free screenings and ticket plans in these two years than in the formative year of 1914. In the historical record, the peak years of 1915 and 1916 dwarf the war years by a factor of at least four or five to one.

Of course, aside from manpower shortages, there is no obvious reason why the war would have impacted free cinema as heavily as the other tactics mentioned in this book. Indeed, the fact that free cinema did not recover after the war seems a clear indication that the impact of the war itself was only part of the problem. I have found evidence of only three free cinema attempts in 1919.[61] In 1920, with the first confirmed Dallas park screenings since 1916, the number was four.[62] As the final four known merchant matinees were all ten-week plans, one only twenty-five miles from Stevens Point, it is reasonable to assume that only one merchant matinee company remained in operation after the war in any significant capacity—the Wisconsin group.

The cause of free cinema's downfall appears to have been a withering attack, both legal and industrial, on all varieties of the form. Though free cinema existed in two distinct types—free ticket as gift and free screening with participating sponsorship—each type drew powerful enemies that emerged either just before or just after the war. For free ticket schemes, the problems were legal, as premium advertising faced increasing state-by-state curtailment through restrictive statutes. For free screenings, exhibitor hostility to nontheatrical screenings was on the rise, as church shows (among other performances) were increasingly considered to be a "menace" to "legitimate business."

In the early twentieth century, states would frequently use statutes to impose crippling taxes and fees on coupon plans—exactly the model of advertising that had been adopted by merchant matinees and other free-ticket schemes. Such statutes were erected to defend both merchants and consumers from the deleterious financial and psychological effects of coupon collecting. In the wake of the advent of United Cigar Store coupons, Sperry & Hutchinson's Green Stamps, and various other turn-of-the-century redemption schemes, several states had passed such statutes on the grounds that coupons "by an appeal to cupidity lure to improvidence"—or, in other words, encouraged reckless spending in a quest for more coupons.[63] Although such a rationale was clearly geared specifically toward loyalty schemes (coupons that only attained worth via repeat purchases), hazy phrasing typically impacted coupon premiums of all types.[64] Such statutes tacitly illegalized ticket schemes in large swaths of the United States by creating licensing fees larger than plausible profits, all in the name of defending the public from a form of advertising that played, potentially improperly, on human desire. Although all such statutes were challenged by Sperry & Hutchinson, with some overturned and others upheld, the coupon as a form of premium advertising was under siege at the exact moment that cinema advertisers attempted to adopt it.

Worse still, although the Supreme Court was to pass judgment in early 1916 affirming that such statutes were legal, statutes remained a state issue and, as such, were wildly inconsistent. The range of possible license fees was enormous. In the state of Washington, the yearly fee was set at $6,000 per county in which the plan operated.[65] In West Virginia, the fee was a more modest $500.[66] Florida opted for a total of $750 ($500 to the state and $250 to the county).[67] Other states either had or were in the process of proposing similar statutes.

The seeming randomness of the valuation and even existence of such license fees would have crippled local ticket schemes in pockets across the country while making life difficult for companies with national pretensions. Robyn-Kander, in particular, ran afoul of anti-coupon statutes on multiple occasions, after which the company almost immediately collapsed (see case study below). Numerous other interactions between state laws and free-ticket companies are likely lost to history. Considering that the Supreme Court decision occurred in the same year that most known free-ticket companies were reaching their peak, this major legal decision was likely the death knell for the ticket-coupon fad.

Within a few years of this attack on ticket plans from outside of the film industry, exhibitors themselves began to rally against other forms of free screenings. Although four-walling, community screenings, and nontheatrical showings of industrial pictures were by no means new, by 1919, the increasing prevalence of screenings at "schools, churches, community centers and other like propositions" caused a sharp negative reaction from some for-profit exhibitors.[68] Although the greatest vitriol, from an East Coast "Grievance Committee" representing Virginia, Maryland, North Carolina, and Washington, DC, was directed toward revenue-generating screenings in locations, like churches, that were unregulated and had no overhead costs (tax-free operation and donated labor), the attack on "nontheatricals" was easily integrated with previous critiques on free park screenings as unfair competition.[69]

Educators attempted to take issue with the "menace" assumption, asserting that exhibitors could simply have staked claim to such screenings, rather than complaining. For example, if the exhibitors had loaned their films to schools (which would have saved the school the cost of renting), the children could have been harnessed as word-of-mouth advertisers for the evening show.[70] Free shows were also frequently defended as a source of the movie habit, rather than a parasite on it.[71] Although the bulk of the debate occurred slightly after the years studied in this book, it is clear that the tide of complaints continued unabated.[72] General hostility toward all nontheatrical screenings was thus likely having a significant chilling effect on park, truck, and touring free shows as well.

What little advertising-oriented free cinema remained after World War I was either highly localized (for example, popular park screenings in Dallas) or operating in regions devoid of legislative restrictions (for example, Wisconsin, which did not attempt to enact stamp legislation until the 1950s).[73] Despite this brief life, advertising-funded free screenings were an important and fascinating interlude in the history of nontheatrical, community cinema and advertising-oriented screening in the United States. And despite persistent antagonism, it has arisen again and again in a patchwork history as yet unwritten. Farmers' matinees recurred in the 1930s.[74] World War II witnessed the rise of an industry-supported National Free Movie Day correlated to war-loan drives.[75] And, of course, this historical web continues to the present; twenty-first-century ticketing company Fandango frequently offers seasonal free-ticket gimmicks, often via an accumulation of packaged goods—an approach not significantly dissimilar to Robyn-Kander's a century before.

Edward Earle was therefore both spectacularly correct and incorrect, depending on one's perspective. Motion pictures did not widely develop into billboard stations. Billboard cinema was as fleeting as the advertisements it contained. In addition to the rise of the feature film and the palatial theater, which were problematic for all cinema-advertising tactics, the historical record indicates that free cinema was often despised, illegal, unprofitable, or all three. However, if one thinks of the mass electric media as interrelated and mutually influencing, rather than rigidly demarcated, then Earle was highly prescient, though a decade ahead of his time. In the 1920s, American broadcasting developed a business model that provided entertainment free of charge and profited entirely from advertising dollars. By the advent of mature radio, and later commercial television, the concept of the downtown billboard station—entertainment provided at no cost through advertising dollars collected from participating sponsors—was a living-room reality. Earle, extrapolating from touring shows, park theaters, and merchant matinees, had predicted the future not of motion pictures, but of broadcasting.[76]

THE TOLLBOOTH THEORY OF ADVERTISING

Although free cinema, as a field, represents a unique approach to the problem of cinema advertising, many models, including park screenings and touring shows, were simply large-scale variants of the tactics discussed in previous chapters, as the cost of the entire show was covered through some combination of slides, trailers, and peripheral signage (and perhaps the odd educational film). As such, the dearth of trade-press remarks on the practice is likely an indication that free-cinema arguments often trod well-worn ground. Captivity, receptivity, combativeness, memorability, and so on would all have returned to the forefront with little variation. The only new element in these discussions would have been the use of an absence of consumer cost as a means to offset concerns about rising hostility. A given provider would therefore have adopted whatever argumentation suited its needs at the time. For example, a touring show would likely assert the captivity thesis when selling slide space while using free-choice arguments for posters on interior walls.

Where debate was published with relative frequency and free cinema had real consequences for the developing cinema-advertising discourse was in the realm of ticket and coupon plans: Merchant matinees, Robyn-Kander, and the like. In this arena, free-cinema theory was as unique as peripheral theory (which had fostered a notion of active audiences specifically to justify its own existence). Free-cinema companies stressed entry barriers not because ticket cost was an inherent evil, but because tickets were a readily established tollbooth between viewers and the cinema screen. Free-ticket companies were selling the right not to the screen, but to the barrier. Robyn-Kander, for example, suggested: "Suppose that the 27,000,000 people who attend the Movies daily *couldn't go* unless they bought your goods" [emphasis added].[77] Of course, no free-cinema tactic ever held complete control over the cinema possibilities of a town; there were always full days and full theaters that were accessible via the direct purchase of a ticket. However, individual screenings were indeed rendered private, unattainable to anyone who had not made a purchase from one of the advertisers supporting the show. Take, for example, the matinee at the Delite Theater in Decatur, Alabama, on September 17, 1915: "No tickets will be sold for the . . .

matinee on this date, the entire seating capacity having been secured by the merchants."[78] The series of farmers' matinees in Kansas in late 1915 were also advertised as "exclusive."[79] Although the patron could simply have opted to attend a different show, the only way through the doors for these particular shows was via a purchase, effectively guaranteeing the result typically only hoped for with an advertising expenditure. As such, the appeal of the cinema, from the perspective of ticket control, was not based on captivity, receptivity, or choice; rather it was based on the preexistence of a culturally acceptable toll. The cinema offered an avenue to profit through the ownership and manipulation of that toll. What was being sold, then, was not the behavior of the audience within the cinema space, but their behavior prior to entry.

This tollbooth concept had its own psychological underpinning: the linkage between a gift with purchase and increased consumer happiness (and spending). The claim that a free ticket would be considered better than cash was made overtly by Robyn-Kander and presumably numerous others.[80] The underlying logic was that the acquisition of a second product—in this case, a visit to the cinema—was interpreted as a bonus, while cash back was interpreted as a sale price. As consumers were considered to be more drawn to acquisition than savings, and a "free" gift concealed any cost increases by distributing them across all other products for sale, a gift would simultaneously increase both revenue and consumer happiness.[81] The gift-with-purchase offer thus increased drawing power to the store while maintaining financial flexibility for the merchant, or so the theory went.

Of course, as mentioned in the above history section, stamp, coupon, and gift schemes were rigorously contested. Statutes effectively illegalizing such schemes on the grounds that they were unethical and manipulative flowered in various states across the country. In short, free cinema was the only field of cinema advertising in which the value of the audience was not the element that was questioned; Robyn-Kander's claim that "people would rather have a theatre ticket than the same amount in cash" was likely taken at face value at the time.[82] Instead, opponents criticized the use of that knowledge in this way as immoral; legally it was defined, in many states, as an act of abuse. In the realm of ticket rhetoric, then, cinema advertising briefly moved past questions of fleeting advertising, receptive audiences, and even class levels and instead discussed whether or not advertising itself could be a problem, even when profitable. In this case, with legislative bodies frequently standing with the opposition, free-cinema advocates were caught up in an argument that unrelated companies had already begun to lose. (It wasn't until the Great Depression that public sentiment began to approve of coupon schemes for advertising.) A key historical element of ticket systems, then, was that they became a point of entry for a caustic debate that predated cinema-advertising arguments.

Such theoretical ruminations were important but represent a minority of published thinking—likely because the competing camps were already rigidly opposed to one another. The bulk of archival material skews toward more practical cost issues. The notion of achieving "tremendous circulation at a small cost" arises, as expected, in Robyn-Kander self-advertising.[83] The fact that gift distribution was being handled by the advertisers themselves also allowed for the free-cinema proponent to stress that cost per prospect could be manipulated while the plan was in progress. Robyn-Kander made a habit of mentioning that the merchant would "distribute [the coupons] with sales to customers in whatever quantity they choose."[84] The variability of merchant matinee plans—with some giving out a ticket for every fifty cents spent, some a ticket for every twenty-five, and a few even giving a ticket for every ten cents—indicates that those plans could be molded to suit as well. As such, although the sunk cost would not change, clients could subtly shift course over the duration of the plan, allowing the advertiser to attempt to find the maximum cost-effectiveness of the plan.

It should not be surprising that the possibility of hidden costs or other financial disasters were likewise prominent talking points. Advertisers heard stories about financial disasters every bit as cautionary as the exhibitors' concerns mentioned in the history section above (such as F. H. Richardson's 1911 condemnation of touring shows).[85] The *Retail Grocers' Advocate*, of San Francisco, considered all coupon schemes to be parasitical "profit sharing" scams aimed at pilfering "the meager profits that are forthcoming for the average retail grocer."[86] The journal refused to print advertising for any such coupon or stamp scheme and vigorously supported then-ongoing legal action in the state of California aimed at illegalizing or crippling stamp and coupon advertising.[87] The *Advocate*'s opposition produced not only numerous small articles warning against movie-ticket schemes but even a front cover. A text box on the cover of the November 5, 1915, issue read simply, "The Movie Ticket Plan costs five per cent of the sales. This means five per cent out of your regular business. You cannot hope to get enough increase to pay for this and besides, you are also paying five per cent on the increase itself. Figure this out and you will be surprised. Keep out of the clutches of the movie ticket schemers."[88]

Mid-century law students Philip Callan, Jr., and Norman I. Jacobs—after clarifying that, among other troubles, any increase in revenue was contingent on one's competitors making no effort to win consumers back—provided an easy formula with which to, as the *Advocate* encouraged, "figure this out and . . . be surprised."[89] Let us assume a retailer had been operating on $10,000 monthly gross sales, then signed the above contract and increased their gross to $12,000 the following month. Paying 5 percent of $12,000 would result in $600 (30 percent of the added revenue) going to the coupon company; only $1,400 of the added revenue would have gone to the retailer, who also had to pay for the extra stock and other increases in operating costs. In short, in this hypothetical, even a 20 percent revenue boost would have been unlikely to cover the costs associated with a 5 percent charge. Knowledge of this jarring math—so easily obfuscated by the figure "5 percent"—would have put numerous merchants off of ticket schemes permanently.

Circumstantial evidence suggests that most retailers who contracted for movie coupons as an advertising scheme learned this lesson very quickly. Most known merchant matinees were described as limited-time events from the beginning, perhaps indicating that the operating companies expected a cool reception afterward. In addition, the one town known to have hosted multiple different merchant-funded screenings—Monett, Missouri—had only one merchant (Cox Brothers Drug) that was financially involved in more than one.[90] Over the course of the three events, the steadily decreasing participation—from eleven to eight to seven contracted merchants, as well as the use of a different theater each time—is also a red flag. It seems clear that for most communities in 1910s America, free cinema was only workable as an occasional aberration. Even with the integration of free and paid tickets, free cinema worked better as a fad than as a permanent business model. It appears that very few advertisers were interested in trying something like this more than once, seeming to confirm the financial concerns described above.

Despite a lack of significant preserved rhetoric surrounding free cinema, specifically ticket coupons, what we know sits comfortably alongside material from the slide, trailer, and peripheral-advertising chapters. It is, in fact, not unreasonable to assume that most free-cinema debates were simply echoing earlier debates; airdomes, park theaters, and touring shows were, after all, integrating advertising, in part, using slides, trailers, and wall signage. It is in the realm of coupon plans where free cinema carved out its own rhetorical identity and added to the conversation of the time, adding interesting questions about legality, ethics, and even whether or not one could turn one's advertising appropriation into guaranteed sales.

CASE STUDY: THE SPONSORED AUDIENCES OF THE ROBYN-KANDER MOVIE TICKET CORPORATION

The Robyn-Kander Movie Ticket Corporation, purveyor of Universal Moving Picture Tickets, was the only advocate of free cinema to regularly identify itself by name in newsprint and trade advertising. The company also had what would be considered, in any other chapter of this book, a shockingly brief life span. In the realm of free cinema, however, it stands out as the most interesting and likely the most successful company of its era. Robyn-Kander was formed in early 1915 in downtown Chicago by newspaperman Allen Kander, with Carl Laemmle's Universal Film Manufacturing Company as (initially) a silent partner.[91] (The "Robyn" in the company name was most likely A. P. Robyn; the previous year, A. P. Robyn was responsible for syndicating the newsprint adaptations of Universal's film serial *Lucille Love, the Girl of Mystery*.[92]) With the date and location of origin both conspicuously close to George P. Loose's, it is likely that the concept was a conscious derivation of the Merchant Matinee Pass. As a case study, Robyn-Kander provides what no other example of free cinema in the silent era can: evidence of the difficulties inherent in nationalizing a tactic born out of a desire to please local advertisers.

As with all case studies in this book, the key at the outset is to understand the ways in which Robyn-Kander's product was unique. From the perspective of distribution, Robyn-Kander tickets were complicated, even overwrought. Rather than simply selling full tickets to merchants, Robyn-Kander sold fragments of ticket vouchers, marketing the tactic as a loyalty scheme that would increase repeat purchasing. With each fragment valued at one-quarter of a cent, a collection of twenty fragments was equal to a nickel admission. Although pricing is unknown (and was likely fluid), a standard markup for coupon plans was roughly 40 percent of the face value; as such, each five-cent cluster of ticket

Figure 4.2. A single Robyn-Kander ticket fragment (one-twentieth of a full admission), still attached to the header and brand-specific footer, as reproduced in an advertisement for San Lac Milk Seals in the trade journal *Creamery and Milk Plant Monthly* (June 1915, 43).

fragments likely cost the merchant about seven cents.[93] Part of this overage would have paid for the printing of informative window signs for both the merchant and the local theaters taking part. (The theaters were not asked to cover any costs.) The printing of the tickets themselves was also a significant cost burden. As was (and remains) standard practice in premium advertising, each fragment was custom printed to include the name of the distributing merchant—an added expense that would hopefully turn a physical gift into a lingering advertisement. Each fragment was also attached to a large instructional header; as only one was to be included with a finished strip, 95 percent of these headers were to be simply thrown away. In short, merchants were purchasing ticket coupons with a significant amount of appended labor and paper waste.

Redemption was equally complex. Merchants would provide fragments to their customers at whatever rate they deemed suitable. (The *Tonawanda Evening News*, for example, included one fragment with each daily paper and four—later five—fragments with the Saturday paper.[94] No retailer rates are known, although one fragment with every five-cent purchase is likely.) With multiple distributors and a standard valuation of one-quarter of a cent per fragment, consumers could collect them when, where, and how they liked, individually or as a team effort. A completed strip would have been given to a participating theater in lieu of a nickel admission; two strips would gain admission to a ten-cent theater. Having accepted completed strips, a theater would send them to the nearest Universal exchange, receiving either the appropriate number of nickels in return or a price break on its next film rental.[95] In this significantly variable system, Robyn-Kander used contracts (with both merchants and theaters) to assure reasonable periods of stability; all evidence indicates that the minimum length of participation required was one month, with an option to renew.

Robyn-Kander thus, via nationalization and diversification, revised three elements of earlier ticket plans, two of which are somewhat obvious. First, the inherently local nature of the merchant matinee was traded for a nationwide plan uniting multiple theaters. Robyn-Kander was thus the only confirmed free-cinema purveyor to attempt to operate on a national scale in the silent era. Second, the relatively steep cost of acquisition, wherein a consumer needed to spend as much as fifty cents in a single store visit, was dispersed among multiple small purchases and potentially various merchants. As with any loyalty scheme, Robyn-Kander tickets helped increase the likelihood of small purchases by encouraging the consumer to see such purchases as components of a larger project.

Third, and much less obvious, the exhibitor's centrality was vastly diminished. Unlike merchant matinees and other free screenings, in which the advertising dollars funded specific shows at specific times in specific venues, Robyn-Kander tickets were good for any random screening and possibly at numerous local theaters. The individual exhibitor was merely a link in a chain for Robyn-Kander. As such, under the Robyn-Kander plan, it was no longer the screen being sponsored; it was the audience. Rather than creating a free screening, Robyn-Kander created free admissions, integrating the free-cinema business model into the film industry's long-standing ticketing model.

Despite the many ways in which Robyn-Kander's service was unique, the company, like most other 1910s cinema-advertising start-ups, had an obvious hope of immediate national relevance. Unfortunately, though the movies may have been a national medium, they were not (yet) a national market. Advertising agencies working in print had taken years to develop a working national system with local papers and mass magazines. Cinema advertisers often hoped such a system would develop overnight. Prior to the existence of massive theater chains, however, most theaters were individually owned mom-and-pop operations, all of which required individual negotiation. Getting a single advertising message approved for screening in multiple theaters required a staggering workload.

Robyn-Kander's historical footprint indicates the difficulty 1910s companies had in learning this lesson. It took Robyn-Kander six months to shift its approach from a single national office to a regional branch system. For half of its first year, the company advertised in national trade presses, downplaying the importance of local merchants and theaters, but also providing minimal evidence that many clients had actually signed on. Known contracts in this period are limited to examples like the Pa-Pro Company, which agreed to circulate tickets nationally through the milk bottlers who were using their San Lac Milk Seals.[96] A sudden tactical shift to local service is apparent on June 20, 1915, when Robyn-Kander sought branch salesmen via a flurry of classified ads in cities across the country: Chicago, Illinois; Charlotte, North Carolina; Indianapolis, Indiana; Lincoln, Nebraska; Little Rock, Arkansas; Muncie, Indiana; Pittsburgh, Pennsylvania; St. Louis, Missouri; and Wichita, Kansas.[97] (Presumably numerous other locations have been missed due to the difficulty of researching local papers on a national scale.) By September 1915, Robyn-Kander had begun to assemble an array of commission-earning offices and jobbers and promised, in print, that a successful regional salesman could expect to earn as much as $100 per week—the equivalent of more than $125,000 per year in current dollars.[98] Simultaneously, national advertising, through trade journals like *Printers' Ink*, effectively ceased.[99]

In addition to this local turn, the company's business boom between late 1915 and early 1916 also appears to have been the result of greater coordination of the business interests of Robyn-Kander and Universal. The bulk of the known contracts were signed to coincide with the arrival, in local theaters, of Universal's new Broadway Features; this new line of films had begun its first run release in July 1915 but was only beginning to reach

Robyn-Kander's many small-town theaters in September and October.[100] Tiny Monett, Missouri, is again a perfect case study. Broadway Features arrived in the Gem Theater in mid-September (two months after first run).[101] The Robyn-Kander plan was advertised and went into local effect the same week.[102] It is clear that either Universal was suggesting the adoption of Robyn-Kander tickets to the exhibitors who signed on for Broadway Features or that Robyn-Kander was using Universal's exhibition data to target particular theaters. Whatever the case, the success of this tactic, however brief, provides clear evidence of the impact of film industry acceptance on the cinema-advertising field; major studio funding, contacts, and data were key elements in the elevation of Robyn-Kander above its peers and into national relevance.

In the wake of these two transitions in the business model, a remarkable flurry of adoption occurred; towns and cities, ranging from 1,000 citizens in McHenry, Illinois, to 700,000 citizens in St. Louis, Missouri, began to sign on.[103] (Surprisingly, there is no evidence of success near the home office in New York.) Despite significant archival limitations, especially in the realm of small-town newspapers, the collected numbers are staggering. Compared to just two known manufacturer contracts through August 29, 1915, seventy different merchant contracts were reported between August 30 and the end of September, with an average of more than one hundred per month through March of the following year. In a suitably large city, roughly one theater per 5,000 residents and one merchant per 1,500, would contract for the plan. Pittsburgh, home of David Simon's wildly active branch office, was the crown jewel. The city redeemed nearly half a million free admissions in December of 1915 and peaked at a reported 2,000 contracted merchants early the following year.[104] Over the course of Robyn-Kander's entire nineteen months of operation, the company published the names of at least 776 contracted merchants and 275 theaters. This total, of course, omits many other contracts for which I have not unearthed evidence or that were never named in print.

Despite the seeming immediacy of success, the Robyn-Kander plan—much like merchant matinees, airdomes, and park and touring shows—took on the tone of a short-lived gimmick, rather than a permanent piece of the local cinema landscape. Contracted cities had a tendency to lapse after a single month, indicating that the bulk of contracted merchants were no more convinced of the value of the Robyn-Kander plan than they had been of other free-cinema schemes. The key task for the historian is to determine the array of reasons for both persistence and abandonment of the plan. What caused the program to falter so regularly in small towns? And what were the triggers for the loss of stable cities? Robyn-Kander's helpful public lists of participating merchants allow us to make educated guesses about the conditions that could have moved the plan from gimmick to quasi-permanence and some of the plausible triggers of swelling disinterest.

Firstly, urban centers appear to have required minimum levels of penetration. Although there is some significant noise in the data caused by very small towns, the few cities and towns that carried their contracts into a second month or more cluster around significantly better contract-to-citizen ratios. Of the twenty-three locations for which significant data exists, only five continued beyond the first month.[105] Four of these lasted for at least two months: Pittsburgh, Pennsylvania (twenty-eight weeks known); Monongahela, Pennsylvania (ten weeks known); Lackawanna, New York (ten weeks known); and Eufaula, Oklahoma (eight weeks known).[106] Tonawanda, New York, with a fifth known week in the historical record, technically makes the cut as well; however, the logical inference, due to the anomalous duration, is that this was a one-month contract severely distorted by supply heavily outstripping demand.[107] At first, this list appears to be completely random, representing only five of the sixteen best merchant-to-citizen ratios; even without Tonawanda, we have only four of the best nine. However, small towns often had an entire population smaller than the ratio average. If one removes the towns of 10,000 population and below (including Eufaula and Monongahela), twelve data points remain; among those twelve, Pittsburgh (first, at roughly 275 citizens per contracted merchant), Lackawanna (second, at 400 citizens per merchant), and Tonawanda (fifth, at 2,445 citizens per merchant) represent some of the best ratios. Note that the order of those three is identical to the list of durations, while the top two have ratios far superior to number three (Guthrie, Oklahoma, at 1,438 citizens per merchant) and Tonawanda. As such, better merchant-to-citizen ratios almost always led to a longer life span for the program, at least in large cities. Though less data exists for theatrical penetration rates, the same pattern is visible. Of the fourteen towns with significant information, the continuing towns represent four of the seven best ratios, in the order of Monongahela, Eufaula, Pittsburgh, and Tonawanda (no theater information for Lackawanna is known). Again, the three outliers are small towns—in this case, all of 4,000 citizens or less. Although the sequence is scrambled, the shortest, Tonawanda, once again appears furthest down the list; eliminate Tonawanda, and the others represent three of the four best penetration rates.

Town-by-town issues are also evident; the plan's incompatibility with local trends could have triggered concern. For example, Robyn-Kander had a clear lack of foresight regarding exhibition. Although the nickel ticket may have been a comfortable standard when Robyn-Kander opened for business in 1915, it was also showing its age. In Mt. Sterling, Kentucky, for example, Robyn-Kander had signed a contract with the Tabb theater and was circulating ticket fragments in town by April 11. The following week, on April 17 and 18, the Tabb was screening *Birth of a Nation* with seats starting at one dollar.[108] As such, for two days in the early stages of Robyn-Kander service, a seat would have cost a citizen of Mt. Sterling four-hundred fragments—an unwieldy and impossible sum. By building a business model on the assumption of a nickel ticket at the dawn of specially priced features,[109] Universal

Moving Picture Tickets were dangerously close to being a historical relic on their first appearance. It is not unlikely that in towns where only one theater was accepting Robyn-Kander tickets, anomalies like this created disinterest and even ill will.

It is possible, of course, that the Robyn-Kander company would have eventually attempted to come to terms with all of these issues. A logical response might have included shifting its business strategy to a constant rotation of active cities (for example, one month per year in each location), instead of aiming for permanence outside of hub cities; with a significant number of participating towns, embracing the status of gimmick might have been sufficient. Likewise, the company may have managed a rapid turn to an alternative price structure, at minimum upgrading the face value of its tickets to ten cents. Before Robyn-Kander could formulate functional responses to the above issues, however, an encounter with anti-coupon statutes scuttled the entire plan.

As indicated in the previous sections, the laws regarding stamp and coupon plans had no national uniformity at this time. It appears that Robyn-Kander successfully strolled through a minefield for several months before finally being made aware of the danger it had been facing. In an October 1915 exchange with the attorney general of West Virginia, Pittsburgh branch manager David Simon learned of the state's $500 fee for the operation of a coupon plan and the fact that this fee had been challenged by Sperry & Hutchinson and upheld.[110] Robyn-Kander had been operating for nearly a year and had spent a small fortune establishing branches and publishing ads, yet the tone of these letters indicates that this is the first the company had heard of such statutes. Robyn-Kander thus provides an important reminder that small start-up companies, seeking to become cinema-centric ad agencies, could and did enter the field with little to no knowledge of business law outside of their home states. And those laws, in the 1910s, could vary widely.

The company could also be remarkably thickheaded once such issues were encountered. Though the West Virginia issue was discovered in October 1915, either Robyn-Kander thought the state an anomaly or David Simon thought it insignificant enough not to inform the head office in New York. By late February 1916, the company had hired a salesman in Seattle and spent a week frittering away funds on newspaper advertising in the state with the most repressive anti-coupon statute in the country.[111] It was not until the US Supreme Court upheld the Seattle law in late March that the upper management of Robyn-Kander appears to have seriously considered the difficulties they were facing. Immediately after the court had given every state in the union carte blanche to erect prohibitive license fees against coupon plans, Robyn-Kander's slim hold on success started to falter. After six consecutive months of relentless expansion, only five known contracts were announced in April. I have found only one new contract announcement for the remaining eight months of the year—an early August pact in the small town of Uniontown, Pennsylvania, located squarely within the region where the company historically had been strongest.[112] Even Pittsburgh went into a steep descent: the peak of 2,000 merchants was reported in mid-February, but by early May, all local publicity had ceased. The situation was dire enough in April that the branch office tried luring new contracts by offering a free share of stock in the company in exchange for a commitment of only one dollar.[113]

In the wake of these many concerns, the unity between Robyn-Kander's various power centers gave way. The company had always been riddled with contradictions: a small-town concept that was more successful in big cities, an independent company that traded primarily on Universal's name, and significant authority figures in four different cities (Chicago, New York, Los Angeles, and Pittsburgh). By the middle of 1916, after two months of grinding rapidly to a halt, the company saw its dissolution occur via a bewildering chain of fraying links. Funding was pulled by a man in California (Laemmle), due to a court decision made in Washington, DC, regarding a law from Washington state, triggering a lawsuit in New York filed by a man from Pittsburgh (branch manager David Simon).[114]

As such, what we have here is a small-time company, wildly out of its depth—in fact, wholly unaware of its own legality—but briefly succeeding due to a confluence of interests. The film industry, and especially Universal, was ramping up its public relations efforts in 1915, and "Universal Moving Picture Tickets" were a novel and seemingly pleasant means of branding.[115] However, within a few short years, the industry was operating almost entirely differently, with theater chains, picture palaces, and an increasingly firm distinction between high-class and low-class business. For Universal, free tickets were simply one of many tactics tried and abandoned during a long-term PR push. Likewise, local merchants interested in film were soon to learn that it was much easier to profit from an association with Hollywood by selling licensed products; Jackie Coogan hats would have hitched a merchant to the movies without requiring the adoption of a problematic and legally questionable coupon scheme.[116] Meanwhile, small-town and neighborhood exhibitors, hanging in the moment before the rise of urban palace envy, were flitting from idea to idea in an attempt to maximize their own notoriety.[117] Robyn-Kander was simply one of the ideas that drew brief attention before those exhibitors moved on.

LESS THAN ZERO

The American film industry's minor dalliance with free cinema in the vicinity of World War I indicates just how invested some were in bringing advertising into a closer relationship with cinema. The brevity of its existence, however, provides equally compelling evidence of just how far outside the norm the idea remained. In attempting to create a completely different method of entry to the cinema, many created entirely new business models that drifted into oblivion almost instantly. As such, though the glimpses are revelatory, free cinema has left the fewest historical details, including an almost complete absence of information on the businesses and people themselves.

What is clear is that free cinema was, in many ways, the evil twin of peripheral advertising. Both were experimented with haphazardly. Whereas peripheral advertising shows a clear tendency toward streamlining (resulting in the dominance of the Publicity Clock Company), free cinema remained eternally wild and amorphous. Free cinema was thus one of the ways in which cinema advertising would clearly differentiate the experience of cinema from location to location. Not even Robyn-Kander managed to integrate a significant portion of the United States into its business. Regional volatility—resulting in different dominant tactics across the country (Robyn Kander in Pittsburgh, park screenings in Dallas, merchant matinees and touring shows in Wisconsin)—renders the entire field of free cinema nearly impossible to pin down as a national movement.

Though free cinema was also perhaps the least common method of cinema advertising attempted at the time, the pushback from the mainstream film industry was no less clear. Indeed, free cinema received what was almost certainly the harshest welcome of any of the tactics discussed in this book. Legal challenges from local exhibitors, direct dissuasion (rather than simple complaints) from F. H. Richardson, and even the financial abandonment of Robyn-Kander by a mainstream production company were all unique challenges faced by free-cinema purveyors and clearly indicate an industry growing openly hostile to a dual-market structure (content sold to an audience or provided for free, with their attention then sold to advertisers). The attempted placement of advertising dollars directly between cinemagoers and exhibitors was a step much too far for many in the mainstream film industry, who preferred to think of their audience as consumers not consumable. It was the alternative cinema—the nascent nontheatrical circuit of educational film—that would eventually adopt many of these ideas as foundational assumptions for its business model.

The growth of the nontheatrical field, however, is not the only way in which free-cinema experiments influenced future developments in the advertising culture of twentieth-century America. If slides mark the advent of the commercial break, and trailers the spot advertisement, the various attempts at free cinema provide the first known example of electric media funded indirectly. As such, free cinema, although it often blurred the lines between advertising and marketing, provides the media historian with the cinema's clearest link to the development of modern American commercial media, connecting the motion picture to the development of broadcasting and to the modern internet. Although cinema remained outside the home and shows were organized and funded individually, the free commercial airwaves were a silent-era experiment abandoned while still imperfect.

NOTES

1. Ernest A. Dench, *Advertising by Motion Pictures* (Cincinnati, OH: Standard, 1916), 141, 145.

2. Compare this to the interpretations of advertising offered decades later by Dallas W. Smythe (entertainment as the bribe or "free lunch" designed to turn leisure time into "labor power" that goes otherwise unpaid) and Sut Jhally (entertainment as the wage paid for the labor of watching ads. Smythe, "Communications: Blindspot of Western Marxism," *Canadian Journal of Political and Social Theory* 1, no. 3 (1977): 5, 11. Jhally, *The Codes of Advertising: Fetishism and the Political Economy of Meaning in the Consumer Society* (New York: Routledge, 1990), 85.

3. "Among the Slide Makers," *MPW*, November 7, 1908, 357; "Advertising Slides," *Nickelodeon*, July 1909, 3; James H. Collins, "Advertising Via the Moving Picture," *PI*, February 23, 1910, 25; Joseph B. Baker, "Examples of Motion Picture Advertising," *Motography*, June 1911, 133; and "Six Advertising 'Talkies' Get Talked About," *PI*, March 26, 1931, 75.

4. Ironically, free screenings were the same tactic that had long frustrated indirect advertisers. Although the history of indirect advertising has

intersected with direct advertising in numerous places, this is the area that would benefit from the greatest additional probing. Did the history of frustration with nontheatrical free shows produce an initial skepticism of free cinema that direct advertisers could not overturn? Or was the billboard screening considered an exciting new means to increase the viability of an advertiser-funded show? Most likely it was a mix of both; initial excitement about ad-funded entertainment screenings probably came under immediate question when park and touring shows came under attack by increasingly hostile exhibitors.

5. For a discussion of serials, cliff-hangers, and audience retention, see Ben Singer, *Melodrama and Modernity: Early Sensational Cinema and Its Contexts* (New York: Columbia University Press, 2001).

6. For a history of the rise of consumer culture at the turn of the century, see William Leach, *Land of Desire: Merchants, Power, and the Rise of a New American Culture* (New York: Vintage Books, 1993).

7. As with most concepts, international experimentation is also evident. In 1908, Mexico City offered free "views" on the city streets interspersed with ads and had a theater operated by a cigarette company that accepted cigarette coupons as tickets. "Cinematographs in Mexico," *MPW*, February 22, 1908, 141. In London, a member of the stock exchange proposed that a theater be taken over in every major city to screen advertising films, using entertainment films as an inducement to attend. "Foreign Trade Notes: British Notes," *MPW*, November 29, 1913, 997.

8. "Free Picture Shows in City Parks," *MPW*, June 17, 1916, 2080.

9. Eric Schaefer, *Bold! Daring! Shocking! True!: A History of Exploitation Films, 1919–1959* (Durham, NC: Duke University Press, 1999), 3.

10. "The Auto Picture Show," *MPW*, June 17, 1911, 1367.

11. One ticket for fifty cents, see Display Ad, *Monett Times*, May 16, 1913, 8. One ticket for twenty-five cents, see Display Ad, *Shreveport Times*, October 20, 1914, 2. Two tickets for twenty-five cents, see Display Ad, *Macon Daily Herald*, August 27, 1914, 4. Ten tickets for one dollar, see Display Ad, *Macon Daily Chronicle*, September 2, 1914, 2.

12. "Free Show For Farmers," *Durant Weekly News*, May 1, 1914, 5.

13. The Delite Theater in Decatur, Alabama, ran a full Friday schedule entirely funded by merchants, with no further dates scheduled: "1200 People Attend Merchants Free Matinee," *Decaturs Daily*, September 18, 1915, 3.

14. Display Ad, *Brainerd Daily Dispatch*, March 24, 1916, 2.

15. Kathryn H. Fuller, *At the Picture Show: Small Town Audiences and the Creation of Movie Fan Culture* (Washington, DC: Smithsonian Institution Press, 1996), 76, 85–97.

16. Ibid., 90. See also Richard deCordova, "Ethnography and Exhibition: The Child Audience, The Hays Office, and Saturday Matinees," *Camera Obscura* 23 (1991): 91–108; Alison M. Parker, "Mothering the Movies: Women Reformers and Popular Culture," in *Movie Censorship and American Culture*, ed. Francis G. Couvares (Washington, DC: Smithsonian Institution Press, 1996,) 73–96; and Jeremy Groskopf, "A Tempest in a Tub: The Atlanta Better Films Committee and the 'Passive Censorship' Experiment" (master's thesis, Emory University, 2008).

17. Barbara Klinger, "Cinema's Shadow: Reconsidering Non-Theatrical Exhibition," in *Going to the Movies: Hollywood and the Social Experience of the Cinema*, ed. Richard Maltby, Melvin Stokes, and Robert C. Allen (Exeter, UK: University of Exeter Press, 2008).

18. James H. Collins, "Advertising via the Moving Picture," *PI*, February 23, 1910, 24.

19. B. F. Goodrich held a one-hour presentation of tire films; see "Los Angeles: Advertising Film," *MPW*, May 13, 1911, 1068. Maxwell automobiles likewise rented a theater in Marion, Ohio; see "Cincinnati," *MPW*, October 10, 1914, 218. In the absence of a theater to rent, other businesses used touring film trucks, rooftop advertising, and daylight screenings near prominent doorways; see "The Auto Picture Show," *MPW*, June 17, 1911, 1367; "Detroit," *MPW*, October 3, 1914, 83; Display Ad, *MPW*, September 15, 1917, 1759; "Moving Pictures in World's Busiest Passenger Terminal," *MPW*, November 10, 1917, 907; and "Films to Help Recruiting," *MPW*, August 28, 1915, 1524.

20. "Notes," *MPW*, December 23, 1911, 975.

21. "Correspondence: Louisville," *MPW*, March 30, 1912, 1185

22. A telling example is the Billiken Shoe Company's funding of a single children's matinee in Atlanta in 1921. As the cost of children's matinees was already the burden of the local Woman's Club and the theater itself, the cost to Billiken was likely much lower than a traditional screening. "Billiken Shoe Story Shown to Children: Fred S. Stewart Co. Host of Little Tots at Howard Theater," *Atlanta Constitution*, September 18, 1921, 7.

23. "In the News Net.," *New York Times*, July 4, 1920, 65.

24. *PI*, December 2, 1920, 41. For a similar example, see "Is Your Movie Theater Empty in the Morning? Then Use It to Show Your Electrical Films!," *Electrical Merchandising* (September 1920): 151.

25. F. H. Richardson, "Projection Department," *MPW*, November 4, 1911, 374–375.

26. "Unfair Competition in Jackson, Tenn.," *MPW*, August 5, 1911, 297.

27. Clement H. Congdon, "Philadelphia," *MPW*, July 13, 1912, 160. "Novel Advertising Scheme," *MPW*, September 11, 1915, 1857.

28. Midwest Special Service, "Correspondence: Indiana," *MPW,* June 28, 1913, 1384.

29. Midwest Special Service, "Illinois," *MPW,* November 7, 1914, 807.

30. *Moving Picture World* argued that cigarette advertising was not a good fit for motion pictures in an era when they were trying to shake the image of being unhealthy for children. The city of Pittsburgh attempted to ban tobacco coupons completely. "A Big Corporation's Pipe Dream," *Motography,* November 23, 1912, 384; Epes Winthrop Sargent, "Advertising for Exhibitors," *MPW,* January 4, 1913, 42; and D. L. Manley, "Correspondence: Pittsburgh," *MPW,* February 1, 1913, 481.

31. "Correspondence: Missouri," *MPW,* July 11, 1914, 320.

32. The copyright was made official on March 15, 1913. *Catalogue of Copyright Entries, Part 4* (Washington, DC: Government Printing Office, 1913): 221.

33. "Amusements: The Palace Theater," *The Eagle,* June 23, 1913, 6.

34. Display Ad, *Daily Free Press,* March 22, 1918, 2.

35. "Merchant's Matinee," *Council Grove Republican,* February 27, 1914, 2; "Merchants Matinee to Begin Thursday," *Macon Daily Herald,* August 26, 1914, 1; Display Ad, *Macon Daily Herald,* August 27, 1914, 4; Display Ad, *Macon Daily Chronicle,* September 2, 1914, 2; "Exhibitors News: Illinois," *MPW,* September 5, 1914, 1394; "Missouri," *MPW,* October 24, 1914, 516; Display Ad, *Shreveport Times,* October 20, 1914, 2; "Princess," *Star Tribune,* November 8, 1914, 53; Display Ad, *Iowa City Press-Citizen,* November 14, 1914, 7; Display Ad, *Iola Register,* December 29, 1914, 3; and Display Ad, *Winfield Daily Free Press,* December 29, 1914, 5.

36. "Free Show for Farmers," *Durant Weekly News,* May 1, 1914, 5.

37. Display Ad, *Holt County Sentinel,* September 24, 1915, 6; Display Ad, *Albany Ledger,* November 4, 1915, 2; and Display Ad, *King City Chronicle,* November 26, 1915, 8.

38. Display Ad, *Stevens Point Daily Journal,* May 22, 1915, 4; Display Ad, *The New North,* June 3, 1915, 1; and Display Ad, *Sheboygan Press,* July 31, 1915, 5.

39. Display Ad, *Brainerd Daily Dispatch,* March 24, 1916, 2; Display Ad, *Evening Review,* September 30, 1916, 5; and Display Ad, *Alton Evening Telegraph,* October 26, 1916, 7. Extant ads for 1917 indicate no change to the pattern. After a break of three years, the 1920 ads had lost all cohesion around screening dates, and the cost per tickets had increased to fifty cents.

40. "Merchants Matinee Is Theatre Feature," *Walnut Valley Times,* March 31, 1916, 4; Display Ad, *Beloit Daily Call,* May 10, 1916, 4; "Trade

with These Merchants," *Hays Free Press*, May 20, 1916, 1; Display Ad, *Holton Recorder*, May 25, 1916, 8; and Display Ad, *Great Bend Tribune*, June 26, 1916, 5.

41. "Dreamland," *Monett Times*, May 16, 1913, 8; Display Ad, *Monett Times*, January 8, 1915, 2; and Display Ad, *Monett Times*, September 17, 1915, 1.

42. "Tickets to Picture Shows," *Retail Grocers' Advocate*, February 18, 1916, 21; and "Schemes That Have Gone Before," *Retail Grocers' Advocate*, August 31, 1916, 57.

43. The US Census shows two plausible Delmar Lees in Illinois in 1910 and one in 1920. The one who appears in both lists was in his late twenties in 1914. He was listed as a teamster in 1910 and as the driver of a coal wagon in 1920. The other Delmar Lee was a real estate agent. "Exhibitor News: Illinois," *MPW*, August 29, 1914, 1258. In the small town of Rossville, south of Chicago, the manager of the Idle Hour Theater was also offering free screenings "on the streets" on Wednesday evenings. However, it is not clear if these were ad funded or simply a public-service advertising gimmick for the theater.

44. Jas. S. McQuade, "Municipal Moving Pictures in St. Louis," *MPW*, August 1, 1914, 689.

45. Ibid.

46. "Free Films in East St. Louis Parks," *MPW*, June 16, 1917, 1823. It is possible that the practice did extend into Missouri on wheels rather than in parks. Two months prior to the East St. Louis plan, the city of St. Louis, Missouri, received a proposal by "an advertising concern" to tour free performances through town showing films on screens mounted on the backs of moving vans. Local exhibitors, in attempting to file a complaint, were told that free shows operating out of a truck required no license. A. H. Giebler, "What Is Doing in St. Louis Film Circles," *MPW*, April 21, 1917, 478.

47. Ibid.; and "Missouri," *MPW*, February 21, 1914, 981.

48. No known estimates exist for the cost of a 1910s park screening, although a 1919 Cleveland city park airdome had an estimated construction cost of between five and ten thousand dollars; see "Renewed Building Activities," *MPW*, March 8, 1919, 1348. For estimates of typical 1910s theatrical expenses, see James F. Hodges, *Opening and Operating a Motion Picture Theater: How It Is Done Successfully* (New York: Scenario Publishing, 1912), 46; Thomas O. Monk, "Theater Competition—An Example," *Motography*, April 1, 1916, 743; Rev. J. J. Phelan, *Motion Pictures as a Phase of Commercialized Amusement in Toledo, Ohio* (Toledo, OH: Little Book,

1919), 29–36; and Richard Koszarski, *An Evening's Entertainment: The Age of the Silent Feature Picture, 1915–1928* (New York: Charles Scribner's Sons, 1990), 10.

49. "Free Picture Show with Ads," *MPW,* June 5, 1915, 1647.

50. "Films in Civic Social Program," *MPW,* February 12, 1916, 992.

51. Debbie Cox, "The Sudekum Family in Nashville, Tennessee," *Family History—And Other Matters* (blog), February 24, 2014, accessed November 30, 2017, http://debieoeser.blogspot.com/2014/02/sudeukum-family-nashville-tennessee.html; and "Free Picture Shows in City Parks," *MPW,* June 17, 1916, 2080.

52. "Free Films in Parks," *MPW,* June 24, 1916, 2276.

53. "Texas," *Motography,* February 19, 1916, 444.

54. W. F. Jacoby, "Report on Playgrounds and Public Recreations," in *Park and Playground System, Dallas, Texas 1921–1923* (Report), 30, 35.

55. Frank H. Madison, "Wisconsin Film Notes," *MPW,* September 9, 1916, 1735.

56. David Simon in Pittsburgh, "Pittsburgh Items," *MPW,* October 30, 1915, 823; Franklin Mettler in Delaware, "Ticket Corporation Gets Charter," *MPW,* March 4, 1916, 1509; H. H. Munro in Seattle, Display Ad, *Seattle Star,* February 29, 1916, 2; and L. M. Baker and A. B. Palmer in Buffalo, Display Ad, *Tonawanda Evening News,* April 27, 1916, 2. The Albany branch provided an address: Display Ad, *Utica Herald-Dispatch,* January 21, 1916, 7. Three Ohio branches were reported, though no locations or managers were announced; see "David Simon Opens Branches," *MPW,* January 1, 1916, 109. One Ohio branch was clearly from Cincinnati: Display Ad, *Cincinnati Enquirer,* December 5, 1915, 20. One was in Little Rock: Display Ad, *Arkansas Gazette,* August 31, 1915, 5. One was in St. Louis: Display Ad, *St. Louis Post-Dispatch,* March 7, 1916, 13. One was in Chicago, in the Mallers Building where the pre-Universal company had been located: Display Ad, *Chicago Tribune,* September 19, 1915. Two others can be inferred: the existence of contracts in both Guthrie and Chickasha, Oklahoma, indicate that Oklahoma City probably had a branch. The California Grocers Association was aware enough of Robyn-Kander to mention it by name; as such, it is likely that there was at least one active branch in California. The existence of a debate with the attorney general for West Virginia indicates that one was likely opened briefly in that state as well.

57. "Brevities of the Business," *Motography,* February 27, 1915, 333; "Illinois Briefs," *MPW,* March 6, 1915, 1472; and Wm. Noble, "Southwestern News," *Motography,* September 16, 1916, 691. See also *Motography,*

September 9, 1916, 630; and Geo. F. Howard, *Biennial Report of the Secretary of State of the State of Texas, 1918* (Austin: A. C. Baldwin & Sons, 1918), 134.

58. G. D. Crain, Jr., "Sunday Show Progress in Tennessee," *MPW*, July 8, 1916, 277.

59. Oil City, PA (ten weeks), Display Ad, *Oil City Derrick*, January 22, 1917, 11; Portsmouth, OH (ten weeks), Display Ad, *Portsmouth Daily Times*, January 27, 1917, 2; Logan, KS (sixteen weeks), "Merchants Matinee Free to Farmers Only Commencing Saturday," *Logan Republican*, February 22, 1917, 1; Connellsville, PA, "The Arcade," *Daily Courier*, March 28, 1917, 10; Concordia, KS, Display Ad, *Concordia Blade-Empire*, April 4, 1917, 3; Oshkosh, WI (ten weeks), "Merchants' Matinees," *Oshkosh Daily Northwestern*, May 5, 1917, 8; Baltimore, MD (at least two months), J. M. Shellman, "Baltimore Newsletter: Co-Operative Plan at New Pickwick," *MPW*, May 19, 1917, 1160; Greensburg, KS, Display Ad, *Kiowa County Signal*, May 24, 1917, 12; Muncie, IN (two weeks), Display Ad, *Muncie Evening Press*, May 24, 1917, 3; and Kingman, KS, "Free Picture Show," *Leader Courier*, October 5, 1917, 1.

60. Carbondale, IL (fourteen weeks), Display Ad, *Daily Free Press*, March 22, 1918, 2; East Jordan, MI (at least two weeks), "Merchants' Matinee Was a Humdinger," *Charlevoix County Herald*, April 19, 1918, 1; and Girard, KS, "Merchants Matinee a Great Success," *Girard Press*, May 9, 1918, 5.

61. Sandusky, OH (two days of merchant matinees), Display Ad, *Sandusky Register*, February 2, 1919, 7; Greensburg, KS (one-off merchant matinee), "Merchants' Matinee," *Kiowa County Signal*, March 20, 1919, 1; and Alton, IL (ten weeks, merchant matinee), Display Ad, *Alton Evening Telegraph*, July 11, 1919, 5.

62. New Philadelphia, OH (ten weeks, merchant matinee), Display Ad, *Daily Times*, April 3, 1920, 5; Sioux Falls, SD (ten weeks, merchant matinee), Display Ad, *Argus-Leader*, April 28, 1920, 13; Wisconsin Rapids, WI (ten weeks, merchant matinee), Display Ad, *Daily Tribune*, November 13, 1920, 4; and Dallas, TX (summer park screenings), "Dallas," *MPW*, September 17, 1921, 315.

63. Phillip J. Callan Jr. and Norman I. Jacobs, "Trading Stamps and the Law," *Boston College Law Review* 4, no. 3 (April 1963): 637–660.

64. "Premiums and Novelties," *Simmons' Spice Mill* (March 1917): 353, 355.

65. "Washington Coupon Law," *Retail Grocers' Advocate*, March 10, 1916, 21.

66. *Twenty-Sixth Biennial Report and Official Opinions of the Attorney General of the State of West Virginia* (Charleston, WV: Tribune Printing, 1916): 337.

67. *Rast v. Van Deman & Lewis Co.*, 240 US 342 (1916).

68. *Exhbitors Herald* referenced its own two years of published opposition in a text box inserted into a report on the rising outcry from Washington, DC; see "Renting Films to Churches Must Stop Warns Crandall," *EH*, January 29, 1921, 53.

69. "'Non-Theatrical' Hurts Regular Trade, Washington Exhibitors Protest in Alarm," *MPW*, March 20, 1920, 1943.

70. "Educator Takes Issue with Managers Who Fear Effect of Non-Theatricals," *MPW*, April 17, 1920, 389.

71. Ibid.; and W. F. Jacoby, "Report on Playgrounds and Public Recreations," in *Park and Playground System, Dallas, Texas 1921–1923* (Report), 35.

72. "St. Louis Mayor Promises Aid in Fighting Censorship," *EH*, February 5, 1921, 37; Jay M. Shreck, "Theatre Men Prescribe Means of Eliminating Non-theatricals," *EH*, August 23, 1924, 21.

73. "Regulation of the Trading Stamp Industry," *Duke Bar Journal* 6, no. 2 (1957): 87.

74. Gregory A. Waller, "Free Talking Picture—Every Farmer Is Welcome: Non-Theatrical Film and Everyday Life in Rural America During the 1930s," in Maltby, et al., *Going to the Movies*.

75. Multipage Display Ad, *Motion Picture Daily*, April 27, 1945, 5–12.

76. See the Picturephone, which could have filled the cultural role that the internet eventually claimed, had the technology been successfully adopted. Kenneth Lipartito, "Picturephone and the Information Age: The Social Meaning of Failure," *Technology and Culture* 44, no. 1 (January 2003): 50–81. In much the same way, the cinema could have been downtown television, given the acceptance of advertising breaks and ticketless entry.

77. Display Ad, *PI*, February 18, 1915, 71.

78. "Merchants Free Matinee at Delite September 17," *Decaturs Daily*, September 11, 1915, 2.

79. Display Ad, *Albany Ledger*, November 4, 1915, 2.

80. Display Ad, *Billboard*, June 19, 1915, 53.

81. Presumably, the explanation was a propensity for the buyer to attribute sales to their own frugality and gifts to the generosity of the seller; although both would have been psychologically pleasant, only the latter reflected positively on the business itself. By the 1950s, the prevailing

wisdom had shifted from this psychology of gift economics to a hobbyist mentality. Studies showed that shoppers were less interested in the value of trading stamps than with the activity of collecting them and filling a book. H. B. Shaffer, "Trading Stamp Boom," *Editorial Research Reports 1956* (Washington, DC: CQ Press). Retrieved from http://library.cqpress.com/cqresearcher/cqresrre1956061400, accessed April 2, 2021.

82. Display Ad, *MPN*, June 19, 1915, 133.

83. Multipage Ad, *PI*, March 11, 1915, 53.

84. "Trading Stamps for Theaters," *Motography*, June 26, 1915, 1039.

85. F. H. Richardson, "Projection Department," *MPW*, November 4, 1911, 374–375.

86. "Movie Coupons Next," *Retail Grocers' Advocate*, August 6, 1915, 27; and "Movie Ticket Man About," *Retail Grocers' Advocate*, April 14, 1916, 19.

87. "A New One Every Minute," *Retail Grocers' Advocate*, August 6, 1915, 7; "Coupon Schemes Are Dead," *Retail Grocers' Advocate*, August 20, 1915, 5; "We Refused Their Ads," *Retail Grocers' Advocate*, October 1, 1915, 23; "Sacramento Local Complains," *Retail Grocers' Advocate*, January 28, 1916, 17.

88. See "Movie Tickets Scheme Here," *Retail Grocers' Advocate*, October 29, 1915, 23; and "Beware of Movie Ticket," *Retail Grocers' Advocate*, November 5, 1915, 15.

89. Callan and Jacobs, "Trading Stamps and the Law," 639.

90. Display Ad, *Monett Times*, May 16, 1913, 2; Display Ad, *Monett Times*, January 8, 1915, 2; and Display Ad, *Monett Times*, September 17, 1915, 1.

91. The earliest advertisement claims that "the ticket is guaranteed to be as good as gold . . . by a concern having millions of dollars constantly employed in their business relations with exhibitors"; the "concern" is clearly Universal. Display Ad, *PI*, February 4, 1915, 81. Universal's Joe Brandt was vice president of the company, while Carl Laemmle and Patrick Powers were on the board of directors. It is plausible that these official positions had been established when the company was in Chicago. *Polk's New York Copartnership and Corporation Directory: Boroughs of Manhattan and Bronx*, vol. 63 (New York City: R. L. Polk & Co., 1915), 877.

92. Display Ad, *MPW*, October 31, 1914, 585; and "Universal Claims Priority," *MPN*, April 4, 1914, 32.

93. Callan and Jacobs, "Trading Stamps and the Law," 637. Callan and Jacobs provide estimates of $14 to $15 per 5,000 (cost) and $2.50 per 1,200 (redemption). Mathematically this works out to a redemption rate of between 69.4 and 74.4 percent—the equivalent of a roughly 40 percent markup.

94. Display Ad, *Tonawanda Evening News*, April 27, 1916, 2.

95. Display Ad, *MPN*, June 19, 1915, 133.

96. Display Ad, *Creamery and Milk Plant Monthly* (June 1915): 43.

97. See *Chicago Daily Tribune* (p. 65), *Charlotte Observer* (p. 22), *Indianapolis Star* (p. 25), *Lincoln Star* (p. 6), *Little Rock Daily Gazette* (p. 38), *Muncie Star Press* (p. 23), *Pittsburgh Post-Gazette* (unpaginated), *St. Louis Post-Dispatch* (p. 40), and *Wichita Daily Eagle* (p. 20). On later dates, at least six further cities are known: *Burlington Free Press* (Vermont, July 14, p. 11), *Atlanta Constitution* (Georgia, August 1, p. 9), *Louisville Courier-Journal* (Kentucky, August 15, p. 27), *New Castle Herald* (Pennsylvania, August 24, p. 9), *Ft. Wayne Journal-Gazette* (Indiana, September 19, p. 30), and *Des Moines Register* (Iowa, October 24, p. 35). A classified ad also appeared in the *Winnipeg Tribune* on August 10 (p. 12).

98. See prior note for list of state offices. It is unclear how many sales positions were salaried and how many worked on commission. The only known salaried position was in Pittsburgh. Classified Ad, *Pittsburgh Press*, December 26, 1915.

99. The only examples of national advertising after July were in *Bakers Review*; see December 1915 issue, Display Ad (p. 96), and "Contracting for Universal Movie Tickets" (p. 78).

100. Display Ad, *MPW*, July 17, 1915, 430.

101. "Movie News," *Monett Times*, September 3, 1915, 8.

102. Display Ad, *Monett Times*, September 17, 1915, 1.

103. Display Ad, *McHenry Plaindealer*, September 23, 1915; and Display Ad, *St. Louis Post-Dispatch*, March 7, 1916, 13.

104. Display Ad, *Pittsburgh Press*, January 13, 1916, 12; Display Ad, *Seattle Star*, March 2, 1916, 6; and Display Ad, *Pittsburgh Press*, February 21, 1916, 8.

105. A further thirteen active cities and towns are known, bringing the total to thirty-six. However, I know of only a single identified merchant contract in each locale.

106. Display Ad, *Pittsburgh Press*, October 13, 1915, 18; Display Ad, *Pittsburgh Press*, April 30, 1916, 6; Display Ad, *Daily Republican*, February 4, 1916; Display Ad, *Daily Republican*, April 17, 1916, 1; Display Ad, *Lackawanna Daily Journal*, April 11, 1916, 4; Display Ad, *Lackawanna Daily Journal*, June 18, 1916, 2; Display Ad, *Indian Journal*, September 24, 1915, unpaginated; and Display Ad, *Indian Journal*, November 19, 1915.

107. "Movie Tickets Free! Enjoy Life's Luxuries," *North Tonawanda Evening News*, April 3, 1916, 1; and Display Ad, *North Tonawanda Evening News*, May 8, 1916, 2.

108. Display Ad, *Mt. Sterling Advocate,* April 11, 1916, 5; and Display Ad, *Mt. Sterling Advocate,* April 11, 1916, 8.

109. Fuller, *At the Picture Show,* 47–49.

110. *Twenty-Sixth Biennial Report and Official Opinions of the Attorney General of the State of West Virginia* (Charleston, WV: Tribune Printing, 1916): 337, 357.

111. Display Ad, *Seattle Star,* February 29, 1916, 2; Display Ad, *Seattle Star,* March 1, 1916, 9; and Display Ad, *Seattle Star,* March 2, 1916, 6.

112. Display Ad, *Uniontown Morning Herald,* August 12, 1916, 1.

113. Display Ad, *Pittsburgh Press,* April 25, 1916, 22.

114. Simon's lawsuit indicates that Universal's removal of funding was a unilateral and abrupt decision. Simon was allegedly compelled to refund the purchase price of $73,000 worth of suddenly unusable tickets. "In the Courts," *Wid's Daily,* January 6, 1919, 2; and "In the Courts," *Wid's Daily,* June 13, 1919, 4.

115. For a brief history of Universal City as a public relations event, see Bernard F. Dick, *City of Dreams: The Making and Remaking of Universal Pictures* (Lexington: University Press of Kentucky, 1997), 37–38.

116. "Wilson's 'Tie-Ups' for Jackie Coogan Win 'The Kid' Thousands in Royalties," *MPW,* November 19, 1921, 323.

117. Fuller, *At the Picture Show,* 112–114.

CONCLUSION

Intemperate Proclamations

> Advertising men are not and cannot be moved by appeals to their aesthetic sensibilities. They have none. They climb . . . our own glorious mountains and upon those awe-inspiring heights, when man is nearest to the blue vault of heaven, they paint the name of some tooth paste with an adjuration to use the same. . . . Men to whom Nature, in her most solemn moods, fails to make the slightest appeal cannot be expected to stand in awe of the screen. I am often surprised that our great dramas are not interrupted at tense moments by the intemperate proclamation of the merits of so-and-so's cigarettes and of so-and-so's cheese.
>
> —W. Stephen Bush (1915)

IN EARLY 1915, *MOVING PICTURE World* columnist W. Stephen Bush published the above sarcastic review of the avalanche of cinema-advertising tactics that had hit his beloved film industry in the preceding few years. In deriding "the screen advertisement" as the greatest "of all the follies of the screen," Bush's article indicates, with calculated overstatement, the fear of a future in which advertising would fundamentally alter the standard business and aesthetic models of motion pictures. Indeed, as is clear from Bush's description, the possibility of the silent cinema becoming aesthetically indistinguishable from the much later television model ("great dramas . . . interrupted at tense moments by . . . intemperate proclamations") was very real.[1] It is not difficult, in fact, to imagine an alternative history in which the movie theater would have performed many of the functions now associated with broadcast television: providing regularly scheduled "free" media produced by large companies for a national audience and fragmented and littered with advertising appeals. As we have seen, however, that possibility remained very distant.

The history of silent-era advertising instead provides evidence of multiple competing models of an ad-supported cinema (ranging from minimal to full funding via onscreen and offscreen tactics) and multiple plausible arguments for why such models would succeed or fail. The appeal of the communicative powers of what was then the most up-to-date medium led advertisers to theorize both temporal and spatial flows of attention and to conceive of restrictions on cinema-advertising effectiveness ranging from the financial (ticket prices) to the psychological (the "combative spirit" or "ill will" caused by compulsory attention). Advertising could have led to a cinema program with frequent direct-advertising caesuras, a proliferation of viewing choices within the theater, or even the above-described proto-television free cinemas. Instead, the lack of easy national circulation through theaters and the relatively unified bloc of opposition from exhibitors and filmgoers (predominantly citing ticket cost and interior design) restrained and marginalized advertising in American cinemas. A "high-class" reconception of the cinema won out, with direct advertising eliminated entirely in almost every theater with pretensions to upper-class spectators.

TO EACH THEIR OWN MARGIN

Despite the marginalization of advertising in the mainstream American silent cinema, the experiments in and debates over cinema advertising were an important stage in the development of twentieth-century advertising. Cinema advertising was part of a larger process of social development. The early establishment of advertising as the low-class boogeyman for American cinema—perhaps the only moment in any medium in which advertising has been almost exclusively defined as bloodsucker rather than benefactor—is a key phase in the history of advertising as an idea in the United States. Failures are never truly gone; the marginalized are not necessarily marginal. To paraphrase Kenneth Lipartito, ideas and inventions that failed in the marketplace can nonetheless undermine or reinforce conceptual and technological paths, having far greater influence than their status as business propositions might suggest. As the media continually define and redefine themselves—branding and rebranding, often in response to the rise of new media forms—failures and resurrections are simply part of the process.[2]

In the 1925 book *Broadcasting: Its New Day,* cinema-exhibition guru "Roxy" Rothapfel asserted, in a direct quote of Secretary of Commerce Herbert Hoover, that "if you try to sell . . . some brand of shoes or anything else over the radio [then] you'll have no radio audience."[3] This restatement of the (still-young) cinema myth of the vanishing audience, in a book by a cinema exhibitor who had been making similar statements since at least 1916, is a clear indication that radio theorizing began where 1910s film theorizing left off.[4] Importantly, the sense that direct advertising would chase audiences away from a temporal, moving medium was not a minority opinion in early American radio. AT&T rented time to advertisers for "selling talks" in the early 1920s under the provision that direct advertising (specific information on product qualities and prices) was forbidden. Hoover made his comments in 1924, declaring, in short, that direct advertising would "kill broadcasting." As networks arose, this opposition to direct advertising was institutionalized; NBC, upon its formation in 1926, specifically declared that radio must function through indirect good-will advertising and could not be "a selling medium."[5] The fact that Rothapfel, AT&T, NBC, and Hoover all believed direct advertising on radio to be a dead end should come as no surprise, considering that opponents of advertising in motion-picture theaters had boisterously argued those exact points for more than a decade.

Radio-advertising theory only diverged from the developed film sense after hesitant experimentation to ascertain its own acceptable margins. Returning to the same ground debated across all cinema-advertising tactics, but without the problem of ticket cost, "receptivity" was eventually rethought in a radio-centric way. Radio appeals, for example, were described as the most powerful due to the idea that the radio voice had the "supple power to move people and mold them, to enlist them and command them. . . . For people do what they are told."[6] Additionally, radio programs created and sponsored by advertisers were considered to "creat[e] a subconscious obligation [to buy] in the mind of the listener" on the grounds that the audience would feel indebted for the free entertainment.[7] The power of the voice and of "public service" (providing freely available entertainment) thus provided enough differentiation for broadcasting to overturn cinema assumptions.

In the wake of modern technology—time-shifting at first, followed shortly by the internet—these long-standing experiments and debates in temporal advertising returned yet again as advertising professionals attempted to differentiate and reconceive advertising for each medium. Silent-era experiments have been reborn in a variety of twenty-first-century media. Time-shifted television has experimented with corner bugs (a modern variant of Hunter's permanent iris) and squeezebacks and frames (Miedreichian screen-crowding tactics). Pre-roll and pop-up ads (slides and trailers), banners (another framing tactic), and progress-bar rollover ads (a variation on Whitaker's elapsed-time clock) populate the internet.

Contemporary interactive media have, of course, received their own receptivity theorizing. Scholar Paul Skalski has described video-game product placement as "a relatively new way to reach . . . not just consumers, but engaged consumers."[8] Internet marketing professional Greg Jarboe has promoted web advertising via a posture argument, asserting its excellence on the grounds that users "come predisposed to 'lean forward' rather [than] 'lean back.'"[9] Reflecting Ted Friedman's notion that technology provides a cultural "utopian sphere" in which "idealized visions of the future can be elaborated without instant dismissal," technological developments, for advertisers, persistently inspire utopian theorizing of the perfect advertising medium.[10] This utopian thinking repeatedly falls into well-worn grooves, regardless of the technology in question.

GONE TODAY, HERE TOMORROW?

Though other modern media have been more receptive to the overtures of the advertising industry, cinema advertising in the late 1920s and beyond retained its silent-era traits: internal conflict (over whether or not advertising was too low class) and hand-wringing over advertising in a ticketed medium. Cinema advertising never truly disappeared, even for a moment. Rather, it settled into a position at the margins with steadily increasing usage (and thus increasing condemnation) at moments of industrial transition.

In the wake of the advent of sound, for example, a J. Walter Thompson Company study found that "more or less regula[r]" advertising film screenings had expanded to "over half" of the sixteen thousand theaters in the country, but this half was disproportionately made up of "the country theatres or hole-in-the-wall type of 10-cent movie houses."[11] After the establishment of television, similarly sharp divisions were evident. Film historian Christopher Anderson has asserted that the American film industry attempted to rebrand itself as highbrow entertainment by referencing its absence of direct advertising—a decades-old tactic given new life for a new competitor.[12] A second J. Walter Thompson Company research report confirms the polarized atmosphere, as "theatres in the eight major metropolitan cities" had become so hostile that cinema advertising was virtually nonexistent anywhere in those locations.[13]

As cinema advertising began its mainstream institutionalization during the late 1970s with Screenvision and National CineMedia, producers like Norman Levy, executive vice president of Columbia, and Irving Ludwig, of the Walt Disney Company's distributing subsidiary Buena Vista, continued to voice silent-era perspectives on cinema advertising. Levy asserted that such advertising was "in terrible taste" and suited only to "low class theaters." Ludwig, by contrast, chose to ignore issues of taste and instead repeated the old obsession with ticket prices, declaring that "a patron [who] has paid $3.50 for a seat . . . [should not receive] three minutes of commercials before my picture." During the early 1990s indie-film boom, Disney, Warner Bros., and Fox were again critiquing direct advertising in theaters, with the first two briefly refusing to circulate their films in theaters that used such advertising.[14]

Exhibitor and advertiser concerns in later eras were likewise strikingly similar to silent-era concerns. Advertising scholar Kim B. Rotzoll used a familiar silent-era phrase to describe 1980s exhibitor concerns when he declared that many theaters were holding out "based on some sense of 'good faith' with the audience."[15] Concerns from the perspective of advertisers, though often given much more up-to-date language, also sound familiar. Joanna Phillips and Stephanie M. Noble's research into current issues in cinema-advertising acceptance addresses a number of issues, including frustrations about captivity (fear of losing your seat or missing some of the film if one leaves), repetition (seeing the same advertisement at successive visits to the theater), unexpected delays prior to a film, preconceptions that ticket price ought to buy "the right to view a movie in a commercial-free environment," and even the assumption that advertisements in a cinema should be entertaining in content.[16] Each of those concerns was voiced in the American transitional era as well. Herbert Jack Rotfeld's notion of theatrical "suicide by advertising" (causing viewers to abandon the theater altogether in order to avoid advertising content) is just a pithier version of Rothapfel's 1920s radio argument.[17]

Despite the entrenched reluctance of both the producers and exhibitors in the American film industry and the continuing fears of advertisers regarding adopting a medium that might produce ill will, cinema advertising did experience a surprising renaissance in these later decades. As Deron Overpeck has observed, the decreasing output and increasing profit percentages demanded by major studios in the late 1970s may have been a key factor in cinema advertising finally reaching widespread general usage, despite ongoing hostility from certain producers and exhibitors. During this transition, both independent exhibitors and large theater chains experimented with pre-film direct advertising as a means to boost receipts, ultimately spurring the formation of Screenvision and NCM. The combination of national chain circulation, a smaller number of tactical choices (only slides and trailers), and simple persistence appears to have increased both viewer and advertiser acceptance of the form. Even the agencies jumped onboard quickly; the J. Walter Thompson Company was a partner in the acquisition of Screenvision in 1981. Over the course of the 1980s, pre-film advertising, under the auspices of the two large-scale space brokers, became the norm in American theaters, with the two companies claiming to screen advertising on thirty-four thousand out of thirty-nine thousand theater screens across the United States.[18] The fragmentation of the television market in the wake of the multichannel transition and the subsequent havoc wrought by DVR and online video only added to the trend, as advertisers sought out new media markets to replace perceived losses.[19]

Rhetoric in support of cinema advertising likewise continued to parallel silent-era claims. Twenty-first-century scholars Michael Ewing, Erik du Plessis, and Charles Foster reference the appeal of "mood carryover," a notion that is effectively identical to old theories of media psychology and receptivity.[20] Cost rationalizations likewise occur with familiar tortured reasoning. For example, compare the following two arguments:

> Francis T. Kimball (1921):
>
> The cost of one page in one issue is about three-tenths of a cent [per] possible prospect. And the "possible" is used advisedly, because it is far from certain that every individual in the total circulation is going to get the message. . . . [Meanwhile] the trailer costs the manufacturer about six-one-hundredths of a cent a prospect—and here the "possible" is advisedly omitted, since in a motion picture theater there is but one attention focus![21]
>
> Kim B. Rotzoll (1984):
>
> Although cinema advertising's costs . . . are four or more times those of prime time television . . . cinema advertising is shown to deliver recall scores 3–5 times greater than that of television ads, so the initial cost disadvantage rapidly turns into a cost efficiency as measured at the more meaningful level of cost-per-thousand-*impressions*.[22]

Despite the shift from magazines to television as the point of comparison and Kimball's elision of the fact that cinema advertising required a larger outlay to reach the superior cost-per-prospect number, the two rationalizations, separated by decades of experience, are nearly identical—greater expense is countered with a claim of greater attention and memorability. Even the voluntary limitations are familiar, as a limit of "two or three" commercial advertisements, rather than a half-hour onslaught of advertising, has been proposed repeatedly and even adopted as a working practice (by Cineplex Odeon in 1989) during the renaissance of cinema advertising.[23] During a simple perusal of the websites for both Screenvision and NCM, the reader will encounter these same arguments.

In sum, all involved parties appear to hold positions remarkably similar to those of their silent-era counterparts, and yet cinema advertising is significantly more common now than it was in the mid-1920s. The pertinent question, then, is: What *has* changed? Overpeck is, of course, correct to point to the changing structure of media ownership and the fall from grace of the television spot. With the same conglomerates owning television and cinema outlets, decreasing reluctance by company heads toward cinema advertising is plausible. As the diminishing returns from television advertising encourages multimedia campaigns, advertisers' attraction to the captive audience of the cinema is also unsurprising.

Cultural preconceptions are perhaps even more important. In the 1930s, the J. Walter Thompson Company's Fred Fidler and Wallace Boren had begun to feel that persistence, even in the face of hostility, could create an "appreciative tolerance" in the audience.[24] Overpeck points to the fact that those who grew up in the United States in the 1980s and beyond have done so in an environment in which advertising has been more widespread; that the young display a general indifference to the question of cinema advertising is part of a trend away from compartmentalizing life into elements where advertising is and is not expected.[25] As the young continue to dominate cinema attendance, their across-the-board tolerance of ubiquitous advertising is an important element. Increasing advertising both on television and in the broader culture may therefore have begun to outweigh the film industry's own precedents.

However, cultural changes—important though they may be—are only a part of the story. More concrete, institutional changes have also been instrumental to cinema advertising's changing fortunes. One important element is the increasing centralization of distribution, culminating in the digital circulation of cinema advertising through the massive systems of both Screenvision and NCM. The ability of advertisers not only to buy significant space from a single company, but also to have the advertisement broadcast to theaters—rather than having to send individual slides or prints and rely on hundreds of projectionists—has both reduced the costs and increased the reliability of cinema advertising. The concept of circulating ads to huge swaths of American theaters via a single contract with a national space broker—first effectively attempted by the Alexander Film Company in 1929—has finally become a stable component of screen advertising.[26] Technological improvements and national oligopoly have thus removed some significant barriers to the circulation of cinema advertisements.

Oligopoly has not just been a factor in distribution, however; it has also simplified tactical choice. Early cinema advertising, as a young theory in a transitioning medium, was awash with competing tactics and theories of the audience. The array of options may itself have kept adoption low by simply bewildering potential advertisers. The recent claim that "low . . . environmental clutter" contributes to a heightening of viewer captivity (there are fewer options when a viewer desires to turn from the screen) not only suggests that simplified architecture of the multiplex era is important, but also implies that the absence of offscreen advertising technologies as an option—there are no more lighted clocks or wall advertisements—is driving renewed faith in the captive spectator.[27] We should, of course, also note that the reduction of "environmental clutter" indicates strongly the importance, to advertisers, of the end of the palatial cinema era. The hierarchy formerly differentiating palaces from hole-in-the-wall theaters has vanished, as the only meaningful differentiation remaining is from television and other forms of home media.

In short, new electronic delivery technologies, cultural acceptance of advertising intrusions into temporally bound entertainment, the increasingly corporate conditions of the American media, and fears that television's advertising value was eroding all helped to finally establish cinema advertising as a piece of the cinema landscape, largely freeing it from associations with hierarchy or spectatorial abuse. However, the practices, concerns, and effects have remained remarkably unchanged over a century. Both the means of integrating advertising into the cinema space and the reluctance advertisers have attempted to overcome in order to do so are legacies of the transitional-era American cinema.

NOTES

1. W. Stephen Bush, "Follies of the Screen," *MPW*, February 27, 1915, 1261.

2. Kenneth Lipartito, "Picturephone and the Information Age: The Social Meaning of Failure," *Technology and Culture* 44, no. 1 (January 2003): 50–81. In addition, see the following studies of failure: Graeme Gooday, "Re-Writing the 'Book of Blots': Critical Reflections on Histories of Technological 'Failure,'" *History and Technology* 14 (1998): 265–291; Scott A. Sandage, *Born Losers: A History of Failure in America* (Cambridge, MA: Harvard University Press, 2005); Randall Patnode, "Path Not Taken: Wired Wireless and Broadcasting in the 1920s," *Journal of Broadcasting & Electronic Media* 49, no. 4 (2005): 383–401; Steven Boyer, "A Virtual Failure: Evaluating the Success of Nintendo's Virtual Boy," *The Velvet Light Trap* 64 (Fall 2009): 23–33; and Paul Atkinson, "The Curious Case of the Kitchen Computer: Products and Non-Products in Design History," *Journal of Design History* 23, no. 3 (2010): 163–179. Related studies of conceptual persistence and the hazy development of new media and technologies include Carolyn Marvin, *When Old Technologies Were New: Thinking About Electric Communication in the Late Nineteenth Century* (New York: Oxford University Press, 1988); John Belton, *Widescreen Cinema* (Cambridge, MA: Harvard University Press, 1992); Rick Altman, *Silent Film Sound* (New York: Columbia University Press, 2005); Lisa Gitelman, *Always Already New: Media, History, and the Data of Culture* (Cambridge, MA: MIT Press, 2006); David Edgerton, *The Shock of the Old: Technology and Global History Since 1900* (Oxford: Oxford University Press, 2007); and André

Gaudreault and Philippe Marion, "A Medium Is Always Born Twice . . .," trans. Timothy Barnard, Wendy Schubring, and Frank Le Gac, *Early Popular Visual Culture* 3, no. 1 (May 2005): 3–15.

3. Cited in Michele Hilmes, *Hollywood and Broadcasting: From Radio to Cable* (Urbana: University of Illinois Press, 1990), 34.

4. S. L. Rothapfel, "First Aid to Theater Men," *Motography* 16, no. 2 (July 8, 1916): 77–78.

5. Cynthia B. Meyers, *A Word from Our Sponsor: Admen, Advertising, and the Golden Age of Radio* (New York: Fordham University Press, 2014), 35, 38, 41.

6. Paul Kesten, *You Do What You're Told!* (New York: CBS, 1935). Referenced in Charles F. McGovern, *Sold American: Consumption and Citizenship, 1890–1945* (Chapel Hill: University of North Carolina Press, 2006), 52.

7. Meyers, *A Word from Our Sponsor*, 49.

8. Paul Skalski, "Video Game Advertising and the Virtual Product Experience," *On Media Theory* (blog), December 25, 2012, accessed January 1, 2013, http://onmediatheory.blogspot.com/#!/2012/12/video-game-advertising-and-virtual.html.

9. Greg Jarboe, "First Person: Greg Jarboe, YouTube Marketing Guru," *InterMedia* 38, no. 1 (March 2010): 38–39.

10. In the Marxist inflection of Ted Friedman's study, technological utopianism is anti-capitalist and is one of the few venues where we can discuss a world in which labor and markets do not hold sway. But capitalists have their utopian fantasies as well. Indeed, Pamela Walker Laird's argument that advertising is in "the business of progress" could be readily rephrased to assert that admen frequently adopt utopian rhetoric. It is likely that capitalist dreams of advertising utopias become, through assertions about audience receptivity, active parts of the adoption rhetoric for new media. The creation of new media is thus a perpetually renewable resource for advertisers' utopian dreams. Friedman, *Electric Dreams*, 4–5; and Laird, *Advertising Progress*, 2.

11. Fred Fidler and Wallace Boren, "Commercial Movies," February 1, 1938, Box 7, Folder "1937 Nov. 9–1938 Oct. 25," JWT, Staff Meeting Minutes, 1927–1938, 5, 7, 12–13. The numbers are difficult to interpret from the extant report. Supposedly both General Screen Advertising Inc. and Screen Broadcasts Inc. had seven thousand contracted theaters. However, the description "over half" implies that there was significant overlap between the two.

12. Christopher Anderson, *Hollywood TV: The Studio System in the Fifties* (Austin: University of Texas Press, 1994), 16–17, 20. As Kim B. Rotzoll put it, "Theater owners are very conscious of the relationship of their medium to television. Perhaps by including overtly commercial fare, drawn primarily from a competitive entertainment form, they feel that the lines are blurred to their disadvantage." See Rotzoll, "The Captive Audience," 84.

13. J. Walter Thompson Media Research, "Report on Theatre Advertising, Revised March 1959," Box 24, Folder "No. 64G," JWT, Information Center Records, T-49.

14. Deron Overpeck, "Subversion, Desperation and Captivity: Pre-Film Advertising in American Film Exhibition Since 1977," *Film History* 22, no. 2 (2010): 219–234.

15. Rotzoll, "The Captive Audience," 85.

16. Joanna Phillips and Stephanie M. Noble, "Simply Captivating: Understanding Consumers' Attitudes toward the Cinema as an Advertising Medium," *Journal of Advertising* 36, no. 1 (Spring 2007): 81–94.

17. Herbert Jack Rotfeld, "Misplaced Marketing: Movie Theaters' Suicide-by-Advertising with Income from Abusing Customers," *Journal of Consumer Marketing* 23, no. 7 (2006): 480–482.

18. Overpeck, "Subversion, Desperation and Captivity," 220–221, 224; Rotzoll, "The Captive Audience," 72–87; and Erich Schwartzel and Nathalie Tadena, "Justice Department Sues to Block Merger of Cinema Advertising Networks," *Wall Street Journal*, November 3, 2014. In the early twenty-first century, NCM claims more than twenty thousand screens, while Screenvision claims roughly fifteen thousand. See "About Us: Overview," NCM.com, accessed December 10, 2017, https://press.ncm.com/about-us/default.aspx ; "About Us," Screenvision.com, accessed March 15, 2013, http://www.screenvision.com/about-us/about-us/; "Number of U.S. Movie Screens," National Association of Theater Owners Online, accessed February 20, 2013, http://www.natoonline.org/statisticsscreens.htm; and Cinema Advertising Council, https://www.cinemaadcouncil.org/.

19. Bruce A. Austin, "Cinema Screen Advertising: An Old Technology with New Promise for Consumer Marketing," *Journal of Consumer Marketing* 3, no. 1 (December 1986): 45–56; Michael T. Ewing, Erik du Plessis, and Charles Foster, "Cinema Advertising Re-Considered," *Journal of Advertising Research* 41, no. 1 (January/February 2001): 78–85; and Amanda D. Lotz, *The Television Will Be Revolutionized* (New York: New York University Press, 2007), 12. It is worth noting that these other media

have, in many ways, adopted the class system of early cinema. Subscription television has long been advertising-free, while online streaming services are developing two service tiers—one with advertising and one without. See, for example, YouTube and YouTube Red.

20. Ewing et al., "Cinema Advertising Re-Considered," 79.

21. Francis T. Kimball, "The Film Trailer and What It Will Do," *MPA*, February 1921, 18.

22. Rotzoll, "The Captive Audience," 83. Though this citation is from a 1987 publication, the essay itself dates to 1984.

23. Rotfeld, "Misplaced Marketing," 480; Phillips and Noble, "Simply Captivating," 92; Overpeck, "Subversion, Desperation and Captivity," 225.

24. Fred Fidler and Wallace Boren, "Commercial Movies," February 1, 1938, Box 7, Folder "1937 Nov. 9–1938 Oct. 25," JWT, Staff Meeting Minutes, 1927–1938, 3, 5.

25. Overpeck, "Subversion, Desperation and Captivity," 227; and Rotzoll, "The Captive Audience," 85.

26. *Alexander Cooperator,* October 1929, Box 8, Folder 1, AIR, 5.

27. Ewing et al., "Cinema Advertising Re-Considered," 79.

SELECTED BIBLIOGRAPHY

PATENTS

Apfelbaum, F. A. Stereopticon Slide Carrier. US Patent 1,116,201, filed December 9, 1913, and issued November 3, 1914.

Barr, John U. Advertising Device. US Patent 1,146,839, filed May 11, 1914, and issued July 20, 1915.

Billings, John W. Automatic Intermittent Projecting-Machine. US Patent 1,321,003, filed November 27, 1916, and issued November 4, 1919.

Broad, Harry L., and Frederick H. Orcutt. Chair Attachment. US Patent 901,065, filed March 19, 1908, and issued October 13, 1908.

Cauger, A. V. Lantern Slide. US Patent 1,142,143, filed June 11, 1912, and issued June 8, 1915.

Cooke, Eugene B., and Chauncey O. Lewis. Advertising Waste Paper Box. US Patent 1,108,066, filed March 5, 1914, and issued August 18, 1914.

Ferguson, Bert C. Automatic Advertising Device. US Patent 946,500, filed March 19, 1909, and issued January 11, 1910.

Fowler, Gloss H. Lighting Fixture for Theaters and Public Halls. US Patent 1,054,759, filed January 16, 1912, and issued March 4, 1913.

Genter, Jacob H. Automatic Annunciator. US Patent 1,101,429, filed May 14, 1913, and issued June 23, 1914.

———. Automatic Annunciator. US Patent 1,147,501, filed May 14, 1913, and issued July 20, 1915.

Gilmore, E. L. Motion Slide for Stereopticon. US Patent 1,083,679, filed January 27, 1913, and issued January 6, 1914.

———. Motion Slide for Stereopticons. US Patent 1,113,610, filed December 9, 1913, and issued October 13, 1914.

Haag, Jacob W. Advertising Apparatus. US Patent 1,004,163, filed December 30, 1910, and issued September 26, 1911.

Hayes, Francis T. Theater, Hall, or the Like. US Patent 1,728,731, filed March 8, 1927, and issued September 17, 1929.

Hunter, T. Hayes. Advertising Film and Method of Producing the Same. US Patent 1,426,567, filed November 6, 1919, and issued August 22, 1922.

Leveen, Samuel. Advertising Waste Paper Box. US Patent 757,403, filed January 21, 1904, and issued April 12, 1904.

May, Jerome W. Advertising Display Means. US Patent 769,868, filed August 24, 1903, and issued September 13, 1904.

Meinhardt, H. A. Slide for Motion Picture Machines. US Patent 1,016,575, filed September 12, 1911, and issued February 6, 1912.

Miedreich, Henry A. Advertising Stereopticon. US Patent 1,362,274, filed April 15, 1920, and issued December 7, 1920.

Miller, Harry. Advertising Clock. US Patent 1,137,512, filed June 24, 1914, and issued April 27, 1915.

Olson, John A., and Perry D. Sherwin. Attachment for Theater-Seats. US Patent 784,590, filed March 4, 1904, and issued March 14, 1905.

Rowntree, Carl B. Apparatus for and Method of Taking Trick and Advertising Moving Pictures. US Patent 1,227,075, filed April 29, 1915, and issued May 22, 1917.

Smith, Richard B. Shadow Clock. US Patent 813,836, filed April 3, 1905, and issued February 27, 1906.

Stambaugh, Reginald V. Process of Making Moving Picture Films. US Patent 1,226,135, filed May 26, 1916, and issued May 15, 1917.

Steinberg, Abraham. Stereopticon Advertising-Clock. US Patent 1,172,844, filed January 25, 1915, and issued February 22, 1916.

Thereault, A. J. Clock Mechanism. US Patent 1,275,791, filed February 12, 1917, and issued August 13, 1918.

Thomas, Frank C. Display Apparatus. US Patent 1,252,629, filed November 1, 1915, and issued January 8, 1918.

———. Method of Combining Advertising with Amusement or Instruction. US Patent 1,200,399, filed June 15, 1916, and issued October 3, 1916.

Van Nostran, Samuel W. Attachment for Theater-Seats. US Patent 741,004, filed August 22, 1902, and issued October 6, 1903.

———. Attachment for Theater-Seats. US Patent 785,987, filed September 29, 1904, and issued March 28, 1905.

Verran, Harry, and Alfred R. Groetz. Advertising Device. US Patent 1,321,863, filed March 10, 1919, and issued November 18, 1919.

Wetzler, Ferdinand, and Max Ornstein. Advertising Projecting Apparatus. US Patent 812,105, filed April 17, 1905, and issued February 6, 1906.

Whitaker, Norman T. Motion Picture Apparatus. US Patent 1,329,216, filed April 17, 1917, and issued January 27, 1920.

Willens, George. Stereopticon Advertising Clock. US Patent 1,218,607, filed February 10, 1916, and issued March 6, 1917.

———. Stereopticon Advertising-Clock. US Patent 1,292,196, filed October 15, 1917, and issued January 21, 1919.

SCHOLARLY BOOKS AND ARTICLES

Abel, Richard. *Americanizing the Movies and Movie-Mad Audiences, 1910–1914*. Berkeley: University of California Press, 2006.

———. *The Red Rooster Scare: Making Cinema American, 1900–1910*. Berkeley: University of California Press, 1999.

Abel, Richard, and Rick Altman, eds. *The Sounds of Early Cinema*. Bloomington: Indiana University Press, 2001.

Acland, Charles R. *Screen Traffic: Movies, Multiplexes, and Global Culture*. Durham, NC: Duke University Press, 2003.

Acland, Charles R., and Haidee Wasson, eds. *Useful Cinema*. Durham, NC: Duke University Press, 2011.

Allen, Robert C., ed. *Channels of Discourse, Reassembled: Television and Contemporary Criticism*. London: Routledge, 1992.

Altman, Rick. *Silent Film Sound*. New York: Columbia University Press, 2005.

Anderson, Chris. *The Long Tail: Why the Future of Business Is Selling Less of More*. New York: Hyperion, 2006.

Anderson, Christopher. *Hollywood TV: The Studio System in the Fifties*. Austin: University of Texas Press, 1994.

Apple, Michael W. "Constructing the Captive Audience: Channel One and the Political Economy of the Text." *International Studies in Sociology of Education* 2, no. 2 (1992): 107–131.

Appleby, Joyce, Lynn Hunt, and Margaret Jacob. *Telling the Truth About History*. New York: Norton, 1994.

Ashcraft, Brian. "Sony Interested in Interrupting Your Gaming with Commercials." *Kotaku*, May 25, 2012. Accessed February 21, 2013, http://kotaku.com/5913268.

Atkinson, Paul. "The Curious Case of the Kitchen Computer: Products and Non-Products in Design History." *Journal of Design History* 23, no. 3 (2010): 163–179.

Austin, Bruce A. "Cinema Screen Advertising: An Old Technology with New Promise for Consumer Marketing." *Journal of Consumer Marketing* 3, no. 1 (December 1986): 45–56.

Balio, Tino, ed. *The American Film Industry*. Madison: University of Wisconsin Press, 1976.

Banet-Weiser, Sarah. *Kids Rule!: Nickelodeon and Consumer Citizenship*. Durham, NC: Duke University Press, 2007.

Barbas, Samantha. "How Movies Became Speech." *Buffalo Legal Studies Research Paper Series*, Paper Number 2012-048: 16–17.

Barnouw, Erik. *The Sponsor: Notes on Modern Potentates*. New Brunswick, NJ: Transaction, 2009.

Barthes, Roland. *Image-Music-Text*. Translated by Stephen Heath. New York: Hill and Wang, 1978.

Baruch, Bernard M. *American Industry in the War: A Report of the War Industries Board*. New York: Prentice-Hall, 1941.

Belton, John. *Widescreen Cinema*. Cambridge, MA: Harvard University Press, 1992.

Bendazzi, Giannalberto. *Cartoons: One Hundred Years of Cinema Animation*. Bloomington: Indiana University Press, 1994.

Benway, Jan Panero, and David M. Lane. "Banner Blindness: Web Searchers Often Miss 'Obvious' Links." *Internetworking* 1, no. 3 (December 1998).

Biltereyst, Daniel, Richard Maltby, and Philippe Meers, eds. *Routledge Companion to New Cinema History*. New York: Routledge, 2019.

Black, Charles L., Jr. "He Cannot Choose But Hear: The Plight of the Captive Auditor." *Columbia Law Review* (1953): 960–972.

Blanchard, Frank Leroy. *The Essentials of Advertising*. New York: McGraw-Hill, 1921.

Boddy, William. *Fifties Television: The Industry and Its Critics*. Urbana: University of Illinois Press, 1993.

Bogost, Ian. *How to Do Things with Videogames*. Minneapolis: University of Minnesota Press, 2011.

Bordwell, David, Janet Staiger, and Kristin Thompson. *The Classical Hollywood Cinema: Film Style & Mode of Production to 1960*. New York: Columbia University Press, 1985.

Bottomore, Stephen. "Rediscovering Early Non-Fiction Film." *Film History* 13, no. 2 (2001): 160–173.

Bourdieu, Pierre. *Distinction: A Social Critique of the Judgment of Taste*. Translated by Richard Nice. Cambridge, MA: Harvard University Press, 1984.

Bowser, Eileen. *The Transformation of Cinema, 1907–1915*. New York: Charles Scribner's Sons, 1990.

Boyer, Steven. "A Virtual Failure: Evaluating the Success of Nintendo's Virtual Boy." *The Velvet Light Trap* 64 (Fall 2009): 23–33.

Braun, Marta, Charlie Kiel, Rob King, Paul Moore, and Louis Pelletier, eds. *Beyond the Screen: Institutions, Networks and Publics of Early Cinema*. London: John Libbey, 2012.

Brooker, Will, and Deborah Jarmyn, eds. *The Audience Studies Reader*. London: Routledge, 2003.

Brown, Elspeth H., Catherine Gudis, and Marina Moskowitz, eds. *Cultures of Commerce: Representation and American Business Culture, 1877–1960*. New York: Palgrave MacMillan, 2006.

Bruner, Robert F., and Sean D. Carr. *The Panic of 1907: Lessons Learned from the Market's Perfect Storm*. Hoboken, NJ: John Wiley & Sons, 2007.

Burgess, Jean, and Joshua Green. *YouTube: Online Video and Participatory Culture*. Malden, MA: Polity, 2009.

Burnes, Brian, Robert W. Butler, and Dan Viets. *Walt Disney's Missouri: The Roots of a Creative Genius*. Kansas City: Kansas City Star Books, 2002.

Burrell, Ian. "Is It Game Over for the Virtual Ad?" *The Independent*, February 18, 2011. Accessed February 20, 2013. http://www.independent.co.uk/news/media/advertising/is-it-game-over-for-the-virtual-ad-2218305.html.

Butsch, Richard. *The Making of American Audiences: From Stage to Television, 1750–1990*. Cambridge, UK: Cambridge University Press, 2000.

Caldwell, John Thornton. *Production Culture: Industrial Reflexivity and Critical Practice in Film and Television*. Durham, NC: Duke University Press, 2008.

Callan, Phillip J., Jr., and Norman I. Jacobs. "Trading Stamps and the Law." *Boston College Law Review* 4, no. 3 (April 1963): 637–660.

Carbine, Mary. "'The Finest Outside the Loop': Motion Picture Exhibition in Chicago's Black Metropolis, 1905–1928." *Camera Obscura* 23 (May 1990): 8–41.

Cauberghe, Verolien, and Patrick De Pelsmacker. "Advergames: The Impact of Brand Prominence and Game Repetition on Brand Responses." *Journal of Advertising* 39, no. 1 (Spring 2010): 5–19.

Caughie, John, ed. *Theories of Authorship*. New York: Routledge, 1981.

Charney, Leo, and Vanessa R. Schwartz, eds. *Cinema and the Invention of Modern Life*. Berkeley: University of California Press, 1996.

Clark, John Maurice. *The Costs of the World War to the American People.* New Haven, CT: Yale University Press, 1931.

Cook, Malcolm. "Advertising and Public Service Films." In *The Animation Studies Reader*, edited by Nichola Dobson, Annabelle Honess Roe, Amy Ratelle, and Caroline Ruddell, 157–168. New York: Bloomsbury Academic, 2019.

———. *Early British Animation: From Page and Stage to Cinema Screens.* New York: Palgrave MacMillan, 2018.

Cook, Malcolm, and Kirsten Moana Thompson, eds. *Animation and Advertising.* New York: Palgrave MacMillan, 2019.

Corbin, Caroline Mala. "The First Amendment Right Against Compelled Listening." *Boston University Law Review* 89, no. 939 (June 2009): 939–1016.

Corn, Joseph. "Selling Technology: Advertising Films and the American Corporation, 1900–1920." *Film & History* 11, no. 3 (September 1981): 49–58.

Cossar, Harper. *Letterboxed: The Evolution of Widescreen Cinema.* Lexington: University Press of Kentucky, 2011.

Cowan, Michael. "Absolute Advertising: Walter Ruttmann and the Weimar Advertising Film." *Cinema Journal* 52, no. 4 (2013): 49–73.

———. "The Ambivalence of Ornament: Silhouette Advertisements in Print and Film in Early Twentieth-Century Germany." *Art History* 36, no. 4 (September 2013): 784–809.

———. "Taking it to the Street: Screening the Advertising Film in Weimar Cinema." *Screen* 54, no. 4 (2013): 463–479.

Crafton, Donald. *Before Mickey: The Animated Film, 1898–1928.* Chicago: University of Chicago Press, 1993.

Crawford, Robert. "Old Debts: The Unsung Relationship Between Australia's Film and Advertising Industries." *Studies in Australasian Cinema* 2, no. 1 (September 2008): 33–45.

Croteau, David, and William Hoynes. *The Business of Media: Corporate Media and the Public Interest.* 2nd ed. Thousand Oaks, CA: Pine Forge, 2006.

Cuff, Robert D. *The War Industries Board: Business-Government Relations During World War I.* Baltimore, MD: Johns Hopkins University Press, 1973.

Curtin, Michael. "Media Capitals: Cultural Geographies of Global TV." In *Television After TV: Essays on a Medium in Transition,* edited by Lynn Spigel and Jan Olssen, 270–302. Durham, NC: Duke University Press, 2004.

d'Astous, Alain, and Francis Chartier. "A Study of Factors Affecting Consumer Evaluations and Memory of Product Placement in Movies."

Journal of Current Issues and Research in Advertising 22, no. 2 (Fall 2000): 32–40.

de Certeau, Michel. *The Writing of History*. Translated by Tom Conley. New York: Columbia University Press, 1988.

deCordova, Richard. "Ethnography and Exhibition: The Child Audience, The Hays Office, and Saturday Matinees." *Camera Obscura* 23 (1991): 91–108.

———. *Picture Personalities: The Emergence of the Star System in America*. Urbana: University of Illinois Press, 1990.

Dench, Ernest A. *Advertising by Motion Pictures*. Cincinnati, OH: Standard, 1916.

Dick, Bernard F. *City of Dreams: The Making and Remaking of Universal Pictures*. Lexington: University Press of Kentucky, 1997.

Douglas, Susan J. *Inventing American Broadcasting, 1899–1922*. Baltimore, MD: Johns Hopkins University Press, 1987.

Du Gay, Paul, Stuart Hall, Linda Janes, Hugh Mackay, and Keith Negus. *Doing Cultural Studies: The Story of the Sony Walkman*. London: Sage, 1997.

Dunnett, Jason, and Janet Hoek. "An Evaluation of Cinema Advertising Effectiveness." *Marketing Bulletin* (May 1996): 58–66.

Earing, Amanda. "The Making of 'How It's Made.'" *Industrial Maintenance & Plant Operation* (July 2008): 12.

Eckert, Charles. "The Carole Lombard in Macy's Window." *Quarterly Review of Film Studies* 3, no. 1 (Winter 1978): 1–12.

Edgerton, David. *The Shock of the Old: Technology and Global History Since 1900*. Oxford: Oxford University Press, 2007.

Ewing, Michael T., Erik du Plessis, and Charles Foster. "Cinema Advertising Re-Considered." *Journal of Advertising Research* 41, no. 1 (January/February 2001): 78–85.

Florin, Bo, Nico de Klerk, and Patrick Vonderau, eds. *Films That Sell: Moving Pictures and Advertising*. London: British Film Institute, 2016.

Fox, Richard Wightman, and T. J. Jackson Lears, eds. *The Culture of Consumption: Critical Essays in American History, 1880–1980*. New York: Pantheon Books, 1983.

Fox, Stephen. *The Mirror Makers: A History of American Advertising and Its Creators*. New York: William Morrow, 1984.

Frank, Thomas. *The Conquest of Cool: Business Culture, Counterculture, and the Rise of Hip Consumerism*. Chicago: University of Chicago Press, 1997.

Friedman, Ted. *Electric Dreams: Computers in American Culture*. New York: New York University Press, 2005.

Fuller, Kathryn H. *At the Picture Show: Small Town Audiences and the Creation of Movie Fan Culture*. Washington, DC: Smithsonian Institution Press, 1996.

Fuller-Seeley, Kathryn H., ed. *Hollywood in the Neighborhood: Historical Case Studies of Local Moviegoing*. Berkeley: University of California Press, 2008.

Gabler, Neal. *Walt Disney: The Triumph of the American Imagination*. New York: Vintage Books, 2006.

Gaines, Jane. "From Elephants to Lux Soap: The Programming and 'Flow' of Early Motion Picture Exploitation." *Velvet Light Trap* 25 (Spring 1990): 29–43.

Garvey, Ellen Gruber. *The Adman in the Parlor: Magazines and the Gendering of Consumer Culture, 1880s to 1910s*. New York: Oxford University Press, 1996.

Gaudreault, André, ed. *American Cinema 1890–1909: Themes and Variations*. New Brunswick, NJ: Rutgers University Press, 2009.

———. *Film and Attraction: From Kinematography to Cinema*. Translated by Timothy Barnard. Urbana, Chicago, and Springfield: University of Illinois Press, 2011.

Gaudreault, André, Nicolas Dulac, and Santiago Hidalgo, eds. *A Companion to Early Cinema*. Malden, MA: John Wiley & Sons, 2012.

Gaudreault, André, and Philippe Marion. "A Medium Is Always Born Twice . . ." Translated by Timothy Barnard, Wendy Schubring, and Frank Le Gac. *Early Popular Visual Culture* 3, no. 1 (May 2005): 3–15.

Gauntlett, Adam. "Sony Could Interrupt Your Games with Ads." *Escapist Magazine*, May 25, 2012. Accessed February 21, 2013. http://www.escapistmagazine.com/news/view/117445.

Gitelman, Lisa. *Always Already New: Media, History, and the Data of Culture*. Cambridge, MA: MIT Press, 2006.

Gitlin, Todd. *Inside Prime Time*. New York: Pantheon, 1985.

Gomery, Douglas. *Shared Pleasures: A History of Movie Presentation in the United States*. Madison: University of Wisconsin Press, 1992.

Good, Owen. "Madden 10 Now Pops Up Ads with Annoying Frequency." *Kotaku*, December 22, 2009. Accessed February 20, 2013. http://kotaku.com/5432396/madden-10-now-pops-up-ads-with-annoying-frequency.

Gooday, Graeme. "Re-Writing the 'Book of Blots': Critical Reflections on Histories of Technological 'Failure.'" *History and Technology* 14 (1998): 265–291.

Gray, Jonathan. *Show Sold Separately: Promos, Spoilers, and Other Media Paratexts*. New York: New York University Press, 2010.

Gray, Lara Cain. "Magic Moments: Contextualising Cinema Advertising Slides from the Queensland Museum Collection." *Queensland Review* 18, no. 1 (2011): 73–84.

Grieveson, Lee. *Policing Cinema: Movies and Censorship in Early Twentieth-Century America*. Berkeley: University of California Press, 2004.

———. "The Work of Film in the Age of Fordist Mechanization." *Cinema Journal* 51, no. 3 (Spring 2012): 25–51.

Grieveson, Lee, and Peter Kramer, eds. *The Silent Cinema Reader*. New York: Routledge, 2004.

Grieveson, Lee, and Haidee Wasson, eds. *Inventing Film Studies*. Durham, NC: Duke University Press, 2008.

Groskopf, Jeremy. "Profit Margins: Silent Era Precursors of Online Advertising Tactics." *Film History* 24, no. 1 (2012): 82–96.

———. "A Tempest in a Tub: The Atlanta Better Films Committee and the 'Passive Censorship' Experiment." Master's thesis, Emory University, 2008.

Gudis, Catherine. *Buyways: Billboards, Automobiles, and the American Landscape*. New York: Routledge, 2004.

Gunning, Tom. "Cinema of Attractions." In *Early Cinema: Space, Frame, Narrative*, edited by Thomas Elsaesser, 58–59. London: British Film Institute, 1990.

———. *D. W. Griffith and the Origins of American Narrative Film: The Early Years at Biograph*. Urbana: University of Illinois Press, 1991.

Gupta, Pola B., Siva K. Balasubramanian, and Michael L. Klassen. "Viewers' Evaluations of Product Placement in Movies: Public Policy Issues and Managerial Implications." *Journal of Current Issues and Research in Advertising* 22, no. 2 (Fall 2000): 41–52.

Haigh, Thomas. "Protocols for Profit: Web and E-mail Technologies as Product and Infrastructure." In *The Internet and American Business*, edited by William Aspray and Paul E. Ceruzzi, 105–158. Cambridge, MA: MIT Press, 2008.

———. "The Web's Missing Links: Search Engines and Portals." In *The Internet and American Business*, edited by William Aspray and Paul E. Ceruzzi, 159–200. Cambridge, MA: MIT Press, 2008.

Hall, Stuart. "Encoding/Decoding." In *The Cultural Studies Reader*, edited by Simon During, 90–103. London: Routledge, 1993.

Hansen, Miriam. *Babel and Babylon: Spectatorship in American Silent Film.* Cambridge, MA: Harvard University Press, 1991.

Hark, Ina Rae, ed. *Exhibition: The Film Reader.* London: Routledge, 2002.

Hediger, Vinzenz, and Patrick Vonderau, eds. *Films That Work: Industrial Film and the Productivity of Media.* Amsterdam: Amsterdam University Press, 2009.

Hervet, Guillaume, Katherine Guérard, Sébastien Tremblay, and Mohamed Saber Chtourou. "Is Banner Blindness Genuine?: Eye Tracking Internet Text Advertising." *Applied Cognitive Psychology* 25, no. 5 (September/October 2011): 708–716.

Hesmondhalgh, David. *The Cultural Industries.* 2nd ed. London: Sage, 2007.

Higashi, Sumiko. *Cecil B. DeMille and American Culture: The Silent Era.* Berkeley: University of California Press, 1994.

Hilmes, Michele. *Hollywood and Broadcasting: From Radio to Cable.* Urbana: University of Illinois Press, 1990.

———. *Radio Voices: American Broadcasting, 1922–1952.* Minneapolis: University of Minnesota Press, 1997.

Hirschman, Elizabeth C., and Craig J. Thompson. "Why Media Matter: Toward a Richer Understanding of Consumers' Relationships with Advertising and Mass Media." *Journal of Advertising* 26, no. 1 (Spring 1997): 43–60.

Holt, Jennifer, and Alisa Perren, eds. *Media Industries: History, Theory, and Method.* Malden, MA: Wiley-Blackwell, 2009.

Horkheimer, Max, and Theodor Adorno. "The Culture Industry: Enlightenment as Mass Deception." In *Media and Cultural Studies: Keyworks,* 2nd ed., edited by Meenakshi Gigi Durham and Douglas M. Kellner, 53–74. Malden, MA: Wiley-Blackwell, 2012.

Howarth, Brad. "The Games Brands Play." *B&T Magazine* (August 7, 2009): 27–28.

Hower, Ralph M. *The History of an Advertising Agency: N. W. Ayer & Son at Work, 1869–1939.* Cambridge, MA: Harvard University Press, 1939.

Jarboe, Greg. "First Person: Greg Jarboe, YouTube Marketing Guru." *Inter-Media* 38, no. 1 (March 2010): 38–39.

Jenkins, Henry. *Convergence Culture: Where Old and New Media Collide.* New York: New York University Press, 2006.

———. *What Made Pistachio Nuts?: Early Sound Comedy and the Vaudeville Aesthetic.* New York: Columbia University Press, 1992.

Jenkins, Keith. *Rethinking History.* London: Routledge, 1991.

Jhally, Sut. *The Codes of Advertising: Fetishism and the Political Economy of Meaning in the Consumer Society.* New York: Routledge, 1990.

Johnson, Keith F. "Cinema Advertising." *Journal of Advertising* 10, no. 4 (1981): 11–19.

Johnson, Martin L. *Main Street Movies: The History of Local Film in the United States.* Bloomington: Indiana University Press, 2017.

Johnston, Keith M. *Coming Soon: Film Trailers and the Selling of Hollywood Technology.* Jefferson, NC: McFarland, 2009.

Jowett, Garth S. "'A Capacity for Evil': The 1915 Supreme Court Mutual Decision." In *Controlling Hollywood: Censorship and Regulation in the Studio Era,* edited by Matthew Bernstein, 16–40. New Brunswick, NJ: Rutgers University Press, 1999.

Jowett, Garth S., Ian C. Jarvie, and Kathryn H. Fuller. *Children and the Movies: Media Influence and the Payne Fund Controversy.* Cambridge: Cambridge University Press, 1996.

Kemper, Tom. *Hidden Talent: The Emergence of Hollywood Agents.* Berkeley: University of California Press, 2010.

Kernan, Lisa. *Coming Attractions: Reading American Movie Trailers.* Austin: University of Texas Press, 2004.

Kiel, Charlie, and Shelley Stamp, eds. *American Cinema's Transitional Era: Audiences, Institutions, Practices.* Berkeley: University of California Press, 2004.

King, Rob. *The Fun Factory: The Keystone Film Company and the Emergence of Mass Culture.* Berkeley: University of California Press, 2009.

Kirby, Lynne. "Gender and Advertising in American Silent Film: From Early Cinema to the Crowd." *Discourse* 13, no. 2 (Spring/Summer 1991): 3–20.

Klein, Hans K., and Daniel Lee Kleinman. "The Social Construction of Technology: Structural Considerations." *Science, Technology, and Human Values* 27, no. 1 (Winter 2002): 28–52.

Kline, Stephen, Nick Dyer-Witheford, and Greig de Peuter. *Digital Play: The Interaction of Technology, Culture, and Marketing.* Montreal: McGill-Queen's University Press, 2003.

Klinger, Barbara. *Beyond the Multiplex: Cinema, New Technologies, and the Home.* Berkeley: University of California Press, 2006.

Koszarski, Richard. *An Evening's Entertainment: The Age of the Silent Feature Picture, 1915–1928.* New York: Charles Scribner's Sons, 1990.

———. *Hollywood on the Hudson: Film and Television in New York from Griffith to Sarnoff.* New Brunswick, NJ: Rutgers University Press, 2010.

Kracauer, Siegfried. "Cult of Distraction: On Berlin's Picture Palaces." Translated by Tom Levin. *New German Critique* 40 (Winter 1987), 91–96.

Kreshel, Peggy J. "Advertising Research in the Pre-Depression Years." *Journal of Current Issues and Research in Advertising* 15, no. 1 (Spring 1993): 59–75.

———. "John B. Watson at J. Walter Thompson: The Legitimation of 'Science' in Advertising." *Journal of Advertising* 19, no. 2 (1990): 49–59.

Kristeva, Julia. *Desire in Language: A Semiotic Approach to Literature and Art.* Edited by Leon S. Roudiez. New York: Columbia University Press, 1980.

Kuhn, Thomas S. *The Structure of Scientific Revolutions.* 3rd ed. Chicago: University of Chicago Press, 1996.

Laird, Pamela Walker. *Advertising Progress: American Business and the Rise of Consumer Marketing.* Baltimore, MD: Johns Hopkins University Press, 1998.

Lash, Lee. *Theatre Curtain Advertising.* Philadelphia: George H. Buchanan, 1909.

Lastra, James. *Sound Technology and the American Cinema: Perception, Representation, Modernity.* New York: Columbia University Press, 2000.

Leach, William. *Land of Desire: Merchants, Power, and the Rise of a New American Culture.* New York: Vintage Books, 1993.

Lears, Jackson. *Fables of Abundance: A Cultural History of Advertising in America.* New York: Vintage Books, 1993.

Lee, Wei-Na, and Helen Katz. "New Media, New Messages: An Initial Inquiry Into Audience Reactions to Advertising on Video Cassettes." *Journal of Advertising Research* (January 1993): 74–85.

Lehu, Jean-Marc. *Branded Entertainment: Product Placement and Brand Strategy in the Entertainment Business.* London: Kogan Page, 2007.

Lessig, Lawrence. *Remix: Making Art and Commerce Thrive in the Hybrid Economy.* New York: Penguin Press, 2008.

Levine, Elana. "Toward a Paradigm for Media Production Research: Behind the Scenes at General Hospital." *Critical Studies in Media Communication* 18, no. 1 (March 2001): 66–82.

Levine, Lawrence W. *Highbrow/Lowbrow: The Emergence of Cultural Hierarchy in America.* Cambridge, MA: Harvard University Press, 1988.

Lindsay, Vachel. *The Art of the Moving Picture.* New York: MacMillan, 1915.

Lindvall, Terry. *Sanctuary Cinema: Origins of the Christian Film Industry.* New York: New York University Press, 2007.

Lipartito, Kenneth. "Picturephone and the Information Age: The Social Meaning of Failure." *Technology and Culture* 44, no. 1 (January 2003): 50–81.

Loter, Jim. "Early Motion Pictures and the 'De-Rationalization' of Advertising." JimLoter.com. Accessed April 16, 2013. http://www.jimloter.com/essays/early.html.

Lotz, Amanda D. *The Television Will Be Revolutionized*. New York: New York University Press, 2007.

MacKenzie, Donald, and Judy Wajcman, eds. *The Social Shaping of Technology*. 2nd ed. Buckingham: Open University Press, 1999.

Maland, Charles J. *Chaplin and American Culture: The Evolution of a Star Image*. Princeton, NJ: Princeton University Press, 1991.

Maltby, Richard, Daniel Biltereyst, and Philippe Meers, eds. *Explorations in New Cinema History: Approaches and Case Studies*. Malden, MA: Wiley-Blackwell, 2011.

Maltby, Richard, Melvin Stokes, and Robert C. Allen, eds. *Going to the Movies: Hollywood and the Social Experience of the Cinema*. Exeter: University of Exeter Press, 2008.

Marchand, Roland. *Advertising the American Dream: Making Way for Modernity, 1920–1940*. Berkeley: University of California Press, 1985.

Marks, Martin Miller. *Music and the Silent Film: Contexts and Case Studies, 1895–1924*. Oxford: Oxford University Press, 1997.

Marvin, Carolyn. *When Old Technologies Were New: Thinking About Electric Communication in the Late Nineteenth Century*. New York: Oxford University Press, 1988.

Mayer, Vicki, Miranda J. Banks, and John Thornton Caldwell, eds. *Production Studies: Cultural Studies of Media Industries*. New York: Routledge, 2009.

McChesney, Robert. "The Market Über Alles." In *The Problem of the Media: U.S. Communication Politics in the Twenty-First Century*. New York: Monthly Review, 2004.

McCray, Patrick. "What Makes a Failure?: Designing a New National Telescope, 1975–1984." *Technology and Culture* 42, no. 2 (April 2001): 265–291.

McGovern, Charles F. *Sold American: Consumption and Citizenship, 1890–1945*. Chapel Hill: University of North Carolina Press, 2006.

Melnick, Ross. *American Showman: Samuel "Roxy" Rothafel and the Birth of the Entertainment Industry*. New York: Columbia University Press, 2012.

Meyers, Cynthia B. *A Word from Our Sponsor: Admen, Advertising, and the Golden Age of Radio*. New York: Fordham University Press, 2014.

Miller, Toby, Nitin Govil, John McMurria, Richard Maxwell, and Ting Wang. *Global Hollywood 2*. London: British Film Institute, 2005.

Misek, Richard. *Chromatic Cinema: A History of Screen Color.* Malden, MA: Wiley-Blackwell, 2010.

Miyao, Daisuke. *Sessue Hayakawa: Silent Cinema and Transnational Stardom.* Durham, NC: Duke University Press, 2007.

Münsterberg, Hugo. *The Photoplay: A Psychological Study.* New York: D. Appleton, 1916.

———. "Social Sins in Advertising." In *Psychology and Social Sanity.* Garden City, NY: Doubleday, Page, 1914.

Musser, Charles. "American Vitagraph, 1897–1901." *Cinema Journal* 22, no. 3 (Spring 1983): 4–46.

———. *The Emergence of Cinema: The American Screen to 1907.* New York: Charles Scribner's Sons, 1990.

Musser, Charles, and Carol S. Nelson. *High-Class Moving Pictures: Lyman H. Howe and the Forgotten Era of Traveling Exhibition, 1880–1920.* Princeton, NJ: Princeton University Press, 1991.

Napoli, Philip M. *Audience Economics: Media Institutions and the Audience Marketplace.* New York: Columbia University Press, 2003.

Neuberger, Roy R. *So Far, So Good: The First 94 Years.* New York: John Wiley & Sons, 1997.

Newell, Jay, Charles T. Salmon, and Susan Chang. "The Hidden History of Product Placement." *Journal of Broadcasting and Electronic Media* 50, no. 4 (December 2006): 575–594.

Newman, Kathy M. *Radio Active: Advertising and Consumer Activism, 1935–1947.* Berkeley: University of California Press, 2004.

Nye, David E. *Electrifying America: Social Meanings of a New Technology.* Cambridge, MA: MIT Press, 1990.

Oakes, Brian. "Building Films for Business: Jamison Handy and the Industrial Animation of the Jam Handy Organization." *Film History* 22, no. 1 (2010): 95–107.

Ohmann, Richard, ed. *Making and Selling Culture.* Hanover, NH: Wesleyan University Press, 1996.

———. *Selling Culture: Magazines, Markets, and Class at the Turn of the Century.* London: Verso, 1996.

Olson, Erik L. "How Magazine Articles Portrayed Advertising from 1900 to 1940." *Journal of Advertising* 24, no. 3 (Autumn 1995): 41–54.

Orgeron, Devin, Marsha Orgeron, and Dan Streible, eds. *Learning with the Lights Off: Educational Film in the United States.* New York: Oxford University Press, 2012.

Overpeck, Deron. "Subversion, Desperation and Captivity: Pre-Film Advertising in American Film Exhibition Since 1977." *Film History* 22, no. 2 (2010): 219–234.

Parker, Alison M. "Mothering the Movies: Women Reformers and Popular Culture." In *Movie Censorship and American Culture*, edited by Francis G. Couvares, 73–96. Washington, DC: Smithsonian Institution Press, 1996.

Patnode, Randall. "Path Not Taken: Wired Wireless and Broadcasting in the 1920s." *Journal of Broadcasting & Electronic Media* 49, no. 4 (2005): 383–401.

Paul, William. *When Movies Were Theater: Architecture, Exhibition, and the Evolution of American Film*. New York: Columbia University Press, 2016.

Phelan, Rev. J. J. *Motion Pictures as a Phase of Commercialized Amusement in Toledo, Ohio*. Toledo, OH: Little Book, 1919.

Phillips, Joanna, and Stephanie M. Noble. "Simply Captivating: Understanding Consumers' Attitudes toward the Cinema as an Advertising Medium." *Journal of Advertising* 36, no. 1 (Spring 2007): 81–94.

Pinch, Trevor J., and Wiebe E. Bijker. "The Social Construction of Facts and Artifacts: Or How the Sociology of Science and the Sociology of Technology Might Benefit Each Other." In *The Social Construction of Technological Systems: New Directions in the Sociology and History of Technology*, edited by Wiebe E. Bijker, Thomas P. Hughes, and Trevor Pinch, 17–50. Cambridge, MA: MIT Press, 1987.

Pope, Daniel. *The Making of Modern Advertising*. New York: Basic Books, 1983.

Presbrey, Frank. *The History and Development of Advertising*. Garden City, NY: Doubleday, Doran, 1929.

Quinn, Michael. "Distribution, the Transient Audiences, and the Transition to the Feature Film." *Cinema Journal* 40, no. 2 (Winter 2001): 35–56.

Rabinovitz, Lauren. *For the Love of Pleasure: Women, Movies, and Culture in Turn of the Century Chicago*. New Brunswick, NJ: Rutgers University Press, 1998.

Rappaport, Stephen D. "Lessons from Online Practice: New Advertising Models." *Journal of Advertising Research* 47, no. 2 (June 2007): 135–141.

Retzinger, Jean. "Spectacles of Labor: Viewing Food Production Through a Television Screen." *Environmental Communication* 4, no. 4 (December 2010): 441–460.

Richardson, F. H. *Motion Picture Handbook: A Guide for Managers and Operators of Motion Picture Theatres*. 3rd ed. New York City: World Photographic, 1916.

Ripley, John W. "All Join in the Chorus." *American Heritage Magazine* 10, no. 4 (June 1959).

Robinson, David. *Chaplin: His Life and Art.* New York: Da Capo, 1994.

Rosewarne, Lauren. "The Men's Gallery—Outdoor Advertising and Public Space: Gender, Fear, and Feminism." *Women's Studies International Forum* 28 (2005): 67–78.

Rotfeld, Herbert Jack. "Misplaced Marketing: Movie Theaters' Suicide-by-Advertising with Income from Abusing Customers." *Journal of Consumer Marketing* 23, no. 7 (2006): 480–482.

Rotzoll, Kim B. "The Captive Audience: The Troubled Odyssey of Cinema Advertising." *Current Research in Film* 3 (1987): 72–87.

Russo, Alexander. *Points on the Dial: Golden Age Radio Beyond the Networks.* Durham, NC: Duke University Press, 2010.

Ryu, Gangseog, Elison Ai Ching Lim, Lynn Thor Ling Tan, and Young Jee Han. "Preattentive Processing of Banner Advertisements: The Role of Modality, Location, and Interference." *Electronic Commerce Research and Applications* 6, no. 1 (Spring 2007): 6–18.

Samuel, Lawrence R. *Brought to You By: Post-War Television Advertising and the American Dream.* Austin: University of Texas Press, 2001.

Sandage, Scott A. *Born Losers: A History of Failure in America.* Cambridge, MA: Harvard University Press, 2005.

Sandler, Kevin S., ed. *Reading the Rabbit: Explorations in Warner Bros. Animation.* New Brunswick, NJ: Rutgers University Press, 1998.

Sargeant, Amy. "Lever, Lifebuoy and Ivory." *Early Popular Visual Culture* 9, no. 1 (February 2011): 37–55.

Sarris, Andrew. *The American Cinema: Directors and Directions, 1929–1968.* New York: Dutton, 1968.

Schaefer, Eric. *Bold! Daring! Shocking! True!: A History of Exploitation Films, 1919–1959.* Durham, NC: Duke University Press, 1999.

Schudson, Michael. *Advertising, The Uneasy Persuasion: Its Dubious Impact on American Society.* New York: Basic Books, 1984.

———. *Discovering the News: A Social History of American Newspapers.* New York: Basic Books, 1978.

Schultze, Quentin J. "'An Honorable Place': The Quest for Professional Advertising Education, 1900–1917." *Business History Review* 56, no. 1 (Spring 1982): 16–32.

———. "Legislating Morality: The Progressive Response to American Outdoor Advertising, 1900–1917." *Journal of Popular Culture* 17, no. 4 (1984): 37–44.

———. "Manufacturers' Views of National Consumer Advertising, 1910–1915." *Journalism Quarterly* 60, no. 1 (1983): 10–15.

Segrave, Kerry. *Product Placement in Hollywood Films: A History.* Jefferson, NC: McFarland, 2004.
Sennett, Mack. *King of Comedy.* Lincoln, NE: iUniverse, 2000.
Singer, Ben. *Melodrama and Modernity: Early Sensational Cinema and Its Contexts.* New York: Columbia University Press, 2001.
Sivulka, Juliann. *Soap, Sex, and Cigarettes: A Cultural History of American Advertising.* Boston: Wadsworth Cengage Learning, 1998.
Skalski, Paul. "Video Game Advertising and the Virtual Product Experience." *On Media Theory,* December 25, 2012. Accessed January 1, 2013. http://onmediatheory.blogspot.com/#!/2012/12/video-game-advertising-and-virtual.html.
Smith, Catherine Parsons. *Making Music in Los Angeles: Transforming the Popular.* Berkeley: University of California Press, 2007.
Smith, Ian Haydn. *Selling the Movie: The Art of the Film Poster.* London: White Lion, 2018.
Smoodin, Eric. *Animating Culture: Hollywood Cartoons from the Sound Era.* New Brunswick, NJ: Rutgers University Press, 1993.
Smythe, Dallas W. "Communications: Blindspot of Western Marxism." *Canadian Journal of Political and Social Theory* 1, no. 3 (1977): 1–28.
Snickars, Pelle, and Patrick Vonderau, eds. *The YouTube Reader.* Stockholm: National Library of Sweden, 2009.
Sobchack, Vivian, ed. *The Persistence of History: Cinema, Television, and the Modern Event.* London: Routledge, 1996.
Spigel, Lynn. *Make Room for TV: Television and the Family Ideal in Postwar America.* Chicago: University of Chicago Press, 1992.
Spigel, Lynn, and Jan Olssen, eds. *Television after TV: Essays on a Medium in Transition.* Durham, NC: Duke University Press, 2004.
Staiger, Janet. "Announcing Wares, Winning Patrons, Voicing Ideals: Thinking About the History and Theory of Film Advertising." *Cinema Journal* 29, no. 3 (Spring 1990): 3–31.
———. *Interpreting Films: Studies in the Historical Reception of American Cinema.* Princeton, NJ: Princeton University Press, 1992.
———. *Media Reception Studies.* New York: New York University Press, 2005.
Stamp, Shelley. *Movie-Struck Girls: Women and Motion Picture Culture After the Nickelodeon.* Princeton, NJ: Princeton University Press, 2000.
Standage, Tom. *The Turk: The Life and Times of the Famous Eighteenth-Century Chess-Playing Machine.* New York: Berkley Books, 2002.
———. *The Victorian Internet: The Remarkable Story of the Telegraph and the Nineteenth Century's On-line Pioneers.* New York: Walker, 1998.

Stewart, Jacqueline Najuma. *Migrating to the Movies: Cinema and Black Urban Modernity*. Berkeley: University of California Press, 2005.

Strauss, Marcy. "Redefining the Captive Audience Doctrine." *Hastings Constitutional Law Quarterly* 19, no. 85 (Fall 1991): 85–121.

Streeter, Thomas. *Selling the Air: A Critique of the Policy of Broadcasting in the United States*. Chicago: University of Chicago Press, 1996.

Suisman, David. *Selling Sounds: The Commercial Revolution in American Music*. Cambridge, MA: Harvard University Press, 2009.

Susanin, Timothy S. *Walt Before Mickey: Disney's Early Years, 1919–1928*. Jackson: University Press of Mississippi, 2011.

Taylor, Timothy D. *The Sounds of Capitalism: Advertising, Music, and the Conquest of Culture*. Chicago: University of Chicago Press, 2012.

Tell, Darcy. *Times Square Spectacular: Lighting Up Broadway*. New York: Smithsonian Books, 2007.

Tungate, Mark. *Adland: A Global History of Advertising*. London: Kogan Page, 2007.

Turow, Joseph. *Breaking Up America: Advertisers and the New Media World*. Chicago: University of Chicago Press, 1997.

Valentine, Maggie. *The Show Starts on the Sidewalk: An Architectural History of the Movie Theatre*. New Haven, CT: Yale University Press, 1994.

Verhoef, Nanna. *The West in Early Cinema: After the Beginning*. Amsterdam: Amsterdam University Press, 2006.

Waller, Gregory A. *Main Street Amusements: Movies and Commercial Entertainment in a Southern City, 1896–1930*. Washington, DC: Smithsonian Institution Press, 1995.

———, ed. *Moviegoing in America: A Sourcebook in the History of Film Exhibition*. Malden, MA: Blackwell, 2002.

White, Hayden. *The Content of the Form*. Baltimore, MD: Johns Hopkins University Press, 1987.

Yumibe, Joshua. *Moving Color: Early Film, Mass Culture, Modernism*. New Brunswick, NJ: Rutgers University Press, 2012.

INDEX

Page numbers in *italics* indicate figures.

Acri, Samuel, 43

Admiral Cigarettes (1897). *See* Edison Film Company

advance slides. *See* coming attractions

advance trailers. *See* coming attractions

advertising agencies, 46, 102n230, 120, 145, 150, 163n34, 268; adoption of cinema advertising, 9, 58, 61, 67, 91n76, 92n84, 105–106, 127, 165n55, 166n58, 233n91, 294; distrust, 6, 105, 147, 148, 160n2; as model for cinema advertising companies, 37–39, 124, 128, 186, 273. *See also* J. Walter Thompson Company (JWT); N. W. Ayer & Son

Advertising Film Producers Association (AFPA), 131–133, 139, 140, 150, 170nn107–108

Advertising Film Service Association of America, 170n108

Advertising Slide Company of St. Louis, 36, 40, 61

Advertising Specialty Company, 36

airdome, 191–192, *192*, 238, 239–240, 264, 271, 281n48

Alexander Film Company, 11, *114*; aesthetic style and perfectionism, 122–123, *125*, 140, 151–154, 166n64, 167n72, 175n175; contracts and space brokerage, 129, 130, *132*, 150, 154–157, 171n124, 174nn165–166, 175n181; Eaglerock planes, 157; lifespan and productivity, 134, *149*, 150, 157–158, 176n187; national focus and standardization, 90n51, 130, 150–151, 161n11, 297; rental pricing, 162n12; salaries, 135–136, 171n121; sales rhetoric, 137, 139, 141, 144, 145, 146, 147–149, 164n44

Altman, Rick, 99n176

American Biograph, 115

American Bioscope Company, 127

American Slide & Poster Company, 76, 78

American Tobacco Company, 40, 115, 224, 245–246

Anderson, Christopher, 292–293

animated letters. *See* trailers

animation (advertising), 120–122; advantages, 138–140, 172n130; disadvantages, 134; influence on mainstream cinema, 10, 18n16, 121; style, 112–113, 118. *See also* trailers

announcement slides, 30, 34–35, 58, 75, 81

Apfelbaum, Fred A., 78. *See also* Perfection Slide Company
Appel, George, 99n175
archiving (digital and physical), 10–11
Arnold Bread Company, 245
Artfilm Studios, *108*, 110, 113.
Artist's Dream, The (1913), 120
Associated Advertising Clubs of the World, 61, 100n184, 131, 170n108
AT&T, 290–291
Atlanta, 117–118, 121, 130, *138*, 168n84, 169n97, 180, 279n22
audiences, 289; abuse of, 262; active vs. passive theorizing, 2, 64, 65–66, 138–140, 141, 210–211; captivity of, 56, 63–64, 85–86, 137, 215; cinema's cross-class reach, 70–72, 173n153; future theorizing, 291–298; hostility of, 50, 68–69, 97n150, 138, 144, 177, 236; illiteracy, 145–146, 173n156; pleasure, 122, 140–141, 159, 213, 261; politics vs. advertising, 54; receptivity vs. ill will, 64–65, 85, 137, 148, 211–212, 215, 225, 299n10; variants of hypodermic theory, 63, 139, 141, 151, 179. *See also* class
Auerbach Advertising Agency, 39, 92n84
automotive industry advertising, 109, 161n11, *203*, 243; B. F. Goodrich, 113, 143, 279n19; Chevrolet, 151; Dodge, 133; Firestone, 168n90; Fisk Rubber Tire, 75; Ford Motor Company, 119

baby shows, 31
Balboa, 124
banner advertisements, 227, 291
Barr, John Upton, 218–219, 224, 234n108. *See also* Publicity Clock Company
Bean, Charles H., 55
Best Slide Company, 47, 50, 77, 78
B. F. Goodrich. *See* automotive industry advertising
billboard advertising, 6, 68, *192*; as adopted for peripheral advertising, 8, 191–192, 201, 202, 203; as adopted for slides, 110; optionality and the ability to disregard, 23, 217; public service advertising, 1, 16n5; speed and brevity aesthetics, 25, 87n13, 173n159, 175n173
billboard slides, 24, 25, 29, 87n12
billboard stations, 236, 238, 253, 259, 277n4
Billiken Shoe Company, 279n22
Birt, George, 36
black-figure vs. white-figure production: in slides, *22*, 24, *27*, 186, 224; in trailers, *108*, 112–113, 118, *138*, 162n26, 163n30
Blackton, J. Stuart, 115. *See also* Vitagraph
Boren, Wallace. *See* J. Walter Thompson Company (JWT)
Braun, William T., 50
Bray Productions, 112, 120
Brayton Manufacturing Company, 31, 32, 35–36, 37, 38, 89n47
Breck, George, 82, 104n269. *See also* Vitaslide Company
Brite-Lite Film Advertising Company, 100n191, 133
Buena Vista, 293
bug, 3, 208, 227, 291
Burden and Salisbury, 38
Burdette, Irvin A., 138–140, 172n130. *See also* Scenic Film Company
Bush, W. Stephen, 56, 288–289

Calkins and Holden, 102n230
Camel Film Company, 131, 168n90, 170n107
captive audience. *See* audiences: captivity of
catalogs (stock slides and trailers): clock and frame companies, 184, 186, 224, 230n23; slide companies, 11, 22, 24–25, 26, 36, 37–38, 40, 46–47, 61,

66, 68, 77–78, 87n12, 95n122, 167n74; trailer companies, *108*, 109–110, 116, 123–124, *125*, 133, 151, 156, 158, 167n77, 175n183
Cauger, A. V., 34, 38, 106, 162n23, 170nn107–108. *See also* Kansas City Slide Company; Neosho Slide Company
censorship of cinema, 57, 98nn165–166, 118, 124–126
charitable organizations as advertisers, 54–55, 67
chaser. *See* intermission
Cheney, George M., 144
Chicago: as advertising hub city, 12, 29–30, 90n50, 91n76; clocks and clock slides, 76, 196, 197, 224; Crystal Theater advertising boards, 201, 203–204; film trucks, 239, 250–251, 281n43; merchant matinees, 246, 248; National Free Movie Ticket Company, 254; park screenings, 251; Robyn-Kander Movie Ticket Corporation, 253, 265, 269, 274, 282n56, 285n91; Rothacker, 98n166, 164n45, 170n108; segregated theaters, 118; as site of standardization and professionalization, 48, 170n108; slide controversies, 50, 91n70, 96n144
cinema advertising: appeal of, 1–2, 17n12, 31; definitions of, 3–7, 8, 19n19, 158–159, 212–213; fears of (by ad industry), 6, 160n2, 165n58; fears of (by film industry), 3, 7, 8, 32, 33, 276, 280n30, 288–289, 293–294; film industry rejection of, 41–42, 59, 65–66, 68–69, 96n144, 97n150, 134–135, 137–138, 144, 159, 177, 202–206, 216, 226–227, 256–258, 276, 289–290; future of, 20–21, 105–106, 136, 159–160, 226, 227, 229n18, 233n91, 259, 276–277, 284n76, 289–298
class: advertising as "low-class," 216, 226, 289, 292–293; cinema as cross-class, 70–72, 145, 173n153; theatrical differentiation by class, 59, 96n144, 107, 134–135, 149–150, 204–205, 227
clocks: clock slides, *74*, 76–78, 82, 83; offscreen projecting clocks, 12, 14, 85, 179, 181, 185–186, 188, 189–191, 193–199, 202–204, 209, 214, 217, 218–226, 227, 229n11, 232n55, 276, 297; other timekeeping devices, 186, *187*, 291. *See also* Publicity Clock Company
Coca-Cola, 40, 114, 168n90, 233n91
color: color photography, 88n22; hand coloring process, 24, 26, 36, 102n218, 113, 223–224; impact of, 64, 80, 152, 153–154, 243
Columbia Slide Company, 38, 91n71
coming attractions: slides, 43–45, *44*, 47, 70, 94n107; trailers, 120, 126, 167n79, 168n81
Commercial Slide Company, 49, 99n175
consumer culture, 119, 179, 237, 260, 277n2, 292; appeal of cinema, 70–71, 139; consumer protections, 256–257; film differentiation from, 3, 4, 7–9, 16n2, 18n14, 276–277; gift-with-purchase, 261, 263; rise of, 1, 9, 238; wartime boom, 31, 53
Cook, Malcolm, 10
Coufal, Joseph F., 48, 49, 58, 59, 61. *See also* Novelty Slide Company; Standard Slide Corporation
coupon plans: bread tickets, 245–246, 250, 253; legality and legislation, 256–257, 273–274; Sperry & Hutchinson's Green Stamps, 256–257, 273; tobacco coupons, 42, 253–254, 256, 280n30. *See also* American Tobacco Company; Robyn-Kander Movie Ticket Corporation
Creel Committee. *See* World War I
Crescent Amusement Company, 239, 252

curtain advertising, 8, 26, 29, 37, 42, 88n30, 89n45, 92n85, 188–189, *208*
Curtainyline Curtain Company, 90n47
Curtis, T. Stanley, 35, 46

Dallas, TX. *See* park screenings, Dallas
Delmar Air Dome, *192*
Dench, Ernest A., 103n261, 236; audiences and class, 71; audiences and compulsion, 65; slide cost (creation), 167n74; slide cost (screening), 66–67; slide screening quantity and the "slide dodge," 50–51, 69–70, 129; trailer cost (production or rental), 123, 142
Dewey, H. H., 134, 142. *See also* Rothacker, Watterson R.
direct advertising: definition, 4–6; in free cinema, 240, 241, 277n4; in peripheral advertising, 216, 228n2; in radio, 290–291; relationship with cinema, 2, 5–6, 8, 13, 15, 54, 83–84, 85, 216, 289, 293; rise of "appreciative tolerance," 105–106, 127, 294, 296; in slides, 28–29, 51, 54, 60, 61, 116; in trailers, 105, 117, 122, 126, 136, 139, 152, 158
Disney, Walt, 18n16, 106, 112, 161n6, 162n23, 293
Dodge. *See* automotive industry advertising
Donworth, Camilla, 170n108, 243
Dorndorf Shoes, 166n62
Dra-Ko Film Company, 113, 122, 140
dual-market structure, 8, 237, 259, 276–277, 301n19
dual-projector system, 13, 45, 48, 59, 94n110, 99n176, 107, 128

Earle, Edward. *See* billboard stations
Economy Slide Company, 95n128, 99n175
Economy Slide Depot, 90n47
Edison Film Company, 163n33, 236; *Admiral Cigarettes*, 2, 114; kinetoscope parlors, 115; Motion Picture Patents Company, 78, 137–138, 154
educational and industrial film, 5, 85, 116–117, 132, 142, 161n5, 163n33, 170n108, 185, 228n2, 239, 242–243, 251, 252, 258, 260, 276. *See also* Donworth, Camilla; Essanay; Rothacker, Watterson R.
elections. *See* political advertising
Emerson Advertising Record, 100n196
Enterprise Optical Manufacturing Company, 79
Erker Bros. Optical, 36, 38, 89n47
Essanay, 116, 163n33
E. T.: The Extra-Terrestrial (1982), 4
Excelsior Illustrating Company, 49, 58
Exploits of Elaine, The (1914), 237

failure, as component of industrial development, 2, 11, 13, 76, 85, 284n76, 289, 290
Famous Players, 126
Fantasmagorie (1908), 112
Farrington, Frank: cinema audiences, 63, 64, 70–71, 72; slide copy, 25, 111; slide screening, 50, 67
feature film, 127, 161n8, 269–270; and announcement slides, 44, 126, 193; linked to palaces and specialty pricing, 1, 8, 205, 206, 259, 272; and seamless (dual-projector) screening, 13, 107, 128, 129
Federal Development Company, 112, 113, 131, 167n77, 170n107. *See also* Harris, W. A.
"feminization" of culture, 18n14
Fidler, Fred. *See* J. Walter Thompson Company (JWT)
film history, approach to, 7–10
film truck. *See* touring show (ad funded)

Fireproofing Children (1914), 119
Firestone. *See* automotive industry advertising
First Circus, The (1921), 162n26
Fisk Rubber Tire. *See* automotive industry advertising
"fleeting impressions." *See under* temporality and advertising
Florida Photographic Concern, 80
Ford Motor Company. *See* automotive industry advertising
Fort Wayne and Northern Indiana Traction Company, 117, 120
four-walling, 238, 239, 242–243, 257–258
Fowler, Gloss H., 182, 184, 193, *194*, 200, 213–214
Fox, 293
frame technologies, 181–185, 186, 188, 193, 199–202, 205–208, 215, 229n11, 291. *See also* Fowler, Gloss H.; Hunter, T. Hayes; Miedreich, Henry A.; Thomas, Frank C.; Verran, Harry
free cinema, 14–15; future of, 259, 276–277, 284n76; merchant screening boom, 246–250; postwar contraction, 255–259; prehistory and context, 236–237, 242–246, 277n4; public rhetoric (for and against), 256, 259–264; ticket coupons, 253–254, 265–275; touring and park shows, 250–253, 281n46; types, 237–242
Friedman, Ted, 292, 299n10

General Sales Company of America (Wonder Clock), 195, 217
Genre Transparency Company, 79, 90n47
Genter, J. H. (Announceoscope), 195, 196, 197, 231n43
geography and the cinema experience, 11, 90nn50–51, 191,199, 226–227, 232n69, 246–250, 253, 258, 269, 272, 276, 289
Gertie the Dinosaur (1914), 121
Gilmore, Earl L., 80, 82, *84*. *See also* Vitaslide Company
Gold Dust Twins, 91n76, 109, 115
Greater New York Slide Company, 36, 40, 49, 77, 99n175
Griffith, D. W., 57
Gude, Oscar, 174n159

Harold Ives Company, 39, 63, 64–65
Harris, D. H., 50, 63–64. *See also* Standard Slide Corporation
Harris, W. A., 132, 137, 139, 167n77, 170n107. *See also* Advertising Film Producers Association (AFPA); Federal Development Company; Screen Advertising, Inc.
Herold, Don, 1, 173n153
Hickey-Freeman Company, 122, 173n155
Hill, Walter K., 127
history: approaches to, advertising history, 9, 21–23, 86, 106, 290; approaches to, general, 11–12; approaches to, media history, 4, 7–9, 10, 159–160, 288–289. *See also* failure, as component of industrial development
Hoover, Herbert, 290–291
Howard, Jonas, 105, 111–112, 129, 140–141
Howe, Frank B., 30, 36, 47
Howe, Lyman, 28
humorous advertising: agency opposition, 103n259, 134; Rothacker opposition, 134, 142; in slides, 30, 79, 82; in trailers, 111, 120, 122, 134, *138*, 140–141, 148, 151, 154, 158
Hunter, T. Hayes, 184, 199, 206–208, *207*, 212, 291
Hunton-Fell-Elliot, 165n55

Illinois Motion Picture Advertising Corporation, 79
ill will. *See* audiences: receptivity vs. ill will

impressionistic copy, 111–112, 120, 153–154
Indiana Curtain Advertising Company, 167n79
indirect advertising, 4–6. 29, 57, 85, 116, 161n5, 228n2, 277n4, 291. *See also* direct advertising; product placement
industrial film. *See* educational and industrial film
Industrial Motion Picture Company. *See* Rothacker, Watterson R.
intermission: and curtain advertising, 8, 29; as participating sponsorship in cinema, 21, 94n110, 289; in single projector theaters, 21, 26–27, 34–35, 43–45, 48, 51, 94n110, 107; as space brokered ad break (chaser), 14, 26, 45, 48, 50, 94n110, 107, 128–129, 131, 136, 159;
international cinema advertising, 16n4, 88n21, 88n30, 103n261, 166n62, 197, 230n34, 278n7
International Harvester Company, 57
International Slide Advertising Company, 48
internet advertising, 227, 277, 291–292

Jarboe, Greg, 292
Jhally, Sut, 272n2
J. Walter Thompson Company (JWT), 58; acquisition of Screenvision, 294; cinema advertising research, 105–106, 109, 127, 130, 135, 151, 160n2, 292, 293, 296, 299n11; opposition to humor, 103n259, 134

Kalck Safety Specialty Company, 196
Kalem, 127
Kansas City, 254; park screenings, 251; space brokerage, 129
Kansas City Slide Company: with AFPA, 131, 170n107; archival sources, 11; catalogs, 38, 87n12; clock slides, 76, 78; formation and growth, 34; "full-service" model, 39; national advertiser contracts, 26; photo slides, 87n9; political slides, 98n162; slide copying and "artistry," 36, 79; slide price stabilization, 37, 46, 66, 95n122; stock-slide aesthetics, 22, 24, 25; trailers, 106, 112, 161n6. *See also* Cauger, A. V.; Disney, Walt
Keeshen Advertising Agency, 67, 92n84
Kimball, Francis T., 167n77, 161n8; theatrical 'class' restrictions, 135; value of cinema audiences, 139, 146, 173n156; value of trailers, 141, 143–144, 172n140, 295
kinetic letters. *See under* trailers
Kineto Machine Company, 196–198, 204, 217, 224
kinetoscope parlors. *See* Edison Film Company
Kracauer, Siegfried, 209–210

Laflin, Fred C., 170nn107–108. *See also* Camel Film Company
Laird, Pamela Walker, 62–63, 299n10
Larson, C. K., 86n5
leader, 98, 118, 127, 188
Lee, Delmar, 250–251, 281n43
Lee Lash Company, 29, 37, 39, 47, 63, 92nn84–85, 137
Levi Company: artistry, 30, 79; catalogs, 38, 92n79; copying, 103n257; eye fatigue, 65, 101n200; patents, 76–77, 78, 79–80; price cutting, 36; slide-making kits, 90n47. *See also* Perfection Slide Company
Levy, Norman, 293
Liberty Loan. *See* World War I
Lipartito, Kenneth, 290
lithograph advertising, 24, 95n133, 120
Loew, Marcus, 97n150, 130
Lombard, Preston, 31, 90n47

Long and Heller Inc., 49, 95n128
long tail, 227, 229n18
Loose, George P., 246–250, 247, 254, 265. *See also* merchant and farmer screenings
Lowe, G. R., 50, 72–73, 75, 146–147. *See also* Neosho Slide Company
Ludwig, Irving, 293
Lux Soap, 160n2

magazine advertising, 4, 46, 70–72, 189; cost-per-reader, 143, 295; decreasing usefulness, 146; "front page" metaphors, 63, 137; medium-specific psychology, 64, 100n196; national campaigns, 67–68, 93n95, 268; optional reading, 22–23, 65, 179, 217; positioning (wraparound vs. integrated), 19n19, 22, 136, 213; space brokerage, 19n19, 38, 131
Mahin Advertising Agency, 91n76
Make 'Em Yourself Slides. *See under* Richardson, F. H.; *see* slide-making kits
Maltby, Richard, 7
Manhattan Slide (and Film) Company, 43, 49, 133, 142
Marshaw Slide Manufacturing Service, 34, 36
Mason, Thomas P., 38, 47
McCay, Winsor, 112, 121
McClure, Arthur, 129
medium-specific psychology: cinema, 64, 140; print, 100n196; radio, 291; recorded sound, 101n196; stage, 101n196
Meinhardt, Hans A., 76–78
merchant and farmer screenings, 238, 253, 259, 265, 278n13; merchant matinee companies, 246–250, 255–256, 264; single-sponsor versions, 245–246; ticket circulation, 240–241, 254, 260–261
Metropolitan Slide Company, 90n47
Mica Non-Breakable Slide Company, 38
Michigan, 52, 56, 67, 96n143, 97n162, 230n31, 248
Midwestern United States: Alexander Film Company contracts, 155, 158; dominance of frame technologies, 199; merchant screenings, 246, 248, 249–250, 255; touring and park screenings, 253, 255
Miedreich, Henry A., 184, *208*, 212, 291
Minneapolis, 130, 182–183, 189, 191, 206, 230n31
mixed media venues, 28, 210, 217, 226
Monache Theatre Company Inc., 141
Monett, MO, 250, 264, 270
Montana, 39, 55, 92n84, 155
Motion Picture Advertising Company, 39, 92n84
Motion Picture Patents Company. *See under* Edison Film Company
Moving Picture Advertising Association of the World. *See* Advertising Film Producers Association (AFPA)
Münsterberg, Hugo, 213
Musser, Charles, 28, 115, 163n32
Mutual Decision, 3
Mutual Film Corporation, 154
mutually defining institutions, 2, 16n1; impact of advertising on cinema, 3, 8, 15, 86, 289; impact of cinema on ad industry, 15, 17n8, 86, 290

Nankivell, Frank A., 122
Nashville, 201, 252, 255
National Advertising Motion Picture Weekly Inc., 118
National Association of the Motion Picture Industry (NAMPI), 49
National Builders Bureau, 142, 146, 156–157, 173n153
National Cash Register Company, 115, 242, 243
National CineMedia (NCM), 3, 20–21, 89n35, 151, 294, 296, 297, 300n18

National Film Advertising Bureau, 151
National Song-Slide Company, 90n47
Naylor, J. E., 90n47
NBC, 290–291
Nebraska, 180, 269
Nelson Motion Picture Studios, 130
Neosho Slide Company, 34, 39, 40, 46–47, 50, 72–73, 75, 90n47
Neuberger, Louis. *See* Publicity Clock Company
New Orleans, 144, 201, 202
newspaper advertising, 46, 71–72, 111, 143, 189; medium-specific psychology, 100n196; national campaigns, 67–68; space brokerage, 38
newsreels, 30, 119, 129, 159, 165nn54–55
news slides, 28, 30
New York City, 251; as advertising hub city, 32–33, 90n50; candidate slides, 57; clocks and clock slides, 76–77, 185, 191, 194–197, 198, 218, 224–225, 226, 227, 232n58, 234n110; early cinema advertising experiments, 28–29, 115, 163n32; electronic billboards, 174n159; patent focus, 90n50; peripheral advertising (non-clock), 182, 189, 209, 233n90; price-cutters (slides), 36; Rialto Theater free screenings, 243; Robyn-Kander Movie Ticket Corporation, 253–254, 270, 274, 275; slide professionalization, 48–49, 59, 99n175; space brokerage, 39; trailer advertising, 130, 133, 164n45; Vitaslides, 81–82; wartime propaganda, 58
Niagara Slide Company, 35, 38, 40, 46, 90n47
No-Destructo Slide Company, 34, 90n56
North American Slide Company, 34, 37, 90n55, 94n118
Novelty Slide Company, 40–41, 43, 45, 48–49, 58, 76, 79, 90n47, 95n122. *See also* Coufal, Joseph F.
N. W. Ayer & Son, 57, 92n79, 98n165
offscreen space, 5, 178–179
Ohio, 33, 52, 56, 96n143, 249, 253, 279n19, 281n48, 282n56
Ohio Transparency Company, 35, 90n47
Ohmann, Richard, 4, 93n95, 102n230
Open Airdome Company of Green Bay, 252–253, 255. *See also* Wisconsin
Oregon, 98n163, 120, 248
Overpeck, Deron, 294, 296

Paradis, H. J., 55
parasite, advertising as, 46, 123, 262–263, 290
Paris Slide Company, 90n47
park screenings, 238, 250, 252–253, 255, 258, 259, 264, 271, 278n4; Cleveland, 281n48; Dallas, 252, 256, 258, 276; Louisville, 251–252; St. Louis and vicinity, 251, 255, 281n46; Tennessee, 239, 244–245, 250, 252,
participating sponsorship. *See* spot
patent medicine, 1, 94n114
Paul, William, 205
Perfection Slide Company, 27, 47, 49, 74, 76–79, 95n128, 103n257, 133. *See also* Levi Company
Perils of Pauline, The (1914), 237
peripheral advertising, 14; boom era, 192–202; future of, 226, 227, 229n18, 233n91; limited evidence of, 179–180; postwar decline, 203–210, 228n5; pre-history and context, 177–178, 181, 188–192; production and aesthetics of, 178–179, 181–188, *203*, *207*, *208*, 222–224, 229n11; public rhetoric (for and against), 210–218; Richardson's theater tour, 202–203
Philadelphia: AACW convention, 131; as advertising hub city, 32–33, 90n50; Liberty Bell Slides, 98n165; Scenic Film Company branch, 130, 169n101; slide companies operating within, 34

picture palaces, 223, 275: design "clutter," 204–205, 209–210, 216, 297; opposition to advertising, 8, 59, 107, 145, 205; rise of, 1, 259, 275
picture settings, 205
Pittsburgh, PA: clocks, 195; Robyn-Kander Movie Ticket Corporation, 254, 270, 271–272, 273, 274–275, 276, 286n98; tobacco coupon ban, 280n30
political advertising: ballot issues, 56; candidates for office, 20, 54–55, 57, 97n162, 98n166, 96n168; voter registration, 56. *See also* World War I
Premo Company, 90n47
Presba, B. S., 37, 41, 91n76. *See also* Thornton Advertising Company
price cutting, 31, 35–38, 41, 46–47, 48–49, 51, 59, 78, 91n78, 94n118, 116, 222
product placement, 4, 5, 8, 15, 52, 85, 97n153, 115, 117, 178, 206, 228n2, 229n11, 292
Publicity Clock Company: infighting, 219–221; lifespan, 198, 209, 218–219, 235nn122–123; market dominance, 224–226, 276; pricing and sales, 196, 198, 222, 235n129; product specifics, 185, 221–222, 234n108; slide aesthetics, 186, 222–224
public service advertising, 1, 75–76, 79, 83, 85, 185, 291
public-service technologies, 181, 185–188, 217

Quality Slide and Photo Makers, 66
Quest of Life, The (1916), 126

radio advertising, 105, 159; critiques, 26, 72, 171, 290–291, 294; dual-market structure, 259, 277; medium-specific psychology, 291; national campaigns, 150, 159; participating sponsorship, 86, 106
Radio-Mat Slide Company, 62. *See also* slide-making kits
Rathbun, John B., 50, 94n110
Raymond Anderson Company, 120, 122
Real Publicity Company, 129, 169n96
reason-why copy, 111, 158
receptive audience. *See* audiences: receptivity vs. ill will
Rembusch, Frank, 181
Richardson, F. H., 12, 180, 200; black masking in theater design, 181, 205; critical theater tour, 201, 202–204, 205, 206, 214, 215; Make 'Em Yourself Slides, 12, 43, 90n57; opposition to touring free-cinema, 244–245, 263, 276; supportive statements, 193–194, 198, 225–226
Richardson, George J., 230n28
Ripley, John W., 29–30
Rittelmeyer, George M., 65–66, 69, 73, 94n111
R. Naylor and Company, 90n47
Robyn-Kander Movie Ticket Corporation, 236, 259; contracts and penetration rates, 253–254, 270–273, 276, 286n105; formation, 253, 265; integration with Universal, 269–270, 285n91; legal problems and dissolution, 254, 257, 273–275, 287n114; regional offices, 269, 282n56, 286nn97–98; ticket structure and philosophy, 241, 254, 260–262, 265–268
Rockwell, Fred G., 77, 78
Rotfeld, Herbert Jack, 294
Rothacker, Watterson R., 98n166; industrial films, 116, 164n39; professionalization, 170n108; trailer pricing, 142; trailer style, 110, 112, 122–123, 129, 134, 141, 142, 164n45
Rothapfel, S. L. ("Roxy"), 51, 59, 96n144, 134, 165n54, 201–202, 290–291, 294
Rotzoll, Kim B., 293, 295, 300n12
Rowntree, Carl A. *See* Scenic Film Company
Ruerup, J. H., 55

San Lac Milk Seals, *266*, 269
Sargent, Epes Winthrop: billposting airdome walls, 191; homemade clock slides, 76, 77; sanctity of the screen, 41–42, 65, 177–178, 201, 228n2
scare copy, 175n175
Scenic Film Company, 165n48, 180; with AFPA, 131, 170n107; heat distortion, 152, 166n67; humor and pleasure, 117, 138–140; kinetic letters, 121; Rowntree process, 112, 113, 118, *138*; space brokerage, 130, 169n97, 169n101; trailer length, 122; trailer pricing, 123
Schultze, Quentin J., 116–117
Scott and Van Altena, 38, 43, 95n128
Screen Advertising Inc., 137; approach, 170n102; space brokerage, 130, 131, 145. *See also* Harris, W. A.
Screen Press Inc., 130
screen size, 180–181, 205–206
Screenvision, 3, 20, 21, 89n35, 151, 293, 294, 296, 297, 300n18
Selig-Polyscope, 127, 163n33
Shredded Wheat, 100n196, 115
Simon, David, 270, 273–274, 275, 287n114. *See also* Robyn-Kander Movie Ticket Corporation
Simpson, James P., 130
Skalski, Paul, 292
slide-making kits, 12, 23–24, 43, *62*, 68, 89n47, 90n57, 102n218
slides (advertising), 13, 87n12; catalogs, 26, 38, 92n79; copying; 36, 103n257; future of, 20–21; guaranteeing screening, 38–39, 69–70, 92nn84–85; national campaigns, 26, 40–41, 51, 67–68, 93n92, 93n95; politics and charity, 52–59, 96n148, 98n166, 98n172, 101n214; postwar stabilization, 59–61; pre-history and context, 21, 28–30; price-cutting war, 35–37, 46–47, 78, 91n78, 94n118, 95n122; production and aesthetics of, 23–26, 88n20, 88n22; professionalization, 37–41, 48–52, 95n128, 99n175; public rhetoric (for and against), 61–73, 101n200; public service slides, 75–78, 83; relationship to motion, 26, 62–63, 79–83; slide boom, 31–35, 86n5, 89n35; slide bust, 41–46; temporal flow (relationship to), 21–23, 26–28, 34–35
Smallwood, Arthur N., 116
Smythe, Dallas W., 18n15, 277n2
song slides, 28, 29–30, 32, 34, 43, 44, 57, 78, 89n35, 89n47, 188
Southern Film Service, 117–118
space brokerage: other media and devices, 189, 197; print media, 37; slides, 20–21, 38–39, 51, 52; theater curtains, 92n85; trailers, 14, 20–21, 113, 128–131, 136, 144, 145, 151, 155, 294, 297
Specialty Slide Makers, 90n47
Spiegel Motion Slide, 79, 104n262
sponsorship, 5, 8, 83, 115, 242, 243, 268, 291. *See also* Robyn-Kander Movie Ticket Corporation; spot
spot, 3, 8, 14, 15, 21–22, 27–28, 106, 159, 237, 244, 277, 296
squeezeback, 3, 291
Stambaugh, Reginald V. *See* Artfilm Studios
Standard Manufacturing Company, 185, 196, 197
Standard Slide Corporation, 59, 60, 61, 63–64, 100n184. *See also* Coufal, Joseph F.
Steurle, Joseph L., 57
St. Louis: 1904 Expo, 115; exhibitors association, 52, 96n143, 168n83; film trucks, 281n46; park screenings, 251–252; peripheral advertising, *192*, 198; Robyn-Kander Movie Ticket Corporation, 253, 269, 270, 282n56; slide companies, 36, 40, 61

Story of the Fountain Pen, The (1912), 119–120
Strauss Theatre Programs, 101n196
Sunkist Oranges, 40, 93n92
Swanson, Wm. H., 90n47

television advertising, 284n76, 292, 294–295, 296; Alexander Film Company, 150, 157; bugs, 208, 227, 291; Bulova time signal, 83; comparison with cinema advertising, 295, 297–298, 300n12; dual-market structure, 237, 259, 277, 301n19; national reach, 159–160, 296; quantity per hour, 239; participating sponsorship, 8, 13, 15, 27, 86, 105–106, 136, 159, 289; repetition, 50
temporality and advertising, 21–23; and copy brevity 25, 87n13, 152–153, 173n159; "fleeting impressions," 26–27, 61, 72–73, 145, 147, 178, 259, 262
Thayer Advertising Agency, 233n91
Thomas, Frank C., 182, 199–200, *200*, 205, 211, 212, 213, 216–217
Thornton Advertising Company, 37, 39, 41, 63, 71. *See also* Presba, B. S.
Three Star Slide Company, 90n47
tickets: as evidence of spending power of audiences, 71; as incompatible with ad funding, 68–69, 97n150, 138, 292–294; and "tollbooth" theory, 260–261
Tilford & Tilford, 118
tobacco coupons. *See* American Tobacco Company; coupon plans
Topeka, 199, 214, 227
touring show (ad funded), 238, 239–240, 244, 250, 251, 254, 258, 259, 271; advertising types, 260, 264; critiques, 244–245, 263, 278n4; film trucks, 238, 239, 250–251, 253, 258, 279n19, 281n46; Open Air Dome Company of Green Bay, 252–253, 255, 276
trailers, 13–14, 85, 106–107; animation era, 120–122; catalogs, 109–110, 123–124; cost, 123–124, *132*, 133, 142–144, 154–156, 162n12, 167n77; future of, 105–106, 136, 159–160; infighting and class segregation, 133–136; invention of, 117–124, 161n8, 154n45; kinetic letters, 118, 121, 166n64; national campaigns, 107, 109, 114, 115, 152, 156–157, 168n90, 170n102; politics and self-promotion, 17n8, 124–127; prehistory and context, 114–117, 161n5, 163nn33–34; production and aesthetics of, 107–114, 122–123, 152–154, 162n26, 167n72, 175n175; professionalization, 128–133, 150–151, 170n107; public rhetoric (for and against), 117, 136–149, 151, 164n44
transient spectatorship, 71, 128–129, 192
transitional era, 4, 7, 8, 64, 226, 294
Triangle Film Corporation, 126, 168n81

Unique Slide Company, 53, 58
Universal Film Manufacturing Company: announcement slides, 43, *44*; "Buy-a-Bale" leader, 126; Robyn-Kander Movie Ticket Corporation, 238, 253, 265, *266*, 267, 269–270, 274, 275, 285n91, 287nn114–115. *See also* Robyn-Kander Movie Ticket Corporation
Universal Moving Picture Tickets. *See* Robyn-Kander Movie Ticket Corporation
Utility Transparency Company. *See* Richardson, F. H.; slide-making kits

Van Nostran, Samuel W., 189
Vedder, George C., 200, 232n67
Verran, Harry, *183*, 206, 211, 212
video game advertising, 292
Vitagraph, 115, 163nn33–34.
Vitaslide Company, 80–84

Ward Baking Company, 233n91
Warner Bros., 293
Washing Day in Switzerland (1896), 114
Wells Enterprises, 90n47
Wheeler, De Witt C., 103n257
white-figure production. *See* black-figure vs. white-figure production
Whitman, Charles S., 57
Willens, George. *See* Kineto Machine Company
Windsor Cut-Out Slide Company, 43–44
Wisconsin, 250, 258, 276; Green Bay, 249, 252–253, 255; Stevens Point ("the Wisconsin Group"), 249, 254, 256
Wonder Clock Company, 196–198, 222
Woods, M. L., 55
World War I, 47, 52, 66, 128, 133, 209, 258–259, 275; Creel Committee, 55, 58, 126–127, 160n2; excess profits tax 53, 59–60; Four Minute Men, 55, 56; industrial films, 170n108; industrial impact, 195, 228n5, 255–256; Liberty Loan, 54, 58, 96n148, 127, 168n87; slides and trailers, 53, 54, 56, 58–59, 96n148, 98n165, 98n172, 124, 126–127, 163n30, 168n87, 199
Wrigley Chewing Gum Company, 115, 233n91
W.S.S. Thriftettes (1918), 163n30

Young, Charles A., 50
Young Advertising Service, 31–32
YouTube, 227, 301n19

Zimmerman, Yvonne, 111

JEREMY GROSKOPF is Instructor of Communication Studies and Journalism at Averett University.

Lightning Source UK Ltd.
Milton Keynes UK
UKHW010749170822
407424UK00001B/48